TEACHING CHILDREN TO READ

TEACHING CHILDREN TO READ

Daisy Marvel Jones

PROFESSOR OF EDUCATION
ARIZONA STATE UNIVERSITY

HARPER & ROW, PUBLISHERS
New York, Evanston, and London

TEACHING CHILDREN TO READ

 For information address Harper & Row, Publishers, Inc., 49 East 33rd Street, New York, N.Y. 10016.

LIBRARY OF CONGRESS CATALOG CARD NUMBER: 76–137815

To Vivian

CONTENTS

FOREWORD

This book is intended for use as a text in courses in the teaching of reading at the preservice level and also for use as a reference for teachers in service. It is not designed as a prescription, but rather as a basis for evaluating materials and practices. It is hoped that the teacher will find it useful in formulating her own opinions, in developing insights and understandings, and in making independent decisions about the *what,* and the *how,* and the *why* of teaching children to read.

Part One presents a background. Parts Two and Three discuss skills and their application. Part Four is evaluative.

The writing of this book is based on years of experience, extensive reading, and much observation of effective teaching. To identify the personal experiences with the children seems unnecessary. To name the teachers in whose classrooms many of the examples have been observed would be endless, but those who see their own practices reflected will recognize themselves. Their contributions are deeply appreciated. Many of the questions have come from students at the university level as well as from teachers at the classroom level. Perceptive listening has revealed the questions. Many of the answers have been verbalized repeatedly before they were ever put in written form. Perhaps the book can rightly be said to be an accumulation of answers rendered over the years.

Much that is in this book may seem oversimplified, but that is because the intent is to recognize the problems of the teacher where she is rather than the ideal where she ought to be and to help her move forward to the next step toward ultimate perfection which so often seems beyond one's grasp.

The teacher who is trying to help the child learn to read is in much the same position as the child who is doing the learning. It is not so much a matter of whether she is right or wrong, up to standard, or approaching perfection, but rather a matter of whether or not she is making progress and is headed in the right direction.

If this book helps to point out that direction, it will have accomplished its purpose.

PREFACE

Dear Teacher,

If you are looking for a recipe for teaching reading, stop right now, for this book does not contain any panaceas nor is it guaranteed to provide a formula to induce all children to read, to make geniuses out of morons, or to transform nonreaders into skilled performers.

There is no "royal road" to success in reading any more than in anything else. However, I am convinced that most children who want to read and who will try can succeed if they are subjected to a good environment. It is the purpose of this book (1) to help the teacher know how to create that good environment, (2) to translate research into everyday language that is meaningful to the classroom practitioner, and (3) to provide an over-all view of the reading process.

There are no guarantees for instant success. There are only some suggestions to pique the imagination and stimulate the enthusiasm of the teacher who cares about children. There are no recommended methods, only appraisal of many methods most of which will have merit when appropriately used. There are no prescribed materials, only a basis for evaluating available materials in the light of evident needs of the learners.

I am convinced that given a child who is capable and wants to learn, a teacher who genuinely wants to help him, and a reasonably satisfactory environment, almost any method and almost any material will work, even the mail order catalogue. All this, of course, is predicated on the assumption that both the child and the teacher work, too.

Daisy Marvel Jones

TEACHING CHILDREN TO READ

Part One

INTRODUCTORY AND BACKGROUND STATEMENTS

or *The Situation in Reading Today*

Part One is planned to give the reader a background for interpreting the suggestions and applications offered in Parts Two and Three.

Chapter 1 puts reading in perspective as it relates to the other language arts and to the child's needs. Chapter 2 is devoted to a brief historical review. An evaluation of achievement, organization, materials, and methods is postponed until Part Four on the assumption that one needs to know what he is doing and how he is doing it before he can evaluate.

The reader may want to skim quickly over Part One and plunge immediately into the more specific and concrete points in Parts Two and Three, coming back later to Part One to read the background material in greater detail in the light of the suggestions offered. He may also want to refer to the evaluative chapters in Part Four as they relate to earlier chapters. Presenting the content of a book in a certain order does not necessarily mean that the reader must consume it in that order. If you feel you already have background from other sources or from experience, if you have an immediate problem that won't wait, then by all means vary your approach. But please do not skip Parts One and Four entirely, because they help to bring into focus the suggestions offered and the observations made in Parts Two and Three. Without this perspective the reading program could become a set of recipes or panaceas. That is just what we are seeking to avoid.

It is hoped that the material in this book will give the teacher a point of view as well as some practical help in solving problems in the teaching of reading.

1

READING IN PERSPECTIVE

or How Reading Fits into the Child's World Today

Reading is important. But so is swimming and typing and talking and running and sewing and playing a musical instrument and dozens of other things a child learns to do. The stress put on reading in the past two decades has almost reached a state of hysteria out of all proportion to its importance. Let's stop to reason sensibly about it and see if we can put it in perspective with the rest of learning.

LANGUAGE AS A MEDIUM OF COMMUNICATION

To begin with, reading is one of the language skills the person in today's society uses as a medium of communication. The language skills are the often quoted foursome: listening, speaking, reading, and writing. These place the user of language in the positions alternately of producer or consumer, and the language itself in the form of either oral or written expression. The relationships of these four elements can be visualized in chart form (See Figure 1).

The Uses of Language Skills		
Form	Purpose	
	Impressive	Expressive
Oral Written	Listening Reading	Speaking Writing

Figure 1. Relationships of the four language skills.

THE TWO CHANNELS OF LANGUAGE

THE IMPRESSIVE PHASE Sometimes the person using language is receiving the message or is acting as the consumer. If the message is coming to him in oral form, he is engaged in listening. If the message is coming to him in written form, he is engaged in reading.

THE EXPRESSIVE PHASE Sometimes the person using language is transmitting the message or is acting as the producer. If the message is being transmitted in oral form, he is engaged in speaking. If the message is being transmitted in written form, he is engaged in writing.

THE TWO FORMS OF LANGAUGE

ORAL LANGUAGE When there is direct communication between two or more persons, the person producing the message may be speaking. The message is spoken on the assumption that the counterpart will be completing the cycle and listening to what is said.

WRITTEN LANGUAGE When the communication is between two or more persons who are not in direct contact, the person producing the message may be writing. The message is written on the assumption that someone will read what has been written.

THE SEQUENCE OF DEVELOPMENT

LISTENING The listener is a consumer of language. The child listens from the day he is born. He listens to the sounds about him, to his mother as she sings to him or talks to him. He soon learns to sort out the sounds he hears and to distinguish the ones which mean approval or disapproval. He associates names with objects and begins to learn language. By the time he comes to school he has learned to attend to the things that fit his needs and to tune out the things that do not concern him. There are many kinds and degrees of listening, some good and some not so good from the standpoint of classroom instruction. Sometimes a child listens for information, for enjoyment, for self-protection, or for the pure joy of rhythmic effect of language. Sometimes he avoids listening because the results are displeasing to him, they interfere with what he is thinking about, or the conflict of sounds may call for discrimination for sheer survival in a noisy environment.

SPEAKING The speaker is the producer. First the child learns to speak because of interest in experimenting with sounds and with the use of his new-found vocal organs. The lip sounds are the most easily made and may result in a repetition of such sounds as m-m-m-m-m-m-m which a fond mother translates into "mama." Sounds made in the fore part of the mouth come early in the development of speech mechanisms. The tongue pressing against the teeth ridge results in a continuation of the sound d-d-d-d-d-d-d which eager parents translate into "dada." When the self-centered infant says "mama" or "dada" and the adults in his immediate environment come running and respond with expressions of approval and adoration, he has made his first conquest through language. Other learnings follow as his needs grow and as his skills in satisfying them increase. His earliest use of speech sounds, then, is experimentation, followed soon after by satisfaction of his personal wants.

Language as a means of communicating ideas comes much later. The young child who says over and over again, "Choo choo train! Choo choo train!" is not telling you there is a train. He is merely practicing a new skill which he is enjoying.

In order to speak in sentence patterns the child must learn a complex array of skills including inflection, word order, accent, pitch, stress, and juncture. He picks up these skills through imitation of the language he hears. If he lives in an environment where the only language he hears is "Don't!" or "Be still!" or "Quit that!" he will learn single words and short terse commands with strong inflection. If he lives in an environment where interested adults take time to explain things to him and answer his questions with language that involves sentence patterns and varied syntax patterns, he will imitate what he hears and develop his language accordingly. The differences in these two backgrounds are well known to teachers of beginning reading.

READING The language which is already familiar to the child is the basis for reading. If the linguistic patterns used in the books are not within the scope of his previous experiences, the learning problems are compounded. There are at least two alternatives in meeting this situation. One is to begin with the language with which the child is already familiar and build on it through the language-experience approach. The other is to familiarize the child with the language of the textbooks through story telling and frequent conversations. This kind of background will lead him naturally into the language used in the readers. There are proponents of both of these approaches. They both have merit. It is highly probable that skillful teachers can be successful with either technique.

WRITING The last of the four language skills to be developed is writing because it calls for finer muscular coordination plus the synchronization of thought and mechanical performance. To be effective it must also encompass both penmanship and spelling to which must eventually be added capitalization and punctuation. There are those who would approach the teaching of reading through leading the child to express his own ideas in writing before he attempts to decipher the ideas of others through reading. Whether reading is approached through decoding the printed symbol to find out what others have written or through using the symbols to encode one's own thoughts, the process still calls for the association of the symbol with the sound and the idea.

THE IMPORTANCE OF READING

How important is reading in today's world? If you stop to think about it, you may not become quite so emotional about getting all the Johnnies and Janies to read, at least not right away. So let's ask, "Why read?"

ORIGINAL PURPOSES FOR READING

SPANNING DISTANCE Probably one of the original purposes for written expression was to communicate with someone removed by space. One hundred and fifty years ago, if Aunt Sally wanted to send a message to her niece whose pioneer husband had taken her to the wilds of the West, she had to pen a note by hand and dispatch it by stage coach. Some weeks later, when the letter arrived, if the niece could not read it for herself, she had to find someone to read it to her. The only means of spanning the distance was the written word. Today if Aunt Sally wants to communicate with her niece whose engineering husband has taken her to the other side of the continent or even to another continent for temporary residence, she just picks up the telephone, dials a series of digits, and has the satisfaction of hearing the beloved voice at the other end of the line. Why wait for a letter to wing its way, even via air mail?

SPANNING TIME Another purpose for the written word is to span time. In the past a person who had profound thoughts he wished to preserve for posterity wrote them down or perhaps had them printed and stored in a book or library for future reference. The only way we can possibly know what man said in the far distant past is to read it from some record that has been preserved. Ancient mariners kept a ship's log. Famous men wrote their speeches. But you don't have to be able to read to find out what the presidents since Franklin D. Roosevelt have had to say. How many times in the past year have you heard a replay of such famous words as, "The only thing we have to fear is fear itself," or "Ask not what your country can do for you, but what you can do for your country." The words of presidents, labor leaders, poets, educators, politicians, theologians, and hundreds of others have been preserved on tape for posterity. Even favorite children's books, poems, and songs are recorded for listening.

It is no longer necessary that we read in order to span either time or distance.

PURPOSES FOR READING IN TODAY'S WORLD

Then why read? That is too often the real question facing the young child who finds the mechanics a bit troublesome and the other avenues to learning not only easier but more satisfying. Telling him he must learn to read because he will need to read when he is in high school or college is not very convincing.

FINDING OUT Unless the child is finding out something he wants to know reading will seem useless and he will soon lose interest. This is based on the theory that the child has natural curiosity, that he is interested in his environment, and that he does want to know something. This implies then that reading must have content right from the very beginning. He can read to find out which book is his, where his playthings are kept, what he is to bring from home, and when Santa Claus is coming.

ENJOYMENT If the child is familiar with books and has heard others read from them, then enjoying stories, poems, and all written material will be a logical development. As he begins to want to know what the stories are about and to read them for himself, he will develop an awareness of the need for reading, a readiness for mastery of reading skills, and maturity which will enable him to attack the printed form with insight and probably success.

When the child's desire to find out, his eagerness to enjoy, his alertness to meaning of the printed symbol have been aroused and his curiosity has been whetted, then he is teachable.

ESSENTIAL LEARNINGS FOR EFFECTIVE USE OF LANGUAGE

Language skills are multiple and complex. They are developed gradually over a long period of time. Many of them are not sequential but parallel. The learner does not master speaking before he begins to write. Neither does he master listening before he begins to read. Each supports the other as the related uses of language grow side by side in an ever expanding spiral.

INVOLVEMENT WITH IDEAS The first step for the child learning to read must be based on ideas expressed through language. He must think about the content and at the same time master the symbols used to express the ideas. Deciding which comes first is futile. They must develop simultaneously. Measuring the skills does not guarantee that the ideas will be forthcoming. Neither does casual attention to ideas guarantee that the skills will be mastered.

MASTERY OF VOCABULARY Learning words is important, but it is not enough. To vocabulary must be added both variety of word meanings and syntax. Words can be very confusing if memory is the only means of mastering them. As soon as the child gets a few words in his recognition vocabulary he begins to get his memory full. Then he must have some techniques for organizing his learnings into some kind of systematic pattern that will enable him to distinguish between the hundreds of similar word forms which have minute differences.

RECORDING IDEAS The child may begin by identifying his own materials with his name. Next he may move into the identification stage where he labels his possessions or the objects in his environment. He may have need for writing down the things he must remember to bring to school. This corresponds to his mother's shopping list. He may have a message to communicate, an invitation to send, or a thank you to express. What is written is meant to be read by somebody. If he sees his writing being read, he develops a desire to read what others have written. The two skills develop side by side.

Writing must begin with an idea to be expressed. It takes certain skills to express the ideas. The symbols to be used are the alphabet and punctuation marks. They are the same tools as those used in deciphering the reading material. The child is somewhat in the same position as the little boy who said, "Writing's easy. Once you know how to make the letters all you have to do is put them together." How true! And how complex!

Spelling then becomes involved in the process. Did you ever stop to think that you can understand a word when listening to someone else without knowing how it looks? Or that you can read a word without necessarily attending to the details of spelling? You can even use a word in oral speech without your hearer knowing that you don't know how to spell it. Not until you commit yourself to putting it on paper does spelling become paramount.

Penmanship is like spelling; as long as you don't attempt to communicate through the written word penmanship is inconsequential. Good penmanship and good spelling are as much matters of courtesy and consideration for the reader as they are matters of correctness. The reason we try to write legibly and spell in the accepted manner is to make communication easier for the receiver of the message. True, Aunt Jane might be able to read my poorly spelled and written letter, with some effort on her part, but if I make it easy for her by putting it in the form to which she has become accustomed, she will welcome my letter and thus regard me more highly.

Formalities of capitalization and punctuation are also part of the written word. In oral communication the pauses, the stops, the surprises, and the questions make their appearance in voice patterns and facial expressions. But words on the cold, expressionless page need some help to carry the writer's message. That's why commas, periods, exclamation marks, question marks, and quotation marks were invented.

When the child first tackles the mechanics of reading he is approaching a new situation like many other new situations he has experienced in his few short years. He has an insatiable curiosity. He wants to know what and how and why. If answers are forthcoming and are satisfying, he continues to learn. But if the learning presents difficulties with which he is ill-prepared to cope, he turns away from it and loses interest.

Learning to read is like a cycle. If the mechanics come easily, the child will read more. If he reads more, he will enjoy it. If he enjoys it and reads more, he will get more practice. As he gets more practice the mechanics become easier and easier and he becomes more and more skillful. On the other hand, if the mechanics present a stumbling block, he will be discouraged. If he becomes discouraged, he will practice less. If he practices less, he will become less skillful. As he becomes increasingly less skillful he will tend to avoid the reading situation more and more. As he avoids it and finds it difficult he will enjoy it less. The circle is never ending. If the circle starts with failure, it draws tighter and tighter. If it starts with success, it keeps on expanding.

And the moral to all this is that nothing succeeds like success. If we want the child to read and to enjoy reading, we must first capture his interest and his curiosity, and then guarantee success in his initial efforts. When that battle is won we are on the way to victory in the other battles which include perfection of skills and reading for meaning.

Which comes first? Both! He won't become skillful until reading makes sense, and reading won't make sense until he becomes skillful.

SOME PERSPECTIVES ON THE PROBLEM

Is reading a problem? Many seem to think so these days. The trend is toward more emphasis sooner in order to get the child to read. Everybody wants him to read. His parents want him to read. The teacher, the principal, and the supervisor want him to read. The special reading teacher wants him to read. In fact, all this wanting has reached a state of anxiety bordering on hysteria.

But what about the child himself? Does he want to read? And if he does want to read, why? Too often his wanting to read is for the wrong reasons. He may want to read to please his teacher, to keep from disappointing his mother, to get the football his father has promised him, to become the center of attention, or "to beat the other kids" in a superficial competition. But all these are external motives. Pressures for unnatural and ill-timed accomplishments in reading have created problems only remotely related to the real issue.

CAUSES OF THE PROBLEM

The causes of the problem are legion. Some are social. Some are economic. Some are political. Some are personal. Some grow out of attempts to fix blame. Some result from lack of understanding of either the reading process or the learner. And some stem from a frantic desire for a cure-all.

DESIRE FOR SOCIAL STATUS Social status is often judged by ability to read. The neighbor's children are reading. Billy's cousin in St. Louis has already started to read. He must keep up. Keep up with what? With his peers? With his parents' friends' children? With the grade standard? With other children who have established the norms? Unless Billy can do what the rest are doing and at the same time provide measurable evidence that he is doing it as well, or perhaps better, then he has not only lost social prestige for himself, but for his whole family. And all this concern says little about what he reads or why. It only reflects how well he reads and how he compares.

URGE FOR ECONOMIC ACHIEVEMENT Economic achievement has become allied with ability to read. Unless you can read you cannot become educated. Unless you become educated you cannot find a place in a profession or a well-paying job. Unless you work at a socially accepted job you cannot earn money. Unless you earn a good salary you cannot become financially and economically successful. Money earned through a job or a profession opens doors to culture, refinement, material possessions, opportunities for advancement, and recognition. The overzealous adult, either parent or teacher, traces it all back to the ability to read. Reading thus becomes the route to the dollar. Wealth begets wealth. This is evident in the form of reading.

POLITICAL ISSUES Those who are seeking a scapegoat to blame for personal deficiences often affix their censure to some issue or to some person outside themselves. If Tommy can't read it must be because the schools don't furnish the right things, the best teachers, the appropriate methods, or effective motives. And the reason they don't is because they don't have the right people at the head of things. These people must have a personal motive for being there. They must be seeking power or prestige at the expense of poor Tommy. Out with them! Elect new officials who will appoint new leaders who will establish practices which will result in success for Tommy.

PERSONAL ASPIRATIONS The ability to read or the lack of such ability reflects in aspirations for personal prestige. Then the pressures build up into anxieties. The anxieties function as blocks to the very thing they seek to build. If only he could read! If only he would read! Read what? That doesn't seem to be so important as the fact that he can read. With this point of view reading ceases to be a source of pleasure and satisfaction or a means of personal growth and development.

ATTEMPTS TO FIX BLAME In order to identify the apparent problem, each person who knows a child whose reading is not "up to standard," whatever that is, immediately starts out to find somebody or something to blame. The parent blames the materials or the method or the teacher. The teacher blames the parent, the frugal taxpayer, or the administration. The principal blames the tight budget or the inefficient teacher. The supervisor blames the system or the teacher. The employer blames the schools. The upper grade teachers blame the lower grade teachers. The lower grade teachers blame the upper grade teachers for their unreasonable expectations. All this round of fixing blame reveals two obvious omissions. Nobody seems to blame himself; and nobody blames the child. He is merely the victim in the controversy.

LACK OF UNDERSTANDING What we really need is a better understanding of the reading process itself. What happens to a child when he learns to read? Do all children do it the same way? We also need a better understanding of the learning process. How does one learn? What are the circumstances which induce learning and which hinder learning? Is there anything we can do about it? And finally, we need a better understanding of the learner. What kind of person is he? How does he function? How can we help him learn to read?

DESIRE FOR A CURE-ALL Probably one of the gravest factors which interferes with meeting and solving reading problems is the insatiable desire for a cure-all. We seem to be looking for *the* method, *the* material, *the* time, *the* setting that will guarantee results. We seem to be seeking a capsule loaded with the necessary ingredients to work a magic charm. If we could administer "still pills," "magic minds," or "ready reading" to all the children on a one-a-day basis with satisfaction-guaranteed-or-your-money-back maybe we would be satisfied. But unfortunately, children do not react like cardboard cartons rolling off the assembly line; each one an exact duplicate of the one before. Children are all different. They react to the same situation in different ways. In fact the same child reacts to the same situation in different ways on different days. All of this means that there is no one recipe for all and the teacher must make a daily individual diagnosis before she can prescribe a treatment to try. Even then she cannot guarantee the day's formula will work the way it did yesterday. She can only suggest and try and try again. The child learns only what he himself accepts.

EMPHASIS ON EARLY READING INSTRUCTION

Much of the concern about reading in the past two decades has centered around beginning reading. As a result we have had many publications, an abundance of materials, an emphasis on research, a concentration on quantitative measurement, and an increase in pressures on young children.

PUBLICATIONS Numerous articles have been published, some written by ill-informed people with "a gripe to air," some by unsuccessful people looking for someone to blame, and some by partially informed critics who demand to be heard. They can point out all the errors and recommend the cures, but many of them have never taught a child to read, not to mention a roomful of children with assorted abilities. They can tell what is wrong, but not what to do about it, or if they do suggest a remedy, they feel sure it would work if someone would just give it a try. They want someone else to "bell the cat." Some publications come from partially informed persons who see an opportunity to "sell" something. They may want personal acclaim or recognition for an idea or perhaps a "quick dollar." They may, or may not, have a product that will provide that much-sought cure-all, but they operate on the theory that "It pays to advertise." All this does not discount the person with a real message and genuine help, but the buyer must know the difference or he may succumb to the same pressures as the gullible bargain hunter who fails to get his money's worth.

ABUNDANCE OF MATERIALS A natural outcome of all this concern has been the production of materials to meet the needs. The market is well-supplied with gadgets, devices, cards, materials, consumables, equipment, machines, and tricks to help teach the child to read. The advertisements in the popular magazines suggest that if your child is having difficulty with his reading he should be using *our* materials, *our* program, *our* devices. Send no money! Free ten-day trial offer! Every one of them will probably work with some child, providing, of course, that the child works; otherwise each one will turn out to be a fad which sells for a while, then joins its predecessors to collect dust in the storage room.

EMPHASIS ON RESEARCH Response to the demand for answers has encouraged research. Perhaps there is no other field which has generated so much research in education as reading, and especially beginning reading. True research is endless and tireless. It is directed toward finding an answer or some answers. It is approached with an open mind and a seeking after truth. Examine some of the short-term studies often quoted in the field of reading. Note that many of them start out to prove a point rather than to seek an answer. By collecting just the data that support a preconceived belief one can accumulate what appears to be research evidence to prove almost anything. Hence, much of the research we are reading sends us around in circles because one study proves one thing and another refutes the first findings. Even the same pieces of research are sometimes quoted or interpreted differently by different observers.

QUANTITATIVE MEASUREMENT Statistics are tools of the researcher. The emphasis which has led to the avalanche of materials and the flurry of hasty research has in turn led to an overemphasis on factors which can be reduced to specific quantities and which can be measured objectively. The statistician can measure how many words the child can respond to correctly, how many right answers he can mark, how long it takes him to make a certain number of responses, and at what age he is able to accomplish certain goals. It is more difficult and less objective when he starts to measure enjoyment, interpretation, judgment, rational thinking, desire, insight, and other behavioral traits based on variable human responses. That is the reason these goals seem to have been omitted in the studies and the emphasis has been placed on measurable skills.

All these studies have resulted in a race to see who can get there first with the most. In order to prove that materials are good, that a particular method is effective, that one school is superior to another, that a teacher is efficient, they must be compared statistically to something else that is claimed to be inferior.

PRESSURES Increased pressures on young children have resulted from these emphases. This means that the child must come forth with measurable traits which can be tabulated, put on punch cards, and reduced to norms, means, medians, percentiles, stanines, grade scores, or deviations. Then these statistics must be subjected to comparisons, analysis of variance, and correlations so that a generalization may be stated that may be statistically true for a hypothetically average child or for a total sampling of the population. But when all is said and done there is no single child who fits the pattern, and the child has been pressured to produce for the sake of the score rather than for the sake of learning.

APPROACHES TO THE PROBLEM

There have been many approaches to the problem of reading based on content, materials, methods, administrative organizations, language tools, time, and sequences.

CONTENT Some have studied the content of reading. As a result we have gone full cycle from literary content to children's experiences to social experience to word lists and back again to where we started. Currently there is a trend for more literature in children's books.

MATERIALS Some have studied the materials of instruction and so we have gone from no pictures to line drawings to full color illustrations to photographs and back again to no pictures. We have gone from miniature books for little people to outsized books for undeveloped muscles. We have gone from small print to large print to charts and back to books. We have gone from elaborate script to clear type to manuscript print and back again.

METHODS Some have studied the methods of instruction and we have oscillated over the years from one method to another, often returning to what was abandoned a generation or two earlier. Phonics, word methods, sentence methods, and meaning have waxed and waned. Analytical and synthetic approaches have had their days. Rote learning and experience activities have shared the limelight. A combination of methods is often recommended and perhaps even a hodgepodge sometimes results.

ADMINISTRATIVE ORGANIZATIONS Some have attempted to solve the problem by manipulation of the administrative organization of the school or the children in the classroom. We have moved from the one-room school to the graded school to nongrading and back to multilevel grouping which is in a sense a replica of the original one-room school with modifications. Teachers have grouped and regrouped children within the classroom to meet different objectives. While the traditional three group arrangement probably predominates, it is not uncommon to find a classroom where all are expected to work as a total group or the opposite extreme of trying to manage six or eight different groups working separately.

LANGUAGE TOOLS Some have attempted to change the tool of language, namely, the alphabet, by introducing simplified spelling, phonetic spelling, and even a revised alphabet that is phonetically reliable. The i.t.a. is probably the most widely used variation built on the principle of altering the tool of reading. The i.t.a. tool can be applied to any method and any material can be printed in i.t.a., so it cannot be considered a method in or of itself.

TIME There are those who have based their suggestions on the time for teaching reading. They may be recommending a time of day for instruction. They may be concerned about the amount of time spent in the teaching of reading. A more recent emphasis has been on the time in the child's life during which the reading skills are taught. Some would spend more time, some less. Some would begin sooner and others would postpone the teaching to adjust to a more advanced level of maturity.

SEQUENCES Some have based their suggestions not so much on what is taught, but on the sequence in which the needed learnings should take place. Some would progress from meanings to skills, and others protest vehemently that progress should go from skills to meanings. Some would present decoding first, followed by encoding. Others would reverse the sequence. Some would teach vowels first and consonants later. Others insist that consonants are easier, more reliable, and carry the burden of communication and thus should not only be taught first, but should be given more emphasis.

WHAT IS LACKING

As we look back over all these approaches to the problem of reading we detect two great lacks, namely, a study of the learner himself and follow-through beyond the stages of initial instruction to maturity in reading.

A STUDY OF THE NATURE OF THE LEARNER Much of the research in reading has been based on how the child reacts to content, materials, methods, organization, language, time, and sequences in learning. But what of the learner himself? What is the optimum time for him to learn a specific skill? What stage of maturity has he reached at the present? What capacity has he for learning? What capacity for learning this specific skill does he have at this time? What is his attitude toward himself, toward reading, and toward learning in general? Maybe we need a study of the child and how he learns and what we can do to help him instead of so many studies of materials, devices, and methods and how he reacts to them.

FOLLOW-THROUGH BEYOND THE STAGES OF INITIAL INSTRUCTION A clear image of the nature of the reader is needed. Many studies are based on beginning reading and confine themselves to a short period of time. While a few studies have followed groups of children for more than one year, the typical pattern is testing in the fall, teaching for a period of twenty-five or thirty weeks, sometimes much less, then retesting all within a single school year. This approach is practical because it prevents excessive attrition from mobility and it gets the job done. But learning to read is not accomplished in a short period of time. And growth studies have told us repeatedly that children grow more or less erratically with spurts and plateaus in their learning curves. Therefore, any such studies must necessarily be influenced by irregularities in the growth pattern. A child who is experiencing a plateau in his learning growth during the interval covered by the study will affect the results adversely, and a child who is experiencing a spurt will affect them unduly in the positive direction. Only long-term studies will level off these irregularities in the learning curve.

What we need, then, is more longitudinal research extending to maturity in reading. We need to study the effects of developmental teaching based on progressive development to higher levels of skills and the application of skills to different types of reading. We need a coordination of the total language arts program including the assimilation of ideas through listening and reading and the expression of ideas through speaking and writing. Unless we finish up the job and see the matured product at the end of three or four, yes, five or six, or maybe twelve or fifteen years, we are not going to be drawing reliable conclusions. Any interim findings or temporary conclusions are just local stops along the way. They are not the destination. And we are letting far too many of the passengers drop off before the train reaches its destination.

The problem is deeper than social, economic, or political concerns. Blame cannot be fixed in a single factor. There is no single cause or cure. Pressuring the child to conform often frustrates him more than it stimulates him. We must take a long-term view and put the emphasis on helping the learner. We must view the objectives in terms of lifetime learning and constant and continuous growth.

THE NATURE OF THE PROBLEM

Problems look different depending on the angle from which they are viewed. The person who stands on the doorstep and rings the door bell gets quite

I can ride my [bicycle rebus].

I can.

I can.

I can ride and ride.

11

Plate 1. Concrete words presented by means of rebus [Mabel O'Donnell and Byron H. VanRoekel, *Janet and Mark,* Preprimer 1 (The Harper & Row Basic Reading Program), Evanston, Ill., Harper & Row, 1966, p. 11].

Come with me, Daddy.

I see something.

I see something I like.

See this swing.

I want to go up in the swing.

20

Plate 2. Concrete words presented by means of labeled illustration [Mabel O'Donnell and Byron H. VanRoekel, *Outdoors and In,* Preprimer 2 (The Harper & Row Basic Reading Program), Evanston, Ill., Harper & Row, 1966, p. 20].

a different view of the mansion than does the traveler who sees it from the distant hilltop. And the person on the inside looking out has a still different perspective. Similarly, the point of view alters the perspective on the nature of the reading problem. It may not look the same at all to the child as it does to the teacher. And how it looks to society at large is quite another matter.

FROM THE POINT OF VIEW OF THE CHILD

How does reading look to the child? Either he can read or he can't read. Either he reads well or he reads poorly. Either he likes to read or he doesn't like to read. Either he sees reading as something important and worthwhile or as a task imposed upon him by the adults in his environment.

Sometimes a child has more insight into the nature and the causes of his problem than anyone else. There is the incident of Fred who had been a problem to all the professional staff. The teacher had tried everything she knew and had referred him to the reading specialist. The specialist had given him tests and had referred him to the psychologist. The psychologist identified a behavior problem and referred him to the principal. The principal suspected a troublesome out-of-school environment and called in the parents. Still there was no solution to Fred's problem.

When Miss Andrews was assigned as a student teacher the room teacher promptly assigned Fred to her for a case study. As a courtesy accorded to teachers in training Miss Andrews was invited to sit in on faculty and staff meetings. One day the discussion centered around reading problems and the case of Fred was brought up. Naïvely Miss Andrews came up with a rather simple statement of Fred's problem and its cause. The teacher, the specialist, the psychologist, and the principal expressed amazement that such a novice in teaching had such perceptiveness.

"However did you find out?" they asked.

Innocently Miss Andrews replied, "I asked him."

Too often nobody asks Fred what his trouble is. Sometimes he can give great insight not only into the problem and its causes, but also into possible corrective measures. Talk over the child's problem with him. Treat him like a person.

FROM THE POINT OF VIEW OF THE TEACHER

How does reading look to the teacher? Is she concerned about scores and norms and impressions made on administrative officials? Is she concerned about keeping pace with the other teachers at the same grade level? Or is she concerned about helping children learn each to the best of his ability? And where does she get her concerns? Is there too much emphasis placed on testing, promotion, comparison? Is she given an opportunity to know each child as an individual? Are her expectations self-imposed or do the pressures come from the nature of the school's organization?

FROM THE POINT OF VIEW OF SOCIETY

How does reading look to society? What do they expect of the schools and why? Are their expectations based on reality? Are they reasonable? Are they fair?

Too often the persons viewing the reading problem, the reading objectives, and the reading class are limited in their point of view and therefore fail to see the total picture.

More than ninety years ago an old Hindu Fable was put into rhyme by John Godfrey Saxe describing the reactions of six blind men who went to view the elephant. The elephant was variously described as a wall, a spear, a snake, a tree, a fan, and a rope depending on what part of the animal's anatomy each blind man happened to feel. The moral was expressed in the final stanza thus:

> So oft in theologic wars
> The disputants, I ween
> Rail on in utter ignorance
> Of what each other mean,
> And prate about the Elephant
> Not one of them has seen!

It seems the fable has a parallel in the way self-appointed critics and experts view the reading class in the present day classroom. The following parody expresses that point of view with apologies to Mr. Saxe.

THE READING FABLE

It was six marms of school room fame
To learning much inclined,
Who went to see the reading class
Though each of them was blind
That each by observation
Might satisfy her mind.

The first observed the reading work
And happening around
When sounds and blends were being stressed
Cried, "This is what I've found.
God bless me! but the reading class
Is merely learning sound."

The second seeing lists of words
Cried, "Yes, I know 'tis so,

Words on papers, boards, in books,
It's words where'er you go.
The magic of your reading is
How many words you know."

The third approached the reading class
And happening to hear
The questions from the story asked
Concluded then and there
That reading is a simple skill
With answers everywhere.

The fourth reached out most eagerly
And found some phrase card drill.
"What most this mystic charm is like,"
She said, "Is just some skill
To make the eye and voice obey
The whim of teacher's will."

The fifth who chanced to come the day
They read a simple text,
Vowed she could see no need to fret
Or grow unduly vexed.
The mystery of their grand success
Was simply reading next.

The sixth no sooner had begun
About the room some swings
Than seeing worksheets everywhere
With pictures, words, and things,
Concluded that to read you need
To draw some lines and rings.

And so these marms of school room fame
Disputed loud and long
Each in her own opinion
Exceeding stiff and strong.
Though each was partly in the right,
And all were in the wrong!

So oft in Academic Wars
The disputants distraught
Rail on in utter ignorance
About each other's thought
And quarrel about the Reading Class
Not one of them has taught.[1]

[1]Daisy M. Jones, "A Reading Fable," *The Clearing House,* 43, no. 1 (September, 1968), 39.

2

A BRIEF HISTORICAL REVIEW

or What We Can Learn from the Past

The past is done, but it continues to have its effect on the present and perhaps even the future. This is no more evident any place than in our schools and in the teaching of reading which is a typical example. Even though needs have changed there is a tendency to retain traditional patterns. Even though new methods have been introduced there are still many who would cling to the good old days. A long-range view of the various plans which have been proposed and an analysis of their strengths and weaknesses should give us enough perspective to take stock of our present status and get a sane point of view.

HOW NEEDS HAVE CHANGED

Can we learn anything from the past? Does history repeat itself? Were "the good old days" better? Do we improve with experience? The only way we can answer these questions is to keep ourselves informed about what has happened, how, and why. Then a critical look at the over-all picture with a perspective on the total situation will at least give us a point of view for a fair appraisal.

In Chapter 1 we discussed the changes that have come about in the need for the reading act itself. It is no longer essential that one be able to read in order to span either distance or time. The telephone, television, telegraph, and tape recordings have taken care of those problems. Modern technology has enabled us to record and transmit the human voice and preserve it for posterity. Listening and thinking may be of greater significance in the communication of thought than mere skill in transcribing the printed symbol.

Even so, there is still need for skill in reading the printed word. How that skill has been acquired, how it is most effectively mastered, and how it is applied in daily life for today's citizens are still causes for much concern among thinking educators and lay people alike. What the consumer reads and the effect it has on his thinking may be of more concern than the degree of skill he possesses and the manner in which he attains it.

HOW METHODS HAVE CHANGED

"That's not the way they did it when I went to school," is an often heard comment from both lay and professional persons concerned with the teaching of reading in our schools. That remark alone bears mute testimony to the fact that methods do change. Some changes have been brought about by the emphasis placed on our national objectives. Some changes have been based on proposed plans for improvement in the teaching of reading. Some changes have been brought about through the influences of pressures and evidences of research.

EMPHASIS OVER THE YEARS

A cursory knowledge of the history of the United States will enable one to see a parallel between areas of emphasis in national goals and patterns of emphasis in the teaching of reading in our schools. These emphases may be divided roughly into five periods: religious, patriotic, industrial, cultural, and scientific.

RELIGIOUS EMPHASIS The period of religious emphasis grew out of the basic reason for the early settlements on the eastern seaboard. The first settlers came in 1620 for the expressed purpose of freedom of worship. It stands to reason then that their basic concern for the education of their children was to teach them to read in order that they might be able to read and understand the Bible. As a consequence the first reading materials were Bible selections and moralistic stories designed to establish fear of God and religious doctrine. This point of view dominated for about a hundred and fifty years. As settlements grew churches and schools were established. Many children did learn to read under those circumstances. History says little or nothing about those who did not. No doubt there were plenty of them who became good, honest, hard-working citizens who were able to cope with pioneer life without benefit of the printed word.

PATRIOTIC EMPHASIS The period of patriotic emphasis was a natural outgrowth of the events in our national history leading up to the Declaration of Independence. During the interval of a century and a half between the time of the landing of the Pilgrims and the conflict with England several generations of Americans had grown to maturity. By the time of the Revolutionary War the "younger generation" looked back on the religious emphasis of their ancestors with some disdain and felt that those goals no longer pertained to their "modern" problems. Religious freedom had long since been established. Communities had grown. Life in small towns had become more complex. Self-government and public relations were of greater concern. The citizenry said, "What we need is loyalty to our country, knowledge of public affairs, ability to participate in self-government, and statesmanship." Then the children were subjected to selections designed to develop knowledge and understanding of the history of our country, to instill patriotism for the United States, and to make them into informed citizens capable of participating in a representative form of government.

The rebellion against English domination, the westward expansion to become landowners, and the desire for a better way of life brought out a more materialistic aspect of educational goals. The citizen who had the potential became the statesman. The masses accepted this leadership and devoted themselves to the daily routine of making a living. Much of this routine was based on "brawn" rather than "brain," on "deeds" rather than "words," and as a consequence those who did not become scholars found their places in a pioneer society. They were getting along all right. They were respected for their deeds. Nobody worried about whether they could read or not. And in many cases they would have lacked books, magazines, or daily papers even if they had been able to read.

INDUSTRIAL EMPHASIS Industrial development in our country brought about new developments and new demands on the schools. The pioneers moved westward. Towns were established. Populations grew. Inventions changed labor patterns. Making a living was no longer a matter of establishing a claim to a plot of ground and tilling the soil. More specialization of jobs, division of labor, and use of machines were part of the industrial revolution. Now the citizenry looked to the schools and again said, "Why don't you do something about it?" As a consequence the schools introduced such practical subjects as manual training, bookkeeping, printing, and agriculture. These learnings were predicated on the assumption that the learner could read the textbook. More books were available and more specific skills were needed.

Reading took on a new importance. The educated person was the one who was prepared to earn money with which to buy the necessities and, perhaps, some of the luxuries of life. As factories and farms produced more than was needed for local consumption and as the new nation began to establish for itself a place in relation to the rest of the world, trade developed. The resulting communication with other parts of the world brought European influences to our schools. Educators began to be concerned about how it was being done in European schools. The influences of such leaders as Pestalozzi and Froebel were felt in educational circles particularly in the larger and more sophisticated metropolitan areas in the East.

CULTURAL EMPHASIS Material progress led to emphasis on cultural pursuits and thus our schools entered another new era. Money from production, manufacturing, trade, and commerce created a new affluent class of citizenry concerned about "the better things of life" for their offspring. The successful financier wanted his sons to have the benefit of the things he thought he had missed as he labored to establish the family fortune. He sent his sons abroad for a liberal education in European schools. Much of that influence permeated the schools in America. This new emphasis on culture led to the classics, languages, literature, the arts, and "the finer things of life" in the curriculum. Those who could afford higher education were concerned about literary pursuits. Those who lacked such concerns or could not afford higher education dropped by the wayside and populated the factories and the farm labor market. They got along in their world without too much emphasis on reading skills. They probably could read the headlines, sign their names to significant documents, vote, and follow the text when the scriptures were read. Beyond this there was little need for reading and probably little material available to be read.

SCIENTIFIC EMPHASIS The onset of the scientific period brought about totally new problems and new needs. All at once the hand labor jobs seemed to diminish. The demands for skill in reading, even for the most menial tasks, increased. The uneducated man became the disadvantaged citizen. This technological phenomenon created unemployment and clamor for more and better education for more people. Universal and compulsory education did not become an actuality until the days of improved roads, better means of transportation, and increased demands for specific skills. Then the public turned to the schools for an answer. Now the demand was to teach them *all* to read and to do it sooner and faster and better. This trend has been gaining momentum for the past half-century or more, until it has almost reached a state of hysteria and unreasonable expectations without consideration for the abilities of the learners or the facilities of the schools. Indeed, it is a compliment to the schools of America that the general public has such great faith in their ability to solve society's problems. At the same time it is a source of great frustration that the solutions are not readily forthcoming without extra expenditure of time, effort, and money.

The scientific age has descended on the schools through demands of society. It has reflected itself in research for better ways, better materials, and better content. All this has resulted in an avalanche of proposals, plans, and recommendations for the improvement of the teaching of reading.

Perhaps a panoramic view of the changes in reading methods will give us a background to help us take stock, find out where we are, what the present situation is, and what we should be doing about it.

A COMPARISON OF PROPOSED PLANS

The fact that so many plans and devices have been proposed to meet the need to teach all children to read with skill and efficiency is evidence of the extent of concern for the problem. All kinds of plans have been recommended, tried, evaluated, and sometimes accepted and sometimes rejected. Each one has entered the scene with glowing promises for curing the ills of the schools. Each one has had its proponents and its critics. Each one exhibits some values and has both advantages and disadvantages. No one proposal exists in a vacuum. Each one must be viewed in its relationship to the total school setting and the total developmental pattern of the learner.

The following comparison of proposed plans is not meant to be exhaustive. There may be others similar in nature but not named specifically. The intent is to examine representative types in order that the reader may have a background for evaluating each new proposal. While the classifications are not mutually exclusive an attempt has been made to divide the proposals into two general categories, namely, plans based on varying the techniques of instruction and plans based on varying the content of instruction.

Each plan is identified, its basic principles established, and some of its advantages and disadvantages pointed out. The purpose of this review is to help the teacher view the proposals unemotionally, see their strengths and weaknesses, and make up her own mind as to which parts of the recommendations she can accept and apply to her present situation.

PLANS BASED ON VARYING THE TECHNIQUES OF INSTRUCTION An analysis of instructional techniques may be further subdivided into those which involve organization for teaching and those which involve materials for teaching.

Organization for teaching may be based on total groups, subgroups, paired learning, or individualized instruction.

Total group or *mass teaching* stems from increased enrollments and demands for universal education. It relates itself to efficiency and technological advances in industrial life. It is based on the assumption that all children are alike, all need the same learnings, and all materials and all methods will get uniform results. It is neither good nor bad in its entirety. It does have advantages and disadvantages, some of which are presented in Table 1.

Table 1. TOTAL GROUP OR MASS TEACHING

Advantages	*Disadvantages*
Is economical of time	Ignores individual differences
Requires single, uniform preparation for teaching	Wastes time for those who deviate from the norm in ability or rate of growth
Utilizes one set of materials for all	Creates unfair competition
Can be compared, measured, and evaluated	Is based on subject matter to be mastered rather than on learners to be taught
Seems fair	

Ability grouping was a natural outgrowth of the recognition of individual differences and the resultant evils of mass instruction. It grew up with the advent of standardized testing, intelligence measurement, and child study. It is based on the theory that children of like abilities placed together for instructional purposes will form a homogeneous group and thus create a setting where mass instruction will work. It has been applied to sectional grouping within a school whereby children are placed in rooms according to ability. It has also been applied to subgrouping within the classroom creating the A, B, C groups, the X, Y, Z groups, the redbirds, bluebirds, and blackbirds, and so on. Regardless of what you call them both teachers and children know which is which. Advantages and disadvantages of the idea are summarized in Table 2.

Team learning has come in for its share of attention in classroom organization. This is similar to ability grouping in that the total class is broken up into subgroups; but it is somewhat different in that a team is ordinarily thought of as a cooperative group working together for the mutual benefit of each. A team may be composed of two or more teachers working with a group of children. It may be supported by para-professional teacher aides

Table 2. ABILITY GROUPING

Advantages	*Disadvantages*
Lessens spread of level of ability within a given group at a given time	Fails to recognize differences in rate of growth
Reduces unfair competition for slower learners	Assumes that reduction in spread of ability eliminates differences
Provides extra challenge for faster learners	Removes stimulus and challenge from lower groups
Reduces teacher preparation if grouping is based on total room organization	Creates status consciousness
Makes possible adjustment of materials to needs of learners	Increases teacher preparation if grouping is based on subgroups within the room
	Increases demand for variety of material

supplementing the work of the professional. It may be varied by the formation of pupil teams whereby learners work together, help each other, and utilize some of the variations of the monitorial system introduced in the earlier schools. The expression "team learning" seems a more appropriate term than "team teaching" to describe the advantages and disadvantages as set forth in Table 3.

Table 3. TEAM LEARNING

Advantages	*Disadvantages*
Puts emphasis on accomplishment rather than on competition	Assumes willingness to cooperate and mutual concern for accomplishment
Takes the learner into the planning stage	Reduces values which might derive from competition
Emphasizes cooperative effort	Lessens individual responsibility

Individualized teaching is the theoretical and ultimate goal of all teaching-learning situations. It is predicated on the assumption that each individual must do his own learning, and, after all, how else can learning take place? Even though the schools are organized around some kind of grouping arrangement, still the modern approach assumes that the teacher must reach each child individually and provide for his unique needs and abilities if real learning is to take place. There are as many patterns of individualized learning as there are proponents of the idea. Individualized instruction is predicated on the assumption that learning tasks will be tailored to meet the needs of each individual. That does not necessarily preclude all group experience. It does involve careful record keeping in order to know what each child is doing and what progress he is making. Some individualized instruction is based on a one-to-one relationship between teacher and child. Some is based on self-instruction or independent study by the child with teacher conference, guidance, and evaluation as needed. Consider the merits of such plans as set forth in Table 4.

Table 4. INDIVIDUALIZED INSTRUCTION

Advantages	*Disadvantages*
Begins where the child is and permits progress from that point forward at his own pace	Increases record keeping
Puts some responsibility for learning and progress on the learner himself	Assumes learner's self-determination and initiative
Eliminates unfair competition	Reduces challenges of competition
Reduces failure	Relaxes striving toward goals based on competition
	May result in satisfied attitude with mediocre attainment

Materials for teaching may influence methods. These overlap to some extent the plans which involve organization because various materials can be used in various organizational setups. However, the following are distinguishable as "methods" by virtue of the emphasis put on the materials being used.

Programed instruction is based on the theory that learning can be broken down into a series of sequential steps and can be presented in such a manner that the learner is constantly aware of his progress, the correctness of his responses, and the transition to the next step. Factual materials, mechanical skills, and memory techniques are particularly adaptable to this kind of device. This technique can be used for whole groups or for individualized instruction. It can be varied as to amount, rate, and level depending on the ability of the group or the individual. The advantages and disadvantages are summarized in Table 5.

Table 5. PROGRAMED INSTRUCTION

Advantages	*Disadvantages*
Works with facts that need to be memorized or with skills that must be mastered	Fails to take into account such cognitive learnings as evaluating and appreciating
Puts all learnings into one of these categories	Is ineffective with child who waits to be told what to do next
Is effective with learners who are self-propelled and who will move on to the next step without directions	Does not recognize insight and intuition as factors in learning
	Presupposes all children need to go through the same sequences

Machines have been advocated as a teaching device or method. The machine is based on the theory that the learner will respond to a given situation and the responses can be programed into the machine in such a way that he becomes self-directive. The value lies not so much in the machine as in the program that is fed into the machine. The machine itself is merely a gadget, a motivating device, a stimulator to entice the learner into activity. Once the novelty of the machine has worn off its value is expended. It will work only so long as the learner makes it work. When he ceases to punch the buttons or pull the levers learning ceases. Some children, however, are enamored of the experience of operating a mechanical apparatus which seems to respond and make them think. It becomes a game in which they match wits with the machine. If the continued practice which comes from the process results in improvement of skill or mastery of facts, then it has served a purpose, but the thinking educator might well question if that is the ultimate goal of learning to read. If used for memory and drill and supplemented with teaching which involves reasoning and thinking, it may make a contribution. For a closer look see Table 6.

Table 6. MACHINE TEACHING

Advantages	*Disadvantages*
Can stimulate the learner to automatic response	Works only so long as the learner works
Can serve as a motivator	Has little effect on reasoning and appreciation
Can lead to independent study and self-direction	Is geared to the average which fails to challenge the fast and lets the slow fall by the wayside
Saves teacher time	
Reduces record keeping	

Recorded materials for learning include television, film, and tapes. All these are based on the premise that what is to be learned can be predetermined, "stored" for use, and produced as needed by "turning on" the gadget into which the program has been fed originally. There are some kinds of learnings for which this may be very effective. Used with discretion such material can do much to supplement and to complement the work of a good teacher. As a total program it leaves much to be desired. For comparison see Table 7.

Table 7. RECORDED MATERIAL

Advantages	*Disadvantages*
May be better than classroom teacher can provide	Puts learner in passive role of receiver
May be more realistic than a written record	Assumes that all need the same kind and amount of exposure to the learnings
Can be adapted to needs of the individual	Requires space and equipment which may be more expensive than the budget will allow
Can be repeated for emphasis	May result in dependence on the gadgets
Can save teaching time	

The Augmented Roman Alphabet was an attempt by Sir James Pitman in England to reduce the sounds of the English language to the forty-four most common and regular ones. He adapted the Roman alphabet to fit the sounds and called his adaptation an augmented alphabet. This alphabet has been utilized in the teaching of reading as an initial approach in which one sound is represented by one symbol and a given symbol represents one sound. In other words the program was designed to produce a one-to-one relationship between sound and symbol in order that the beginner might have a tool on which he could depend. This is one of the few attempts to vary the approach to the teaching of reading by manipulating the medium of instruction rather than the method or the content. Because of its use in the beginning stages only, it has been called an *i*nitial *t*eaching alphabet and the terminology has been shortened to i.t.a. in popular parlance. Numerous research studies have been conducted and scores of articles have been written on the subject. The reader is left to explore the research for himself and to draw his own conclusions. The summary of advantages and disadvantages in Table 8 may lend perspective to the study of the problem.

Table 8. I.T.A.

Advantages	*Disadvantages*
Simplifies sound-symbol relationships in beginning reading	Is highly regular but not completely regular in sound-symbol relations
Can be adapted to various methods or materials	Is founded on need for automatic mastery of mechanics
Can be utilized with any content	Requires an adjustment on the part of the teacher
Encourages written expression and independence in early stages in the learning-to-read process	Demands a transition to traditional orthography

PLANS BASED ON VARYING THE CONTENT Plans based on what to teach are perhaps the best known and most familiar to the general public. The controversy about what the child should be taught has raged for centuries, and no doubt discussion will continue for years to come. The controversy involves not only what to teach, but also where to begin and in what sequence the essential learnings should be developed. The differences are not in what the child shall learn, but rather in the area of emphasis and the sequence in which the learnings shall take place.

Most lay and professional critics agree that the accomplished reader knows the alphabet, understands phonic principles, and can pronounce the words. They also agree that he is able to put the words together into sentences, can combine these techniques into experiences utilizing language, is familiar with linguistic patterns, and can use the skills at a satisfactory rate. Furthermore, he can combine all the knowledges and understandings into a total learning pattern that involves an eclectic approach which results in the reading act. The differences of opinion center about which one of the various learnings is more important at each step of development. Attempts to isolate one of these objectives and make it the basic approach have resulted in a variety of so-called methods each of which has its proponents as well as its critics.

It is doubtful if the proponent of a single method has actually used it to the exclusion of all others. Much of the claim for a given method may well be attributed to the skill and creative ingenuity of the teacher. While it is improbable that any one of the following methods has been used in isolation, an attempt will be made to identify the major characteristics of each, putting it in perspective by pointing out its advantages and disadvantages in order that the unbiased observer may see it in relation to the total learning-to-read process.

The *ABC method* is probably the one the uninformed critics think is basic to all reading. There are those who would go so far as to say, "Teach the child his ABC's and he will learn to read." It is true the workman must know his tools, but being able to identify a hammer, a saw, and a chisel doesn't make a carpenter. Neither does identifying the abstract symbols by name make one a reader. For a summary of the advantages and disadvantages of the ABC method see Table 9.

Table 9. THE ABC METHOD

Advantages	*Disadvantages*
Recognizes alphabet as basic tool of English language	Slows reader's responses through overemphasis on minute detail
Relates reading to spelling and writing	Assumes ability to spell a word guarantees ability to pronounce it
Contributes to phonic study	Assumes ability to pronounce words gives meaning
Promotes left-to-right movement of the eyes	Emphasizes short recognition span
Leads to effective use of such tools as the dictionary	Is highly mechanical

Phonics is a study of sounds as expressed in symbols. These are related to the pronunciation of words. The study of phonics is based on the study of the alphabet. There are proponents of the so-called phonic method who believe that the name of the letter is not so important as the sound represented by the letter. Actually, letters do not "have" sounds. It is even questionable whether phonics as such is a method. Technically, it is a scientific study of the symbols and the sounds they represent. Phonics can be taught by various methods such as rote memory, inductive reasoning, discovery, and drill. It is commonly thought of as a method and for that reason will be considered here. It does have merit. It should be viewed in relation to the total reading process and in terms of the entire learning sequences. A summary of its advantages and disadvantages is presented in Table 10.

Table 10. THE PHONIC METHOD

Advantages	*Disadvantages*
Gives the learner a tool which leads to some degree of independence in word attack	Can be confusing when words do not fit regular pattern
Aids in pronunciation and spelling of words which follow a regular pattern	Can lead to mispronunciation and misinterpretation
Provides measurable evidence of learning	Puts emphasis on mechanical performance
Emphasizes systematic left-to-right movement	Develops habits of slow, laborious decoding of words
	Ignores the significance of word meaning in context

The *word method* grew out of a dissatisfaction with the results of overemphasis on letters and letter sounds. The first advocates of the whole word method, long before 1900, produced sound evidence that it was quite possible to recognize a total pattern without necessarily being aware of its separate parts. For example, one can recognize a person without being aware of the color of his eyes. A child can recognize a favorite toy without knowing how many wheels it has. Experimentation has proved that a reader can distinguish highly dissimilar words from one another without knowing the letters that make up the words. The theory that words, not letters, express ideas and that communication is the main purpose of reading led to the development of the word method in teaching beginning reading. Out of these theories and this philosophy has grown the practice of teaching

Table 11. THE WHOLE WORD METHOD

Advantages	*Disadvantages*
Leads to immediate success in interpretation of meaning	Provides no immediate means of decoding new words
Lengthens the eye span	Overemphasizes memorizing words without related meanings
Increases speed at the outset	Can be abstract and mechanical
Gives the beginner early satisfaction	Emphasizes words rather than thought units

beginning reading by familiarizing the child with whole words, first concrete words such as nouns and action words and later more abstract words. Telling apart the ones that are similar in appearance was a later step. More than a hundred years ago children were learning to read with this approach. It has experienced popularity and condemnation and has been subjected to variations over the years. As a beginning step in learning to read it bears examination. For a summary of the advantages and disadvantages see Table 11.

The *sentence method* was a natural next step after the emphasis on the word method. It was reasoned that if the child is to learn to read for ideas, the logical place to begin is with the idea not the symbol. Since many words, particularly such abstract words as *could, which, of,* and *was,* did little to convey meaning when they were presented in isolation, then putting them into meaningful settings would enhance the reading act. While *could* by itself expressed little or no meaning the phrase "could not come" began to take on meaning. Putting it in a complete sentence, such as "Billy could not come to the party," added still deeper meaning. The theory back of this approach was that reading should begin with the expression of an idea. Then the child should be shown how it looks in print. He could distinguish between different sentences expressing different ideas because of their differences in general configuration, their location on a chart, the chalk board, or the printed page, or by their association with a picture or object related to the expression. Later steps included identifying separate parts of the sentences, breaking them down into phrases or words, and eventually analyzing the words for structure. Sometimes the follow-through missed some of these later steps and critics claimed children were not learning to read; they were merely memorizing the stories. However, some capable children did succeed with this approach, and some teachers did follow through and lead children to measurable success with skills as well as meanings. It bears closer inspection. See Table 12.

Table 12. THE SENTENCE METHOD

Advantages	*Disadvantages*
Begins with meaning	Offers no means of attack on words at the beginning
Emphasizes expression	Requires much meaningless repetition of content to fix learnings
Increases speed	Utilizes stilted sentence patterns
Includes all the elements of mature reading when carried to its ultimate conclusion	Permits guessing

The *story method* was designed to carry forward the theories attributed to the sentence method and at the same time to overcome the criticisms. It was based on an expansion of the theory of meaning as an essential approach to the learning of reading. Recommendations included the reading of the entire story to the children. After this reading by the teacher the children were encouraged to retell, dramatize, and illustrate the story, and to listen to it over and over again until the vocabulary, the word patterns, and the plot were thoroughly familiar. Then the children were introduced to the printed page. The sequence was from the meaningful story back to print, to sentences, to phrases, to words, to sounds, and finally to the letters of which the words were composed. Examine its possibilities as set forth in Table 13.

Table 13. THE STORY METHOD

Advantages	*Disadvantages*
Starts with literary content Represents good composition Has interest appeal Assures meaning by familiarizing child with plot Establishes familiarity with the linguistic structure of language before the child is asked to read	Introduces difficult vocabulary when based on traditional stories Encourages overdependence on context clues Permits memorizing and guessing Encourages random eye movements seeking elements of familiarity Is less appropriate with informational material

The *intrinsic method* was based on the development of mechanics in a meaningful setting. For example, the child was asked to scrutinize such an expression as:

The train runs on a trick track truck.

Here the technique is to decide what makes sense, then select the ending which fits. This involves first of all meaning, then the ability to analyze the words for structure and select the right one. In actuality the process is a recognition of the differences in the vowel sounds of *i*, *a*, and *u*. This recommended procedure was an attempt to satisfy both the proponents of the meaning approach and the advocates of the importance of mechanics. Its merits as well as its dangers are pointed out in Table 14.

Table 14. THE INTRINSIC METHOD

Advantages	*Disadvantages*
Is based on meaning combined with mechanics Provides sequential development Gives meaningful practice Tends to become self-teaching Provides effective checking for both accuracy of skill and meaning	Is highly individualized requiring personal teacher-pupil contact Was the forerunner of excessive test-type busy-work exercises May result in paper-and-pencil drill rather than in reading for meaning May be interpreted as a lack of phonics

The *experience activity method* grew out of the emphasis on child development as an approach to education as opposed to the theory of structure of the discipline. For years curriculum has been planned as the academician saw the organization of a body of knowledge to be taught. Then the child development movement caused curriculum planners to take a new look in terms of how the learner reacts to the content rather than to the systematic organization of the content itself. The reasoning was that the child should have meaningful experiences. These experiences should be expressed in language. The language should be expressed in symbols. The child should be shown how it looks in print. Then he should be led to recognize, remember, analyze, and eventually gain independence in associating symbol with sound that makes sense. The whole philosophy led to such proposals as natural or incidental learnings, chart lessons, experience activities, language experience, and even some of the more recent linguistic approaches. The idea that the language pattern must be familiar to the child and that it must make sense to him was basic. The sequence from meaning to form to analysis was recommended. An analysis is presented in Table 15.

Table 15. THE EXPERIENCE ACTIVITY APPROACH

Advantages	*Disadvantages*
Is based on children's incidental experiences	Lacks systematic sequence in mastery of skills
Introduces print as "talk written down"	Offers little or no method of word attack in beginning steps
Begins with familiar vocabulary	Introduces the learner early to vocabulary which is mechanically difficult and phonetically irregular
Uses linguistic patterns that are familiar to the child	Permits memory reading
Leads child to plan content of his own learning	Depends on the creativity and ingenuity of the teacher
Emphasizes thought	
Integrates reading with learnings in other areas	

While *speed* cannot rightfully be called a method it did come in for its share of emphasis in the teaching of reading and in some cases influenced methodology. There are advocates of speed in pursuit of the printed page and in the instantaneous recognition of words and symbols. Out of this craze has grown the development of devices to increase speed. Flash cards, eye pacers, speed machines, mechanical flash devices, and controlled rate techniques have been introduced. The theory is that the fast reader grasps ideas quickly. This approach lends itself to mechanical drill, objective measurement, and statistical evidences of accomplishment. Perhaps the idea has made a contribution to the teaching of reading. However, one must remember that speed exercises do not teach word recognition or develop ideas. An accurate response can be speeded up. An inaccurate response subjected to excessive drill will only fix the inaccuracy. In order for speed drill to be effective it must fix learnings into quick and accurate responses. For a summary of the advantages and disadvantages of an emphasis on speed see Table 16.

Table 16. SPEED READING

Advantages	*Disadvantages*
Encourages reading for ideas	Stimulates hasty response
Helps establish skill	Encourages superficial reading
Conserves time	Permits guessing
Lends itself to measurement and record of growth	Lacks mechanical accuracy
	Creates tensions
Is applicable to many reading needs	Is not appropriate to all reading needs

The *eclectic approach* was an attempt to meet all the criticisms and to capitalize on the desirable qualities of each of the various methods and at the same time to circumvent or at least suppress the major criticisms. It is often thought of as a combination of methods. Literally, it means selecting from various sources or systems according to taste or opinion. This selection might be made by the teacher in the classroom. More often the selections have been made by the writers of basal readers, the manuals, or the workbooks. Most basal reading programs, while subscribing to a basic philosophy of reading, do make such selections. The careful observer will find elements of all, or almost all, the popular theories and proposed methods. This is true for several reasons. The first is probably an honest conviction that each has its merits which should be utilized. The second is probably an attempt to satisfy the customer regardless of his personal convictions. The third is probably a recognition that such published materials will be used by both experienced teachers and novices. They will be used by both alert and dull children. They will be used by children with rich backgrounds as well as by children from disadvantaged areas with meager backgrounds. When a basal reader uses an eclectic approach in its content and in its suggestions in the manual, it is actually depending on the skill and good judgment of the teacher to select what fits the needs of her children in the immediate situation. Any basal reading program used in its entirety as a prescriptive dose for all children alike is doomed to criticism from some source or other. Without straddling the issue it does depend on a good teacher and it does have merits as set forth in Table 17.

Table 17. THE ECLECTIC APPROACH

Advantages	*Disadvantages*
Encourages pupil growth as well as perfection of mechanical skills	Places responsibility for planning and deciding on the teacher
Incorporates the good qualities of a variety of approaches	Is suggestive rather than prescriptive and may lead to overdoing if all suggestions are followed literally
Is adaptable to varying situations and levels	May lack organization and sequence in the hands of an inexperienced teacher
Frees the teacher to select learnings in terms of pupil needs	

All the plans described above, whether they are based on varying the techniques of instruction or on varying the content to be taught, have emerged as natural consequences of the pressures of the times. They have all been tried in various settings. They have all claimed some success. They have all been criticized. I am convinced that a really good teacher who understands the structure of the language with which she is dealing, the child with whom she is working, and the learning process which is going on can take any one of them, or any combination, and produce commendable results.

INFLUENCES WHICH HAVE BROUGHT ABOUT THESE CHANGES

The American public expresses great faith in its schools. Whenever any need exists, whether it be for industrial know-how, physical health, or psychological adjustment, the public always turns to the schools and the teachers, saying, "Why don't you do something about it?"

Educators always respond to these demands with an attempt to meet them. Such demands sometimes leave the school personnel in a quandry as to what is the best thing to do. Too often trying to please everybody results in disaster.

Sometimes it seems that educators have been swayed by public criticisms and demands. Some questions might well be raised. Are the educators surveying the problems, making the decisions, and prescribing the actions or are they merely trying to keep abreast of the demands? Are they exercising leadership or succumbing to pressures? Are they proposing a program or defending a situation not of their own making? Both pressures and research findings have influenced changes.

PRESSURES Public opinion has brought about many of the changes which have taken place in the teaching of reading throughout the history of the American schools. The parent wants his child to excel, to have a better life than he did, to succeed. The politician wants the comparison to show favorable results in terms of measurable goals. The businessman wants skilled workmanship and performance. Meeting all these demands in schools designed to teach all the children of all the people in a melting pot of assorted abilities, needs, interests, and backgrounds too often results in "hash," that is, a mixture of whatever is available. Sometimes the end product leaves much to be desired. The question might well be raised, "Is succumbing to the pressures exercised by lay critics, the public press, and the advocates of pet theories the best way to teach reading?"

RESEARCH The advent of the scientific period has had its influence on instructional techniques and materials. Research has led educators to examine proposals not so much in terms of what they claimed, but what trial and experimentation proved about them. There has been research into the use of devices, materials, techniques, and plans of all kinds. Most of it is designed to compare one situation with another and to come up with an answer as to which is better. Some of the research has been conducted by individuals with prejudices or preconceived ideas which they were trying to prove. Some of it has been conducted by interested persons in order to support the sale of certain products. And some of it has been an honest seeking for the answer to definite questions.

Too often the questions asked by research are unanswerable. It is like asking which is better, a bathing suit or a formal? It all depends on where you are going. Or which is better for the child, meat or oatmeal? Again, it all depends. One probably should have both in balanced amounts. Any research which proves that one is better than the other must first say, "better for what?" So much depends on the objective. And in education we need to define our objectives before we can decide on materials or techniques. Yes, research does make its contribution, but the informed teacher will examine the research in the light of its purpose and her pupils.

A SANE LOOK AT THE SITUATION

Where are we now? We are being buffeted about by influences outside the schools. We are still trying to please everyone. We are still being influenced by nonprofessionals, by salesmen, by critics. We are listening for leadership from administrators, research workers, and professionals.

All this is brought about not only from pressures outside the classroom but from an element of unrest which exists within the classroom. The turnover in teaching staff, the lack of continuity from year to year and from level to level, the constant bombardment from outside to meet demands and use materials often leave the teacher confused about what she should do.

What we need is more individual classroom teachers who are willing to square their shoulders, look the situation in the face, and say, "I am a professional. I am willing to make a decision and face the responsibility."

THE TEACHER AS A PROFESSIONAL

Once that position has been taken by the teacher she must follow through with the assumption of responsibility for her own decisions and her own actions. She can no longer say, "It isn't my fault; that's what the principal said to do." Or "I can't help it, this is what the public demands." Or "I don't see why they didn't learn, I followed the manual carefully."

Follow-through is also more than assuming responsibility. It means a professional approach with an on-going program. The teacher who teaches a year or two and quits is not a professional. The teacher who gets the children through the examinations at the end of the year and assumes no feeling of responsibility or concern for what comes next is not a professional. The teacher who refuses to accept the child who is "not ready for her grade" is not a professional.

When the teacher reaches that point where she can face responsibilities and is willing to make decisions then she is truly a professional. A professional teacher will be aware not only of the historical background, the present situations, and the current demands, but also of the needs of the children. Then she will be able to diagnose the situation and prescribe learning experiences in terms of the accepted goals and the needs of the children.

FIXING RESPONSIBILITY

Follow-through means accepting a lifetime responsibility for the development of the profession. It means seeing the total program of the school. It means fitting the teaching-learning activities of a given day, a given week, a given school year into the total developmental processes of the learner. It means putting the emphasis on helping the learner learn.

Yes, we have changed with time. Some changes have been good; some have been not so good. It is not so much a matter of whether we are right or wrong, but whether we are headed in the right direction.

Part Two

DEVELOPING READING SKILLS

or
So Much to Teach

Have you read Part One yet? If so, you are already aware that the mastery of mechanics has long been a controversial issue in the teaching of reading. You are also aware that mechanics cannot be separated from comprehension. Therefore, you may decide to alternate your reading of Part Two and Part Three to get the blending of skills and meanings in the total reading program and the teaching steps which help the learner.

For purposes of organization the skills are discussed separately in Part Two. They include readiness, vocabulary development, phonics, linguistics, oral and silent reading, and speed.

This treatment of skills is not a set of recipes. Neither is it a technical analysis of research. It is intended as a translation of research findings into the language which helps the classroom teacher answer such basic questions as:

How will I know?
What shall I do?
What shall I use?
How shall I go about it?

3

THE IMPORTANCE OF READINESS

or Are You Ready?

Readiness is a much abused term. It is easy to excuse lack of success on the grounds that the child was not ready, but such an excuse represents a passive attitude, waiting for time to take care of readiness. Pointing out immaturity as a basis for lack of progress is an escape from responsibility. We need to define what we mean by readiness, by maturity, by progress. It is equally important that we know how to encourage these qualities in reading and learning. Time may take care of the ripening of the apple, but waiting for time to pass will not get the child ready for school intellectually any more than it will physically. The child who sits on the edge of the bed for an hour will be no nearer ready for the arrival of the school bus than he was at the beginning of the hour. The hour must be used with purposeful activities designed to get him dressed and his school supplies assembled so he will be standing at the end of the driveway when the bus comes.

The child who meets school in a state of readiness is the one who has used his time appropriately in the years or months or days which precede school entrance. If he is not ready when he comes, there are some things we can do about it after he gets there. And the teacher who is aware of the needs is the one who will lay a foundation for successful reading later. In order to capitalize on the principles of readiness the teacher must first of all be able to recognize its existence or its lack. When it does exist she must know where to start and what to do next. When it does not exist she must know how to meet the situation and develop a state of readiness that will ensure success with next steps.

RECOGNIZING READINESS

"How can I tell when Johnnie is ready to read?" That is the question often asked by the teacher as well as by the mother. You can pinch the peaches to tell if they are ripe. You can use the touch test on wet paint. The cooking thermometer will help you know whether the candy is ready for beating. Unfortunately, you can't pinch the children, touch them to tell, or apply a thermometer guaranteed to give you an accurate reading on readiness. But there are some very practical ways to tell.

There are readiness tests on the market. Many of them are designed by experts and yield valuable information. Some of them provide predictive scores which support subjective judgment. Some of them are divided into parts indicating kinds of readiness. Administering a readiness test wholesale to all the children near the end of kindergarten or at the beginning of first grade is often a waste of time, both the child's time and the administrator's time. Some of the children are so obviously ready that there is no point to testing them. Some of them are so obviously not ready that a test will serve little purpose except to support the judgment of the teacher. There are, of course, others who will be on the border line. The results of a readiness test may sway the teacher's judgment one way or the other. Test results in such cases, however, may fail to take into consideration such factors as health, experience, will to learn, or general maturity and so lead to wrong decisions. The child who possesses the above qualities and is almost ready will probably succeed, while the child who lacks these qualities yet attains the same score on the test may not succeed. Much is still left to the judgment of the teacher. Then how will she tell?

EVIDENCES OF READINESS

The evidences of readiness are as much subjective as objective. No test score can give the final answer. The best it can do is to support the subjective judgment of the teacher. The child needs to be physically ready, socially ready, intellectually ready, and psychologically ready. Collecting evidence under these headings will help the teacher decide.

PHYSICAL READINESS A general state of good health including hearing, seeing, and muscular coordination is essential to success in beginning reading.

Since the child uses his ears for communication through listening, an appraisal of *hearing* might be a logical first step. Can he hear? Does he listen? There is quite a difference between hearing and listening. Hearing is a physical process. Listening is a mental process which includes conscious attention.

Since the child uses his eyes to view the printed symbols, an appraisal of *sight* is also important. Can he see? How well? Does he observe? There is quite a difference between seeing and observing. Seeing is a physical process. Observing is a mental process which includes conscious attention to visible phenomena.

Since the child must handle the books and other learning tools while he is using them, *muscular development* is significant as a factor in readiness for the reading act. There is quite a difference between muscular development and muscular coordination. The child may be able to use his eye muscles, his large body muscles, his finer hand muscles, and his locomotion skills; these are physical processes. Coordination involves a blending of the various movements into a smooth mechanism which operates as a unit; this takes both thought and practice.

SOCIAL READINESS Recognizing social maturity is more subjective than measuring physical factors, but it is nonetheless important. A child who has been shut up in a third story room with high windows for five or six years may have a strong physical body because he has had adequate food and bodily care and still be socially unready to cope with the tasks demanded of the beginning reader. The child needs social experiences with things such as animals, toys, pets, other children, adults, nature, and science in order to read about them. The child needs social experiences and interpersonal relations in order to develop his own personal maturity.

INTELLECTUAL READINESS An even more elusive quality is intellectual development. It is one which psychologists and educators have been trying to "pin down" for the past century. It is revealed in the way a child reacts to his environment and even more specifically in his use of language.

There is a difference of opinion as to whether native ability is fixed at birth or is subject to stimulation from the environment. There are those who believe that all children have ability if it can be aroused. Regardless of whether it is native or acquired the teacher who faces twenty-five or thirty 6-year-olds soon becomes aware that they are not all alike. They do not all respond to the same stimulation in the same way or with equal amounts of insight or perception. Some seem alert and "catch on" right away. Some seem uninterested, respond with a blank stare, give vague responses, and even turn away from the learning tasks.

The language the child uses when he comes to school, and that includes the 12-year-old as well as the 6-year-old, is indicative of his intellectual maturity as related to the skills needed in learning to read. If he knows the words to name objects, to identify actions, to describe feelings, to express ideas, he is exhibiting both intellectual ability and linguistic maturity. If he can put those words together into meaningful patterns that communicate his thoughts to others, he is ready to use those same linguistic patterns to absorb the thoughts of others through reading.

Whether one considers present intellectual level or rate of intellectual growth, real differences do exist and the teacher who attends to these differences is making a sound appraisal of readiness.

PSYCHOLOGICAL READINESS The child's psychological readiness is somewhat elusive and some tend to ignore it altogether. It is basic to his attitude toward himself, toward others, toward school, and toward the reading act itself. An objective measure of psychological development is difficult to obtain, but that does not make it any less real. You may be able to count how many times a child can skip a rope without tripping and come up with a fixed number which changes with time. That is objective. But you will have more difficulty arriving at a numerical term which will measure how well he likes school, how he feels about himself, or how much he wants to learn to read. Just because you cannot furnish a score does not mean these attitudes do not exist. Psychological readiness is a genuine factor in learning to read and must be taken into account.

SEX DIFFERENCES There is plenty of evidence that girls mature linguistically younger than boys and that the vast majority of cases in remedial reading clinics are boys. This cannot be used as a blanket statement, however. Some boys who are especially alert or who come from reading-oriented backgrounds may be more nearly ready for beginning reading at a given age than girls without these advantages. Some girls who lack rich backgrounds or native intelligence may not be as nearly ready for reading as boys with more of the advantages. One cannot generalize on sex as a basis for deciding on readiness. All one can conclude from the statistics is that, other things being equal, one can expect more immaturity in the reading act among boys than among girls. But great caution must be exercised in generalizing. Each case must be judged on its own.

READINESS FOR INITIAL INSTRUCTION

The teacher who looks for evidences that the child is ready for initial instruction in reading must be aware of the multiple facets of readiness. They include meaning, perception, and ability to generalize on word patterns.

READINESS FOR IDEAS The child needs first of all to be aware of ideas. The teacher needs to communicate with the child on an intellectual level through conversations, questions, answers, and observations about things and incidents. The child needs many experiences with literary materials, both prose and poetry. The child who communicates, the child who enjoys stories, the child who uses language is the child who is ready for that next step.

RECOGNIZING WORDS When it comes to word forms the identification of readiness is a bit more specific. The child who notices labels, who points out words he knows, who asks, "What does this say?" is the child who has become aware that the abstract symbols stand for ideas. The child who discriminates between words that are similar in appearance has shown an awareness of word form. The child who says, "This says, 'John,' and that's my name. It begins like Jane's name but it is not the same," has revealed a degree of readiness for word recognition that is helpful to the teacher in identifying the stage for which she is looking.

GENERALIZING In attacking mechanics in reading the insight of the learner is a bit deeper. The child who notices similarities and differences in color or form, who hears similarities and differences in tone or word pattern, and who comments on these characteristics is beginning the first steps in inductive reasoning and generalization. Until the child can make such generalizations much of his mastery of mechanics will be rote memory resulting from telling and drilling. When he shows evidences of insight into patterns, he is beginning to understand how words are formed from the tool which is used to record his language, namely, the alphabet.

A check list will be helpful in deciding who is ready for reading and who still needs help in maturing before attacking initial instruction. Such a device is offered in Table 18. This is not a test. It is not an objective set of criteria with a score. It is merely a guide to help the teacher view the child in his entirety and to direct her thinking in making the necessary decisions.

If you look at a child with these questions in mind and if you come up with mostly "yes" answers, then perhaps you are dealing with one who shows a degree of readiness for beginning reading. The "no" answers will serve as warning signals. If there are too many of them, perhaps you should proceed with caution. If you find mostly "no" answers, then per-

Table 18. IS JOHNNY READY TO READ?

Physical Readiness	*No*	*Yes*
Does he appear healthy and free from frequent illnesses?	______	______
Is he well fed, properly nourished, and energetic?	______	______
Can he hop, skip, and march in rhythm?	______	______
Can he jump rope, turn summersaults, walk a straight line?	______	______
Can he bounce and catch a ball?	______	______
Can he manipulate puzzles, blocks, scissors, etc?	______	______
Does he show a definite hand preference?	______	______
Can he grasp a pencil in position for writing?	______	______
Can he draw a man or representative human figure?	______	______
Does he seem to hear accurately?	______	______
Does he follow simple directions?	______	______
Does he notice similarities in sounds, tones, pitch, etc?	______	______
Does he look at the speaker while he listens?	______	______
Is his look direct, free from squinting, head tilting, etc?	______	______
Can he distinguish differences in content, size, and shape?	______	______
Does he hold a book a suitable distance from his eyes?	______	______
Can he recognize his own name when he sees it?	______	______
Is he one of the larger children in his group?	______	______
Does he compete successfully in physical activities?	______	______

Social Readiness	*No*	*Yes*
Is he willing to listen as well as to talk?	______	______
Is he willing to share toys, books, etc?	______	______
Does he assume responsibility for his own materials?	______	______
Is he eager to participate in new activities?	______	______
Does he respond positively to others?	______	______

Psychological and Emotional Readiness	*No*	*Yes*
Is he interested in pictures, books, and stories?	______	______
Is he willing to work at a task alone without constant help?	______	______
Does he stick to a task until it is finished?	______	______
Does he profit from his mistakes and correct his own errors?	______	______
Does he see good in the work of others?	______	______
Is he willing to share "center stage" with his peers?	______	______
Is he willing to listen and sometimes take "no" for an answer?	______	______

Intellectual Readiness	*No*	*Yes*
Does an intelligence test indicate ability at or above normal?	______	______
Does he show evidence of orientation in time by recognizing today and tomorrow, last week and this week, the days of week, the months of the year, and the seasons?	______	______
Does he know when his own birthday is?	______	______
Does he show evidence of orientation in space by recognizing near and far, up and down, high and low, big and little, in and out, over and under, etc?	______	______

Table 18. (Cont.)

Intellectual Readiness (Cont.)	*No*	*Yes*
Does he know his own address and telephone number?	______	______
Does he show evidence of orientation to his physical world by recognizing hot and cold, pretty and ugly, loud and soft, kind and cruel, smooth and rough, etc?	______	______

Linguistic Readiness	*No*	*Yes*
Does he articulate consonant sounds accurately in ititial, medial, and terminal positions?	______	______
Does he articulate vowel sounds accurately in such words as *pin* and *pen, him* and *hem, doll* and *ball,* etc?	______	______
Does he speak in thought units rather than in single words?	______	______
Can he relate in sequence a personal experience or a story?	______	______
Does he react to a story picture by interpretation rather than by description or mere enumeration?	______	______
Does he differentiate between fact and fancy?	______	______
Is he conscious of need to get his ideas across to listeners?.	______	______
Does he pick up and use new words readily?	______	______
Does he call his teacher and classmates by name?	______	______
Does he use proper terminology in naming pets, objects, etc?	______	______
Does he notice signs, labels, etc?	______	______
Does he enjoy singing, dramatic play, and rhymes?	______	______
Does he memorize rhymes, jingles, and songs easily?	______	______
Can he predict the outcome of a story?	______	______
Can he repeat a series of numbers, colors, objects, etc?	______	______
Can he count rationally five or more objects?	______	______
Can he say the alphabet in sequence?	______	______
Can he identify the letters in isolation?	______	______

General Readiness Factors	*No*	*Yes*
Is the child a girl?	______	______
Are the parents at least high school graduates?	______	______
Is the family income at least $3000 a year?	______	______
Does he have siblings?	______	______
Does he live with both parents and without other adults?	______	______
Does he have adequate play space?	______	______
Is English the language spoken in the home?	______	______
From your observation do you think the child is now ready for more formal instruction in reading?	______	______

haps you are dealing with a child who lacks a sufficient degree of readiness to ensure success at the start. The "yes" answers will indicate the strengths on which to build. The "no" answers will furnish leads for readiness activities.

If the answers are about half "yes" and half "no" you may be confronted with a questionable decision. Perhaps you need the support which will come from an objective score on a readiness test. Perhaps you need a consultation with the parent, the supervisor, the psychologist, or maybe with the child himself. If there is any doubt, the wiser decision is to delay the attack on beginning reading until you have some assurance of success at the outset.

In addition to this suggested check list you will find other helps in most manuals accompanying basic programs. One example is in the Teacher's Guidebook for *Starting Out with Pictureforms.*[1] The introductory discussion of readiness presents "Earmarks of Readiness" under the headings of good health, good vision, good hearing, adequate motor control, initiative and responsibility, social and emotional adjustment, communication, concepts, memory span, and relationships. Many of these guides are helpful, or you may wish to develop your own.

READINESS FOR READING AT ALL LEVELS

The principle of readiness carries forward to all reading experiences as the learner progresses to higher levels of insight, understanding, and application. Ideas, word perception, and reasoning continue to be significant. These are expanded through broadening background of experiences and increased independence in the use of the skills.

BACKGROUND OF MEANING Meaning is essential for any reading. The second grader reading about a sea coast when he has never seen one needs a background of understanding which he may get from vicarious sources such as pictures, movies, TV programs, or verbal explanations. At best these are only substitutes for real experiences. The fourth grade child who reads about "table land" and visualizes a table as a piece of furniture is not ready for the reading even though he may be able to pronounce all the words. The same is true of other concepts couched in familiar vocabulary but unfamiliar ideas; for example, a range as a mountain range or a cooking surface, a palm tree or the palm of your hand, a pen as an enclosure or as a writing implement, and fast as speed, adhesion, or refraining from food.

The geometry student reading about parallels or angles needs the experience of handling concrete objects or visualizing real examples before he can properly interpret the abstractions in the geometry propositions. The student of political science needs a background of meanings established through experience, listening, wide reading, or extensive discussion and application before he can properly comprehend and interpret such terms as propaganda, academic freedom, free trade, open market, tax support, governmental responsibility, or balance of power. Knowing how to pronounce the words is not enough. Knowing the meanings of words in isola-

[1]Teacher's Guidebook for *Starting Out with Pictureforms* (The Harper & Row Basic Reading Program), Evanston, Ill., Harper & Row, 1966, pp. vii–viii.

Plate 3. Concrete words presented by means of picture dictionary [Mabel O'Donnell and Byron H. VanRoekel, *Around the Corner,* Primer (The Harper & Row Basic Reading Program), Evanston, Ill., Harper & Row, 1966, p. 50].

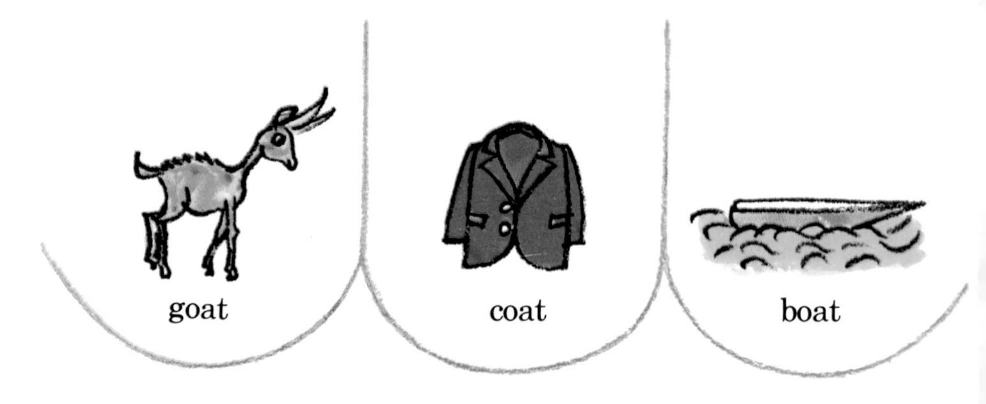

I may see a goat.
He will have a red coat.
The goat in a coat
will ride in a boat.

Is this what I will see
at my door?

49

Plate 4. Pictures and rhymes as clues to word recognition [Mabel O'Donnell and Byron H. VanRoekel, *Just for Fun,* Preprimer 4 (The Harper & Row Basic Reading Program), Evanston, Ill., Harper & Row, 1966, p. 49].

Plate 5. Picture dictionary used to introduce new words [Mabel O'Donnell and Byron H. VanRoekel, *Around the Corner,* Primer (The Harper & Row Basic Reading Program), Evanston, Ill., Harper & Row, 1966, p. 112].

Helping Yourself with New Words

Picture Dictionary

apple barn pony

Words You Can Get by Yourself

far	show	faster	sing
farm	grow	master	spring

morning	at	spring time
morn	pat	springtime
born	patted	

any way	play time	far away
Anyway	playtime	Faraway

blue eye	new born	work out
blue-eyed	newborn	workout

Let the Sentences Help You

Mark is my best friend. friends

I want to learn how to skate. learn

Talk softly
so that no one can hear you. softly

152

Plate 6. Clues to word recognition [Mabel O'Donnell and Byron H. VanRoekel, *Real and Make-Believe*, Basic First Reader, Strand 1 (The Harper & Row Basic Reading Program), Evanston, Ill., Harper & Row, 1966, p. 152].

tion is not enough. The teacher needs to anticipate the voids in the learner's background and see that the reader comprehends the meanings implied in each specific situation.

INDEPENDENCE IN SKILLS Eventually the time comes when the reader must have complete independence. When the concepts become uppermost in the reading act, the reader who has to stop and struggle with the mechanics is indeed impeded in his communication with the author. The sixth grader is not ready to read about the geography of India if he is still in the developmental stage in word pronunciation. The eighth grader is not ready to discuss the implications of the Stamp Act if he is still reading word by word without the advantages of total meaning patterns in figures of speech and differences in semantic word meanings and usage.

This kind of readiness can be checked informally. Most of the questions in the readiness chart in Table 18 are based on readiness for initial instruction in beginning reading. With a bit of rewording many of them can be adapted to readiness for reading activities at advanced levels. Others might be added, for example:

	Yes	*No*
Is the child reading for ideas?	______	______
Does he know how to attack mechanics independently?	______	______
Does he have an adequate background of meanings before he is introduced to new vocabulary?	______	______
Has he reached independence in his skills?	______	______
Has he become skillful to the point of automatic response in word analysis techniques?	______	______

DEVELOPING READINESS

Once we have determined the degree of readiness for the reading process we are in a position to diagnose the situation and do something about it. Let us not fall into the trap of telling the parent that the child is immature and we must wait. That is merely a delaying tactic which lets the teacher "off the hook" temporarily and puts off the parent for awhile. It doesn't help the child. Time brings healing, but medication helps. Time brings growth, but nutrition helps. Similarly time brings an element of maturity, but experiences help. What should be the nature of those experiences in order to further the maturing process? Many of them will be designed to provide background for reading. Useful commercial materials are available. There are ways in which the parent can help.

PROVIDING BACKGROUND

The experiences designed to develop a background of readiness must include physical and social activities, intellectual challenges, and support for the emotional state of the learner.

IMPROVING PHYSICAL SKILLS Physical skills can be developed. Refer to the check list in Table 18 to see what skills the child lacks. Then provide activities which involve experiences related to his needs. These might include skipping, drawing, handling books, tumbling, playing ball, cutting, building with blocks, sawing, talking, listening, watching, swinging, and so on. Make your own list to fit the needs of your children. And it won't be the same for every child.

PROVIDING SOCIALIZING EXPERIENCES Social skills can also be developed. Provide opportunities to play with first one, then two children, and eventually with a whole group. Show the child how to share toys and tools through parallel play as well as cooperative play. Encourage participation in new experiences which help him gain success and security. Teach him how to assume responsibility for his own things and follow up by having him report his successes. Introduce him to new children and new adults and help him make the transition in acceptance of new persons in his environment.

PROVIDING INTELLECTUAL CHALLENGES Intellectual readiness can be developed. Study the results of the intelligence test. Did he give an inadequate response because he lacked the experiences which would enable him to respond acceptably? Intelligence tests are very revealing, but the modern educator has learned to accept them in relation to the background of the child. They may not reveal real native ability, but they do reveal the level at which the child was performing at the time the test was administered. In that sense they are measures of expectancy. The real question is, "Can the expectancy be raised with carefully planned experiences?" This is where the discriminating observation and the reasoned judgment of the good teacher work to the advantage of the child. This understanding provides the teacher with the clues as to what to do for the child.

Language practice which involves communication is one of the most effective intellectual challenges the teacher can provide. Talk about time—today and tomorrow, now and then, summer and fall, Monday and Tuesday. Keep a record of time lapse by marking the calendar or watching the clock. Point out space relationships such as near and far, right here and over there, up high and down low, right and left. Play games which call for recognition of such relationships. Help the child to make a record of his own address, his birthday, the appearance of his home, the identification of his clothing and materials, his seat, his place in line, and his family. Talk with him. Listen to him.

Content learnings stimulate reading readiness by providing intellectual challenges which keep the mind expanding. Provide experiences with real things which will enable the child to touch hot and cold, soft and hard, slick and rough, and thick and thin. Help him learn the names of his classmates. Count objects. Label toys. Identify pets, animals, tools, furniture, and garments by their exact names. Help him differentiate between a sweater, a jacket, a coat, and a cape. They are all types of wraps but knowing the difference is a higher level of learning. Practice nursery rhymes and jingles which give repetition in alliterative sounds. Let the child participate in dramatic play, retell stories, engage in role playing, and relate incidents from his own experiences.

Understandings basic to terminology must be built before the introduction of vocabulary. The child who meets the situation, understands the concept, and then is supplied with the correct term builds meaningful vocabulary rather than verbalism. The child who memorizes the definitions for numerator and denominator continues to have great difficulty in verbalizing the statements and moreover in remembering which is which. But the child who meets the parts of the fraction and discovers through repeated experiences that the numeral below the line points out or names while the numeral above the line tells how many is ready for the terms to express the ideas.

All these activities are purposeful, meaningful, and direct. They tend to develop the very skills which have been pointed out as indicative of the kind of maturity needed for reading. They must be tailored to fit the needs of the child. When the needs are recognized and met readiness will be established. When readiness exists success becomes possible.

ENCOURAGING EMOTIONAL STABILITY Emotional stability comes through the development of a positive self-concept. It can be stimulated and encouraged. Help the child succeed in little things. Comment on these successes and encourage him to try more new things. Show him his progress. Accept small failures as a matter of course and lead him to try again. Give him as much help as he needs to get started but let him do it himself. When he finds out he can he will be more willing to try next time.

Along with all the developmental experiences comes the attitude the child is developing toward himself as a person, as a learner, and as a potential reader. If he is constantly placed in situations which are too much for his level of maturity, if he sees himself lagging behind the group in all the planned activities, whether physical or intellectual, if he meets constant failure, then he will come to accept himself as one who can't and consequently as one who doesn't. Once he has established that attitude he will cease to put forth effort because he will be convinced before he tries that there is no use. It is important that the child experience consecutive successes.

Begin with what the child can do. The first step is to provide the child with activities commensurate with his present stage of development.

Find out what he can do and give him a chance to do it. If he cannot skip, beginning with skipping is inviting failure. Perhaps he can stand on one foot. Then let him try hopping on that one foot for a step or two. When he has mastered that he will have experienced success and will have grown. Then you are ready to say, "That's fine! If you can stand on your right foot perhaps you can stand on your left foot. Let's try it. Then how about hopping on your left foot? Now let's try hopping on first your left foot then your right foot. Good! You're skipping before you know it." Now the child has both grown and succeeded.

Challenge for growth. The next step is challenging for growth. As the child is led to try something new and finds success in the undertaking he feels the satisfaction of "I can" rather than the discouragement of "I can't." Shaping attitudes toward self in this manner is a most important step toward an adequate self-concept. The same idea works with more academic tasks. Let him draw a ball. Add a smaller ball at the top. Call it a head. Ask where the eyes and mouth go. Add them. Later add arms and legs. He has grown in his concept of the parts of the human body and has seen himself progressing.

Provide continuous success. The work each day must build on what has gone before. Only one step forward is an achievement. When the child learns to expect new experiences each day and to anticipate success in his undertakings his whole attitude toward self, toward school, and toward learning takes on a new aspect.

Record accomplishments. The child needs to be told what he has accomplished. He needs to go home with the report to his mother about his achievements. He needs to see the gains listed and checked off. The tabulation will be impressive and will convince him that his efforts are worthwhile.

The entire process of developing an adequate self-concept revolves around these basic steps. (1) Find out something the child can do. (2) Let him do it and experience success. (3) Show him the next step. (4) Challenge him to try. (5) Watch for evidences of growth or improvement. (6) Help him to see and recognize his own progress. (7) Keep him succeeding by providing for constant forward steps. As he sees the record of his accomplishments he will begin to see himself as someone who can. This attitude will eventually condition him for beginning reading and for other learning experiences throughout life.

USING COMMERCIALLY PREPARED MATERIALS

Most publishers of reading programs provide materials to help in the development of readiness. These are built on the assumption that certain experiences and skills will be common to many children. It is still the task of the teacher to select from available materials the ones that are pertinent to the needs of the children within her class group.

An example of such commercially prepared material is the prereading booklet *Starting Out with Pictureforms* and the accompanying charts from the Harper & Row Basic Reading Program.[2] The picture reproduced in Figure 2 illustrates the materials needed for the planned exercise. The back-

PICNIC

Lesson 1

Figure 2. Example of materials for use in readiness activity [Teacher's Guidebook for *Starting Out with Pictureforms* (The Harper & Row Basic Reading Program), Evanston, Ill., Harper & Row, 1966, p. 1].

ground board is similar to a flannel or a magnet board. The pictureforms can be added to the board one at a time and in a variety of arrangements. The example given is based on a picnic in which the family participates. The discussions which go with the use of these pictureforms may extend over as many days or class periods as the teacher feels will be beneficial to the children selected for this readiness activity. The manual suggests activities which will lead the children to engage in:

[2] *Ibid.*, p. 1.

Sharing experiences
Extending word concepts
Classifying ideas
Classifying items
Role playing
Recalling details
Matching shapes
Drawing conclusions
Developing number experiences
Identifying and classifying by color
Establishing listening habits
Listening purposefully
Recalling story content
Listening for directions

The teacher who uses these or similar materials will be responsible first of all for determining which children will benefit from them. Using them with all the children in the room may result in a waste of time and cultivation of habits of inattention. There may be some children who are more mature and who will not need these activities because they have already had them at home, in nursery school or kindergarten, or in independent play. There will be others who are inattentive because they lack the maturity to see the relationships and therefore may need more individual activities before engaging in group experiences. There will be others for whom a little of such activity will be sufficient. There will be still others who are experiencing their first success and for whom a great deal of this kind of practice will be beneficial.

The materials cannot do the teaching. They can only furnish the teacher with the tools. The manual cannot dictate the amount or the sequence of the activities. It can only furnish the teacher with the ideas. She is still the diagnostician who knows each child as an individual and who must prescribe the activities, keep the records, note the progress, and decide when to move forward to higher levels of learning.

GUIDING THE PARENT IN HELPING THE CHILD

One of the additional tasks of the teacher of the beginner is helping the parent help his child. Make sure the mother understands why you are playing games, working puzzles, cutting out pictures, organizing like things together, putting away toys, cleaning up play areas, washing paint brushes, identifying objects, sharing toys, counting things, and so on. Then encourage her to follow through with these activities and learnings at home. These will do far more good in developing readiness than any amount of time spent on drill on the ABC's or in counting by rote.

The well child, the alert child, the experienced child, the eager child is easy to teach. That is what readiness is all about.

THE IMPORTANCE OF READINESS

Need we belabor the fact that readiness is important? The following generalizations may give the observant teacher food for thought when she is tempted to plunge ahead for purposes of getting all children reading, keeping up with the other classes, satisfying parent expectations, or attaining scores on competitive examinations.

EFFECT OF OVERSTIMULATION

Overstimulation may burn out the bearings before the child has had an opportunity to learn. Such overstimulation may result in frustration which could impede or retard learning instead of encouraging it as was obviously intended. Beware of excessive pressure.

CONSEQUENCES OF CONTINUED FAILURE

Continued failure may become an accepted pattern. The child may assume that he is a failure. His parents may refer to him as one who can't. His siblings may deride him. His classmates may call him "dummy." Once he accepts that appraisal of his own abilities it is very difficult to change his point of view. He will withdraw from new learnings and become less and less capable.

REWARDS OF SUCCESS

Success breeds success. When the child succeeds at doing something he enjoys it. Then he practices the new skill and becomes even more successful at it. As he gains more successes he gains more skills. This builds up his personal evaluation of himself and causes him to be not only willing but eager to try more new things. He assumes that he can. He tries. He succeeds. He enjoys the success and the performance. He gets more effective practice and becomes more skillful. The cycle applies whether he is learning to crawl, to swim, to color a picture, to balance on a walking board, to catch a ball, to imitate a sound pattern, to analyze a word, to read a story, or to enjoy a book.

ROUTE TO SUCCESS

The readiness route to success in reading, then, is one of sequential steps toward maturity. These questions might be worth cogitating at this point. They will be developed more fully in later chapters. Watch for them.

- Should reading be approached through mechanics or understanding?
- Should routine learning or insight be the basis?
- Which leads to true learning, verbalism or meaning?
- Is effective learning accomplished through positivism or negativism?
- Does teacher direction or self-propulsion result in more permanent learning?

In summary then, let us conclude that if reading is approached through understanding, insight, meaning, positivism, and self-propulsion, learning will result.

4

VOCABULARY DEVELOPMENT

or Words! Words!! Words!!!

One teacher remarked "They must learn their words before they can read." Her neighbor promptly reacted with, "Oh! They won't really learn the words until they have read."

These two comments are the clue to how children acquire reading vocabulary. It is true that reading is made up of an expression of ideas in symbol form. The symbols include stories, paragraphs, sentences, phrases, words, syllables, phonemes, and letters. It is equally true that houses are made up of rooms, roofs, floors, windows, walls, plumbing, and wiring. Must one be able to identify tile, glass, wood, brick, metal, and cement in order to identify a house? Must one be able to identify the parts in order to recognize the whole?

The analogy is not a matter of whether the parts are significant, but rather the sequence in which the learnings take place. No thoughtful and discriminating teacher will question the value of knowing the alphabet and the relation between sounds and symbols. The point is not whether these facts should be learned. The real issue is when, in what sequence, and how they should be learned.

First the child must accumulate a stock of meanings. Then he must acquire vocabulary to express them. In order to use that vocabulary in reading he must arrive at a code system which he eventually masters to become an independent reader.

ACCUMULATING MEANINGS

Since reading is based on association of meanings with printed symbols, acquiring a rich storehouse of meanings is the first essential in reading readiness, not only in the initial stages but also for the reading of any material at any level. Let us think about how either children or adults acquire meanings to go with sound patterns.

ACQUIRING SOUND PATTERNS

Sounds reach the child as he listens. When he experiments with sounds through imitation he develops the linguistic patterns which constitute meaningful speech. The sequence leads to meaningful background for reading.

LISTENING TO SOUNDS The child experiences sounds in his environment from birth. He soon learns to interpret them. He recognizes footsteps approaching his crib. He knows his mother's voice as she talks to him. He learns to respond to his own name. He soon learns what "No! No!" means. He recognizes the sounds accompanying the preparation of food, drawing bath water, the entrance of a stranger, and presence of danger. He learns to respond to these sounds with pleasure, satisfaction, fear, or sometimes indifference. Before long he associates names with objects as someone says, "Where's your nose?" "Show me the kitty." "Bring me your rattle."

EXPERIMENTING WITH SOUNDS Before long the young child starts experimenting with the sounds he hears and with his own speech mechanisms. His earliest efforts are merely aimless prattle, but soon he begins to notice and imitate specific sounds. Then he learns to cry for attention, to express feelings of hunger or pain, and to satisfy his desires. As his awareness of his environment unfolds he is filled with curiosity about things and names and words. Watching a young child develop vocabulary is not only fascinating but awe inspiring. The wonders of language and the skills with which young children acquire it are even more marvelous than the invention of the steam engine or the discovery of atomic power.

DEVELOPING LINGUISTIC PATTERNS Experimentation with sounds and speech mechanisms leads to the linguistic patterns which result in intelligible speech. The child soon learns "the tune." He detects the difference in the inflection of his mother's voice when she says, "No! No! Bad Boy!" and "That's a good boy." Even before he fully understands the actual meanings of the words he reads approval or disapproval into the intonation and pitch of the voice. He soon learns where to put the emphasis. When he says "Me go, too," his emphasis naturally falls on the word *me*. He gives the other words less stress because it is himself in whom he is most interested. He soon learns where to make appropriate pauses to convey meanings. In saying, "My dolly, my blocks, my kitty," he gets the junctures in their proper places. He would never say, "My dolly my, blocks my kitty."

Thus linguistic patterns are formed early and center around ideas and total meanings rather than around isolated words. His first expressions are made up of concrete words which name objects or actions, such as kitty, baby, drink, go, bye-bye, and so on. Next come descriptive words, such as pretty, ooooooh, cold, etc. Abstractions come into speech patterns only after the child has learned to form sentences; then they take their proper place as service words used as auxiliaries or connectors, such as and, is, could, and if. He never mouths such words in isolation. The stress and juncture patterns come naturally and incidentally.

ACQUIRING MEANING PATTERNS

Sounds take on meaning when they are blended into patterns which represent ideas. As concepts and terms are refined meanings become more concrete.

IDENTIFYING IDEAS The identification of ideas as differentiated from objects comes much later in the development of speech. Concepts such as yesterday and tomorrow are more abstract. It takes a level of some maturity to generalize on abstractions such as fair play, share with our friends, take your turn, and be good. These meanings come through repeated experiences. They develop gradually and are refined as they take on deeper meanings related to actual happenings.

REFINING CONCEPTS The refining of concepts and the development of shades of meanings can come only with experience and maturity. The word *good* may apply to the taste of a favorite food, the appearance of a garment, the quality of a piece of furniture, the appeal of a well-loved story, the actions of a person, or the character of the child himself. The young child may translate the word into meaning in one situation without necessarily transferring the concept to another situation. Not until he has met a term in many different settings and has generalized on its abstract meaning has he really added it to his vocabulary with its various shades of meanings. Ideas and concepts need to be expressed in specific terms.

REFINING TERMS The same principles apply to the refinement of terminology. To the young child all four-legged animals may be dogs. It takes a bit more maturity to differentiate between dogs, cats, ponies, and goats. And it takes even more maturity to differentiate between poodles, bulldogs, pomeranians, and mutts. Add to this the generalization that all these are also dogs and the child may be confused about how a pet can be a poodle and a dog at the same time, as well as how both a pomeranian and a poodle can be dogs.

To the very young child all food may be either good or bad. He needs experience and maturity to distinguish between sweet, sour, salty, tangy, delicious, and spicy. This calls for experience both with food and with language. The child who hears these terms used will pick them up and use them too. Lack of knowledge of the terms may indicate lack of experience rather than lack of intelligence. Concepts need to be developed and refined. Language must also be presented and developed. Refinement comes from continued experimentation and use. The child who comes to beginning reading with this kind of rich background of concepts and language to express them is quite a different child from the one who calls all animals "gogs," and expresses his dislike by wrinkling up his nose or turning his head.

ACQUIRING VOCABULARY

The young child acquires a speaking vocabulary by imitating the words he hears. The richer the environment and the more alert the child the greater will be the vocabulary. All children come to school with a speaking vocabulary pretty well established. This background may or may not be conducive to the teaching of reading. If the child can verbalize about his experiences, retell stories, identify ideas with appropriate labels, and communicate with others, he is more nearly ready for reading than if he has never had an opportunity to talk with adults, listen to stories, or acquire experiences that are linguistically meaningful.

When the child starts to attach ideas to printed symbols he is beginning the reading process. Not all words are alike in their relation to learning. Some are concrete and some are abstract. Some are needed constantly and some are of only temporary value. Some are regular in their phonetic pattern and some violate the rules. Some are related to familiar concepts and some introduce new ideas. All these factors are closely related to when and how to teach.

TYPES OF VOCABULARY

The vocabulary the child acquires and which he will need in learning to read may be roughly divided into concrete words and abstract words. Each presents different kinds of learnings and different problems in teaching.

CONCRETE WORDS Label words are concrete. They include many nouns and some pronouns. The child learns to recognize the labels on the colors in his crayon box, the door, the chair, the table, the window, the bird cage, the pencil sharpener, and so on. He associates the labels with the objects. He recognizes them first by location and later by general appearance.

Many action words are also concrete. They include verbs such as run, skip, hop, jump, swim, fly, draw, color, cut, and so on. These can be dramatized to give them reality and concreteness. They can be illustrated through action pictures. The pictures can be reduced to semi-concreteness through the use of stick figures and symbolic drawings.

Some descriptive words, including many adjectives and some adverbs, are also concrete. The color words are good examples. Others are such concepts as big and little, old and new, pretty and ugly, and tall and short. These words, when used to describe, are fairly concrete. Adjectives such as good and bad, kind and unkind, happy and sad are not quite as concrete but can be explained through experiences.

Some adverbial uses can be experienced and understood, for example, "He ran *fast*," or "He walked *slowly*." Such ideas as "right here" or "in a minute" can be dramatized and understood, but these are quite a bit more removed from the concrete.

Textbooks frequently present concrete words through labels and illustrations. Plates 1, 2, and 3 illustrate this point. The child who meets a new word in a rebus is able to supply the missing word by naming the object in the picture. This tends to expand his reading experience without overburdening his vocabulary learning in the early stages. The child who sees a familiar object in a picture and finds it conveniently labeled is able to match word forms and grasp the new vocabulary independently. A picture dictionary presents concrete words. These techniques enable the child to arrive at the recognition and pronunciation of words independently and they give him a reference point to which he can return if he needs some reinforcement later.

ABSTRACT WORDS How can you show a child what you mean by *could, but, what,* or *that?* These kinds of words represent the real causes of difficulties in word recognition. They are abstract words. They cannot be pictured. They cannot be attached to real objects. They cannot be dramatized. They have little or no meaning when they stand alone. And frequently they are quite similar in appearance. That is the reason the child often confuses *no* and *on, now* and *how, that* and *what,* was and *saw,* and many others. Such words must be heard in relation to a total idea before they take on real meaning. You get meaning when you say "*could* not come," "all *but* Mary," "*what story,*" or "*that* house."

Concrete words include mostly nouns, actions words, descriptive adjectives, and some adverbs. They can usually stand alone. Abstract words include mostly prepositions, conjunctions, articles, linking verbs, auxiliary verbs, and some adverbs. Even then you cannot generalize. In the sentence, "Democracy is a desirable form of government," the word democracy is a noun and the subject of the sentence, yet it is quite abstract as a concept. In the same manner, the word run may be concrete to the child in reference to running a race, but when it is used in the connotation of a "run on the bank," it takes on an abstractness for which the reader may have no background.

TYPES OF LEARNING

Too often the teacher proceeds on the assumption that anything worth teaching is worth teaching thoroughly, and anything taught should be learned for permanent and everlasting mastery. That isn't necessarily the case. We learn many things for temporary use and promptly dismiss them from our minds when the need has ceased to exist. If you are spending the summer in a strange town you will learn your way around to the places you need to go. If you do not return to that town for many years, you may forget the names of the streets, the way to the museum, and the telephone number. Does that mean you did not know or learn those facts at the time? Not necessarily. Some things we learn for temporary use only. Some are learned for permanent mastery. And others are learned as basic principles which can be analyzed and recalled as needed.

FOR PRESENT AND TEMPORARY USE ONLY You needed the facts about the strange town during the six weeks you were there. You ceased to have use for them when you left. Lack of use caused you to forget the details such as the telephone number. Does that mean the learning was inadequate? No, it merely means you have no further use for it. The same might be true of some of the vocabulary the child uses in the early stages of learning to read. He may be reading a story in which the name of the main character is Bartholomew. He will recognize it at a glance when it appears in the story, but he may not be able to spell it or divide it into its phonetic parts. Actually he may recognize only that it is long and begins with a capital *B*. Does that mean he does not know the word? Not necessarily. He can use it as he needs it. If, some six or eight weeks later, the teacher suddenly puts the name Bartholomew on a flash card and asks what it is, the child may be stumped. He may cock his head to one side, squint at the word, wrinkle up his brow, and look puzzled. The question is not, "Did he learn it originally?" but rather "Should he have fixed it for permanent mastery?"

FOR PERMANENT MASTERY It is difficult to visualize reading material at any level which does not make use of such words as is, in, and, the, was, saw, that, can, do, of, for, and so on. Dolch has compiled a list of 220 words which he considers a basic sight vocabulary.[1] They occur so frequently that one might just as well learn them once and for all. The learner will gain nothing by passing them by for temporary learning. He is going to need them and many of them are abstract and unphonetic in nature. This constitutes a learning problem which cannot be dealt with through the picture dictionary technique or through the phonic analysis approach.

FOR ANALYSIS AND RECALL AS NEEDED Some words are highly regular in their phonetic structure and can be analyzed according to the basic principles of word patterns. They do not need to be memorized in isolation. The child who is familiar with the principle of a single final vowel in a one-syllable word will not need to memorize such words as he, so, go, and my, but when he tries to apply the same principle to such words as to, do, the, who, and ski, he will be in trouble. In the same way the child who is familiar with the concept of the closed syllable with a single vowel will expect to find a short vowel in such words as can, glad, pen, doll, pin, but, and hot, but he will find the rule doesn't work on such words as car, roll, put, and comb.

Some words may not be used for a long time, but when they do recur they are so regular in their pattern that recognition is not a matter of memory, but rather a matter of the application of a well-understood principle. Plates 4, 5, 6, and 7 illustrate some principles. The picture rhyming words shown in Plate 4 give the child two clues to independence in word recognition. The picture dictionary page shown in Plate 5 provides repetition and introduces the concept of the addition of the letter *s* to form the plural, thus utilizing a basic principle which can be applied to many other situations. The words which the child can get by himself as shown in Plate 6 are illustrations of consonant substitution, consonant elimination, and consonant annexation sometimes at the beginning and sometimes at the end of a word. The principle of the compound word is an early step

[1]Edward M. Dolch, "A Basic Sight Vocabulary of 220 Words," *Methods in Teaching Reading,* Champaign, Ill., Garrard, 1955, pp. 373–374.

leading children to analyze words for known parts as a technique for independent attack on unfamiliar words. The logical next step after compound words is the dividing of words into pronounceable parts or syllables as shown in Plate 7. Showing the child how and giving him confidence in his own ability to "do it by myself" leads him toward the ultimate goal of independence in reading.

Before deciding whether to demand permanent mastery the teacher should ask herself, "Is this a word the child will continue to need in most of his reading from now on? Is it one he will use in this situation and then have no further use for in the immediate future? Is it one which is phonetically regular and therefore one which he can analyze and reconstruct independently whenever he needs it?" Answers to these questions will guide her in deciding how to teach the word.

CONDITIONS TO BE MET

The conditions which the child meets will affect the nature of the learning involved in attacking new vocabulary. Sometimes the concept will be familiar and only the form will be new. Sometimes the form will be familiar and the concept will be new. Sometimes both the form and the concept will be new and unfamiliar to the child.

FAMILIAR CONCEPT, NEW FORM When the child is observing labels on familiar objects such as the desk, chair, table, door, doll, book, and coat, he knows the objects. He knows the words that name the objects. All he needs to learn is the appearance of the printed form.

FAMILIAR FORM, NEW CONCEPT The child may know the word watch when it is applied to the time piece worn on the wrist, but when he meets the same word in such expressions as "stood watch in the night" or "watch word," he is confronted with a puzzle which may block his recognition of the seemingly familiar word or, if he does recognize it, he will call up wrong associations and get vague or incorrect impressions. Imagine the impressions gleaned by the child who knows that his mother has a "charge account" but reads about "a charge of electricity," or the child who knows that his mother cooks on a range and thinks a "mountain range" is the kind of stove they cook on in the mountains, or the impression of the child who knows about writing notes, then meets the term in "musical notes" or "take note of certain facts."

NEW FORM, NEW CONCEPT The child who has never heard the words peninsula or vertical or llama has no idea how to pronounce them much less what meanings to associate with them. He may be able to apply some of his knowledge of phonics and figure out a reasonably accurate pronunciation and still not have the slightest idea of the meaning. If he does pronounce the word either through phonetic analysis or through repetition, he will be engaging in mere verbalism without meaning. Next time he comes to the same word he will probably stop for prompting before proceeding. The teacher who points out the vertical flag pole, the vertical lines in the corners of the room, or the vertical position of the table legs is developing meaning. The child who has heard the term in conversation and has repeated it in oral speech is ready to recognize its printed form when he sees it.

HOW TO TEACH

These principles lead to some basic recommendations about how words should be taught.

- Concrete words can stand alone. If they represent familiar concepts, they are learned readily. If they follow regular patterns, they can be recognized independently.
- Abstract words call for use in meaningful settings. If they are part of the child's conversational vocabulary, learning the printed form will call for recognition rather than for comprehension.
- If the word has only temporary use, practice and permanent mastery may be an unwise use of time and effort.
- If the word has lasting value, practice to the point of permanent mastery may be justified.
- If the word is phonetically regular, drill on the word may be of less value than help on word analysis.
- If the concept is familiar, mere introduction of the form may be sufficient.
- If the form is familiar but the concept is new, experience should precede the presentation of the form.
- If both the form and the concept are new, the child needs to be familiarized with the idea and with the sound of the word before he is introduced to the printed form or is asked to apply phonetic principles to its pronunciation.
- If we begin with the form and seek to give it meaning, we invite rote memory, abstraction, and verbalism.
- If we begin with the idea and seek to give it meaning and form, we encourage understanding and insight leading to independence.

Then begin with the idea. Use it in conversation. Illustrate. Dramatize. Be sure the children grasp the concept. Then present the form. Show them how it looks. Analyze the word. Work for meaning first and pronunciation afterwards. Make sure the mechanics become the means to the end and not the end in themselves.

ARRIVING AT THE CODE SYSTEM

Associating symbols with meanings is the initial step in beginning reading. To the adult who already knows how to read it all seems so simple. Very few adults can actually remember how they learned to read and practically none of them realizes how it feels to be confused with all those strange hieroglyphics at one time. Repeated experiences with printed forms over many years have made them so familiar that the mature reader thinks no more about the system and the symbols than he does about which foot he puts forward first to walk.

HOW IT FEELS TO BE A BEGINNER

In order to know how it feels to be a beginner, in order to empathize with the neophyte in reading, one must place himself in a comparable position. One way to do this is to attempt to learn a new language. Another way is to attempt to learn a code for the language one already knows.

Study the lessons in Figure 3.

Page 1. The little boy's name is Sam. It is under his picture.

Page 2 shows Daddy. Find his name.

On page 3 Sam is talking. He wants Daddy to look. Read what he says. In the second line you see the same word twice. In the third line he wants Daddy to look at something. What does he say?

Now how did you learn these words? You learned to attach the names *Sam* and *Daddy* to their pictures. You got the word *look* from the discussion and you found it repeated four times on page 3. The sentence "Look at me," was developed through meaning. No, you did not guess the word *me*. You arrived at it from context. As an adult with reading background already established you had some advantages over the 6-year-old. You could see at a glance that there were only two symbols in the final word and you would never have guessed that the word was *this*. Neither would you have guessed *my* because that would not make sense.

The boy on page 4 is Dick. Sam is still talking. He wants Daddy to look at someone. In the last line he doesn't say, "Look at me." What does he say?

Note that the teacher supplies the meanings and interpretations. The child has no way of knowing that it is still Sam who is doing the talking on page 4. If he jumps to the conclusion that because it is Dick's picture Dick is doing the talking, he will come up with a wrong impression. The teacher who helps the children discover what Sam says to Daddy about Dick is helping them make effective use of context and picture clues. This is *not* guessing.

Now turn to Figure 4. On page 5 Sam is still talking. He wants Daddy to *watch*. (The repetition of the word watch four times in succession gives practice and association as well as meaning.) In the first line he is talking to someone. In the second line what does he tell Daddy to watch? What is the difference between line two and line three? In the last line Sam

Figure 3. Learning to read by code, pages 1, 2, 3, and 4.

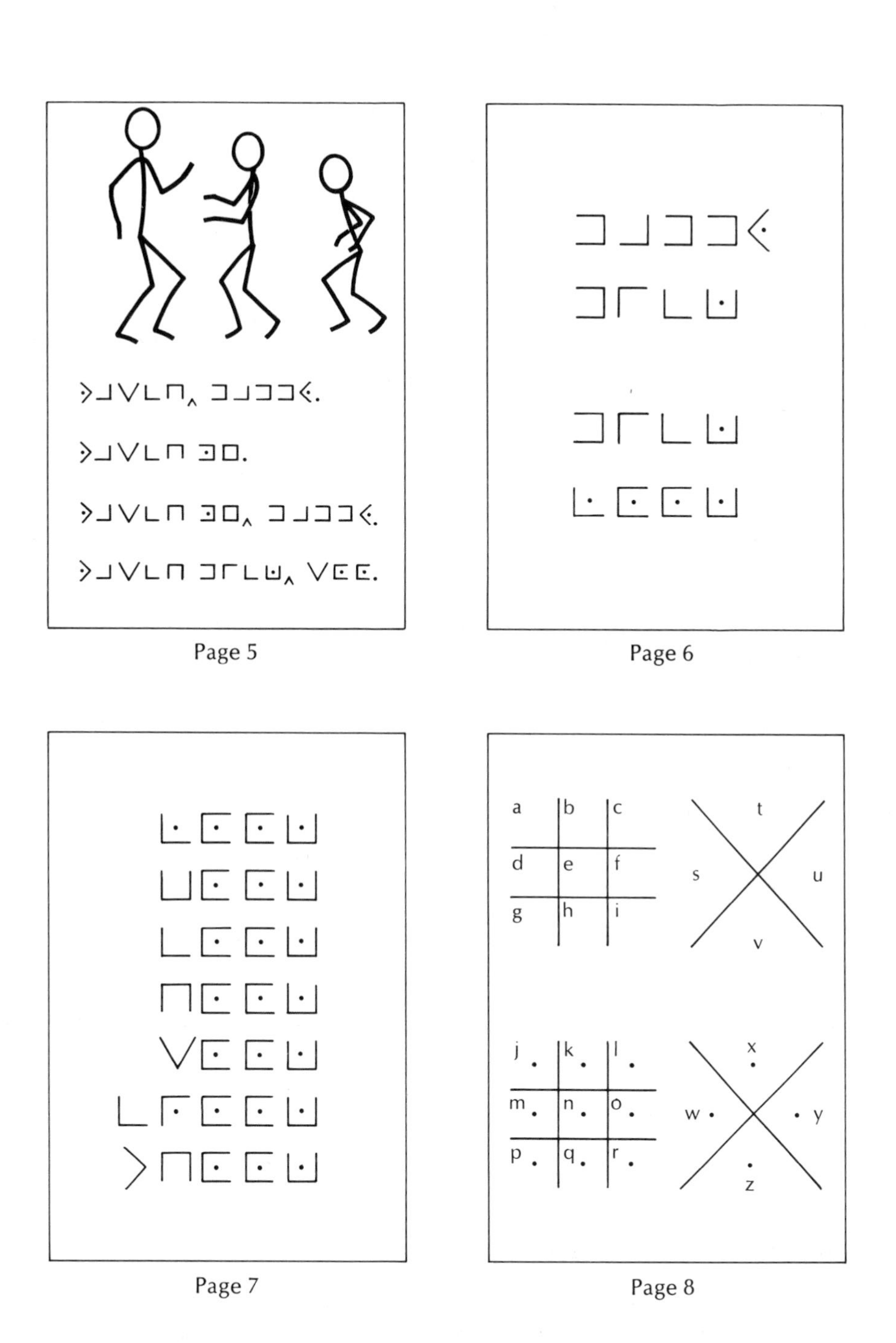

Figure 4. Learning to read by code, pages 5, 6, 7, and 8.

wants Daddy to watch someone else. What do you think the last word is?

As an adult you probably figured out the final word must be *too*. You did not guess. You used your powers of reasoning. It comes at the end. It is preceded by a mark that indicates a pause. It has three symbols. (A 6-year-old would not be able to use that clue.) It makes sense. You have used a context clue plus what you know about word structure to arrive at a sensible conclusion.

Now we are ready for a bit of word analysis. Look at page 6. Notice that *Daddy* and *Dick* begin alike. Notice that in *Daddy* you find the *d* repeated two more times. Listen for the *d* sound.

Notice that *look* and *Dick* end alike. Listen for the *k* sound at the end of each word.

The chart on page 7 leads to word building based on the principle of substitution for the initial consonant sound. We already know the first word is *look*. All the rest in the list end the same way. Thus we find *book, cook, hook, took, crook,* and *shook*. Now the child is ready to identify the letters that make the difference.

There! It wasn't easy, was it? And you had all the advantages. You already knew the principles of sound. You knew about the alphabet and the spellings of words. All you needed to do was to set up a new set of associations with different symbols. The child who is just beginning to read lacks that background. He must acquire both the symbols and the meanings. With a little practice and daily repetition you could become so familiar with these symbols that you could read them at sight recognizing the words instantly. It would be easier for you if you knew how the symbols were developed. Page 8 gives you the "key" to the code. Now you need no longer memorize the isolated symbols but can understand the principle. Now you can build or rebuild the code for yourself.

Organized knowledge makes you an independent learner. It's a long road for the young child who has to learn the associations, become familiar with the concepts, practice until he becomes proficient, and organize his knowledge so that he is independent in its application. He needs time. That doesn't mean a mere fifteen-minute drill period a day for the duration of first grade. It means repeated exposures during the day, return to the relationships at intervals over and over again, not for days, not for weeks, not for months, but for years. If he becomes a skillful and independent reader in two or three, maybe five or six years, he will have made good progress.

WORDS IN MEANINGFUL SETTINGS

Learning a code system calls for use of words in meaningful settings. Some words take on meanings at once. Others must be in appropriate context in order to clarify meanings. When the child is guided in the acquisition of these meanings, he is able to take on each new learning as he comes to it with confidence and success. A textbook which provides these experiences for the learner is helping him to grow in reading skill.

CONTEXT CLUES Using context clues is not guessing or reading the pictures. It is reasoning based on the evidence available. An example of the use of context clues is illustrated in Figure 5.

THE GLOSSARY Much information about words, not the least of which is meaning, can be gleaned from a glossary. Use of a glossary does not just happen. The children do not just "pick it up." They need to be taught its value and how to use it. Providing the children with exercises and direct instruction in the use of a glossary will aid them on their road to independence. In Figure 6 you will see a sample teaching page to help the child learn to use a glossary. Note the pronunciation key at the bottom of the page.

WORDS WITH MORE THAN ONE MEANING Being able to pronounce a word is not enough. Being able to spell a word is not enough. Being able to use it in a sentence is still not enough. Not until the word appears in its proper setting can the real meaning be determined and that meaning can change by changing the setting. Plate 8 illustrates this point.

WORD ORIGINS How words have acquired their meanings and sometimes a reason for spellings which seem to vary from the phonetically regular patterns can often be learned from a study of word origins. Even children as young as fourth grade can often benefit from this kind of insight into words. Presenting "word highlights" to add more information and deeper insight into vocabulary is a challenge for the alert child. See Plate 9. Once the child has his curiosity aroused he can be encouraged to pursue this type of word study independently for the rest of his life.

SIGHT WORDS VERSUS PHONETIC ANALYSIS

What is a sight word? When should a word be analyzed for phonetic structure? How can one decide? Can one word be both? Or either? Answering these questions calls for some explanations.

SIGHT WORDS The expression "sight word" has more than one interpretation. When the child recognizes at sight a word simply because he has seen it many times and knows how it looks, he has applied one interpretation

Let the Sentences Help You

I said good night to Daddy before I went to bed.	before
There is a picture on page 5 in my book.	page
The street stops here. This is the end of the street.	end
I write words on paper with my right hand.	write right
I have read this book. I am ready to start a new one.	read ready
You could hear me call you. Why did you not answer me?	answer
Who ran away with the apples? There is just one apple left.	left
We are lost. Have you any idea how to find the way home?	idea
No one will stay at home. Everyone will be here.	Everyone

179

Figure 5. The use of context clues [Mabel O'Donnell and Byron H. VanRoekel, *Real and Make-Believe,* Basic First Reader, Strand 1 (The Harper & Row Basic Reading Program), Evanston, Ill., Harper & Row, 1966, p. 179].

Glossary

be lieve (bi lēv′), to think that something is so.

bra vo (brä′vō), a cry or shout to show that something is well done.

bray (brā), the noise made by a donkey. **brayed**

budge (buj), to move.

ex claim (eks klām′), to cry out in surprise. **ex claimed′**

gath er (gaTH′ər), to bring into one place. **gath′ered**

har ness (här′nis), the straps and other things that fasten an animal to a wagon or cart.

live ly (līv′li), full of life.

Mar co (mär′kō), a boy's name.

mar ket place (mär′kit plās), a place where things are sold.

mer ri ly (mer′ə li), in a happy way.

mer ry (mer′i), happy.

oats (ōts), a grass used as feed for animals.

pas ture (pas′chər), a grassy field.

Ser a fi na (sãr ə fē′nə), the name of a donkey.

stub born (stub′ərn), wanting to have one's way.

tem per a men tal (tem′pər-ə men′təl), changing one's way of feeling and acting often and without reason.

tie (tī), to fasten something with a cord or string so that it will not come undone. **tied**

to ward (tôrd), in the direction of.

tune (tün), a piece of music; a melody.

Zi Peppi (zi pep′i), a man's name.

cap, fāce, cãre, fär; let, bē, wėre; it, īce; hop, gō, ôrder; voice, house; cut, pu̇t, tülip, ūse; th, thing; TH, then; zh, garage; ə stands for *a* in about, *e* in mother, *i* in animal, *o* in actor, *u* in surprise

41

Figure 6. The glossary as an aid to independence [Mabel O'Donnell and Byron H. VanRoekel, *From Faraway Places,* Basic Third Reader, Strand 1 (The Harper & Row Basic Reading Program), Evanston, Ill., Harper & Row, 1966, p. 41].

of the expression sight word. The response is instantaneous and automatic. He has made a sight word out of it for his personal use.

Another interpretation of the expression sight word is a developmental concept. The first time the child sees the word island, for example, he may be helped to recognize the two syllables and he may be told that the *s* is silent. He may be given an explanation of the meaning. After he has experienced the word a few times he accepts the meaning and the pronunciation and recognizes it instantly at sight and no longer questions the phonetic irregularity. Then it has become a sight word.

Some words are presented as sight words for immediate use. This may be because they are so phonetically irregular that analysis would be a waste of time, or it may be because the phonetic principles involved are not yet within the child's grasp and he needs the word for immediate use. Some words initially presented as sight words may later be analyzed phonetically. Some words are analyzed phonetically for original presentation and later become sight words through repeated use.

Sight reading is still a different concept which will be discussed in greater detail in connection with silent and oral reading in Chapters 7 and 8. At this point we will define it as reading new material at sight without previous preparation. That is quite a different concept from the teaching of sight words.

PHONICS AND WORD ANALYSIS Phonics and word analysis will be discussed in detail in Chapter 5. Suffice it to say at this point that phonic principles need to be discovered by the learner. They are vitally important in the development of a mature and independent reader. They are a tool not a method. They are a part of a reading program and need to be kept in their proper place in relation to the total reading process.

TRAVELING THE ROAD TO MASTERY AND INDEPENDENCE

The road to mastery is a long one with many side roads and many alternate paths. It is quite possible for different people to travel from here to there and both arrive without traveling identical routes. In reading the same is true. But everyone who learns to read has to start somewhere. To my knowledge research has not yet produced evidence that any of them were "born that way."

The reader must learn some techniques and he must become skillful in their use. If he is to be the master of his language, he must know and use it both from the standpoint of the producer and the consumer. And the teacher who is trying to help him learn must see not only the over-all program and the broad perspective, but also the minute details such as the word he doesn't know in relation to the present purpose for reading.

HOW TO DEVELOP MASTERY

Mastery depends on understanding and independent application of principles. Recognition and analysis are learning steps. Recognition tends to fix learnings, but total language patterns are essential to comprehension.

WORD RECOGNITION TECHNIQUES The initial techniques used for teaching vocabulary vary depending on the type of word and the purpose for learning it. Sometimes a new word will be presented as a sight word. Sometimes it will be analyzed for structure. Sometimes it will be derived from context clues. The teacher will have to make these decisions based on what she knows about the word, what she knows about the child, and what she knows about the immediate purpose. A teacher's manual accompanying a basic text can be helpful. The author of the manual may know more about the lesson, more about the reading program, and more about the vocabulary control plan than does the teacher, but the teacher knows more about the child than anyone else and her decision is final. That decision is final for two reasons: first, it is, of course, the teacher not the children who reads the manual and it is the teacher who presents the material to the children; second, the teaching cannot be based on what a general program recommends, but must be based on the child and what he needs.

WORD ANALYSIS TECHNIQUES An analysis of word structure is a means of helping the learner observe patterns in words which follow basic principles. When the learner masters a principle he has mastered a generalization which expands his capacity for remembering. Grouping together items of like structure and organizing them increases the scope of understanding. This is just as true of word patterns as it is with mathematical patterns, science principles, or social phenomena.

One approach would have the child memorize the rules, practice on the patterns, and come up with automatic response. This may produce skill without understanding. Another approach would have the child meet the words, observe their similarities, discover the principles involved, and eventually apply those principles in new situations. The latter approach is more likely to result in understanding and insight.

RELATION OF DRILL TO MASTERY Drill or practice involves repetition to the point of mastery. Isolated drill may result in automatic response without understanding about how and when and why to apply the principles. A few repetitions on a well-understood principle will do much more to fix learning than will numerous repetitions of abstract ideas. Mastery has come about when the learner has made a learning his own, when he can use it independently, and when he knows how and when the principle applies.

Some things are so meaningful and so important that one presentation will be sufficient. If you were introduced to the President, you would not need to be told again who he is. Once would fix it for mastery. But if you were introduced to twenty-five strangers at a meeting, you would probably forget most of them before the next meeting. The ones you did remember would be any who made a profound impression for some specific reason. The same is true of words. Most children learn their own names readily. It is not at all uncommon for them to have to be told numerous times the pronunciation of some of the abstract words. The amount of repetition needed for mastery depends on the intensity of the impression and the value to the learner.

MASTERY OF THE TOTAL LANGUAGE CONCEPT Mastery is more than saying the sounds represented by the symbols. Word mastery also includes meaning, spelling, and writing as well as recognition and pronunciation. The child who uses a word in speech but hesitates to use it when he writes a story because he does not know how to spell it has not really mastered it yet. The child who pronounces a word orally when he is reading from a book but who avoids it when he is speaking has mastered only the form, not the idea. A child needs to be comfortable with words. Until he reaches that point he has not attained true mastery.

WHAT TO DO WHEN A CHILD COMES TO A WORD HE DOESN'T KNOW

Then there is always the question of what to do when a child comes to a word he doesn't know. The answer, like so many others, must be, "It all depends."

It depends on whether he is reading orally for an audience or in a testing situation. It depends on whether he is reading silently in an instructional situation or for his own personal pleasure. It depends on the child and his potential for independence. It depends on the nature of the word itself. Let us imagine ourselves to be a teacher in these different situations and see if we can follow her thought to arrive at some practical answers.

WHEN READING ORALLY FOR AN AUDIENCE When the child who is reading to an audience comes to a word he doesn't know my first reaction is, "I wish I had anticipated that difficulty and had prevented the situation from arising. If I had known the child well enough and had studied the material carefully enough, I might have developed that concept and have supplied the new term before I asked the child to read orally. But since I didn't I'll have to do something about the situation I have allowed to arise. What shall I do?" The next reaction is to think about the purpose for reading. If the child has an audience, they are counting on him to relay meaning.

Stopping to struggle with a vocabulary problem won't help them. Let's discount that as a possible approach this time. Notice that I said "this time," because there may be another occasion on which I will stop to work with word analysis.

Furthermore, if he has an audience, he feels some responsibility for getting his message across. Again, stopping to struggle with the mechanics will not get the message across and thus accomplish the purpose for the oral reading at the moment. And what's more, stopping to work out a word he obviously doesn't know, and perhaps wishes he did, will only embarrass him before his peers. Such embarrassment will only make him more reluctant to read orally on future occasions. The decision in *this* situation just has to be to tell him the word and let him go on. But I'll make a mental note of the child, the word, and the nature of the difficulty and watch for an opportunity to do a little constructive teaching later.

WHEN READING ORALLY IN A TESTING SITUATION Remember, this has been identified as a testing situation. If I am trying to check on him, I won't be doing it before an audience. This will be our private affair, his and mine. He is here to find out how he is doing and I am here to help him. He knows why he is being measured and I hope he has learned to trust me as a teacher, one who will help him over his hurdles rather than one who will try to catch him in difficulty and reprimand him for not knowing better. This is a situation when I may stop to help him work out the word independently, then go back to put it in its setting so it makes sense. But again, that depends on those other factors I mentioned earlier, the nature of the word and the nature of the child. More about that later.

WHEN READING SILENTLY IN AN INSTRUCTIONAL SITUATION Here is my opportunity to apply a little preventive medicine. I shall try to vaccinate him against difficulties. My purpose for the guided silent reading is to help the child learn how, then give him a chance to do it. I shall do the developmental teaching that leads him to read to himself to find out the answers to some carefully worded questions. After he has read silently I shall check to see if he got the idea. In the discussion period, when he is expressing his ideas or answering my questions, he will reveal his understanding and possibly expose his lack of knowledge of certain words in the context. This is my opportunity to use that word in a conversational situation so its meaning and its sound will become familiar. If I can get the child to use the word in oral speech first, he will be less likely to hesitate when he comes to it in oral reading. This is what I call the ounce of prevention. The oral reading which follows then is not a test to see if he knows all the words because he does know them; I made sure of that in the guided silent reading experience. Then the oral reading becomes his personal triumph because he has an opportunity to do something he has just learned how to do. Now it becomes an exercise in making right associations.

WHEN READING SILENTLY FOR PLEASURE When a child is reading by himself I won't even know if he comes to a word he doesn't know unless he asks for help. If he doesn't ask for help with an unfamiliar word, it may mean he can get the idea without it so he decides to "skip it" and go on. That is his right. That is what an adult does in much of his recreational reading. But if he does ask for help, I still have to make a decision. I'll have to decide whether to tell him the word or help him work it out. Again it all depends. It depends on what I know about the child and what I conclude about the nature of the word itself.

WHEN THE CHILD'S POTENTIAL VARIES Let's take a look at the child first. There are some children, I must admit, who seem to lack the mentality for abstract reasoning and application of principles to new situations. I have learned from experience that if I attempt to help Paul with a word by recalling phonetic principles, by indicating meaning clues, or by putting it in a new setting, I may approach it from every angle I know and still I'll come up with a blank expression and a futile effort that results in frustration for both Paul and me. After I have had enough such experiences I might decide not to struggle with Paul in working out a new word, not because Paul doesn't need it and not because it is impossible, but because I have twenty-nine other children in the room and I have to think about what is good for the greatest number under the circumstances. Perhaps fifteen minutes spent with Paul under these circumstances would be like Ben Franklin's whistle. The cost is too great in relation to the results. Perhaps Paul should be handled with less pressure in the classroom and be referred to the reading specialist or the clinic for the individual attention he seems to need and which is too expensive in terms of time taken from the majority.

On the other hand, if the child who asks for such help is a capable child like Alan and I know from experience that a gentle hint or a quick comparison with something he already knows will result in an insight so that he can go it alone from there, then I'll give him the help I know he can handle and take one more step in establishing his independence. That step may be covering a prefix or a suffix to reveal a known root word; it may be calling his attention to a phonetic pattern we have studied; it may be a thought provoking question that will reveal a context clue; or it may be a reference to an illustration.

WHEN THE WORD PATTERN VARIES Let's take a look at the word itself. Shall I try to get the child to work it out phonetically? Shall I utilize a context clue? That depends on the nature of the word.

Suppose he is reading a story about sea life and does not recognize the word fish. I take a quick look at the word. I recall that we have had the word wish and decide to give him a phonetic clue. I don't put him in a testing situation which will lead to another defeat and further frustration by saying, "What's this?" then nag him by saying, "You ought to know that. We've had it before." Instead I will try to put him in a situation where he feels confidence in his own ability because I have given him a tool which he can use. I will say, "Oh! We've had the word wish. Take a look at it. If I take off the *w* and put an *f* in its place what would I get?" If I have done a good job teaching initial consonant substitution and if he is an alert child, he will probably take up from there and go on. If not I may try a context clue by asking next, "What kind of animal might we find living in a pond?" If that's doesn't work, I might suggest that he look at the picture. By this time if I haven't gotten results I may conclude that his interest in the reading act and his personal integrity are more valuable at the moment than success with word pronunciation. In that case I might give up for the time being and tell him the word hoping for another opportunity later to take up the task and try again.

We used the word fish to illustrate our point above. It is phonetically regular and it is concrete. A phonetic clue or a meaning clue—either one seemed feasible. But suppose he meets a word like enough or could or either. Attacking such words phonetically would frustrate the teacher even more than the child. I cast about for another approach. I can't think of any thought-provoking questions that will bring out the word. The picture doesn't help. What shall I do? I try having him read the whole sentence leaving out the word he doesn't know to see if he can fill in the blank with something that makes sense. If that doesn't work, I'll try reading the sentence to him myself leaving out the word. If that doesn't work either, my judgment tells me that it might be wiser to tell him than to keep on. Even then I won't tell him just one word in isolation but will be careful to put it in a meaningful phrase.

One teacher has worked out with her children a chart entitled, "What To Do When You Come To A Word You Don't Know." On it are the suggestions the children developed in a conversational lesson. Now don't go make a chart just like it and post it in your room! Work out a plan with your children and record for them what they help you decide. It will probably be the same general idea, but it will be in their words and if they help work it out they will know how to use it. It might go something like this:

When I Come To A Word I Don't Know

I read on to the end of the sentence.
I read again to see if I can figure it out.
I look to see how the word begins.

I look to see if I know a part of it.
I look to see if it is like a word I already know.
I read the sentence again.
Then I ask for help if I need it.

Now when the child asks for a word and I decide to help him help himself what do I do about it? First, I look at the word, then I look at the child, then I appraise the situation, then I decide what is the best thing to do with this word, for this child, in this situation. The answer won't always be the same. If it were we could put teaching on a phonograph record and dispense with the teacher. And you're the doctor. You have to diagnose each case and make a decision. And the decisions will vary with the situations.

But suppose you decide to help the child work out the word. Here are some things to try:

- Cover up an ending revealing a smaller known word.
- Cover up a beginning consonant or blend to reveal a known phonogram or smaller word.
- Mention a word he does know that is similar or rhymes.
- Ask a thought-provoking question which will draw out the meaning.

For example, suppose he asks for the word *brown.* Say, "Oh, that's a color word." Pause. If there is no immediate response suggest that it rhymes with *down.* Pause. If there is still no response suggest that he can tell the color of the boat by looking at the picture. If he says *tan* accept his answer but give further guidance with a remark such as, "Yes, it is a shade of tan, perhaps a bit darker. But if it were *tan* it would begin with a *t* and this begins with *br* like *bread* and rhymes with *down.*" If he still does not get it you might decide to tell him. Even then you can still do a bit of constructive teaching by suggesting that he listen to *down* and *brown* to see if they really do rhyme. Then have him repeat *bread* and *brown* to see if they really do begin alike. Put them on the chalk board for visual comparison like this:

bread	down
brown	brown

My! That was a long answer to a simple question, "What shall I do when a child comes to a word he doesn't know?" But as I said in the beginning, "It all depends." And unless you know what it depends on, you can't decide. Now I might have given you a formal answer such as:

- Utilize context clues.
- Apply phonetic analysis.
- Adjust the technique to the nature of the word.
- Adjust the technique to the ability of the child.

But if those suggestions are mere verbalisms to you as a teacher then you might resort to some of the all-too-often-used nagging procedures such as saying, "Now think!" or "Sound it out," which we have been using for years and which result in failure for the child and in frustration for the teacher. Of course that is what we have done, but we taught the child how and led him through the process instead of telling him to do it and deciding that he had failed.

One teacher said, "I never tell a child a word. I always make him work it out. Wouldn't you?"

My answer has to be, "No. It all depends."

Another teacher said, "I never let a child struggle with a word. If he doesn't know I tell him. Wouldn't you?"

And again my answer has to be, "No, not always. It all depends."

5

THE RECOGNITION OF WORD PATTERNS

or What About Phonics?

What about phonics? That is the way the question is usually asked. There are many answers ranging all the way from "Drill! Drill! Drill!" to "Beware! Poison! Let it alone!"

There have been numerous research studies based on what to teach, when to teach, how to teach, and what materials to use. If you are a bit confused, uncertain, do not always know just what to do, and are not sure what you think, take courage. If you read the research, you will find conflicting conclusions. If you want some down-to-earth answers which will help you decide what to do about Sally and Tommy who are in your room now, I'll try to provide some help in making up your mind so we can get on with the teaching of reading.

Let the Syllables Help You

November	No vem'ber

101

Let the Syllables Help You

member	mem'ber	winter	win'ter
remember	re mem'ber	middle	mid'dle
remembered	re mem'bered	dinner	din'ner

132

Plate 7. Principle of syllabication presented to aid word recognition [Mabel O'Donnell and Byron H. VanRoekel, *All Through the Year,* Basic Second Reader, Strand 1 (The Harper & Row Basic Reading Program), Evanston, Ill., Harper & Row, 1966, pp. 101, 132].

Some Words Have Different Meanings

Did you see him scramble to his feet?
Please help me scramble the eggs.

I will wash my hands at the sink.
He wanted to sink into the ground.

Jack drove a truck that dumps the sand.
The unhappy boy felt down in the dumps.

Did you see him field the ball?
We walked across the green field.

The hen can perch on the fence.
We ate the fresh perch for lunch.

Fred, bring water from the pump.
See his legs pump over the ground.

He will pitch the last game today.
The room was as black as pitch.

The newsmen sat in the press box.
Press down on the lid of this box.

Plate 8. Examples of words with more than one meaning [Eldonna L. Evertts and Byron H. VanRoekel, *Trade Winds,* Basic Fourth Reader, Strand 1 (The Harper & Row Basic Reading Program), Evanston, Ill., Harper & Row, 1966, p. 52].

Circus is a Latin word meaning "circle" and is related to the Greek word for "ring." When we talk about a three-ring **circus,** we are really repeating ourselves.

23

In France long ago, a foot soldier who went ahead of the main army was called a *peonier.* Our word **pioneer** means "a person who does something first." An early settler or anyone doing original work is known as a pioneer.

59

Plate 9. Word origins for insight into vocabulary [Eldonna L. Evertts and Byron H. VanRoekel, *Trade Winds,* Basic Fourth Reader, Strand 1 (The Harper & Row Basic Reading Program), Evanston, Ill., Harper & Row, 1966, pp. 23, 59].

EXTRA! EXTRA! TOO MANY NUMBERS

Clues, or not? Most cases for which a detective is hired are not simple, but very difficult. Among the most difficult are those in which the real clues are intermingled, or mixed, with false clues which often lead him off in the wrong direction. He must learn to recognize quickly those clues which are helpful and disregard, or forget about, those which are not. But false clues are not easily recognized.

In many arithmetic problems there are false clues also. These are the extra numbers which may easily lead you off on the wrong track if you, as a "problem" detective, are not careful.

Plate 10. Scanning for essential details in mathematics problems [Mabel O'Donnell and J. Louis Cooper, *From Codes to Captains,* Basic Fourth Reader, Strand 2 (The Harper & Row Basic Reading Program), Evanston, Ill., Harper & Row, 1963, p. 257].

I shan't attempt to review the research or the history. That has been well done by others. You can read it for yourself. I shan't attempt to evaluate the commercial programs. The advertisements will do that and each one will make you think it is the cure-all which will guarantee quick and easy results. I shall only attempt to give you some basic information which will help you make up your own mind about what to do in your situation. There is no one right answer. There are only some answers that will be helpful in dealing with cases. First we shall attempt to answer the questions about what the teacher wants to know; then we shall suggest some things she should know about phonics.

WHAT THE TEACHER WANTS TO KNOW ABOUT PHONICS

I will attempt to answer the questions, but you must promise to read on to the end because, otherwise, you may be like the blind teachers who went to observe the reading class. Remember them? If you read my first answer, which is going to be "yes" to the question, "Shall we teach phonics?" but do not go on to get the rest of the answers, you are going to end up interpreting phonics perhaps differently and arriving at conclusions different from what were intended.

Let's begin with the questions: (1) Shall we teach phonics? (2) What do we mean by phonics? (3) Why should phonics be taught? (4) To whom should phonics be taught? (5) When should phonics be taught? (6) How should phonics be taught? (7) What is the place of phonics instruction in a total reading program? (8) What is the present status of phonics programs? (9) What should be included in a phonics program? Some suggested answers follow.

SHALL WE TEACH PHONICS?

Yes, *if* we agree on what we mean by phonics; *if* we know why; *if* we are certain to whom to teach phonics; *if* we do it at the appropriate time; *if* we go about it in the right way; *if* we use appropriate and effective materials; *if* we relate it to the total reading program; *if* we keep abreast of new findings; and *if* we include the right things for the right child.

WHAT DO WE MEAN BY PHONICS?

Perhaps the place to begin is with definitions of phonics and phonetics. These two words are often used interchangeably. Technically, most dictionaries indicate that phonetics is the oral productions of sounds and phonics is the application of those sounds to the written forms used in the teaching of reading. Perhaps quibbling over the difference is a matter of technicalities or a matter of semantics. Perhaps it is just as well to accept either and get on with the business of using phonetics or phonics in helping children master the intricacies of the reading process.

WHY SHOULD PHONICS BE TAUGHT?

Since I started out with a positive "Yes" about whether or not to teach phonics and since I posed a number of "if's" in the answer, I must justify the qualified "yes" with some reasons based on the advantages and the limitations of a good phonics program.

ADVANTAGES There are at least two good reasons for teaching phonics, one based on the system of our language and the other based on how learning takes place.

Organization based on an alphabetical system with a phonetic pattern typifies the English language. In spite of all its irregularities there are enough regularities to be worthy of note. You have probably read statements that the English language is less than 50 percent phonetic and claims that it is at least 85 percent regular. Which of these claims you accept depends on what you are counting. The word *pat* is probably completely phonetic because both the consonants are regular, representing no more than one position of the vocal organs, and the *a* is a medial vowel with a short sound. Not all words are that regular.

Consider the word *house*. Is it phonetic or irregular? That depends! The sound of the consonant *h* is probably used to represent a regular sound which is consistent for that symbol (unless it is used in a digraph as in *th* or unless it is silent as in night). The sound of the *s* may be considered regular unless you point out that sometimes it sounds like a z as in has. Is the *ou* combination an irregular vowel sound or can it be construed as a diphthong which is regular for that combination? Usually we expect a terminal e in a one-syllable word to make the intermediate vowel long, but since there are two medial vowels and they form a diphthong, then perhaps the e serves no purpose and is irregular. Now we have confused the issue. We have not decided whether to tabulate the word *house* among the regular or the irregular words from a phonetic point of view.

Even if we considered the extent to which the word is regular within itself we could come up with different answers. If we considered it a five-letter word with two consonants only one of which is always associated with the sound we hear in this word, then we might claim that the word is only 20 percent phonetic. If we accept the *s* sound as regular, then perhaps the word is 40 percent regular. If we count the diphthong as a regular sound, then perhaps the word is actually 80 percent regular. You can see how different evaluators come up with different answers. It would appear that those who doubt the value of emphasis on phonics might make one decision and those who feel that mastery of phonic skills is basic to beginning reading might arrive at a different answer. I fear the decision is too often colored by the prejudices of the judges. Nevertheless, the word still has enough regularity so that, if the child is familiar with the alphabet, he will not call it *pony* or *box,* but he just might call it *horse* unless context caused him to feel concern for what makes sense.

Generalized learnings result in economy of time and effort. The person who memorizes isolated facts eventually gets his memory full and the only way to make room for more is to eliminate some. If some of the facts can be related to each other and "tied up in bundles" that are based on common principles, then the learnings can be reduced to generalizations and the details can be temporarily discarded until they are needed. The child who understands the principle of consonant and vowel substitution does not need to memorize list of words such as can, man, mat, met, pet, pen, pin, etc.

Instruction in phonics will help the learner see sense, organization, and pattern in his language. It will help him to learn basic principles instead of isolated facts. It will lead him toward independence in his attack on the printed page. It will help him to unify the total language process of both encoding and decoding to the end that he sees the interrelationships. It will help him view spelling as going from sound to symbol and reading as going from symbol to sound. When taught inductively so that there is insight and understanding, it will develop an appreciation and respect for our wonderful language. It will lead to deeper meaning and greater skill in reading.

LIMITATIONS When phonics is taught as mere rote memory without insight, understanding, or meaning, it may result in robot performance and actually deter communication with the author. The child who learns to think of reading as a mechanical process may become proficient at pronouncing words without getting meanings. The child who gives undue attention to the details of word structure may become a slow laborious word caller. As a result he may fail to get enjoyment and satisfaction from the reading act, so that he views it as a school chore from which he will be forever relieved when he is old enough to quit school. If this attitude makes him into an adult who evades or avoids reading, then the whole purpose for teaching reading itself will have been missed. Only when the child becomes so skillful in the use of mechanics that he performs automatically and gives his total attention to the gathering of thought from the printed page will his mastery of phonics have functioned as it was intended to function.

TO WHOM SHOULD PHONICS BE TAUGHT?

Some say not all children need to be taught phonics. Some firmly believe that not all children are able to master the abstractions of phonics. Those generalized statements are not very helpful, but perhaps we can arrive at some guide lines which will steer us in deciding each case on its own merits. Otherwise, too many teachers end up doing nothing about phonics or else giving the same dose to everybody. Either approach is a waste of time and effort and a source of frustration for some of the children as well as the teacher.

Granted there is no such thing as a typical group, yet statistics verify that in large unselected groups the normal curve is a reliable expectancy of distribution. If we had a theoretical 100 children they would probably represent varying degrees of mentality and maturity and would distribute themselves along a continuum which we can divide into subgroups for practical consideration. Consider them on a horizontal line thus:

10% to 20% — 60% to 80% — 10% to 20%

At the upper end of the scale there are probably from 10 to 20 percent of the children who are highly intelligent and who come from a reading background. They have already observed printed forms and noticed similarities and differences in word patterns through recognition of their own names, labels on boxes, and captions under pictures. They have already learned incidentally to apply the basic principles of phonics to recognition of words. They may not be able to verbalize the rules, but they instinctively make the correct associations. They seem to get along adequately in reading without formal instruction in phonics. They are able to pronounce phonetically such nonwords as *fam, wam, fot,* or *sim* because they can apply the principles. They may not need to be taught phonics in the sense that they need the knowledge to pronounce words, but they will be helped by some guidance in the organization of what they have observed about language.

There are probably some 10 to 20 percent of the children at the other end of the scale who seem to lack the ability to see relationships, to generalize, and to draw conclusions which they can apply independently to new situations. Whether that lack is due to limited intellectual ability or to meager background of experience with words it still exists. This is the child who seems to know today and seems to have lost all recollection tomorrow. This is the child who stops on the same word every time he meets it. This is the child who can mouth the sounds yet never seems able to put them together into a whole word. This is the child who memorizes the rules yet seems unable to understand the concept or to see its application even when it is pointed out to him. The teacher with thirty children may be making a wise decision when she ceases belaboring the point short of frustration and rebellion on the part of the slow child and sacrifice of time for other children who would benefit from instruction.

That still leaves us with a large middle group of from 60 to 80 percent of the children. These are the ones who are not quite sharp enough to figure it out for themselves. But they are sharp enough to see through it if it is explained to them. They are the ones for whom a phonics program will be most helpful. To deny them such help in seeing pattern in their language would leave them with no tools for independence. To wait for them to see through it and eventually figure it out for themselves would leave some of them without ever attaining that goal and would be a needless delay and waste of time for others who could be utilizing that knowledge much earlier with the help of a sound instructional program. They are the ones who can benefit by some help in phonetic analysis of language and who will not get it by themselves.

The teacher who can identify the independent learners, the ones who seem unable to generalize, and the ones who can understand generalizations when they are explained to them will have identified the basic groups. Then she will know to whom to teach phonics and why. She will at least have eliminated some of the boredom for those who need only a bit of organization for their understandings. She will have eliminated the frustrations for those who seem not to get the point. And she will have provided helpful instruction for those who need it and can benefit by it.

WHEN SHOULD PHONICS BE TAUGHT?

This question really has two parts: (1) When in the school day? (2) When in the reading sequence?

WHEN IN THE SCHOOL DAY Some would have us teach phonics in a separate period apart from the reading class. Others would say to intersperse the teaching of phonic principles into the total reading program as the need or the situation arises. Either way will get results.

If the teacher is aware of all the implications of phonics as a help in word recognition, if she is skillful at taking advantage of these opportunities for helping the child to help himself, if she is keenly sensitive to individual differences in capacity and background for capitalizing on the potential learnings in phonics, and if she can manage to keep accurate records so that she knows what she has taught to whom, then perhaps relying on incidental teaching of phonics as the need arises or the situation presents itself will get the job done. The teacher who is working in a tutorial relationship with one child can probably make this work. The teacher who has had many years of experience with various methods and materials may be able to get most of the skills taught in this manner. The teacher who is working with exceptionally capable children who will already be aware of most of the phonic principles and merely need to have their understandings organized into meaningful patterns may be able to clinch phonic principles in this manner. But too many teachers are not in the categories described above. Planning a sequential program and a definite time is merely a matter of self-discipline to make sure the jobs get done.

One can start with a logically organized listing of the skills to be taught and follow through day by day making sure each one is presented. This is a subject-centered approach to curriculum. It makes sure the topics get presented. It does not necessarily make sure all the children learn. Or one can start with a complete listing of the skills to be covered, but instead of pursuing them one by one down the list, watch for opportunities to insert each of the learnings into meaningful situations. As each new learning is introduced it can be checked off the list. This involves a psychological approach based on the needs of the learner and calls for record keeping after the teaching is done. As skills are checked off and the list becomes shorter the teacher may find it necessary to watch for specific situations or even to create situations to present the learnings not yet developed.

Whether these learnings are presented during the reading class or in a separate period depends on the management of the teacher. The important thing is that they get done. Each teacher knows her own routine best. It is quite possible for one teacher to do it at one time and for her neighbor to do it at another. Both may be equally successful. Instead of asking yourself when it should be done, ask yourself, "Am I getting the job done? Which time works best for me and for my children?"

WHEN IN THE READING SEQUENCE Deciding when in the learning sequence phonics should be taught involves the dichotomy over synthesis and analysis. Synthesis involves learning the separate parts and attempting to put them together to make phonograms, words, and meanings. Analysis involves beginning with meanings and attempting to analyze the patterns to see of what they are composed. Both ways work. The teacher who is concerned about the child and how he learns may be using a bit of both.

HOW SHOULD PHONICS BE TAUGHT?

The difference between synthesis and analysis is a matter of sequence and also a matter of methodology.

SYNTHETIC APPROACH The teacher who depends entirely on synthesis will structure the program around the organization of the discipline and seek to fit the child to the pattern. She will begin with a formula, a pattern, an organized set of learnings, probably a workbook or a textbook and pursue the lessons page by page seeking to establish a base on which to build future learnings. She will teach phonics first on the theory that the child must learn the parts before he can put them together into the whole. This approach begins with letters and sounds.

ANALYTICAL APPROACH The teacher who depends entirely on analysis will structure her program around the interests, abilities, and learning patterns of the children and will seek to fit the program to the child. She will attempt to show him how his ideas look when recorded in print. This approach will be followed with an analysis of the printed forms and a discovery of similarities and differences as a basis for drawing conclusions. With this approach the formal work in phonics will come after the child has had some experience in reading.

The synthetic approach demands memory for abstractions. It requires drill on skills. Its ultimate goal is reading for meaning. The teaching and reasoning will be deductive. The analytical approach calls for insight and understanding at the outset. It leads the child to discover relationships and basic principles. The thinking will be inductive.

I am convinced that it is possible for the child to learn to read by either approach. If the goal is measurable attainments based on objective scores at an early age, then the synthetic approach may show up favorably. If the ultimate goal is insight and understanding with emphasis on comprehension of ideas and independence in attack and the emphasis is put on long-term goals, then the analytical approach has merit. Too often we settle for a few right answers and high scores without developing real insights. I am convinced that the teacher who begins with the idea of establishing communication with the author and proceeds through the discovery of principles is going to be ahead in the long run.

WHAT MATERIALS SHOULD BE USED IN TEACHING PHONICS?

Durkin, in discussing materials for teaching phonics, says, "of all the various skills comprising reading, phonics is the juiciest from an economic point of view."[1] Then she asks why and answers her own question by pointing out the anxieties of the parents and the inadequacies of the teachers.

There are many prepared programs on the market with exhibits, advertisements, and demonstrations to promote their sale. This may be due to the great faith many people put in a panacea. Probably most of the materials advertised have worked for their creators. Most of them will be helpful for some children if used consistently and appropriately, but expecting any one technique to produce results for all in a quick and easy manner without any

[1]Delores Durkin, "Phonics Materials: A Big Seller," *The Reading Teacher, 20,* no. 7 (April, 1967), 610–614.

effort on the part of the learner or the teacher is to invite failure and disappointment.

The teacher is faced with the problem of what materials to use. The decision may be made for her in a program which adopts basic materials. Such materials used uniformly for all may turn out to be a waste of time for half to two-thirds of the children in the average classroom. There may be some children who already know and who do not need the drill. There may be others who are too immature or too incapable to understand. There are others who need a little help and lots of independent application and still others who need a great deal of teaching before they are left to work alone.

The teacher who is allowed to select her own materials may have to make some decisions that will not be easy. She must know what materials are available, what they are supposed to accomplish, and what her children need. Even then she cannot expect to make a single selection for the entire group. Once the materials are selected there is still the problem of how to use them. And remember, the authors who developed the materials and wrote the manuals may know more about the phonics than you do, but they don't know as much about your children as you do. The decision about when and how much and how is still up to you.

There are materials on the market from thirty or more different publishing companies. They include basal readers, phonics texts, workbooks, phonograph records, programed exercises, duplicating sheets, kinesthetic materials, filmstrips, color charts, games, puzzles, wall charts, talking typewriters, flash cards, and revisions or modifications of the alphabet itself.

Of course, there is the rare teacher who seems to sense instinctively what the learner can do and who seems to have great skill in helping him to move forward in his learning. She has such keen insight into the structure of the language that she is always able to put her finger on exactly the technique and the example that will meet the situation. Since we are not all that gifted or that skillful perhaps we need some of the materials.

Extensive research studies have backed up many of the materials now offered to the educational buyer. Competition for the dollar is keen. The teacher who understands the problem and really wants to help the learner will probably experience a measure of success with a variety of materials. What the teacher and the child do with the material is far more important than what material they use. Perhaps the first caution which should be offered is not to confuse the child with too much material at one time. The phonics programs may be one as good as another, but too many different programs running concurrently may leave the child in the same quandry as the traveler who has been given three or four alternate sets of directions for finding his way to his destination.

Select materials in terms of children's needs. Use them cautiously and well. Keep uppermost in mind at all times how the material is helping the child with his learning problems. Never lose sight of meaningful reading as the ultimate goal. Keep phonics in perspective as an aid to independence.

WHAT IS THE PLACE OF PHONICS INSTRUCTION IN A TOTAL READING PROGRAM?

A USEFUL TOOL Phonics is not a method. It is a tool. It is a useful tool in the mastery of the reading process. It is only one of the useful tools. Used alone to the exclusion of all other word recognition tools it will have limited value. Combined with those other tools it can become invaluable. Putting all your faith in one tool or one technique to teach reading may produce an automaton who can perform but cannot learn, who can achieve scores but cannot think, decide, and act.

PART OF A BALANCED PROGRAM Phonics is related to word recognition through decoding. It is related to spelling through encoding. It is related to word meaning through recognition of meaningful parts such as suffixes and prefixes. Phonics may tell you how to pronounce or spell the word fast, but it will not tell you whether it is referring to a rate of speed, a condition of being attached to something, a looseness of morals, or a long interval without food. The setting in which the word occurs must be given equal consideration.

The learner who can utilize the principles of sound-symbol relationships in connection with context clues and good judgment will become the mature reader who can get the idea. As a tool its value must not be overlooked, but as a panacea its dangers cannot be overemphasized. By all means use it. Don't become a slave to it.

WHAT IS THE PRESENT STATUS OF PHONICS PROGRAMS?

The pendulum continues to swing. Over the years we have oscillated from overemphasis on phonics to complete exclusion of it from the teaching of reading. Research has been conducted. The findings have often been interpreted in the light of the prejudices of the researchers or the interpreters. Each time the pendulum swings it is to be hoped that it goes a little less to the extreme. There is still hope that we can settle down to a sane and sensible middle of the road practice. And that doesn't mean straddling the issue or evading a decision. It means seeing the value of phonics and capitalizing on its contribution to the maturity and insight of the skillful reader. It means, at the same time, seeing the limitations of a program which gives the learner only one tool to use in the complex process of becoming that skillful reader.

Present-day reading programs nearly all recognize the values of phonics.

Most of the phonics programs are now presented as one element in a good reading program. Even the researchers tell us that there is more difference between two teachers using the same program than between groups of teachers using different programs. In the hands of a teacher who knows the phonetic structure of the English language and the growth patterns of the children a sound phonics program based on careful research can be helpful and valuable. I believe we are reaching some middle grounds that are sensible.

WHAT SHOULD BE INCLUDED IN PHONICS INSTRUCTION?

Include that which is practical and useful and within the comprehension of the learner at the moment. That is a qualified answer. It takes a bit of explaining. One might logically follow with the questions: What is practical and useful? What is within the comprehension of the learner?

UTILITY OF PHONIC GENERALIZATIONS A generalization of sufficient dependability that the learner will find it applicable in future word analysis is a principle which perhaps should be learned. Clymer's well-known study on the utility of phonic generalizations caused considerable question about the value of teaching such old reliables as when two vowels go walking the first one does the talking.[2] Some follow-up studies, including one by Bailey, have revealed that when the rule is broken down to more specific examples it is more reliable.[3] For example, if you tabulate all the examples you can find of words containing two vowels side by side, you will have numerous exceptions to the rule of the long first vowel and the silent second vowel. Some may reveal a long second vowel, as in thief, break, and believe. Some may reveal a short vowel sound, as in bread, friend, and sieve. Others may actually constitute separate sounds in separate syllables, as in diet, coincide, and create. But if you take specific combinations there is much more regularity of pattern, such as the *oa* in boat, float, road, toad, moan, loan, etc. Perhaps the teacher could select her own phonic elements to be taught by making her own studies, but there is considerable question as to whether this would be good use for her time. Perhaps it would be wiser to accept a recommended list based on findings of research and use that for curriculum content. Such lists can be found in research reports and in textbooks and workbooks based on such studies.

SCOPE OF COMPREHENSION OF THE LEARNER The part of the question about the comprehension ability of the learner may be more dependent on

[2]Theodore W. Clymer, "The Utility of Phonic Generalizations in the Primary Grades," *The Reading Teacher, 16* (January, 1963), 252–258.

[3]Mildred Hart Bailey, "The Utility of Phonic Generalizations in Grades One through Six," *The Reading Teacher, 20,* no. 5 (February, 1967), 413–418.

the judgment of the teacher. If the phonic principles are understood by the child and are useful to him in his reading, then go ahead and teach them. And many times the teacher will find herself in the position of helping the child "try them on" to see if they fit. In other words, she will often provide contact with phonic principles, encourage the child to try them out, and help him see the application. If he gets the idea, she will encourage him to proceed along that path. If he misses the point, resists the gentle urging, or turns away, she might be wiser to wait a bit, take a different approach, or try again later. Only the teacher working with the individual child can decide what to include in the phonics program for that child at that time.

WHAT THE TEACHER SHOULD KNOW ABOUT PHONICS

The teacher should know considerably more than she ever expects to teach to the children because she needs a reserve on which to build. Having such a reserve of knowledge will enable her to answer children's inquiries with insight and intelligence. But even more important such knowledge will give her background on which to base decisions when she faces the issue of how she will handle a particular word structure problem. Knowledge of the structure of the word pattern will enable her to decide which principles should be shown to the children and which are not regular enough to teach as generalizations. She will know how to lead children to discover the generalizations for themselves.

The teacher's learnings might be divided into four categories: (1) the alphabet, (2) word structure, (3) word meanings, and (4) the dictionary.

Many teachers think they already know all these things, but a survey test conducted by Spache and Baggett revealed many deficiencies in these learnings. Their study of what teachers know about phonics and syllabication concluded that information is often sketchy and inaccurate at best.[4] The fact that primary teachers tend to have a better background in phonics than intermediate grade teachers may be partly due to the fact that they have studied the manuals and have attempted to teach it to the children. No doubt many of them learned it after they became teachers.

Let us turn our attention for the rest of this chapter to a brief summary of the main points of phonics and word structure needed by teachers as professional background for effective teaching.

THE ALPHABET

To begin with the teacher should know about consonants and vowels, what they are and why. Let's take the consonants. They are the framework on

[4]George D. Spache and Mary E. Baggett, "What Do Teachers Know About Phonics and Syllabication?" *The Reading Teacher, 19, no.* 2 (November, 1965), 96–99.

which the sound-symbol relationship is based. If you don't believe that, try reading these two sentences. They both say the same thing:

> Cxnsxnxnts xrx mxrx xmpxrtxnt thxn vzzzls.
> Xoxxoxaxxx axe xoxe ixxoxxaxx xxax xowexx.

CONSONANTS AND CONSONANT COMBINATIONS It is not enough to know that all the letters which are not vowels are consonants. The teacher must also know why they are consonants. What makes them consonants? When the outgoing breath stream is obstructed by the organs of articulation the resulting sounds are consonants. The obstructions vary. The manner of release varies. And the vibrations of the vocal cords vary. These variations result in a classification of consonant sounds in three different categories.

Whether or not the vocal cords are vibrating forms the basis for one kind of classification of consonant sounds.

• When the vocal cords are vibrating the resulting consonant sounds are *voiced* or *vocalized* and are called *sonants.*

(b, d, g, m, n, ng, l, w, y, v, z, th, r, j, zh)

• When the vocal cords are not vibrating the resulting consonant sounds are *unvoiced* or *unvocalized* and are called *surds.*

(p, t, c or *k, wh, f, s, th, sh, ch, h)*

• Some of these consonant sounds come in pairs, that is, they use the same vocal organs and are formed alike, the difference being in whether they are voiced or voiceless. These pairs are called *cognates.*

(p-b, d-t, g-k, w-wh, v-f, s-z, th-th, sh-zh, j-ch)

The manner in which the air is released through the obstruction created by the position of the organs of articulation provides another basis for classification of consonant sounds.

• When the air is completely blocked then released with an explosive force the resulting sound is called a *plosive* or a *stop. Stop* is the term used to describe the manner in which the air is impeded. *Plosive* is the term used to describe the manner in which the air is released. The stops or plosives are *b, d, g, k* or *c, p,* and *t.* Plosives cannot be vocalized without the accompanying vowel sounds. Separating them from the word in which they occur results in a distortion such as buh-ig or duh-ot. The release of the consonant is different depending on the vowel sound which follows. Experiment with the vowel release of the *b* in *bi-t, boo-k, ba-ll, ba-t, bu-t,* and *bi-te.*

• When the air is only partially blocked and released with a continuing flow of the breath stream, the resulting consonant sound is known as a *continuant* or a *prolonged sound.*

• Some continuants are released through the mouth with the organs of speech setting up an impediment which creates a friction through which the breath is forced in the release of the sound. These are called *fricatives.*

(f, h, j, r, s, v, w, y, z, ch, sh, th, th, wh, zh)

• Some continuants are released through the nasal cavity with the oral cavity completely blocked forcing the outgoing breath stream through the nostrils. These are called *nasals.*

(m, n, ng)

The organs of speech used to form the obstruction provide another basis for classifying consonant sounds. Sometimes more than one organ is used.

• Some obstructions are formed with the lips. These are called *labials* or *bilabials.*

(p, b, m, w, wh)

• Some obstructions are formed by pressing the teeth against the lip. These are called *labio-dentals.*

(f, v)

• Some of the obstructions are formed by the tongue touching the teeth or the teeth ridge known as the alveolar ridge. These sounds are referred to as *alveolar sounds.* Sometimes it is the tip of tongue and sometimes the blade of the tongue which contacts the alveolar ridge. It might be noted that not all people make these sounds in identically the same way.

(t, d, n, l, s, z, r, sh, zh)

• Some of the obstructions are formed by placing the tongue between the teeth. These are called *interdentals.*

(vocalized *th* as in this, that, then)
(voiceless *th* as in thin, thank, thought)

• Some sounds are formed by placing the middle of the tongue against the hard palate. These are called *palatal sounds.*

(y, j; the *j* sound is sometimes described as a glide from the *d* to *zh)*

• Sometimes the obstruction is formed with the tongue against the soft palate or velum. These are called *velar sounds.*

(k, g, ng)

• Sometimes the obstruction is formed back in the throat or glottis. This is called *glottal sound.*

(h)

Figure 7 summarizes the classification of consonant sounds as follows:

p and *b* are labial plosives. (One is voiced and the other is voiceless. They are cognates.)

w and *wh* are labial fricative continuants. (One is voiced and the other is voiceless. They also are cognates.)

m is a labial nasal continuant. (It is voiced.)

f and *v* are labio-dental fricative continuants. (One is voiced and the other is voiceless. They are cognates.)

Place of Articulation	Manner of Release		
	Plosives	Continuants	
		Fricatives	Nasals
Labials	p b	w wh	m
Labio-dentals		f v	
Alveolars	t d	l r s z sh zh	n
Interdentals		th (voiceless) th (voiced)	
Velars	k g		ng
Palatals		j y	
Glottals		h	

Figure 7. Classification of consonant sounds.

t and *d* are alveolar plosives. (One is voiced and the other is voiceless. They are cognates.)

l, r, s, z, sh, and *zh* are alveolar fricative continuants. (While their formations are similar they are not identical: *s* and *z* are cognates; *sh* and *zh* are cognates; *l* is sometimes called a lateral fricative continuant; *r* is the most elusive for description and appears late in speech development.)

n is an alveolar nasal continuant. (It is voiced.)

voiced th and voiceless *th* are interdental fricative continuants. (They are cognates.)

k and *g* are velar plosives. (One is voiced and the other is voiceless. They are cognates).

ng is a velar nasal continuant. (It is voiced.)

j and *y* are palatal fricative continuants. (They are not quite identical and are not usually considered as cognates.)

h is a glottal fricative continuant. (It is unvoiced.)

m, n, and *ng* are nasal continuants. (All nasals are voiced. Experiment with them and feel the movement from lips to alveolar to velar positions.)

The above classification might well exclude:

c which is sometimes equated with *k* as in call, cut, and come, and sometimes with *s* as in cent, city, and cyst

q which is actually a *kw* blend as in quick
j which is a glide from *d* to *zh*
ch which is a glide from *t* to *sh* (Note that *d* and *t* are cognates and *zh* and *sh* are cognates, thus making *j* and *ch* cognates.)
s which is a *zh* sound as in treasure
x which is sometimes *ks* as in box or anxious and sometimes *gz* as in exact or exist (Note that *k* and *g* are cognates and *s* and *z* are cognates, thus making the two sounds of *x* cognates.)

While the consonants are not so irregular in their sounds and spellings as the vowels they do present variations which complicate the learnings. Cordts gives a list of different spellings for the same sound and different sounds for the same letter which provides convincing proof of the irregularity of the phonic system in the English language.[5] A few are cited below.

The following are examples of more than one spelling for the same sound:

f as in if, off, laugh, graph
k as in kite, come, truck, ache, antique, quick, choir
ng as in sing, finger, handkerchief
s as in some, city
z as in has, zebra, buzz
sh as in ship, sugar, mansion, patient, machine, ocean, anxious, precious, conscious, sufficient, tissue
zh as in pleasure, seizure, garage, division
j as in jump, germ

The following are examples of more than one sound for the same letter:

f as in if, of
n as in an, thank
ng as in wing, plunge, congratulate, stronger
s as in sit, his

These are only representative. See Cordts for a more complete list.

Notice the sound of the c in such words as cat, cut, cold, clay, and cry. This is a hard c. Notice the sound of the g in such words as game, go, gusty, gray, and glad. This is a hard g. Observe that in each case c or g has been followed by *a, o,* or *u* or has been used in a consonant blend.

Now notice the sound of the c in cell, cinder, cyst, and cycle. This is a soft c. Notice the sound of the g in such words as ginger, gem, and gypsy. This is a soft g. Observe that in each case c or g was followed by *e, i,* or *y*.

These observations lead to a generalization which is useful. Again there are some exceptions, but the observation helps us see system and pattern in our word structure and provides one more aid to independence in word recognition.

[5]Anna D. Cordts, *Phonics for the Reading Teacher,* New York, Holt, Rinehart and Winston, 1965, pp. 121–128.

Next we come to the consonant combinations. When two or more consonants appear in sequence in the same word or the same syllable they present a new learning. Sometimes you hear them both and they are called *blends* or *clusters*. Sometimes you hear only one sound and they are called *digraphs*. Sometimes they are sounded in separate syllables.

Consonant blends or consonant clusters are formed when two or more consonants appear together in the same syllable and when both can be heard, for example, *sp*ell, *st*ay, *gl*ad, *fl*at. Note that both can be heard distinctly, yet a distortion is created when an attempt is made to separate them as in *fuh-ul-at* or *guh-ul-ad*. They must be kept intact and must be blended with the vowel which follows to give an accurate articulation, thus: *fla*-g, *sto*-p.

Digraphs are formed when two or more consonants appear together in the same syllable and when neither one is heard but a new sound is formed, for example, the *f* sound in phone or laugh, the *sh* in ship, the *ch* in chair, the *th* in that or thin.

Some sources include the *ck* in a word like stick as a digraph. In that case the two letters represent a single sound but the sound is the same as one of the letters. This leads to a more simplified definition of a digraph which is two letters representing a single sound whether that sound is a new sound or the same sound as one of the letters. The wise teacher will be aware of both interpretations and will prepare to help children accept without confusion the one which happens to be in the program they are using.

Adjoining consonants may be sounded in separate syllables as in *in-side, pic-ture, pen-cil,* and *bas-ket.*

VOWELS AND VOWEL COMBINATIONS The teacher should know not only what the vowels are but why they are vowels. Ask the average person, teachers included, "What are the vowels?" and most of them will tell you *a, e, i, o,* and *u,* and sometimes *y,* and a few will add *w* to the list. This is rote learning memorized in the early stages of learning to read. Ask them *why* these letters are vowels and most of them will have no idea. They have never experimented with their vocal mechanisms and have not discovered that the sounds represented by these letters are all open sounds in which the breath stream flows from the resonance chamber without any obstruction from the organs of speech. The differences in the sounds are caused by the shape of the resonance chamber rather than by the use of the organs of articulation. As one little boy said, "It all depends on the way you hold your mouth."

Long and short vowel sounds are basic. The teacher should be able to distinguish the long sound of each vowel as heard in common words and as marked by the macron. Listen to the long a in make, baby, day, and potato; the long e in see, me, green, and complete; the long *i* in high, ripe, die, and decide; the long *o* in go, open, home, and grow; and the long *u* in mused, mule, music, united, and use.

She should also be able to distinguish the short vowel sound as heard in the following words and as marked by the breve. Listen to the *a* in cat, candy, basket, and man; the *e* in pet, red, federal, and bell; the *i* in sit, mix, spin, and assist; the *o* in hot, box, doll, and pond; and the *u* in us, sun, bug, and rubber.

Irregular sounds of the vowels should be recognized as those which are neither long nor short. Dictionaries use different systems for marking them. Notice the different sounds represented by the *a* in said, saw, father, and again; by the e in her, they, been, and eight; by the *i* in bird, police, view, and notion; by the *o* in done, who, women, and ribbon; and by the *u* in tune, put, minute, and burst.

This is only a sampling of the various sounds expressed by the vowels. Cordts points out that the various sounds for the letter *a* are represented by sixteen different spellings, the sounds for the letter e by twenty-three different spellings, the letter *i* by nine different spellings, the letter o by twenty-six different spellings, and the letter *u* by ten different spellings.[6] And this list does not include vowel combinations or silent vowels.

Vowel combinations represent still different sounds. The combination of two vowels in one syllable representing only one sound is called a *vowel digraph*. Like the consonant digraphs, there are two interpretations of the vowel digraph, both of which the teacher should understand. One interpretation restricts the meaning of the term to include only two-vowel combinations which produce a single new sound, not the sound of either of the vowels alone, for example, said, been, good, food, blood. Another interpretation accepts any two adjacent vowels in one syllable whether they represent the sound of one of the vowels or a new sound. This may be the sound of either one of them and, furthermore, it may be either long or short. This definition would encompass not only all the words above, but also such words as believe, boat, friend, great, and bead.

Two vowels together within a syllable may represent a glide from one position to another, thus changing the shape of the resonance chamber during the articulation of the syllable, for example, in such words as coin, house, down, and boy. These are called *diphthongs*. (Be sure to note the *ph* digraph in the first syllable of that word. It is pronounced "dif-thong.")

Y and w as vowels or consonants is another distinction which must be recognized. Sometimes both teacher and children fall into the trap of identifying a *y* or a *w* as a consonant or a vowel by its position in a word rather than by the way it is formed by the vocal organs. It is misleading to conclude that *y* is a consonant when it is at the beginning of a word and a vowel when it is at the end of a word because that is not necessarily always

[6]*Ibid.*, pp. 163–167.

true and besides it may occur in the middle of a word. The same is true of the *w* as a consonant or a vowel.

In the word *yes* the sound of the *y* is formed by impeding the breath stream and is therefore a consonant. In the word *my* the *y* represents an open and an unobstructed sound like a long *i* and is therefore a vowel. But in the word *beyond* the *y* appears in the middle of the word and is a consonant because the breath stream is obstructed, while in the words *cycle* and *myth* the *y* appears in the middle of the word and is a vowel. In *cycle* the *y* has a long *i* sound and in *myth* a short *i* sound, but both are open unobstructed sounds and are therefore vowels.

The same is true with the *w*. To conclude that it is either a vowel or a consonant depending on its position in the word may be misleading. In the words *wing* or *want* the *w* represents a sound which is obstructed by the lips and is therefore a consonant. In the words *wring* or *write* the *w* is silent and presumably a consonant which was probably sounded in the original form from the Anglo Saxon. In the word *blow* we hear the long *o* sound but not the *w* sound at all. There are different interpretations which can logically be placed on this construction. The *w* might be construed as a silent terminal consonant. Or the *ow* might be construed as a vowel digraph in which case the *w* would be a vowel. But when the *ow* appears in such words as *now* or *down* there must still be a different interpretation. Here the *ow* is definitely a diphthong with a glide from one vowel position to another within the same syllable. The *ow* sound in *down* is exactly the same as the *ou* sound in *house*. Since *ow* is a diphthong sound the *w* must be construed as a vowel.

Both *y* and *w* are consonants when the breath stream is obstructed. They are vowels when the breath stream is unobstructed.

WORD STRUCTURE

Many of the rules or generalizations stated about word patterns have so many exceptions that the wary teacher, as well as the pupil, is likely to lose confidence in them. Some of the patterns common to one-syllable words can be applied to the syllables in multisyllabic words.

COMMON PATTERNS IN ONE-SYLLABLE WORDS There is enough regularity in word pattern in the English language to merit calling attention to similarities as a basis for arriving at independence in attacking pronunciation. Examining words which follow a common pattern can aid the children in discovering principles for themselves. Exceptions can come later and can be recognized as such. But if the rule is memorized first then the exceptions seem to break down what has been learned.

Examine the following words: hat, sad, ten, bed, win, did, hot, box, cut, and mud. Each one begins with a single consonant. Each one ends with a single consonant. Each one has one vowel in the middle. Each one represents a c-v-c (consonant-vowel-consonant) word pattern. In each case the vowel is short. This is a useful word pattern to recognize. It also appears in the accented syllable of multisyllabic words, such as *bas'*ket and *pen'*cil.

A similar principle is evident in such words as in, on, if, at, ax, up, and us. In these words there is a v-c pattern. The consonant follows the vowel and closes the syllable. The vowel is short. This also applies to many accented syllables in multisyllabic words such as *un'*der and *en'*ter.

Usually, when a syllable has only one vowel and when that vowel is followed by a consonant which closes the syllable, the vowel is short. The exceptions can be observed later, for example, saw, car, ball, cold, climb.

Another common pattern which can be generalized is the c-v pattern (me, be, go, so, my, and by). Here the vowel sound ends the syllable leaving it open and the vowel is usually long. This also pertains to accented syllables in words of more than one syllable such as *la'*dy, *no'*tice, and *mu'*sic. The exceptions can be dealt with after the basic principle has been discovered, for example, do, to.

Another common word pattern is the c-v-c-v which utilizes the long vowel and the silent terminal e in such words as name, theme, ride, home, and mule. Such exceptions as *come, give,* and *have* will need to be recognized. The child will find that the word *have* violates the rule and is pronounced with a short *a* in spite of the generalization; then when he comes to the word *behave* he finds it reverts to the original rule.

Another pattern worth noting is the two vowels together in such words as goat, read, pail, sleep, eat, and train. In each case the child can be led to observe that there are two vowels together, the first one is long, and the second one is silent. There are many examples of words which exemplify this pattern. Clymer's study has pointed out that this rule may lack utility as a generalization, but if it is observed as a common pattern in many words, it becomes useful as a possible clue in identifying an unknown word.

A rule does not necessarily say a principle always holds true. The discovery of the principles merely leads to the statement that in many of our words we can observe these patterns. Such patterns are worth knowing as aids in attacking new or unfamiliar words. Try them. If they work and yield words that make sense in context, then they are helpful. If they create words or sounds that do not make sense, then teach the child to use his judgment and try something else.

These are only a few of the more common word patterns but they illustrate the point about phonetic regularity, or irregularity, in our language and about principles for teaching the more common ones.

APPLICATION OF PATTERNS TO MULTISYLLABIC WORDS Children who know word parts can usually put them together and develop new words or attack longer words independently. Root words can be expanded by adding affixes. These include both prefixes and suffixes. Some authorities differentiate between suffixes which change the meaning of a word, such as kind*ness* and laugh*able,* and inflectional endings which merely change the tense or degree of a word, such as do*ing* and kind*er.* Many accept all parts affixed to the end of a word as suffixes. The teacher would be wise to note the difference but to accept the classification used by the author of the children's text.

The principles of syllabication and accent are helpful in arriving at the pronunciation of a word, but generalizations must be stated with caution lest a rule be formulated which does not hold true in all cases. It depends on whether there are one or two consonants in the middle, whether the accent is on the first or second syllable, whether the vowel is long or short, and whether there is a blend or a digraph. Figures 8 and 9 show these conditions as a basis for arriving at some dependable generalizations. Even then this analyzes only two-syllable words and does not differentiate between such seemingly different words as *model* and *hotel* or *message, massage,* and *passage* where the accent shifts from one syllable to another.

There is no rule that always works to tell where the division comes, whether the vowel is long or short, and where the accent falls. Many times it is practical to try more than one pronunciation pattern to see which one makes sense in context. If there is uncertainty consult the dictionary. The child who develops respect for the authority of the dictionary is doing more for independence than the one who relies on rules.

If the teacher calls attention to common patterns, recognizes exceptions, and frequently refers to the dictionary to verify a pronunciation, she will gradually lead the children to follow these same techniques. When the child learns this approach he is becoming independent.

WORD MEANINGS

COMPOUND WORDS The recognition of word parts in such words as into, bedroom, sometimes, playhouse, and bookcase helps to establish both pronunciation and meaning. Compound words are common in the English language and should be taught. Children meet them as early as first grade.

SYNONYMS The user of language who knows more than one way to express an idea has a richer vocabulary than the one who depends on such platitudes as cute, pretty, and nice. The speaker who differentiates size by using synonyms such as tiny, miniature, and dimunitive or other traits with such terms as clever, attractive, picturesque, valuable, and vigorous has at his command language which is more useful, more forceful, and more interesting. Synonyms are worth cultivating.

Two consonants together					Only one consonant	
Consonants alike		Consonants not alike				
Unrelated	Related in root word	Unrelated	Related		Short vowel Closed syllable	Long vowel Open syllable
			In a blend	In a digraph		
Divide between two conso-nants	Divide after double con-sonants	Divide between two conso-nants	Do not divide the blend	Do not divide the digraph	Divide after consonant	Divide before consonant
Examples dol'lar hap'pen bot'tom	*Examples* tall'er fall'en roll'er	*Examples* pic'ture sil'ver pen'cil	*Examples* help'ing start'ed farm'er	*Examples* moth'er wash'er meth'od	*Examples* fin'ish mod'el riv'er	*Examples* mo'tor ba'by pa'per

Figure 8. Dividing two-syllable words when accent is on first syllable.

<table>
<tr><td colspan="4">Two consonants together</td><td>Only one consonant</td></tr>
<tr><td rowspan="3">Alike and unrelated</td><td colspan="3">Not alike</td><td rowspan="3">Open unaccented first syllable</td></tr>
<tr><td rowspan="2">Unrelated</td><td colspan="2">Related</td></tr>
<tr><td>In a blend</td><td>In a digraph</td></tr>
<tr><td>Divide between the two consonants</td><td>Divide between two consonants</td><td>Do not divide the blend</td><td>Do not divide the digraph</td><td>Divide before the consonant</td></tr>
<tr><td>Examples
col-lect′
sug-gest′
com-mand′</td><td>Examples
con-trol′
al-most′
for-get′</td><td>Examples
a-fraid′
be-stow′
re-ply′</td><td>Examples
a-chieve′
a-shamed′
ma-chine′</td><td>Examples
ca-noe′
re-view′
be-lieve′</td></tr>
</table>

Figure 9. Dividing two-syllable words when accent is on second syllable.

ANTONYMS Similarly, antonyms are useful and effective. The speaker or writer who contrasts huge and diminutive, ancient and modern, miserable and pleasant, and wise and foolish is adding not only to his vocabulary but to his appreciation and understanding of language.

HOMONYMS The English language is plentifully supplied with homonyms, for example, by and buy, I'll and aisle, soul and sole, pride and pried, course and coarse. A class can soon accumulate several hundred examples. Even first graders who have experienced *hear* and *here* or *to* and *two* are ready to start such a list.

Word Patterns in English				
Word Types	Meanings	Spellings	Pronunciation	*Examples*
Synonyms	Similar	Different	Different	big—large old—ancient trip—journey
Antonyms	Opposite	Different	Different	good—bad hot—cold up—down
Homonyms	Different	Different	Same	here—hear bury—berry groan—grown
Heteronyms	Different	Same	Different	read—read wind—wind present—present

Figure 10. Differentiation among word patterns.

HETERONYMS Still another interesting phenomenon of our language is illustrated in expressions such as, "You are sitting *close* to the door, so please *close* it" and "*Record* the scores in the *record* book." The only way to decide whether to pronounce the *s* in *close* with the voiced or the voiceless sound is to try it both ways and see which fits the context. The only way to decide where to put the accent in *record* is to decide which fits the meaning. There are many other examples such as "*live* in a house" or "a *live* pet" and "make *use* of it" or "*use* it." These constructions are known as heteronyms. Context clues are of paramount importance in arriving at correct pronunciations for such words.

Figure 10 summarizes synonyms, antonyms, homonyms, and heteronyms. The facts plus the examples will enable you to construct your own definitions.

THE DICTIONARY

The teacher should be aware of alphabetical arrangement, pronunciation systems, word origins, and word usage as revealed in the dictionary.

ALPHABETICAL ORGANIZATION Familiarity with alphabetical sequence both forward and backward and its application to word listings even to the second, third, etc., letters within a word is essential for effective use of this tool. The guide words at the top of the page in most dictionaries speed up the application of this skill. Rote memory of the alphabet is not sufficient. Practice in using the dictionary will help to fix the learnings.

PRONUNCIATION SYSTEMS Dictionaries use different devices for indicating pronunciation, the most common ones being diacritical markings, pronunciation keys, and phonetic respellings.

Diacritical markings are used by most dictionaries. Since dictionaries vary in the patterns employed it is more helpful to teach the use of the key in the dictionary than to teach a diacritical marking system itself. The most common markings are the macron for long vowels and the breve for short vowels. Some dictionaries even reduce this to only the long vowel on the assumption that unless otherwise marked the vowel will bear its short sound. More complex markings such as the diaeresis, the semidiaeresis, the modified macron, the circumflex, and the tilde are less and less frequently used.

The *schwa* is increasingly used in dictionaries to represent the unaccented vowel sound in multisyllabic words. It is best described as a guttural grunt. Some programs equate the schwa sound with the short *u* sound. They are not quite the same. Compare the sound of the *u* in *cut* and in *circus*. The schwa sound in the unaccented syllable is the same for various vowel spellings. Note the sound of *a* in *about*, *e* in *decide*, *i* in *pencil*, *o* in *conduct*, and *u* in *circus*.

Pronunciation keys are given in most dictionaries either in the front or the back, and many of them have a simplified key at the bottom of each page. Such a key is designed to help the user determine sounds by comparing with familiar words. Teaching the use of the key is more valuable than teaching a marking system.

Phonetic respellings are frequently used to indicate irregular sound patterns. For example, it is simpler to respell *bureau* as *bur′o* or *road* as *rod* than to attempt to mark the irregular vowels and the silent vowels.

WORD ORIGINS Dictionaries also give information about word origins and their derivations from other languages. Calling attention to this information extends and expands appreciation for the flexibility of the English language and helps to explain some of the seeming inconsistencies in spelling and pronunciation.

WORD USAGE The dictionary shows how words may be used as different parts of speech and with different meanings. Notice: I can *picture* it in my mind, and I drew a *picture* of it. Here we have the word *picture* used first as a verb then as a noun. The dictionary is also a source of different meanings for the same word. Notice: He will *fast* during lent. He can run *fast*. She is a *fast* woman. He is tied *fast* to the post. It is not enough to look up the word. One must select the pronunciation and the meaning that fits the context in which it has been used.

Teach the uses for the dictionary; then teach respect for the authority of the dictionary. These will be more valuable than the rules. Remember, the dictionary does not make the rules. The authors merely record accepted practices.

Yes, teachers should know a great deal more about structure of the language than they ever expect to teach to a particular class of children at any given grade level. They should know about the alphabet, about word structure, about word meaning, and about the many contributions which can be made by the dictionary. Then they will be in a position, not just to teach the children right answers and dependable rules, but to lead them to use their knowledge to become independent in studying language patterns for themselves. Not until the child reaches that stage of maturity is he truly master of his language.

Perhaps one of the greatest deterrents to teaching such independence to children is the lack of such independence on the part of teachers themselves. What an indictment!

6

THE IMPLICATIONS OF LINGUISTICS

or How Can the Linguist Help Me?

If you have taught for more than ten years perhaps your first question will be, "What do you mean by linguistics? I went through elementary school, high school, and college and I never heard tell of it."

If you are a brand new college graduate ready to teach your first class of children to read you may ask, "What is linguistics? I had a course in college called linguistics, but I don't see what that has to do with teaching children to read."

WHAT IS LINGUISTICS?

Defintions can be so wordy, so misleading, so vague. Like the 10-year-old you may read the definition, then look up and say, "What's that?" And no wonder!

SOME DEFINITIONS

One junior dictionary does not even list the word. One adult dictionary defines a linguist as a student of languages and linguistics as "the science of language, the comparative study of the origin, growth, likeness and differences of languages." Webster's *New World Dictionary* defines linguistics as "the science of language including phonology, morphology, syntax, and semantics, or the study of the structure, development, etc. of a particular language."

SOME INTERPRETATIONS

There! That should be sufficient to convince you that linguistics is far more than just another way to teach phonics. It goes far beyond the study of sounds and words. It involves uses of words in settings that include meaning. Language must express ideas. Various languages have different ways of expressing meaning. Some depend on inflection of word form; some utilize word order in the sentence; some depend on the pitch of the voice, the point of emphasis, and the placement of appropriate pauses to convey shades of meanings; and some depend on the relation of words in a total setting to arrive at different meanings for the same words or expressions.

Shane concerns himself with the physiology of speech, the physics of sound, the phonology, grammar, and semantics of English, and the study of language and culture based on the sociology of a people and the relations to human behavior.[1] For the purpose of the teaching of reading the chief concern is study of phonology, grammar, and semantics. Phonology has to do with word structure. Grammar has to do with syntax in the English sentence. Semantics has to do with shades of meaning based on word usage.

The introduction to the teacher's edition of *New Directions in English* has this to say about linguistics:

> The term *linguistics* is capable of two meanings. The first is the narrow, technical meaning; the study of the structure and systems of language; the study of phonology, morphology, and syntax; the study of grammatical statements about language. The second meaning of linguistics is the study of language in all of its manifestations.
>
> The survival of civilization will be little threatened by a misplaced comma or a misspelled word. The survival may, however, depend on a genuine understanding of what language is and does in the fabric of society, which is to say that linguistics in the human sense of the word is far more important

[1]Harold G. Shane, *Linguistics and the Classroom Teacher: Some Implications for Instruction in the Mother Tongue,* Washington, D.C., Association for Supervision and Curriculum Development, NEA, 1967, p. 120.

as the core of a language program than is the study of linguistics in the technical sense of the word.[2]

The same is true of reading. The course of human history will be little affected by the scores the child makes on an objective test. It will be greatly influenced by whether or not the child becomes a reader and by what he reads. It will be even more affected by the ideas, ideals, and impressions he forms as a result of the meanings he derives from his reading. If he grows up to be a reader who is influenced by shallow propaganda, glaring advertisements, misleading political statements, and emotion-packed vocabulary, his reading will readily change the course of history through his purchasing power, his voting habits, and his social relationships.

It is not enough to teach the child to pronounce the words. The study of language must teach him to understand, interpret, and think and, as a result, to act, that is, to determine his own destiny. Unless the attention to linguistics in the teaching of reading directs itself to this end, it will do no more than dozens of other recipes or formulas designed to make a more perfect robot out of the young learner.

With that background let us look into the field of linguistics as it is currently affecting the teaching of reading. Let us consider the areas of emphasis and the patterns of analysis as a basis for identifying the relationships between the study of linguistics and the teaching of reading.

AREAS OF EMPHASIS AND PATTERNS OF ANALYSIS

We have been hearing a lot about linguistics lately. Many people, both professionals and laymen, are looking for a technique, some material, a recipe, or something that will guarantee that, if applied in the right amounts at the right time, perfect performance every time will result. But it is not quite that simple. There are a number of reasons why this is so. English is not consistent enough to guarantee uniform stimulus-response patterns. But even more so, the learners are not like automobiles coming off the assembly line. They don't all respond in the same way. Each learner is a custom job, and it is the responsibility of the teacher to help him learn in his own unique way.

ORIENTATION

Let us take a look at linguistics and the work of the linguists to see what they have to offer us. Let's begin with some of the terms.

Linguistics as a study is a branch of anthropology. Anthropology is defined as the science that deals with the origins, development, races, cus-

[2]Freeman B. Anderson *et al.*, *Teacher's Edition, New Directions in English,* New York, Harper & Row, 1969, pp. T9–10.

toms, and beliefs of mankind. In as much as languge is a part of the development and customs of mankind it is a branch of anthropology.

A linguist is one skilled in language or a student of language who studies the history and structure of language.

Linguistics, then, pertains to the study of languages, their origin, and growth, and the likenesses and differences in languages.

RELATION TO READING

Now how does all that relate to the teaching of reading and to the other language arts? This treatise is not designed to add new information to the subject. It is merely an attempt to interpret linguistics in the light of classroom teaching in order to give perspective on the subject.

First, let us consider what linguistics is not. It is not a method or a technique. It is not a tool. It is not another system of phonics. Then what is it? It is an organized body of knowledge about the tool we use in communication. It is something the teacher should know. It is not necessarily something she will relay to the children.

If you have been confused in your interpretation of linguistics, it is probably because you have read different authors who were talking about different facets of the subject. Perhaps an organizational pattern will help us to see what the linguists are talking about. Figure 11 identifies the areas of emphasis as historical and geographical, and as descriptive and structural; and it identifies the patterns of organization as word patterns and meaning-bearing patterns.

Pattern of Organization	Areas of Emphasis	
	Historical or Geographical	Descriptive or Structural
Word Patterns	Word origins and derivations New words New meanings Coined words Colloquialisms	Phonemes, morphemes, and sound-symbol relations Word patterns Syllabication and accent Word structure—root words, affixes, inflection
Meaning-bearing Patterns	Influence of other languages Word order Sentence patterns Structure of English Historical influence Regional speech	Semantics Syntax Sentence parts Punctuation Pitch, stress, juncture Spelling Context Informal language

Figure 11. Organizational pattern of linguistics.

IDENTIFYING THE PHASES OF LINGUISTICS IN READING

Historical and geographical implications of linguistics may be applied to either word patterns or meaning patterns. Descriptive and structural implications of linguistics may also be applied to either word patterns or meaning patterns.

The historical linguist attempts to trace the history and origin of the language. He may also try to isolate certain linguistic patterns in geographical settings.

The structural linguist attempts to describe the language as it now exists. He, too, may deal with word patterns. He also deals with meaning-bearing patterns which may include isolated words, phrases, sentences, or even whole groups of sentences which are needed to give complete meaning.

HISTORICAL OR GEOGRAPHICAL STUDY OF WORD PATTERNS

Figure 11 shows some of the subjects involved in the historical or geographical study of word patterns. It is doubtful if much of this will be taught to the elementary school child as an organized body of knowledge. Some of it may be challenging to a few of the more superior intellects. It is part of the "stock in trade" of the professional educator. A thorough understanding of this phase of linguistics will help the teacher to recognize patterns in the language, to be cognizant of the difficulties encountered by the learner, and to make judgments about what to teach to whom and when. Some examples of the historical and geographical emphasis on word patterns might help to clarify this point of view.

WORD ORIGINS AND DERIVATIONS Other languages have made abundant contributions to English. The *pend* derived from the Latin word meaning "to hang" is evident in such words as pendant, independent, suspend, and dependable. The Latin root *porto* meaning "to carry" is evident in such words as portable, import, transport, and export. The dictionary points out word derivations from Old English, Old French, Anglo-Saxon, Latin, and Greek, and other sources.

NEW WORDS New needs cause us to create new words. A dictionary bearing a copyright date before 1900 probably would not include such words as astronaut, refrigerator, or helicopter. Intermediate grade children gain much from making a collection of such words and comparing an old dictionary with a current one.

NEW MEANINGS Familiar words frequently take on new meanings. The child who thinks of a diamond as a gem may miss the point when the word is used in reference to a geometric shape or a baseball field. He may be confused by the use of the word spring referring to a flexible piece of steel, a source of water, or a season of the year. The changing meanings of the word square are illustrated in such expressions as "a square box," "a square deal," or "a square."

COINED WORDS The acronyms formed from first letters of words referring to organizations or special meanings are examples of coining words. UNESCO comes from *U*nited *N*ations *E*ducational, *S*cientific, and *C*ultural *O*rganization. A scuba diver is one who uses a *s*elf-contained *u*nderwater *b*reathing apparatus. Another type of coined word comes from the name of a person. Louis Pasteur gave his name to the process of pasteurization.

COLLOQUIALISMS Words take on different meanings in different geographical settings. To the people in some parts of the country *poke* means to punch, to others it means a sack. To some *reckon* means to calculate, to others it means, "I suppose so." Every student of language has his own list of examples.

HISTORICAL OR GEOGRAPHICAL STUDY OF MEANING-BEARING PATTERNS

Historical and geographical studies may also be based on meaning units. Figure 11 lists some of the fields of inquiry in this area. Historically languages have developed to meet the needs of the times. Geographically languages have developed to meet the needs of the people in a given place. A study of this development of languages leads to the study of the sentence patterns which have evolved in different languages and in different regions.

INFLUENCES OF OTHER LANGUAGES It is evident that English has borrowed much of its structure from various sources. A study of the dictionary will give information about derivations as they pertain to form, meaning, and spelling. Unabridged dictionaries give complete details.

WORD ORDER In the English sentence word order helps convey meaning. Usually the modifier precedes the substantive it modifies, for example, "the clever dog," and the modifier follows the verb it modifies, for example, "Dogs learn quickly." Some of these patterns are reversible without distorting the meaning and some are not. You might say, "Dogs quickly learn," but you would not be likely to say "the dog clever." There is quite a difference between "Boys eat hot dogs" and "Hot dogs eat boys." In Latin the verb comes last and the subject and object are indicated by the case of the substantive rather than by the sequence in the sentence. Many of the amusing expressions which result from confusion of one language pattern with another are explainable if one understands the source, for example, "He went the stairs up."

SENTENCE PATTERNS The following sentences illustrate some of the more common patterns with which children are familiar long before they start learning to read.

Boys run. (subject–verb)
Boys are noisy. (subject–linking verb–adjective)
Boys run fast. (subject–verb–adverb)
Dogs are animals. (subject–linking verb–noun complement)
Boys like dogs. (subject–verb–object)
Boys teach dogs tricks. (subject–verb–indirect object–direct object)
Boys teach dogs clever tricks. (same as above plus modifier)
Boys teach dogs clever tricks quickly. (same plus two modifiers)

These are only some of the simple sentences children use freely. Many children use compound and complex sentences with subordinate clauses, relative pronouns, prepositional phrases, and even participles with ease, although they have not learned to identify them by name.

STRUCTURE OF ENGLISH Many of the inflections from other languages have been dropped in English. Much of the meaning is conveyed through the sequence of the words within the sentence, the emphasis given in vocalization, and the inflection of the voice to convey elements of surprise, determination, or inquiry.

HISTORICAL INFLUENCE Pioneers used expressions and figures of speech which have added color to the meaning of language, for example, "soft soap," "slick as a greased pig," "sharp as a tack," and "apple polishing." Most modern children have never seen soft soap, have not experienced the pioneer frolic of catching a greased pig, and may never have used a carpet tack for its original purpose, and might not be familiar with the concept of apple polishing. Therefore, these expressions must be explained if they are to have meaning when they occur in literature. Logging camps, military life, the gold rush days, and World Wars I and II have added their own expressions to our language.

REGIONAL SPEECH Localization of cultural groups in certain geographical areas account for dialects peculiar to certain sections of the country and the expressions which take on specific meanings in family groups. There is a growing tendency for local or regional speech to fade and for greater uniformity in speech throughout the country due to the influence of nation-wide mass media.

DESCRIPTIVE STUDY OF STRUCTURES OF WORD PATTERNS

Another area of emphasis in linguistic studies is descriptive or structural linguistics which deals with word patterns in language as it is used as a tool of communication (see Figure 11).

PHONEMES, MORPHEMES, AND SOUND-SYMBOL RELATIONS Much of the research in recent years has been based on word patterns as represented by symbols. Many of the proposed reading programs center on word patterns in beginning reading. A study of phonemes includes the isolated sounds and the letters which represent them. A study of morphemes includes the unit of structure, the pronounceable parts of words such as the *am* in *ham* or the *our* in *sour*. The emphasis is on a regular pattern of sound-symbol relation.

WORD PATTERNS The analysis of common word patterns was presented in Chapter 5 in connection with the study of phonics. There we identified such common patterns as c-v-c, v-c, and c-v-c-v. In each case we pointed out the regularity of the pattern and the effect on the sound of the vowel in the word. We also showed the application of the principles to syllable parts in multisyllabic words.

SYLLABICATION AND ACCENT Dividing words into pronounceable parts may aid in spelling and sometimes in analysis for meaning. Accent varies with the word pattern and the meaning. Compare these two lists of words.

visit	control
habit	patrol
gravel	regret
label	decide
shovel	equip
signal	accent
neighbor	suggest

All of these are two-syllable words, but the first list consists of words with the accent on the first syllable and the second list consists of words with the accent on the second syllable. There is nothing about the structure or spelling of the words that will tell the reader the difference.

Mispronunciation often results from the application of rules of syllabication and accent where they do not fit. One may have formed the habit of placing the accent on the next to the last syllable in words of three or more syllables, for example, in-ter-*lo*-per, au-to-*mat*-ic, in-di-ca-tion, in-vi-*ta*-tion. The same principle applied to the word *determiner* results in mispronunciation, det-er-*mi*-ner instead of de-*ter*-min-er.

Sometimes more than one pronunciation is acceptable. Many diction-

LESSON I.

GIRL AND DOLL.

girl	left	would	ver′-y	tell
doll	nice	like	whip	play

The girl has a doll. Do you see it′? Do you see her lift it up′? Is it a nice doll′?

Ann′, would you like a doll′? O yes‵, I would like one very much‵? Will you get one for me′?

Has the boy a doll too′? No‵; the boy has a whip. Can not you tell a whip from a doll′? Do you think the boy wants a doll to play with′?

I have a little doll;
  I take care of her clothes;
She has soft flaxen hair,
  And her name is Rose.

She has pretty blue eyes,
  And a very small nose,
And a sweet little mouth—
  And her name is Rose.

You must take good care of the doll, and good care of her clothes.

Can you make a hood′ or a bonnet for her′, and little shoes for her feet′?

Do you think she needs them to keep her warm′? Can you tell me why a doll can not be cold′?

Plate 11. Sample pages from children's books over a period of more than a century.
(a) *The Second Reader of the School Family Series* by Marcius Willson (New York, Harper & Row, 1864, p. 9).

Helping Yourself with New Words

Picture Dictionary

bicycle

dog

doghouse

garage

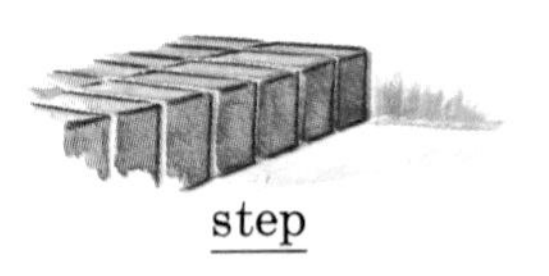
step

Questions and Answers

A day or two went by.
The doghouse sat
all by itself in the sun.

Then one morning Mr. Wells
was at work in the garage.
Janet went inside to talk to him.
Then what did she see?
Over in one corner was a bicycle.
A not-too-big bicycle!
Just about big enough for Janet!

"What is that doing there?"
she asked. "Can you ride on it?"

Plate 11.

(b) *All Through the Year* by Mabel O'Donnell and Byron H. VanRoekel [Basic Second Reader, Strand 1 (The Harper & Row Basic Reading Program), Evanston, Ill., Harper & Row, 1966, pp. 6, 24].

aries give the word illustrate with the accent on either the first syllable or the second, *il*-lus-trate or il-*lus*-trate. But when the verb is changed to the noun construction the major accent is moved to the third syllable with the minor accent moved back to the first syllable, il-lus-*tra*-tion.

WORD STRUCTURE—ROOT WORDS, AFFIXES, AND INFLECTIONS Adding a prefix to a word can change its meaning as in *re*word, *un*tie, *dis*agree, and *anti*climax. Adding a suffix to a word can change its meaning or its structure as in invita*tion,* help*ful,* port*able,* and move*ment.* Adding an inflectional ending to a word can change the degree or the tense as in old*er,* old*est,* call*ed,* call*ing.* A suffix can denote agent as in call*er,* farm*er,* or sing*er.* Some linguists distinguish between a suffix and an inflectional ending. There is an increasing trend, especially in practice material for children, to classify all affixes on the ends of words as suffixes.

DESCRIPTIVE STUDY OF STRUCTURES OF MEANING-BEARING PATTERNS

Descriptive or structural linguistics may be based on meaning-bearing patterns as well as on word patterns (see Figure 11). Meanings are expressed not necessarily by single words, but by larger syntactical units made up of phrases and frequently whole sentences. We need to teach larger segments of sound in order to maintain meaning in its entirety. Many children who seem deficient in reading at higher grade levels are really deficient in general language ability. This justifies time and effort spent in the development of oral language prior to and along with the use of language in the reading situation. Beginning reading should be couched in the spoken language that is familiar to the child. Reading stories to children and talking with them helps them to become familiar with language patterns they will encounter in reading.

Lefevre proposes attention to larger structural patterns. He refers to this as a syntactic-semantic approach.[3] For this the teacher needs a knowledge of the structural system of English, not necessarily in order to relay it to the child, but in order to know what, how, and when to point out organizational patterns which exist in the child's language. This is what Lefevre calls the "meaning-bearing pattern."

SEMANTICS A semantic study of words moves beyond mere recognition and incorporates knowledge of the various meanings of particular words. Consider the different meanings illustrated here.

[3]Carl A. Lefevre, "A Comprehensive Linguistic Approach to Reading," *Elementary English,* October, 1965, pp. 651-659.

A *rose* is a flower.	He *rose* to his feet.	
He caught a *fly* ball.	Airplanes can *fly*.	
It is the *fall* of the year.	He can *fall* asleep quickly.	Do not *fall* down.
We played a *game* of checkers.	He is *game* to try anything.	We killed wild *game* for food.
The grass is *green*.	He was *green* with envy.	Blackberries are red when they are *green*.

Add to this the variations caused by homonyms and heteronyms which depend on recognition of spelling and sometimes origin for both pronunciation and meaning. It is more complicated than merely sounding the letters and pronouncing the words. Even correct pronunciation from a mechanical basis does not guarantee meaning.

A method of reading which stops with recognition of words assumes that the pupils will assemble the words into meaningful relationships. Bright children from highly literate environments may learn to read this way, but children who are linguistically deprived may progress no farther than the mechanical process of association of sound with symbol. Mere recognition of words is not reading. Reading is finding out what the sentences say. Too great an emphasis has been placed on words and their pronunciations. What really matters is the function of the words in the utterance of sounds which express ideas. Some linguists seem to think that it makes no difference whether the words are meaningful or not. Some will even accept those of the nonsense variety such as *fam, cum, wid,* etc. Others seem to be of the opinion that children ought to read meaningful words from the beginning. Some say that right from the start all reading activity should be based on meaning of the whole sentence.

SYNTAX A functional knowledge of the English sentence is necessary in order to get the full meaning from the spoken or written words. The child needs to learn to interpret the sentence in its entirety and in its relationship to the rest of the sentences in the total setting. This involves the use of the word in phrases, in clauses, or even in whole sentences, the arrangement of words in the sentence, and the grammar dealing with the sentence parts. It also involves interpretation based on punctuation, figures of speech, and meaning patterns as revealed by change in pitch, stress, and juncture in oral speech.

SENTENCE PARTS Meanings are altered when only parts of sentences are quoted out of context. Notice what the addition of the final word does to the meaning in the following sentences.

The girl wanted the dress.
The girl wanted the dress discarded.

In one case she wanted the dress; in the other case she did not want it.

PUNCTUATION Meaning is influenced by punctuation marks. They indicate the inflection of the voice in interpreting the printed word. Consider these sentences.

> You went to the mountain.
> You went to the mountain?

Unless the reader is aware of the terminal punctuation mark and its implication for meaning as well as for vocal inflection, he may see no difference between the two and thus miss the point.

Read the following pairs of sentences. Note the effect of the punctuation marks in each case.

> Woman without her man is a raving maniac. (Woman is the maniac.)
> Woman, without her, man is a raving maniac. (Man is the maniac.)

> This bears watching. (You are watching.)
> This bear's watching. (The bear is watching.)

> Next stop, the moon. (We'll stop at the moon.)
> Next, stop the moon. (The moon is being stopped.)

> Let me call you sweetheart.
> Let me call you, sweetheart.

PITCH, STRESS, AND JUNCTURE How one pitches his voice, where he places the emphasis, and the point at which he pauses all alter the meanings. Consider the different points of emphasis in reading the sentence "He hit him" in response to each of the following questions.

Who hit him?	*He* hit him.
What did he do to him?	He *hit* him.
Whom did he hit?	He hit *him*.

Notice the difference in stress in reading the expression "an elevator operator" when answering the following questions.

Is he a telephone operator?	No, he is an *el*evator operator.
Is he an elevator repair man?	No, he is an elevator *op*erator.

Again, in Matthew 26:27 we read, "Drink ye all of it." Does that mean for all of you to drink of it or does it mean for you to drink all that is in the cup? Try reading it aloud each way.

SPELLING When vocalization is identical in speaking the words we can still get different meanings. Spelling is often the clue. For example:

> The consecrated cross I'd bear.
> The consecrated cross-eyed bear.

The sun's rays meet.
The sons raise meat.

CONTEXT Even when the words are identical you may have to decide on pronunciation based on how they are used in the situation. Study these.

Those garments are 89 centers from the bargain counter.
We plan to work in 89 centers for social improvement.

How do you pronounce the italicized words below? How can you tell?

He removed the *minute* speck in her eye in a *minute.*
Real *live* bears *live* in the park.
You may *present* the *present.*

And sometimes the same word can serve several different functions, often in the same sentence. This headline appeared in a newspaper.

Police police police picnic.

The first *police* is the subject of the sentence. The second is the verb. The third is an adjective modifying the word picnic. Notice the change in voice inflection as you read it aloud.

Sometimes the change of just one word will change the meaning and even the grammatical structure of the entire sentence. Consider these.

The body's calcium needs are balanced daily.
The body's calcium needs to be balanced daily.

By simply changing "are" to "to be" we have changed the entire meaning as well as the grammatical structure of the sentence. In the first sentence the word calcium modifies the word needs and is therefore an adjective, while in the second sentence it is a noun and is used as the subject of the sentence. In the first sentence the word needs is the subject and in the second it is the verb.

INFORMAL LANGUAGE Conversational language is often quite different from what appears in print. The importance of the total setting is often essential in order to understand the conversation. Consider these: hafto, didja, whadja, wuz-a-goin', etc. One girl said to another, "Squp." It was obvious what she meant when the two turned and started up the stairway. Then there is the question, "Jeet yet?" and its answer, "No, twirly teet."

Even though one has a functional knowledge of syntax, understands the sentence parts, interprets correctly the punctuation, gets the implications of the spelling, and even uses context clues he still cannot be completely sure of the meaning of some passages. Examine this one for instance.

I saw the man on the hill with the spyglass.

What image does the sentence create? Where was the spyglass? Did I have it? And was I using it to look at the man on the hill? Or did the man have it? And was he using it to look at me? Or was it on the hill with the man and referred to merely as a means of identifying on which hill the man was located?

Words or sentences or even paragraphs are islands in the sea of meanings. We need to teach the total relationships for real meanings. This story illustrates the point that knowing the words does not necessarily prove that the meaning is clear.

> A lobbyist was opposing a large appropriation for a state college. He sent the following letter to the legislators:
>
> Dear Congressmen:
>
> Before you cast your vote on Senate Bill No. C-192a please give careful consideration to the following facts gleaned from the campus. You should know that up at the state college the men and women students use the same curriculum. The men and women students often matriculate together. A young woman student cannot get an advanced degree until she shows her thesis to both male and female professors.
>
> Signed: Bill Smith, Lobbyist
> for economy in government
>
> Note: Senate Bill No. C-192a was defeated 187 to 3.

THE LINGUIST AND THE EDUCATOR

The linguist is a student of language and its structure. The educator is a student of human growth and development and the resulting learning patterns. Each has something to contribute to the other. The linguist needs to know more about how learning takes place. The educator needs to know more about how the language is structured. Both points of view are necessary before either can presume to prescribe the work of the other.

DIFFERENT POINTS OF VIEW

Most linguists and most educators tend to agree that the ultimate goal of reading should be the use of words in meaningful settings. However, they may disagree on the most effective approach to that goal.

Many linguists would organize the learning program around the structure of the language and attempt to help the child adapt his learning techniques and sequences to a logical order. Many educators would organize the program around the developmental steps in the child's growth and attempt to help him discover and organize his understandings about the structural pattern observable in the language which he uses.

RESPONSIBILITY OF THE TEACHER

The good teacher should understand thoroughly the linguistic structure of the language she is using as a medium of teaching. The good teacher should also understand the learning patterns, levels of development, and sequences in child growth and should therefore be prepared to help the learner progress along parallel lines. This includes developing concurrently such concomitant learnings as concepts on which reading is based, familiarity with both the aural and the visual stimuli, acquaintance with sentence patterns, awareness of word structure, and generalizations about frequently recurring and useful patterns. In this way she may lead the learner to independence in both mechanics and in the acquiring of meaning.

The teacher who understands both the learner and the language is in a position to introduce one to the other in a mutually beneficial setting.[4]

LINGUISTIC PRINCIPLES AND READING

Much has been done to help the teacher introduce the learner to his language in meaningful settings. Teachers' manuals offer helps in planning exercises and activities to give meaning to language patterns. Some examples are cited below.

MODIFIERS

Say, "When I tell you about Janet, I like to use more than one word. I do not say just *red* when I talk about her hair. I talk about her *pretty red* hair. Can you use more than one word and tell me about her eyes? about her shoes? about her dress? Start with, 'Janet has ------' "[5]

PREPOSITIONAL PHRASES

Say, "Who can tell me where the tomatoes are? Use the words *in* or *on* when you give your answer."[6]

ANTONYMS

Hold up the card *come* and have the pupil do as the card directs. Then hold up the card *go* and have the child go back to his place. Say "*Come* and *go* have different meanings. They are called opposites."[7]

[4]Daisy M. Jones, "The Implications of Linguistics for the Teaching of Reading," *Elementary English, 46,* no. 2 (February, 1969), 176–183.

[5]Mabel O'Donnell and Byron H. VanRoekel, *Janet and Mark,* Preprimer 1, Teachers' Edition (The Harper & Row Basic Reading Program), Evanston, Ill., Harper & Row, 1966, p. T42.

[6]*Ibid.,* p. T46.

[7]*Ibid.,* p. T68.

Tell the pupils that there are other words that are opposite. Through discussion, make it clear that *up* is the opposite of *down, in* is the opposite of *out, here* is the opposite of *there,* etc.

NOUN PHRASE SUBSTITUTION

Use word cards: the, monkey, stop, shadow, girl, ball, and puppy. Build "The monkey stops," in the card holder. Place other cards at the bottom of the holder. Say, "Here is a two-part sentence. Who will read the sentence? Show us the first part and read the words (The monkey). Now show us the second part and read it (stops). Read the whole sentence.

"Now we will make some changes in the first part." (Remove monkey.) "Who will find another word to take the place of monkey?"

Have a pupil choose one of the other noun cards, insert it in place of monkey, and read the sentence. Let other pupils take turns removing the noun card left by the pupil just ahead and replacing it with one of their own choice. Each time a substitution is made have the sentence read aloud. Let pupils work orally giving words of their own to complete the first part (clock, bus, record, etc.).[8]

NOUN PHRASE EXPANSION

Hold up the word cards one at a time: the, puppy, eat, big, little, good. Build "The puppy eats," in the card holder; place other word cards at the bottom of the holder. Say, "Read the sentence. How many parts has this sentence? Who will read and frame the first part? Now we need someone to read and frame the second part. Let's read the whole sentence again.

"Today we are going to make our two-part sentence grow. We can do it by adding a word to one of the parts. We will add a word only to the first part." Have the first part, "The puppy," framed and read again. Hold up the word card *little*. Say, "We are going to add this word to the first part of the sentence right here." Place *little* between *The* and *puppy*. Say, "Which part of the sentence has grown larger? Read it and frame it."

Remove *little* and substitute *big* or *good*. Other possible words the children may contribute are nice, cute, spotted, brown, hungry, etc.[9]

PAST TENSE SIGNAL -ED

Say, "Here is a simple little sentence which says 'I work.'" (Place cards in rack.) "When I say 'I work' I mean that I am working right now. We do

[8]Mabel O'Donnell and Byron H. VanRoekel, *Around the Corner,* Primer, Teachers' Edition (The Harper & Row Basic Reading Program), Evanston, Ill., Harper & Row, 1966, p. T60.

[9]*Ibid.,* pp. T68–69.

not say, 'I work last week' or 'I work early this morning.' But I can make the word card mean something that I did a minute ago, last week, or last year. With this extra bit added to *work* I have the word worked. You say words all the time with *ed* on the ends to show that you are talking about something that has already happened. We can see this with our word cards. Here are a few more little sentences." Add: I look. I rest. I stay. "Let's read each of them with the word *yesterday* before them. 'Yesterday I worked. Yesterday I looked. Yesterday I rested. Yesterday I stayed.' "[10]

PRONOUN SUBSTITUTION

Say, "I am going to tell you a little story. It may sound funny because I will not say things the way you are used to hearing them. Listen: 'Mark Park and the puppy walked down the sidewalk. Mark Park and the puppy saw a man selling popcorn but Mark Park and the puppy didn't have any money, so Mark Park and the puppy couldn't buy any.' What was wrong? I said Mark Park and the puppy too often, didn't I? We try to say things in shorter ways than that. Usually I would say just one word instead of Mark Park and the puppy. What is this word? It is *they*. Now I will tell the story again with *they* in it and I think it will sound better."[11]

OTHER LINGUISTIC PRINCIPLES

And so there are carefully planned lessons to guide the teacher in the development of linguistic abilities utilizing the principles of communication intonation, juncture, pitch, stress, sentence patterns, sentence transformation, exclamation, negative noun phrases, verb phrases, punctuation, questions, structure words, clause markers, question markers, verb markers, word form changes, modifiers, adjectives, adverbs, changing class forms, noun verb agreement, plural signal, verb inflection, word study, figures of speech, rhymes, and vocabulary expansion.

Throughout the intermediate grades the child's understanding of his language and its ability to express meanings is strengthened and deepened through exercises in making inferences, expanding vocabulary, using similes and metaphors, studying structural analysis, reading dialect, classifying, generalizing, summarizing, organizing, understanding figures of speech, experimenting with intonational patterns, interpreting analogies, and many other exercises some of which are in the pupil's text and some recommended in the teacher's edition for use with the text.

[10]Mabel O'Donnell and Byron H. VanRoekel, *Real and Make-Believe,* First Reader, Teachers' Edition (The Harper & Row Basic Reading Program), Evanston Ill., Harper & Row, 1966, pp. T45–46.

[11]*Ibid.,* p. T102.

The child first applies linguistic principles in speaking and later transfers them to oral reading when he is able to communicate the ideas of the author through vocal expressions.

The application to silent reading comes when the child is able to read for ideas and total thought concepts rather than for word pronunciation. In order to do this he must move beyond the stage of finger pointing and subvocalization of every word through whispering, lip movement, or tenseness of the organs of articulation.

The application of the patterns and principles of linguistics comes in the independent stage where the child gets the idea without necessarily being conscious of the mechanics. Perhaps the highest level of application comes when he is able to appreciate a good joke based on the peculiarities of our language. When the third grade child thinks the jokes like the one about the man who cut a hole in the rug because he wanted to see the floor show are funny, it means he has gotten the point to the different meanings and implications of word usage.

7

THE PLACE OF ORAL READING

or Johnny's Reading, Who's Listening?

There was a time when "reading" meant "reading out loud." At one time in our nation's schools reading was synonomous with declamation or elocution. This may have been partly due to the scarcity of reading material in the hands of the masses and partially to the lack of skill in the reading act by a great majority of the people. The implication here is that the reading act was not only for the information of the reader himself but also for the edification of the listener who was dependent on the reader for his information.

When that situation existed the teaching of reading put the emphasis on accuracy of pronunciation, effectiveness of oral expression, and artistic delivery. Much time was devoted to practice in oral reading in order that the reader might be able to perform effectively. As printed materials became more abundant and as more and more people learned to read for themselves that need became less of a primary purpose for reading. The change in need led to a change in emphasis. Reading for self-enlightenment demanded more silent reading. Even though this changed need and consequent change in emphasis had come about, tradition caused the schools to maintain long-established practices.

Perhaps the purposes for oral reading in today's schools need examining. This will lead to a reappraisal of present patterns and recommendations for effective relationships between silent and oral reading and for appropriate uses for the oral reading act itself.

PURPOSES FOR ORAL READING

When we think of oral expression, whether it be speaking or reading, as a means of communication between producer and consumer of language, then the only justifiable reason for oral reading will be the communication of a thought to a listener. The listeners may be individuals, small groups, or a large audience. Unless the message is conveyed the act cannot be construed as "reading" in the strictest sense of the word. If the audience is already familiar with the message, if the audience holds a copy of the printed message in hand, if the rendition is such that the audience does not get the intended communication, then the act cannot be called reading but is merely an exercise in association of sound with symbol on the part of the performer.

Perhaps we should ask, "Who is reading? Why?" And add to that "Who is listening? Why?"

Unless the listener is getting information or is being entertained there is no point to listening. The only other excuse for the oral exercise might conceivably be to test the abilities of the reader. This point will be discussed later under legitimate uses for oral reading.

RELATION OF ORAL READING TO SILENT READING

If the reader is reading orally to communicate to a listener, then the reader himself must have obtained the message before he could possibly pass it on to his hearers. That leads to the logical conclusion that he must have read it for himself first. The implication here is that the reader must have had some direction in reading the material silently before he rendered it orally. The purpose of that kind of directed silent reading is to make sure that he has gotten the information. During this directed silent reading experience he will use his mechanical skills and will comprehend the total idea. Then when he reads orally he can devote his attention to the interpretation of the ideas expressed by the author rather than to the articulation of the sounds which the symbols represent.

MASTERY OF MECHANICS

Mastering the mechanics so that they do not interfere with the expression of the ideas is a first major step. This involves recognition of the symbols, a rate of recognition that is at least in keeping with the tempo of the speaking voice, the ability to articulate the sounds, the establishment of an eye span and an eye-voice span that will enable the reader to take in the total ideas rather than isolated words, and the ability to interpret the ideas with effective use of thought units and the helps derived from punctuation and sentence structure. Blending all these skills into a smoothly coordinated whole is a complicated process calling for practice and growth over an extended period of time.

WORD RECOGNITION

Word recognition has been treated extensively in Chapter 4 in connection with vocabulary development and in Chapter 5 in the relation of phonics to the total reading program. Suffice it to say at this point that obviously the reader cannot read orally unless he can make the appropriate associations. In silent reading he may be able to theorize about the possible meanings, skip the words he doesn't know, and arrive at a general idea of what the author is talking about; but when he reads orally wrong pronunciations and omissions interfere with the message and lead to ineffective reading habits. Accuracy in word recognition is essential to effective oral reading.

RATE OF RECOGNITION

The rate at which the oral reader recognizes the words on the printed page is basic to effective communication. Who has not heard the young child who reads with long pauses between words. When word recognition is so slow meaning is lost. The child might just as well say the words in reverse order.

The child who sees oral reading as pronunciation of the words on the printed page often mouths the words one at a time. He would get much the same effect if the words were printed in a vertical column like a spelling list. There are two reasons he proceeds in this manner. The first may be that he conceptualizes reading as "telling the teacher what the words are." The second may be that he sees the words one at a time, that is, he looks at each word and says it before he looks at the next word. His rate of recognition as well as his unit of recognition is based on a mechanical approach to words.

RATE OF ARTICULATION

The rate at which the reader articulates the words is directly related to the oral reading act. How fast can you speak? How fast can a child speak? Some of the most nimble commentators on the air may articulate at a rapid rate. Certainly the well-known chant of the auctioneer clips off the words at a pace seldom equaled by most of us in normal speech. Ordinary conversation proceeds at about 100 to 150 words per minute. The young child may be doing very well to vocalize 100 words per minute. By the time he is ten or twelve years of age he may have speeded up to 150 words or so per minute. Even the adult who is reading familiar material is going at a fast pace when he reads 200 words per minute orally.

Compare that with the rate at which the child can recognize the words represented by the printed symbols. If he has been taught to scrutinize the words carefully and make sure he is aware of the initial consonants or consonant clusters, the phonetic principles involved in long or short vowel sounds, and the ending sounds, not to mention the intricacies of multisyllabic words, then he will pause to analyze each word as he reads. When he is sure of the pronunciation he will say the word. Then he must pause to work out the next word before he says it. This means that his rate of recognition is much slower than his rate of articulation in normal speech. Obviously, since he cannot say the words any faster than he can recognize them, he is forced to adjust his rate of articulation to his rate of recognition. He says the words one at a time, thus becoming a word caller.

EYE SPAN

What we call eye span develops as the child becomes more skillful at word recognition. As he becomes so familiar with many of the words, especially the service words, he no longer needs to analyze them for pronunciation. Then he will be able to take in larger "eye-fulls" at a glance. Just as one can see a whole person without noting the color of his shoes or the size of his ears, so the reader can learn to take in a group of words at a glance. Experimentation with tachistoscope devices which provide drill on short exposure has proved that it is possible to perceive a phrase of several words in one-fiftieth or even one one-hundredth of a second. The work of Renshaw during World War II in spotting airplanes and taking in a series of digits supports this fact.[1] Harris points out that the value of tachisto-

[1]Samuel Renshaw, "The Visual Perception and Reproduction of Forms by Tachistoscopic Methods," *Journal of Psychology*, 20 (October, 1945), 217-232.

scopic training is still a subject of controversy.[2] If, however, the child can take in at one eyeful the whole phrase "in the house," it no longer becomes necessary for him to look at each word separately and say "in - the - house." The perception of this larger unit of recognition is known as an eye span. Eye span can be increased with purposeful practice. It does speed up the recognition act.

EYE-VOICE SPAN

When the reader becomes so proficient at taking in a whole group of words at a single glance that he is able to let his eye skip along ahead of the point at which his voice is articulating, he has developed what is known as an eye-voice span, that is, he creates a span between the place where the eye is looking and the voice is articulating. This is well illustrated in the oral reading act when the reader can glance up at his audience while he finishes the sentence or the phrase. This act is evidence that he has already taken in what is coming and is therefore able to articulate it without actually looking at the printed page while he is saying the words. In other words, he reads more rapidly silently than his voice is able to articulate orally. The development of an adequate eye-voice span is dependent on accuracy of word recognition, development of a lengthened eye span, the ability to think about what is coming while the voice is still articulating what has already been assimilated, and skill in oral rendition. This is a complicated process. The principle of eye-voice span is graphically represented in Figures 12, 13, and 14.

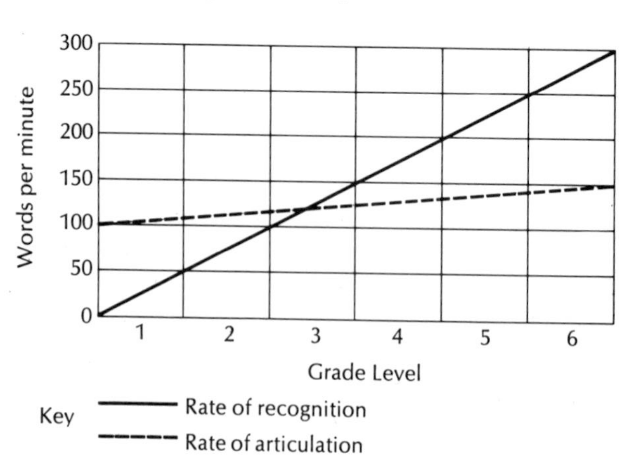

Figure 12. Rate of articulation and rate of recognition based on regular theoretical growth patterns.

[2]Albert J. Harris, *How to Increase Reading Ability,* New York, McKay, 1951, pp. 526–527.

Figure 12 shows a schematic representation of the theoretical growth of a child's rate of articulation and his rate of recognition. Obviously, before he has been introduced to the reading act the child cannot recognize any words per minute. If he arrives at 300 words per minute by the end of the sixth grade he has done very well. Many readers do not attain that speed. The ratio of his rate of word recognition to the rate of articulation will change as he progresses. At first he may be able to articulate more than 100 words per minute, but he can recognize far fewer words in the minute. If he attempts to read new material at sight without previous preparation, he will be forced to slow down his rate of articulation to keep pace with his rate of recognition. This makes him a slow, word-by-word reader. The antidote for this is acquiring the idea for himself before he attempts to communicate it to a listener. His silent reading may need to be carefully guided by the teacher. She may say, "Read the next line to yourself to find out what Bob said to his mother." Pause for silent reading. "What does he want mother to do?" Answer: Come to see the boat. "Good! Read it to us." Now the child does not need to "work out the words" as he goes along. He can devote his energies to conveying the message.

When the child has developed an adequate eye-voice span he is actually reading silently before he reads orally because his silent reading for meaning is taking place in that interval between the point of eye fixation and the point of voice articulation. In other words, when he is able to let his eye skip on ahead of his voice he is actually looking ahead for the total idea while his voice trails along at a slower pace relaying to his audience what he has already found out for himself.

The point at which this eye-voice span develops varies. It comes much

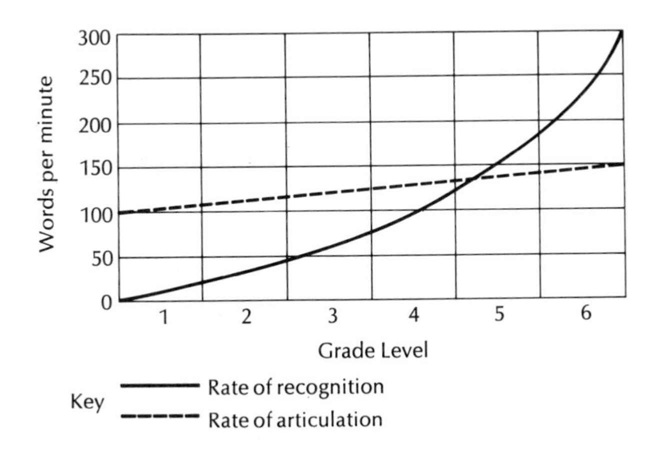

Figure 13. Rate of articulation and rate of recognition based on positive acceleration learning curve.

earlier with some children than with others. It is determined by the skill with which the learner masters the mechanics of word recognition and acquires a lengthened eye span. Figure 13 illustrates what happens when the child follows a normal pattern of growth in rate of articulation but gets off to a slow start in word recognition. For him the two lines may not cross until he has been working at the reading act for four, five, or even six years. He still needs guided silent reading for meaning before he is asked to perform orally.

Figure 14 illustrates what happens when the child follows a normal pattern of growth in rate of articulation and gets off to a rapid pace in word recognition. For him the two lines may cross quite early and he may be able to use an eye-voice span by the time he is a first or second grader. He needs less guidance in the silent reading period because his command of the skills is adequate and he can devote his attention to the message the author has to express. He is one who reads smoothly and fluently in phrases and with expression.

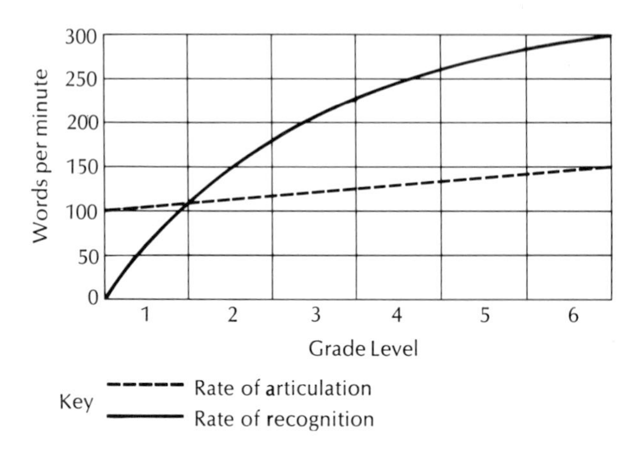

Figure 14. Rate of articulation and rate of recognition based on negative acceleration learning curve.

Another factor which influences the development of the eye-voice span is the difficulty of the material. The teacher who can read a child's story at sight with a long eye-voice span is dealing with material much below her normal reading level. Presented with a technical paragraph from a chemistry manual she would experience quite a different reaction. Another example of shortened eye-voice span is evidenced when one attempts to read in a foreign language. When the words are unfamiliar and the meanings must be checked with a dictionary the reader finds himself figuring out one word at a time, pointing with his finger to keep the place, and regressing to pick up meanings lost during the delays.

The eye-voice span, then, is determined by the extent of mastery of mechanics and the level of difficulty of the material to be read. It varies from one individual to another. It also varies for an individual reader from one kind of material to another. Regardless of the cause of the variation the reader should not attempt to convey to a listener a selection from which he has not previously gotten the idea for himself whether that be in the time devoted to silent reading for meaning or to the interval represented by the eye-voice span. Otherwise, he will be telling the listener what the words are instead of what the message is.

INTERPRETATION

The purpose for oral reading is the interpretation of the message for a listener. No other excuse for oral reading is acceptable in an audience situation whether the audience consists of one person or a roomful of listeners.

PUNCTUATION

The writer conveys to his reader his pauses, emphases, and vocal inflections by means of punctuation marks. This is an item of mechanics that must be developed along with word recognition if the reader is to be effective in the interpretation of the printed page. This can and should be done quite early in the reading program. Let's take an example from the preprimer level:

> Don, Don.
> Here I come.
> Go, Don, go.

The speaker makes appropriate pauses when he speaks. The young child experiencing the printed page for the first time has not learned this interpretation. He needs the help which can be given by the teacher who does more than tell the words and have the child repeat them in a testing situation. The lesson might go something like this.

> Look at the picture. Who are the children? What are they doing? Sarah is doing the talking. In the first line you can find out that she is talking to someone because she calls him by name. She called him once and he did not seem to hear so after a pause she called him again. The author put a mark called a comma there to tell us about the pause. After the second time she stopped to see if he was listening. The author used a period like this to tell us about that stop. Let's say it the way Sarah did.
>
> In the second line Sarah is telling Don what she is doing. What is it? Read what she said.
>
> In the third line she is still talking to Don. Notice that she uses his name again. What does she want him to do? How many times did she use the word *go*?

Point to them. Notice that one begins with a capital and the other with a small letter. The one at the beginning of the sentence must have a capital letter. Notice that she paused both before and after she said Don's name. Point to the marks that tell us to pause. We call them commas. Let's read it the same way Sarah said it.

When the teacher discusses with the children the meanings of the punctuations marks in an informal way as they appear in the printed matter and helps them utilize them as a means of interpreting the author's meaning, such marks will become a familiar part of the printed page. The teacher should call the marks by their correct names without necessarily dwelling on them or asking the children to use the technical terms. Eventually the child will pick up the terms and use them. When he meets them later in the more formal situations of a language lesson, they will seem like old friends and will not have to be taught as totally new concepts.

In many basic reading programs imperative sentences are used in the early preprimer selections. The child must depend on the pictures to carry the action of the story and on the teacher to help with the interpretation. The actual printed material often carries only the words of the speakers. Such material must be interpreted in terms of the plot of the story so that the words do not become mere verbalisms devoid of meaning.

At the third or fourth preprimer level the child is usually introduced to declarative sentences and direct discourse. The wise teacher will know when the quotation marks indicating direct discourse are coming and will provide readiness. Consider this example.

Stop here, Mother.
Stop here.

The picture shows Sarah and her mother on the street waiting for the bus. The teaching might go something like this.

Who is in the picture? Where are they? What are they doing? Sarah is talking. How can you tell? What did she tell her mother to do?

We have to depend on the picture here to tell us but I can make the words tell it. Look at the chalk board.

Sarah said, Stop here, Mother.

But when I tell you that Sarah said it I must use some special marks to show you exactly what part of the sentence tells what Sarah said, so I shall use these marks (") to tell you where she started to talk and these marks (") to show you where she stopped talking. Then it will look like this.

Sarah said, "Stop here, Mother."

Now we are ready for a new story. I can make it say the same thing in different ways. Watch what happens when I move the sentence parts around. [Teacher builds the sentence in the pocket chart.]

Sarah said, "Stop here, Mother."
"Stop here, Mother," Sarah said.
"Stop here, Mother," said Sarah.

The child who has had this kind of developmental readiness from the teacher in interpreting quotation marks is ready to attack a page including such punctuation with a minimum of help. Now he can tell who is talking without relying on the pictures. He can find where a speaker started to talk and where he finished. Meanings become clear.

What teacher has not heard a child verbalize the words and lose the meaning when he interpreted the sentence, "'Come here, Daddy,' said Don," as if it were punctuated "'Come here,' Daddy said — Don."

This child has learned to accustom himself to the noun preceding the word *said* and thus thinks "Daddy said" is more logical than "said Don." He fails to recognize the quotation marks as signals telling him where the speaker started and stopped; therefore, he ignores them and devotes his energies to pronouncing the words. As a consequence he misses the point entirely and finds himself with one word, Don, left over at the end which he does not know how to use in the sentence and he merely pronounces it with a rising inflection showing his puzzlement.

Yes, effective oral reading must be preceded by getting the idea for oneself before attempting to relay it to an audience. In order to do that the reader must master the mechanics and that involves far more than mere word recognition. It requires a satisfactory rate of recognition adjusted to the rate of articulation. This involves the use of an effective eye span and eye-voice span plus the utilization of punctuation marks to help in interpretation. This kind of reading leads to the interpretation of the thought expressed by the author when he recorded his ideas through the medium of cold impersonal symbols on the printed page.

PATTERNS OF ORAL READING

When we accept the definition of reading as getting the meaning from the printed page and recognize that oral reading must include the transmission of that meaning to a listener, then we will have to reevaluate some of the common oral reading practices which too often appear in the classroom. Let's classify them in two categories: questionable practices and effective practices.

QUESTIONABLE PRACTICES

When the teacher says, "You may read next, Mary," she is implying that she wants to hear Mary read presumably to see if she can. She does not offer any guidance in interpretation. She does not give Mary any reason for oral reading. She does not give the audience any purpose for listening. The reading class becomes merely an exercise to practice the mechanics of sound and symbol association and a check on the accuracy of the performance as a basis for passing judgment and perhaps the awarding of marks or the keeping of a record.

Mary visualizes herself as a performer being tested. She is anxious to read without making a mistake. She fears the criticism of the teacher. She dreads the ridicule and scorn of her more capable classmates. Or if Mary happens to be one of the better readers she covets the praise that comes from the teacher, enjoys the applause of her classmates, and looks with derision on her less capable peers. To her the oral reading act is a check on her ability. She will stop to struggle with a word she doesn't know while the other children sit and wait. The child who can read fast without making mistakes may hurry over the end of a page or the end of a paragraph trying to display more of her superior ability before the teacher can call on the next reader.

Reading "next" or reading "around" the class by turns in order to give each one some practice for the day has little or no value.

EFFECTIVE PRACTICES

If reading around is to be condemned as a procedure in the reading class we must substitute something better. Here are some ideas.

SHARING AN IDEA WITH A LISTENER Consider the following illustrations as valid uses for oral reading.

> "Mary has found out what Jean put in the box. Read it to us."
> "Betty knows why she hid it. Let's listen while she reads."

RELAYING INFORMATION TO AN AUDIENCE Throughout life one of the most practical uses for oral reading is passing information on to another. The children have many such uses in school.

> The teacher says, "Tom has an announcement. It tells us about the plans for this afternoon. Read it to us, Tom."
>
> And Tom reads, "The bus will be in front of the schoolhouse at ten o'clock. We are all to be ready with our sack lunches and our tickets. We will return at three o'clock."

INTERPRETING A PASSAGE When several children or a whole class have read the same selection and are discussing it, then reading becomes a sharing experience.

> The teacher guides a discussion by saying, "Read to yourself to find out what Fred said. How do you think he felt? Why do you think so? Read it to show us his excitement. (Daddy was here!) Now read it as if he were merely telling us a fact. (Daddy was here.) Now read it as if he were asking a question. (Daddy was here?)"

REPORTING A reporter has a message which it is assumed the listeners want to hear. This is a common use for reading both in and out of school.

The teacher introduces new material by saying, "Bobby has found out some interesting information about butterflies. It came from the encyclopedia which he has at home. His father has helped him rewrite it in words he can use in reading. He is going to read to us what he found out."

ENTERTAINING A mother reading to a young child is a highly valued use for oral reading. Teachers read to classes. Children can read to others in their own classes or to children in other classrooms. They can read to younger brothers and sisters at home or to other children in the neighborhood. Being prepared for such oral reading calls for more than just knowing all the words.

"Patty has a new book her aunt brought. She says she has read it at home and has practiced till she is sure she can read it to us. I am sure we will enjoy the story. It's about a little train that could talk. Let's listen to Patty's story."

There! See the difference between reading in order to be tested and reading in order to convey a message? So much depends on the teacher. Unless the child has that kind of teacher he may learn many attitudes and responses which will interfere with effective reading rather than develop skill and purpose in the reading act. The teacher sets the stage, provides the stimulus, builds purpose, invites response, and guides the learner. If the teacher sees herself as a taskmaster who tells her students what to do, checks up on them to see if they did it, then rewards them for success or reprimands them for failure, she will be testing them instead of teaching them. But if the teacher visualizes herself as a helper and a guide and the teaching act as stimulation of learning, then she will teach them how, provide an opportunity for successful performance, and guide the learners toward growth.

LISTENING—THE CORRELATIVE OF ORAL READING

In Chapter 1 we identified the four phases of language as communication. We indicated that listening is the correlative of speaking. Except for early babyhood prattle which is merely experimentation with the newly discovered vocal organs, most speech is produced for the benefit of a listener. The 3-year-old who insists, "This is my book," is telling listeners that it is his, not theirs. He is establishing ownership and wants others to be aware of the fact. The young child who says, "What's this?" wants to know. He demands an answer. The kindergartener who comes to school with the announcement, "I have new shoes," isn't satisfied with the fact that the shoes are new. He wants others to know about it. He demands a listener for his announcement.

WHO IS LISTENING AND WHY?

The child who learns to view oral reading as communication needs listeners. What takes place in the reading circle too often discourages instead of helps the reader as well as the listener. Let's eavesdrop on some questionable classroom situations:

> Read next, Patty.
> Watch your place, Mary. I might call on you next.
> All right. Did anybody hear any mistakes?
> What is that word, John?
> Weren't you watching?
> Who does know?
> Tell her, Sally.
> That's right. Go on, Patty.

No wonder Patty dreads to read. No wonder Mary points with her finger and keeps her eyes glued to the book. No wonder the children are watching for the words. And what do they hear? Words! Mistakes! That's why they were listening.

And what was the message? That wasn't the reason for listening. After the reading is over the teacher may feel a compulsion to check on comprehension and may ask such fact questions as, "Who went to the party? What color was Mary's dress? How many children were there? What did they do?"

These questions following the oral reading exercise call for mere rote repetition of isolated facts. Most of them can be answered with one word. Frequently the children cannot answer them without rereading the selection because they were not listening for information. To encourage them to listen for the message the oral reading might have been preceded by such suggestions as the following.

> Listen to find out what happened at the party. See if you can tell how Mary's costume looked.
>
> The story doesn't say how many children were at the party, but if you are a good detective you can figure it out.
>
> List as many things as you can which they did at the party. Add to the list other things they might have done.

Now the oral reading will be for the purpose of conveying the message and the follow-up discussion might be more like this.

> Describe Mary's costume.
> Tell about the games at the party.

These questions or guiding suggestions cannot be answered with one word. They take insight, understanding, and verbal response based on sentence structure and language usage to convey a series of related ideas.

True, the answers may be varied and cannot be marked right or wrong and counted to determine the score. But what was the purpose? Was it to determine a score or to guide interpretation?

WHAT IS THE LISTENER DOING?

Then what should the listener be doing while the reader is reading orally? Some teachers have the children watch the book and some have them watch the reader. The appropriate use for the listener's time will vary depending on the immediate purpose.

Looking at the book might sometimes be a legitimate use for the child's time while he is listening to another read, but if he does so he must be looking for something besides mistakes. Perhaps in a group situation he may gain more impressions by seeing, hearing, and saying the words or sounds that accompany the symbols. In that case it can be a developmental learning situation for the immature reader. Perhaps noting how it looks as another child renders the oral interpretation may help to fix his skills and give him some additional impressions.

Following the reader in the text may have a place in a reading class, but if all reading follows this pattern it may lead to some undesirable habits. It may eventually interfere with listening as a technique for learning. It may have a retarding effect on eye-voice span when the child reaches the point where he can read more rapidly silently than orally. It may retard the speed of the capable reader by forcing him to gear his eye movements to the rate of articulation of the child who is reading orally so that if he is called on next he will "know the place." If he is not afraid of "getting caught," then he may skip on ahead and read for himself and not stay with the reader.

Watching the child who is reading rather than the book might be a better use of time for the child who has an adequate eye-voice span. In that way he can keep his mind on the message instead of on the mechanics and thus learn to utilize effective listening skills. He can combine his listening with watching the expression on the face of the reader and noting the changes in voice inflection as the message is interpreted. At the same time he can avoid the unfortunate experience of losing his place. He will no longer be slowing down his pace of word recognition to stay with the reader.

Deciding whether to have the listener look at the book or watch the reader will have to be based on the purpose for reading, the level of maturity of the listener, and the skill of the oral reader. One cannot give a rule which covers all situations. The teacher will have to decide what is most effective for a particular child in a particular situation. They may not all do the same.

LEGITIMATE USES FOR ORAL READING

We cannot judge the appropriateness of any action unless we know the purpose for which it is taking place. To say that *all* oral reading should be for the entertainment of an audience is to deny the actuality of other classroom functions. It is true that I do not read a newspaper before an adult audience to prove that I know how to pronounce all the words or to practice my skills in oral articulation. My only reason in such a situation would be to convey a message. But to apply this analogy to all classroom situations would be to deny the teaching-learning function of the schoolroom setting.

In order to learn the child must first be exposed to new concepts. Then he must have an opportunity to practice them until he becomes proficient. Finally he needs an answer that tells him whether or not he is making progress. This puts a different light on uses for oral reading in the classroom. Let's consider oral reading in the curriculum under the headings of testing, practicing, and communicating.

TESTING

Testing is strictly a private affair. The teacher may feel the need for hearing the child read aloud in order to note whether or not he knows the words, to find out how he uses his phonic skills in the attack on unfamiliar words, and to measure his speed of recognition. The rest of the children are not interested in hearing another child tested. They register their disinterest by looking around, losing the place, talking to their neighbors, leafing through the pages, looking at the pictures, and distracting their classmates as well as the teacher. They should not be exposed to sitting through a test for a classmate.

Also, the child who is being testing may want to know how he is getting along, but he certainly does not want to be held up as a bad example to his peers. He has a right to the privacy of an evaluation in which only he and his teacher participate. In other words, oral testing is a matter of communication between teacher and learner and does not need an audience.

PRACTICING

Practicing is a necessary step in the perfection of skills. No one enjoys hearing the learner practice on the piano, but this is a phase through which long-suffering families must go unless they have soundproof practice rooms. Even then, those within hearing distance do not sit down in an audience situation and concentrate on listening. Instead, they are more likely to close the door or go for a walk. The learner may benefit from having someone listen while he practices. That is the function of the private teacher or sometimes the mother, who endures endless hours of such routine because it is helpful to the learner.

The same might be said for developing skill in reading. The child who learns to recognize words and interpret meanings still has a long way to go before he is ready to entertain an audience. The audience is not going to enjoy the performance until he has acquired sufficient skill to put the emphasis on the meaning instead of on the mechanics. But how will he acquire this skill unless he has an opportunity to practice?

Practice in the reading circle subjects the listeners to an experience which has little or no value for them and perhaps may lead to habits of inattention and attitudes of boredom. The child who is doing the reading may learn to dread the practice because he feels inadequate and unprepared. If he dreads it, he will gain no skill and then dread it even more. The situation gets progressively worse. There are also disadvantages to practicing alone. The child who always practices alone may lose interest and perpetuate wrong responses, poor habits, and ineffective reading. Even an adult needs a lot of self-determination to pursue a routine task alone indefinitely.

Young children need the support of another person. The child may work in a one-to-one relationship with his teacher. He might get his mother, a brother or sister, or a doting aunt to listen while he practices. Another device which will be helpful in a classroom is for him to have a partner, one who will listen to him while he practices and to whom he listens in return. In this way children may get considerable practice and at the same time avoid the undesirable features of reading around the class. Not only does this scheme provide a useful setting for the practice but it provides much more oral practice for each individual. Reading in pairs, with several pairs working concurrently, may result in much vocalization at one time, but the children will be concentrating on their own reading and will not be disturbed by the others. Only the teacher or a visiting adult who misunderstands the purpose will be bothered by such a situation.

Yes, practice is valuable, but it certainly is not appropriate for an audience.

COMMUNICATING

Communicating with a listener is the other purpose for oral reading. Communicating implies that someone is listening. The listeners may range all the way from one individual to the assembly in the auditorium to the unseen radio or television audience. Whatever the size of the audience the reader should visualize himself as responsible to his audience for communication.

The reader's responsibility may take many forms. Perhaps he must convey a message or provide enjoyment or both. His reading should give the audience his own interpretation of the ideas or relay the rhythm and beauty of the expression even though the message or the story is already familiar. But whatever his purpose he must prepare to be able to fulfill his responsibility.

By way of summary then let us conclude:

- Silent reading in some form must precede oral reading so that the reader has the message in mind before he attempts to relay it to his listeners.
- Oral reading which involves a struggle with mechanics and practice for the purpose of testing is highly questionable as a group process.
- Oral reading should involve sharing an idea, relaying information, interpreting a passage, reporting, or entertaining.
- The listener must listen for the message not the mechanics and must gear his accompanying attention to the printed form in terms of his own stage of development.
- Testing may be a legitimate use for oral reading, but it must be a private affair between teacher and child and not a public performance before an audience.
- Practice may be a legitimate use for oral reading, but it must be for the purpose of perfecting skill before facing an audience.
- Basically, the purpose for oral reading is communicating with others, either to inform or to entertain.

8

SILENT READING

or When Johnny Reads to Himself

The classroom was reasonably quiet. The teacher was working with a small group. All the rest of the children were busy at various tasks—working puzzles, drawing pictures, writing, reading. Suddenly Alan said in a loud clear voice, "Atta boy!" Everybody stopped and looked up. Alan became acutely conscious that all were looking at him. The wise teacher looked pleased, stopped what she was doing, and said, "Tell us about it, Alan."

Alan had just given his first indication of complete absorption and comprehension in silent reading. Up to that time reading for Alan had been an exercise to be performed in class. Today he had given his undivided attention to a book of his own choosing and had actually read and comprehended. The excitement of the story had completely captured his attention. He was totally unaware of the other children. For him reading had at last become a means of getting the message the author was trying to communicate through the printed page.

When a child chuckles to himself over a good story, he is using silent reading effectively. When the dismissal bell rings and he does not hear it because he is absorbed in a story, he is comprehending in silent reading. When he says to his mother at bedtime, "Wait till I finish my chapter," he is involved in a story. He is reading in the truest sense of the word. This stage of development comes gradually. No teacher, no parent, no child can name the time or a place it happens. For some it seems as if it will never come; and for others it seems to come early and almost automatically. The best thing the teacher can do to encourage purposeful silent reading and individual growth is to create a rich environment, offer help with skills, and watch for the buds to open.

Silent reading may be of different types for different purposes. We need to examine the abilities used in effective silent reading. We need to make sure we know the uses the learner has for his silent reading skills both in school and out. We need to judge the uses for silent reading against the oral reading practices and help the child establish a balance so he will use each effectively and gain an independence which will be useful to him throughout his educational program and throughout the rest of his life.

THE WHAT AND WHY OF SILENT READING

What happens when one reads silently? What does one gain from his silent reading that is different from oral reading? A look at the types and purposes will answer these questions.

TYPES OF SILENT READING

Perhaps we should begin with the reading act itself and with ourselves as readers in order to understand the learner and what he is doing. What kinds of silent reading skills do adults use in their daily lives? Some things we read in a cursory manner, some things we read carefully, some things we read with the thrill of a creative mind.

CURSORY READING The term cursory reading implies a hasty or superficial manner. It is the type of reading employed by many adults who go over the daily newspaper. They are not necessarily looking for anything. Different readers will be attracted by reports of stock transactions, announcements of bond issues, facts about new fertilizer, scores from yesterday's game, and so on. Each person who reads the daily paper will be giving it a superficial and cursory examination. He will skip some parts and pause to read others.

The sixth grader who is looking for information may comb through encyclopedias, geographies, and periodicals picking out what he wants and skipping the rest. The graduate student who is looking for evidence to support his thesis may skim dozens of references before he finds one which suits his needs. This kind of reading does have its place. It is nearly always silent reading. It is directed toward a preconceived purpose.

CAREFUL READING The term careful reading implies taking pains or exercising caution. It involves a watchfulness in terms of a specific purpose. Now the sixth grader or the graduate student may follow up with careful reading to glean the exact information he needs for his study. He may deliberately take notes as he reads. The care with which he searches for details is quite different from the attention he would give to a fast moving story. Careful reading takes time. This, too, is practically always silent reading.

CRITICAL READING The term critical reading also implies great care. It is for the purpose of making a judgment, providing a logical basis for action. Too often the term critical is associated with a negative reaction. If one does critical reading only in this sense, he may become not a critical reader, but a fault finder. True critical reading can be quite positive. The citizen who reads the political speeches to decide where to give his allegiance in order to provide more constructive government is using critical reading to make a positive judgment and to provide a logical basis for action, namely, voting at the election booth. The teacher who reads the suggestions in the professional magazine and evaluates them in terms of the needs of the children in her classroom is doing critical reading in relation to a specific problem. If she reads and accepts all the slanted research, all the glowing advertisements, all the emotional outbursts, she may be led into classroom procedures which will be unsuccessful and disappointing. But if she reads these same materials critically, she will be sifting and weighing the evidence as a basis for deciding what to do about her own problems. Then she is a critical reader.

The student who stops to ask "Why?" when he reads about inventions or voyages of discovery or crops to raise in the jungle or animals that hibernate is reading critically. He is not satisfied with finding out what happened so he can answer the fact questions. He is concerned with depth and insight into causes and effects as a basis for understanding and applying knowledge to new situations.

Most critical reading is done in a deliberate and thoughtful manner. It is a personal affair. It is usually done silently.

CREATIVE READING The term creative reading implies productivity. The creative reader does much more than absorb. He goes beyond the facts. He gets the point and applies it to a new situation, to his own problems, to the future. To be creative the reader must see relationships beyond those expressed on the printed page. He must be original, inventive, and innovative. He must see new uses for familiar materials and accepted ideas.

The seamstress who sees possibilities for altering a pattern or the cook who improves upon a recipe is reading creatively. The middle grader who reads biographies omniverously and discovers in his heroes the qualities he would like to emulate in his own life is creating for himself a set of principles or an ideal. He is getting more from the biographies than a mere accounting of the acts of the heroes.

Creative reading demands time for reflective thought. It is nearly always a personal and a private perusal of reading matter. It, too, is nearly always silent reading.

Cursory, careful, critical, and creative reading all have their places in silent reading. To do any one of them to the exclusion of the others is to settle for half-a-loaf, or perhaps a quarter of a loaf. The mature reader must know how to do all these types of reading. And knowing how is not enough. He must also know when to read carefully, when to read critically, and when to read creatively, as well as when to settle for a cursory perusal of reading matter. Until he can select his materials for a definite purpose and apply his skills accordingly he is merely waiting to be told or following a recipe. This kind of judgment does not come from telling; it does not happen all at once. It comes after repeated experiences with many kinds of reading material for many different purposes.

The teacher who visualizes her task as giving directions, checking, and evaluating is merely training performers. The teacher who would develop effective silent reading habits will stimulate, lead, encourage, challenge, and question. This teacher will give children opportunities to express opinions, compare and evaluate, challenge one another, and even challenge the author. These activities do not lend themselves to right and wrong answers. They stimulate cursory perusal of material to find out what is available. They cause a reader to pause and read carefully when he comes to a point that is pertinent to his problem. They encourage him to examine printed material critically before accepting it just because "it's in the book." They encourage him to go beyond the thoughts of the author and to be creative in reconstructing the ideas into new patterns and new applications.

PURPOSES FOR SILENT READING

Why read? Why do adults read? Why do people read outside of a school setting? Why do children read?

There are many invalid reasons for silent reading. Some children read because the teacher has assigned a chapter or because they have a book report to give. Some read because they want to be well prepared in case they are "called on." This implies that they view the reading act in terms of satisfying an external force and acquiring an artificial reward. The external forces are the demands of the teacher, of society, of the situation. The rewards are the approval of teacher or peers, the grade, the promotion, the recognition. If these are the purposes for silent reading, the learner is not developing into a reader; he is merely acquiring some techniques for collecting extrinsic rewards.

But there are many valid reasons for silent reading. When the reader is pursuing information meaningful for him, when he is enjoying the content during the recreational period, and when he is developing habits and tastes which he will continue to apply the rest of his life, then he is reading with purposes related to the reading act itself.

TO GET INFORMATION One of the basic reasons for reading is to get information. The adult reads because he wants to know who is running for Congress, the price of sugar, how to put the do-it-yourself picnic bench together, the bus schedule, the weather prediction, and so on. Reading to "find out" is equally applicable in the classroom.

The teacher who asks fact questions such as, "What color was Sarah's dress? Who went to the picnic? How many balls did Fred buy?" is asking questions to which she already knows the answers. The children who have studied the lesson also know. Their answers merely prove to the teacher that they have prepared for the recitation. They are being tested and rewarded.

On the other hand, the teacher who raises the question, "Which is the better way to get the boat ashore?" is inviting the children to assemble the facts and use them to draw a conclusion, prove a point, or support a judgment. The teacher's question is a real one to which she wants an answer because she does not already know. The children present the facts, not to prove that they have studied and know, but to support the point of view they have established. Now the gathering of information becomes a matter of personal use rather than self-defense. Children need lots of information. Much of it can be supplied through reading.

For example, the children may wonder why the main part of their own city grew up on the east side of the river. In their reading they will uncover many facts. Early settlers moved from east to west. Many of them traveled in covered wagons with all their possessions. Most of the roads were poor or even nonexistent. There were no bridges over the rivers; therefore rivers had to be crossed at the time of the year when the water was low. Sometimes they came to a river and couldn't get across for days, for weeks, or even for months. By the time the water had receded they had settled down into homes which eventually became permanent. They had established a new town on the east bank of the river. They became permanent settlers and never did move on west. It was many years before a bridge was built. Thus the older part of town grew up on the east bank and even today the local community is affected by that sequence of events.

This information is quite different from that which results from answering questions which come from memorization. This kind of reading calls for gathering of information to support a point of view or give insight into a situation. It calls for thinking and application beyond the mere recording of yes-no or one-word answers. Gathering information can be one of the more useful and most used purposes for silent reading.

TO ENJOY THE CONTENT One who likes to read for self-entertainment is never without friends, never bored, never without something to do, never without stimulation for a richer and fuller life. He does not need to depend on others, on radio, TV, or public entertainment, or even on money for his personal entertainment. Personal enjoyment is one of the major purposes for learning to read. And most of that kind of reading is done silently.

TO DEVELOP TASTES AND LASTING INTERESTS Cultivating taste in reading lays a foundation for future enjoyment. Taste comes with experience. The child who has never read anything but comics may continue to read comics because he has nothing to take their place. The child who has been exposed to all kinds of reading such as factual materials, nursery rhymes, fantastic stories, realistic stories, science fiction, love stories, fairy tales, biographies, myths, and historical narrative will be the one who develops tastes which discriminate between fact and fiction, between matter-of-fact and artistic expression, and between realism and idealism. He will be able to select different kinds of reading matter to meet his different moods, his varying needs, and his developmental stages in life. He can be exposed to these varieties both through listening and through guided reading. The teacher who whets his appetite and invites him to partake is doing far more to develop his tastes and to create lasting interests than is the one who assigns, monitors, and examines.

ABILITIES NEEDED FOR EFFECTIVE SILENT READING

The child who reads in a cursory, careful, critical, or creative manner needs some mechanical and intellectual skills to make his reading fruitful. The child who would read with a measure of success needs to establish some skills and some insights in order to get information, to enjoy the content, and to develop tastes and lasting interests. Let us examine these abilities first as mechanical skills, then as intellectual achievements which lend themselves to success and maturity in the reading act.

MECHANICAL ABILITIES

Mechanical skills do not constitute the whole of the reading act, but certainly one cannot read without some skill in the mechanics of reading. One needs to learn the skills, reduce them to subconscious and automatic response, then use them to get on with the business of finding out what the author is talking about. This takes lots of practice. It does not come about automatically. Maintaining a fine balance between meaning, enjoyment, and skill calls for a willing and eager learner and an insightful and creative teacher. Knowing when to provide new insights, when to work for perfection of skill, when to encourage more practice, when to release the pressure and let the child move on his own momentum calls for a delicate touch.

SATISFACTORY RATE Our discussion of the relation between eye span and thought getting in Chapter 7 brought out the importance of satisfactory rate. The reader must develop a rate that is conducive to reading for total meanings. The reader who has to stop and labor over each word loses the idea when it takes a group of words such as a phrase or a sentence to express a total concept. In the final analysis rate is determined by the type of content and the purpose for reading.

ACCURATE PERCEPTION In order to get correct information the reader must perceive accurately the printed symbols. He must glean from the printed page the impressions intended by the writer. There is a lot of difference between "He *was* a boy" and "He *saw* a boy." A child who reads *palace* as *place* in the sentence "The princess went to the *palace*" loses the glamour of the fairy story. Reading *persevere* as *preserve* in the sentence "He who *perseveres* will succeed," may give the reader the image of one who saves or maintains something or who makes jellies. Unless he perceives accurately the minute details of the mechanics of word structure and does it with a degree of speed commensurate with getting meaning, he will either lose the idea or get a wrong idea.

WIDE RECOGNITION SPAN The reader who detects at a single rapid glance the difference between "*on* the house" and "*in* the house" is taking in a complete concept instantaneously and noting at the same time the minute difference in the two ideas as indicated by the first letter in the first word of each phrase. It makes a lot of difference whether Santa Claus was in or on the house so far as the story goes.

In the same way the reader must detect instantly the difference between *house* and *horse* in the phrases "in the house" and "in the horse." Actually there is only one letter difference between the two phrases but unless the child sees that *u* and that *r* as a detail within the whole and instantaneously translates that minor difference into a difference in total meaning, he may come up with a rather unusual concept in the sentence which says, "They built a large wooden horse and hid the army inside it." If he sees a *u* instead of an *r* or if he thinks of an army as more likely to be in a house than in a horse, he misses the whole significance of the story of the capture of Troy.

RHYTHMIC MOVEMENT WITHOUT REGRESSION Efficient use of mechanics as well as free flow of thought depends on rhythmic movement without regression. The reader must learn to move rhythmically and easily from one concept to the next so that his train of thought moves forward with the story. This calls for not only accuracy, speed, and wide span of recognition, but also a steady forward movement without unnecessary regressions either in eye movements or in articulation. The child who hesitates over pronunciation, repeats phrases or parts of sentences, and keeps looking back to verify what he has just read is exhibiting an uncertainty about the mechanics as well as the meaning.

Sometimes a child fails to put the words together in the correct linguistic patterns and as a consequence misses the point. He may reread attempting to recheck the mechanics or to restructure the meaning. In doing so he may further confuse the issue. For example, if he reads the sentence, "Gray heads the swimming team," and sees *gray* as an adjective modifying *heads* he may wonder why the swimming team must have gray heads. Does it mean they should be old? At the same time his pitch and stress in reading leaves the sentence dangling because when he gets to the end there has been no verb and he doesn't quite know what happened. If he can go back and reread the sentence changing the pitch and stress so that *Gray* becomes the subject and the name of a man and *heads* becomes the verb, he gets a totally new meaning out of the sentence and a feeling of completion when he comes to the end. These rhythmic movements and forward progressions help to insure meaning. Acquiring such skill comes only with experience.

ACCURATE RETURN SWEEP A smooth flow in reading depends on the mechanical ability to move from the end of one line of print to the beginning of the next line. In the early stages of learning to read the child does not meet this problem as long as only one line of print appears on a page. It is minimized when there are only two or three lines on a page with wide leading between the lines. When the reader reaches that stage where he sees a solid page of print, paragraphs which extend over ten or more lines, and sentences which carry over from one line to the next with the breaks at the ends of lines coming in the middle of an idea, then he is facing a more complex reading problem. Line markers may be helpful to the reader at this stage. A 3 by 5 file card works very well. Sometimes the reader finds it helpful to run his index finger down the left-hand margin of the page guiding the eye to the next line of print. Books with wide pages and long lines of print present greater difficulty than those with shorter lines. Many wide books reduce this difficulty by using a two-column format in printing.

RECOGNITION OF THOUGHT UNIT The reader's first experience with a two-line sentence presents still a different learning. Now he must not only return to the next line below, but he must carry the thought over to complete the idea. If the break in the sentence coincides with the idea thus,

> The children put all their toys
> in the big wooden box.

the thought units are kept intact and a slight pause at the end of the line even though there is no punctuation mark will not cause him to lose the idea. But if the break in the sentence is made to maintain an even right-hand margin, regardless of the break in the thought unit, and appears thus,

> The children put all their toys in the big
> wooden box.

then he has the problem of returning to the beginning of the next line to complete the idea. The recognition span is now spanning the return sweep. This is even more difficult. Having to turn the page to complete an idea adds still another dimension to the difficulty of the mechanical feat. Now the child must have not only an adequate eye span, but also eye-voice span that will enable him to hold in mind the beginning of the phrase or idea at the bottom of the page while he does the physical feat of holding the book with one hand, turning the page with the other hand, and at the same time grasping the rest of the thought for himself before he articulates it using the beginning part which he has carried over from the preceding page.

Yes, these mechanics are complicated. They may be learned one at a time. They may be practiced in isolation. They may be perfected step by step. But until the child can do all of them with ease and can synchronize them into a smoothly flowing unit, he will not make the mechanics of reading serve his purpose, which is effective silent reading for thought.

INTELLECTUAL ABILITIES

If practicing on mechanics were all there were to reading, we might teach a robot to read. We might reduce the skills to automatic responses. We might condition the learner to give the desired response every time a given stimulus is presented. But to get meaning he must do more than respond to a stimulus. He must think, decide, act purposefully, and perform judgments. These intellectual abilities are what add the dimension of thinking to the reading process.

INTERPRETING INFORMATION Being able to find the answers to the fact questions provided by the teacher is not enough. Being able to quote a factual statement after the silent reading is still not enough. The effective reader must learn to set his own purposes for reading, establish his own questions, locate the answers, and select from available information those facts which answer his questions.

A group of children studying about Eskimos was given the task of listing the foods the Eskimos eat. One child went through the reading material and picked out all the names of foods. In her list she had among others, these words: meet, candy, and bred. She had copied those words from the passage which said, "If you meet an Eskimo child eating the blubber from whales which are bred in the ocean do not be surprised because they like blubber as well as you like candy."

No, decoding the words is not enough. Even knowing their meanings is still not enough. Before the child can get the idea he must get the total concept and not only locate the information but also interpret pertinent facts in terms of the question.

EVALUATING AND ORGANIZING INFORMATION Simple recall of factual information may result in isolated and useless facts unless the reader can organize his information into useful bundles of related facts. Making a list of the commodities that pass through the harbor at New Orleans is a mechanical process. Sorting them into lists of imports and exports gives new insights into the facts gleaned. Dividing the imports into raw materials and manufactured goods gives still another point of view. Doing the same for the exports will provide information to help the learner discover whether the port is used as an outlet for raw products or for the manufactured products that result from the labor of the people. This same type of organization of the imports will lead to similar conclusions. It may also lead to forming a judgment about whether the types of imports and exports are good for the economy of the region. Reducing these facts to diagrams may help the child visualize his conclusions.

RECALLING AND SHARING INFORMATION Information collecting can be mere busy work if the child sees no use for it except to write out his lesson, recite when called on, and regurgitate when tested. If each child in the class has collected the same information, the only reason he can think of for reproducing it is to prove that he has gleaned it. But if different children have collected different information from different sources, the interchange in class will be for the purpose of sharing with others. Then his selection, evaluation, organization, and recall will take on a new meaning. Now he has something to contribute to others who want to know.

ANTICIPATING OUTCOMES AND SENSING IMPLICATIONS The creative reader is the one who goes beyond the facts on the printed page. The child who gains insight into the why and the how as well as the what, the who, and the when will be formulating a basis for generalizations which will enable him to anticipate outcomes and sense implications in what he reads. When he generalizes that shipping by boat is cheaper because there is no need to build the thoroughfare, then he is beginning to sense the implication that there is an advantage to building a city on a major navigable waterway. Now he sees seaports and river ports with a new perspective. When he finds out the cost of constructing highways or railways through mountainous terrain, he begins to see why larger cities have grown up in areas where level ground provides reasonably easy access. When he sees the difficulties involved in tilling soil which is so steep that erosion and use of tools create problems, he begins to see why mountain slopes are more often used for grazing than for farming. On the other hand, if population is dense and tillable soil is scarce, terracing may be practiced. Now he is able to anticipate what to expect in a new region and to sense the implications of attempting a financial venture which is unrealistic in terms of the natural geography of the region.

APPLICATION OF READING ABILITIES

The above discussion leads up to the conclusion that the child must eventually learn to use his silent reading skills, both the mechanical skills and the intellectual skills for a variety of purposes. In making appropriate use of silent reading he arrives at outcomes which make him a more mature reader.

USES FOR SILENT READING

The child has use for silent reading constantly. Most of his uses in school parallel similar uses which adults have for reading and which he will continue to have for the rest of his life.

FINDING ANSWERS The reader needs to know how to find answers to questions. He needs to know where to look. He needs to know how to locate the specific facts he wants. He needs to know when he has found the answer which fits the specific situation. This is one important use for silent reading both in school and throughout life.

FOLLOWING DIRECTIONS It is not enough to be able to read directions. One must also be able to translate them into action. This calls for careful reading and comprehension of the highest order. Repeating what has been read is one thing; doing it is a much higher order of learning because it calls for translation and application.

CHECKING OF FACTS The mere collection of facts is not enough. The learner who has use for the facts will also need to know how to check on the facts he has collected to make sure they are pertinent to the problem. The question "What color is the grass?" may seem like a very simple one and the answer green may seem obvious. But if the reader is reading about a long dry summer, the answer may be brown, and if he is reading about a forest fire, the answer just might be black.

SELECTING A CENTRAL IDEA One of the more difficult learnings for the immature reader is that of selecting the central thought. Sometimes he needs to know how to select from a longer selection the central idea the author was trying to convey. He may read a lengthy description of a covered wagon trip to a new home in the wilderness, but his reading may be merely listing of facts unless he reaches the general conclusion that the pioneers worked hard and endured much privation for a way of life which meant more to them than the ease and comfort of their original homes.

ANALYZING A PROBLEM Insight is needed in order to analyze the problem in terms of the facts given. Perhaps the story was about a flood and some stranded animals. Was the problem how the animals got there? How to build an ark? How to save the animals? Which animals to save? Unless the reader can identify the crucial problem he may spend time discussing the wrong issues while the animals drown.

ORGANIZING, SUMMARIZING, AND REACHING A CONCLUSION Some readers come up with lots of miscellaneous facts but never reach a conclusion. They grow up to be the adults who can discuss an issue endlessly but never reach a point of action. They are unable to organize their facts and to summarize them in terms of generalizations. Being able to name all the states and their capitals is rote memory. Being able to group the capital cities as inland cities and seaport cities lends organization which helps to reach conclusions about what kinds of commerce to expect. Being able to organize the cities into groups indicating in which cases the capital city is the largest city in the state provides a basis for inquiring why it is or is not the largest city and why it became the capital.

EVALUATING All the above purposes for reading help to lead the reader to evaluate what he has read in terms of the question or the original purpose for reading. If the purpose was to obtain or use information, he will apply it meaningfully. If the purpose was to entertain himself, he will be able to select and enjoy with independence.

OUTCOMES OF SILENT READING

The pupil who learns to use silent reading independently will grow into the self-actualizing learner who is gradually liberated from the direction of the teacher and will become the student who sets his own purposes and plans his own activities.

BROADENED EXPERIENCES One who travels vicariously can relive the historical past with famous heroes. He can visualize an act, a situation, a character, a theory, and use his insight as a basis for planning his own future. Eventually his reading becomes a matter of dealing with ideas on a higher plane than mere fact gathering.

WIDENED INTERESTS AND DEEPER APPRECIATION Concrete experiences provide a solid foundation for early reading. As soon as the learner has enough background of concrete experiences on which to generalize, he can begin to visualize mentally the situations described in his reading. Then he can reconstruct for himself through his imagination the situations described by the author. These mental images may vary depending on the background of the reader. The more experiences he has the wider will be his interests. The wider his interests the greater will be his understandings. To understand is to appreciate.

ECONOMY OF TIME, EFFORT, AND ENERGY The more rapidly and efficiently the reader can read the more territory he will cover. The less effort and energy he must expend to get the thought from the printed page the more reading he will be able to do. Truly, greater comprehension in silent reading will result from the economy of time, effort, and energy which grows out of perfection of mechanical skills and expansion of intellectual ability.

POWER OF COMPREHENSION AND INTERPRETATION The slow, laborious reader who is distracted by effort with the pronunciation of words is easily diverted from the idea to the skill and as a consequence loses the trend of thought. The reader who can proceed with the mechanics without having to give conscious thought to the effort is truly the one who can use silent reading as a means of communing with the author. If his mind is centered completely on the information, the ideas, the implications, he can devote himself to thinking, evaluating, analyzing, organizing, concluding, applying, and anticipating. This kind of mental activity is creative reading. It is the highest goal of silent reading.

PROGRESS TOWARD MATURITY

The truly mature reader understands the difference between silent and oral reading and can use each effectively. When he reaches independence in his skills, he is ready to soar on his own.

RELATION BETWEEN SILENT AND ORAL READING

Teachers frequently ask, "How much oral reading should we have the children doing?" "Isn't silent reading much more important in the upper grades?" "What use does the older child actually have for oral reading?" "Should they always read silently first?" The answers to these questions are relative. To give a simple brief answer is to open the way to differing interpretations and consequently to misinterpretations. Let's take some examples.

PERCENTAGE OF ORAL AND SILENT READING If you are talking about the proportion of the material in the basic reader which will be articulated orally by some member of the class, then perhaps we can say that at the lower grade level there will probably be more of it read orally and the amount will tend to diminish proportionately as we progress to higher grades. This relationship is illustrated in Figure 15.

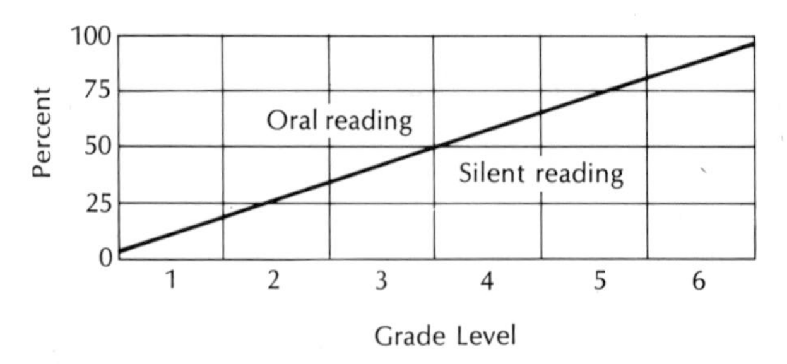

Figure 15. Percent of basic text which might be read orally in class.

If you are talking about the proportion of the reading material in the basic text the individual child will read orally, you get a different answer.

Even that may have to be broken down into different situations. Suppose the story in the primer consists of four pages and Mary reads orally only the part that tells about the item purchased at the toy shop. Perhaps she has read orally only two or three lines out of a story consisting of twenty or thirty lines. In that case we will have to conclude that, even though all the story may have been read orally in class, Mary read orally only 10 or 15 percent of it. That proportion and its change through the years is represented in Figure 16.

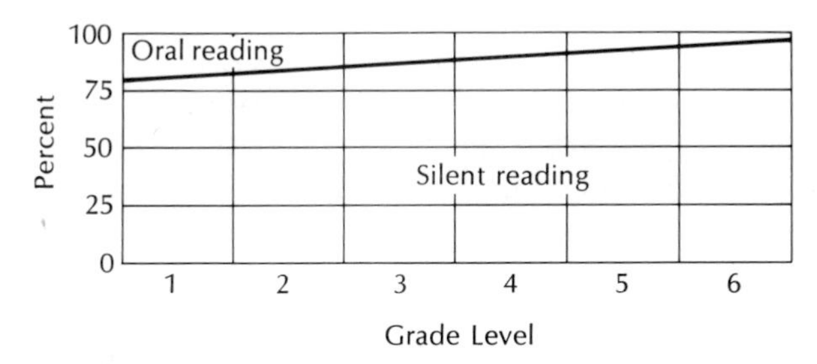

Figure 16. Percent of material an individual child might read orally in class.

If Mary reads with a partner, then perhaps she reads at least half the story orally for practice. Or she might read all of it to her partner who in turn reads all of it to her. Or Mary might take the book home to show her mother how well she can read the story in which case she reads all of it orally. This gives a different proportion and, even then, as she progresses through school she will tend to do less of such oral reading. See Figure 17 for this comparison.

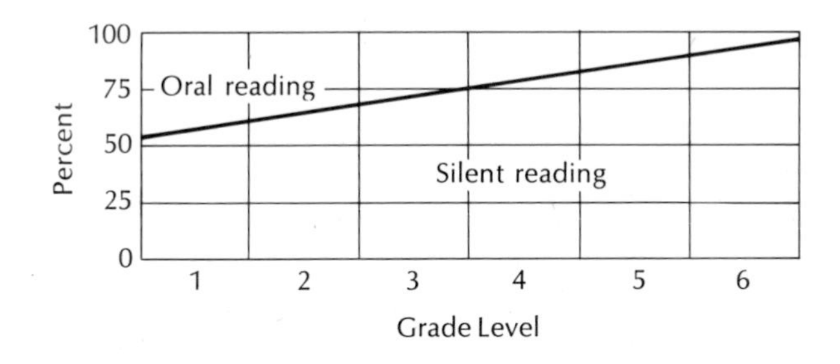

Figure 17. Percent of material an individual child might read orally, both in and out of class.

Perhaps we can say that in the lower grades, particularly in the stages of initial instruction, there may be more need for the teacher to hear the children read orally in order to fix impressions, verify learnings, and provide practice. As the mechanical skills become more firmly fixed perhaps silent reading of a story followed by a discussion which brings out meanings and insights will verify the effectiveness of the reading without the teacher actually having to hear each child read orally in turn. How much of each? It all depends. The teacher who knows the children, the material, and the purpose will be in a position to decide in each situation, and the decision will vary from one time to another. She must diagnose and prescribe. All that can be done at this point is to present principles on which to base the diagnosis.

NEED FOR PRELIMINARY PREPARATION The question about preliminary preparation through silent reading preceding oral reading was discussed in connection with the principles of eye span and eye-voice span. Suffice it to reiterate at this point that the oral reader should have enough preliminary preparation to ensure satisfactory oral performance which will result in meaning for the listener. Whether that preparation comes the day before, the minute before, or the eye-voice span before will depend on the maturity of the reader's skills and the difficulty of the material. But no reader should ever attempt to transmit to a listener a message which he himself has not yet obtained from the printed page.

NEED FOR MASTERY OF MECHANICS Mastery of mechanics and use of skills differ somewhat in silent reading as compared to oral reading. Silent reading calls for sufficient ability in word recognition so that the reader can glean accurate impressions. It also calls for sufficient speed so that he can keep his attention on the thought expressed. Oral reading calls for these skills plus accuracy in word pronunciation and a sufficiently long eye-voice span to enable the voice to convey the meaning while the eye is collecting the impressions and the brain is translating the ideas. In silent reading it is possible to get the idea without being able to pronounce all the words. Not so in oral reading.

SELECTION OF APPROPRIATE SKILLS Even mastering the skills of mechanical performance and of comprehension is not enough. Since different skills are needed for reading directions, story action, conversation, poetry, factual information, argumentation, and essay type material, the reader must not only have a variety of skills at his command, but must also be able to select the ones appropriate for the situation at hand. It is not enough for the teacher to say, "This is an arithmetic problem. Read it first to see what the problem is. Read it again to find out what to do. Read it still a third time to pick out the pertinent facts needed in the solution." Eventually the child must learn to recognize a problem for himself and do his own deciding about how it should be read and which of his reading skills he will use. When he is "weaned" from the teacher and can set his own purposes and decide on his own procedures, then he is an independent reader.

INTERPRETATIONS OF SIGHT READING The expression *sight reading* has been used both with challenge and with derision. Saying how and when a child should learn to read "at sight" calls for interpretation. There are different interpretations of the expression sight reading. One refers to *sight words* taught in beginning reading. The other refers to reading new material "at sight" without preliminary preparation.

Sight words may be learned initially or may be acquired through familiarity. In beginning reading when the child is merely told that this word is *cat* and that one is *elephant,* he can tell them apart simply because they do not look alike. He recognizes them at sight. He knows such words at sight the same way he knows his mother at sight. He recognizes them because he has seen them before and he knows how they look. This interpretation of sight reading has come in for considerable derision from the critics who see this early learning-to-read process going no farther than merely telling the child what the words are and expecting him to remember them. Such critics have seen only one small part of the total learning-to-read process and have drawn a hasty conclusion that is partly right and mostly wrong.

This kind of rote memory bogs down when the learner simply cannot absorb any more new words. Unless he is given some techniques for identifying similarities and differences and putting together words with common elements so that he has a basis for analyzing them, he will eventually reach the saturation point. For example, the first grader may learn the word *Tam* as the name of a character in a story. It is phonetically regular and can be used to identify related words, such as am, ham, and Sam. At first it may have been presented as a sight word, but when he meets it again as a fifth grader spelled with a small *t* as tam and referring to a kind of cap, he recognizes the pronunciation of the word because of its phonetic regularity but may have to learn the new meaning.

Thus the child who starts out with sight reading by this definition and progresses into organized knowledge which gives him insight into the structure of words in his language will acquire an independence that eventually forms a pattern. Thus some words that were once sight words by this definition become phonetic words when subjected to analysis and organization. Whether a word is a sight word or a phonetic word depends on the nature of the word itself and moreover on the manner in which the learner attacks it at the time. Some words which were introduced as sight words in the early stages of learning may later become phonetic when the child masters the skills of word analysis. Some words which were originally introduced as phonetic words may later become sight words if the child uses them so often that they become permanently fixed without need for attention to their component parts.

Reading at sight is another interpretation that needs clarifying. The expression sight reading is sometimes used in referring to the reading of new material at sight without preliminary preparation. If the teacher begins the lesson with, "What page are we ready for today? What is the name of the story? You may read first, Tom," then what Tom is doing is sight reading. If this interpretation of sight reading is used, then perhaps the answer is that the child should not be asked to read new material at sight unless he has an adequate eye-voice span. That means that he must have reached that stage when his rate of word recognition exceeds his rate of articulation by enough so that he is able to let his eye skip on ahead of his voice and find out what is coming before he vocalizes it for his hearers. This calls for skill in thinking about what is coming while voicing what has already been taken in by the eye and interpreted by the brain. This depends partly on the stage of maturity of the reader and partly on the difficulty of the material being read.

INDEPENDENCE IN READING

The truly independent reader has mastered the skills at his level so that he no longer has to think about them. He is both capable of and willing to select his own reading matter. He knows how to adapt his rate and his techniques to the task at hand. And he has established some habits and interests which will go with him beyond the classroom.

MASTERY OF SKILLS Mastery of skills is essential but to devote full attention to skills while comprehension waits is to make of the reader an automaton and to deny the purpose for which reading is done. You can't wait till one skill is perfected before starting another. They must develop simultaneously, alternating attention first to one then to the other.

ABILITY IN SELECTION OF MATERIAL When the child reads of his own volition and selects the materials he can read and wants to read, then he is an independent reader. Such independence comes gradually. In the beginning he may need to be led into the situation. He may need a little help and some urging to get him to try. He may need some convincing that he really can do it. For a while he may need a limited quantity of books from which to select in order to keep him from going in over his head or from wasting his efforts on material which will not challenge him to growth.

The mature student should not always expect to be told what to read and how much. The high school or college student who expects to be told which chapter to read and what answers to find is still a dependent reader. He has not yet learned the basic principle of self-selection. Long before the college level he should have learned how to find material to support a point of view. Instead of asking, "Is this what you want?" he should be coming forth with, "This is what I have found."

ADAPTATION OF RATE AND TECHNIQUE TO PURPOSE The reader must learn to adapt his rate and his techniques to the material at hand and to the purpose for reading. He must recognize that a story may be read rapidly to find out what happened; a set of directions must be read carefully and followed explictly; a beautiful poem may be read aloud for the effect of rhythm and play on words; and a newspaper may be read casually for general information. When the reader can establish his own purpose for reading, can recognize the type of reading that will aid in the accomplishment of the purpose, can select from his repertory of skills the one to use under the circumstances, and can glean from the reading material what he needs to accomplish his purpose, then he is a mature and independent reader.

ESTABLISHMENT OF PERMANENT HABITS AND INTERESTS The establishment of appropriate habits and permanent interests which lead to complete independence in reading is the ultimate goal. The teacher who teaches children how to read, how to select reading material, how to establish purposes, and how to fit the skills to the situation is building for them a foundation which makes learning a lifetime process. And the teacher who follows through by gradually withdrawing the guidance and by giving the child the reins for himself is helping him toward maturity in his reading skills. That is the ultimate goal—complete independence.

9

THE IMPORTANCE OF RATE OF READING

or How Fast Can They Read? How Fast Should They Read?

Speed is a by-product of skill. In no case is speed the first objective or the initial learning. As learnings are mastered and blended together into a smoothly operating performance speed seems to come automatically. It grows out of familiarity with the processes and repetition of the performance. Speed follows vocabulary mastery, insight into language structure, development of adequate eye span, accurate return sweep, and ability to read for meaning. Any drill for speed which precedes these skills dooms both the teacher and the learner to frustration and disappointment. The child cannot develop speed in doing something he cannot already do. He cannot learn to recognize words faster until he can first recognize the words. He cannot learn to move rhythmically across the line of print taking in whole phrases at a glance until he has first learned to take in a larger eyeful.

Much has been said about the value of speed in reading. Sometimes it becomes a false god, an artificial goal, a skill to be acquired for the sake of the skill itself. Many of the advertisements directed at adult readers guarantee to increase your speed and make you a more efficient reader, but they can't increase your speed unless you already possess the skills. And even the acquiring of speed alone does not necessarily bring efficiency in reading. Not all reading material should be read at the same rate. A good reading program is one which teaches the child to *fit speed to needs.* This is far more important than mere increase in speed.

RATE

In Chapters 7 and 8 we pointed out the relationship between silent reading and oral reading. We discussed the rate of articulation and the rate of recognition as a basis for differentiation between speed in oral reading and speed in silent reading. The rate at which one can say the words and still enunciate clearly is bounded by a physical limitation. This varies with age, with personality, and with experience. Mere speed for the sake of speed may deter rather than increase the value and the effectiveness of the oral reading act. The rate at which one can see and recognize the meanings expressed by the words need not be limited by the rate at which one can articulate. This makes it possible for one to read silently at a rate in excess of the rate of articulation, but such a skill depends on the suppression of speech and the ability to read ideas rather than words.

RATE IN ORAL READING

Sometimes a child gets the impression that he is a good reader if he can read fast and say all the words without making a mistake. To him this means he has "studied his lesson." He is obviously the child who views oral reading as a test of skill rather than as a means of sharing an idea. If the teacher asks him to "read next," there is no obvious terminal point other than for the teacher to stop him. But if the teacher asks him to read "the part that describes the boat," then when he gets the boat described he has made his point and that is the place to quit. If oral reading is merely a test exercise, then the speed he demonstrates may accomplish his goal. But if oral reading is the communication of an idea to the listeners, then speed as such is no longer a major objective. Not all material needs to be read at the same rate. Consider the appropriate tempo for reading each of the following passages:

Quickly Jim rushed to the barn, threw open the door, and led the frightened horses from the blazing building.

Jim dreaded to meet his father. He edged haltingly and reluctantly toward the closed door of the darkened study.

RATE IN SILENT READING

In the same manner speed in silent reading depends on the purpose for which the reading is done. If the reader is looking for the date on which an event happened, he may skim rapidly over the printed material letting his eye pause only where there is evidence that a date is being presented. If he is eager to find out how a story comes out, he may skip along rapidly over the paragraphs getting the general idea but not pausing for details. How much he can take in at an eyeful depends on his skill in word recognition, on the difficulty of the material being read, and the purpose for which he is reading. It is possible to take in whole phrases, whole sentences, and even whole lines at a glance and still get the point. Many mature adult readers who have made a practice of wide reading claim to read down the page instead of across the page. Even they sometimes pause for a closer inspection of some point that needs to be impressed more firmly in mind.

SELECTING SUITABLE RATE

How fast one *can* read and how fast one *should* read are two different questions. One might be able to say the words at a rapid clip, in fact so rapidly that they lose significant meanings which can come only with suitable emphases and pauses and with appropriate voice pitch to convey meaning. Then perhaps the rate at which one can read has reached the point of diminishing returns and should be reappraised.

One might be able to move his eyes rapidly over the printed page and get the general idea at a rate of a thousand or two of words per minute. Some speed readers claim to do so and some advertisements promise to teach you to perform this remarkable feat, but if one picks up general ideas and gets wrong interpretations because he missed the details or the qualifications of the statements, he may have made his reading not only fruitless but actually harmful. A fleeting glance at a news story may leave one with a completely erroneous interpretation of an incident. Sometimes sensational headlines and slanted news stories are designed to do just that.

To work for speed before correct habits are formed only causes the reader to make his errors faster. That is negative learning. It may do far more harm than good. Speed in reading must first of all be an outgrowth of practice on related skills. It represents efficiency and coordination of those skills.

Furthermore, speed is relative. The reader who develops a rate of speed and attempts to adapt it to all his reading is defeating the purpose for the skill. The reader who learns to adapt his rate to his needs is making his habits serve his reading. This means that he must know how to read rapidly and how to read carefully. And finally he must be able to set his own purposes for reading and to select the speed he will use to accomplish the purposes.

VALUE OF SPEED

Research has shown that once skills have been established comprehension does increase with speed. Shores concluded that "fast readers are the good readers when reading some kinds of materials for some purposes," and that "in general the fast readers are the good readers on the reading tasks presented in the standardized tests of general reading ability."[1] That makes sense if you stop to think about it. The reader who has to stop and work out the pronunciation or the meaning of a word loses temporary communication with the author. The reader who says one word at a time and regresses to pick up thought units is giving his attention to mechanics instead of to ideas. The reader who glides along smoothly and quickly over the ideas on the printed page without letting the mechanical problems interfere with his communication with the author is reading for ideas. Since the mind can move from one idea to the next more rapidly than the voice can articulate the words, the reader must make the adjustments.

A listener often finds his mind wandering because he is a jump ahead of the speaker. His rate of listening is automatically limited to the rate at which the speaker is articulating. But when he is reading silently he can control the rate of intake by the speed at which his eyes travel across the line of print. If he forces his eyes to move at the same rate at which he can vocalize the words, he is automatically slowing down his pace of comprehension. But if he can learn to suppress inner speech and comprehend the ideas without saying the words, he can increase his rate of recognition to keep pace with his rate of comprehension. By gearing his rate of recognition in this manner he uses up the slack that lets his mind wander and is able to keep his mind on the author's thoughts. Thus, the increase in speed actually increases skill in comprehension.

The child needs guidance while he is establishing his skills and experimenting with their use. He needs direct instruction in meeting situations and making decisions. He needs to experiment with different rates of reading for different purposes and to discover for himself not only which ones work best in each situation but also why they are better.

Once the reader has generalized about appropriate rates of reading for different purposes, he is able to make decisions when he meets new situations. Only then will he be a mature reader. The reader who thinks speed for speed's sake is a desirable goal will tend to try to read rapidly no matter what the material. If he reads a mathematics problem, a science experiment,

[1] J. Harlen Shores, "Are Fast Readers the Best Readers? A Second Report," *Elementary English, 38,* no. 4 (April, 1961), 236–245.

or the directions for a game rapidly and depends on reading only once, he may find he has failed to grasp the necessary details. Then he will see the necessity for reading, or rereading, more deliberately. If, on the other hand, he reads the exciting account of a thrilling adventure slowly and deliberately, he may find himself bogged down in the details and miss the excitement of the story.

TYPES OF READING DEMANDING DIFFERENT RATES

When the reader learns how to read and how to select the appropriate skills to meet different purposes, then he is ready to work on his own. He must first identify the type of reading material he is using. Then he must identify the type of reading skills he will need to suit the situation. Finally, he will need to know how to adjust his speed to his needs.

IDENTIFYING THE TYPES OF READING

Since not all reading material is handled in the same way and the reader must fit his skills to his needs, he will need to know when to skim and when to scan. He will need to know when reading demands only a cursory perusal of the material and when it demands more careful reading. He will need to know when and how to preview, to take notes, and to use reviewing techniques effectively.

SKIMMING Skimming means to read or glance at hurriedly or superficially. Another meaning associated with skimming which can be applied to reading through analogy is to skim cream from the surface of the milk. Sometimes the word skim is associated with inferior quality. It could just as well be used to mean "select the quality from the top" as in the case of the cream. The reader who is able to glance quickly over a passage in a book and select the part that tells him what he wants to know or find the specific information that meets his immediate needs without belaboring the details is an efficient reader as well as a rapid reader. He may go back later for the details, but they will be to support his major finding rather than to establish his point of view.

Children reading a well-motivated story are eager to find out what happened. They won't want to stop and labor over a few words. This is the time to let them read on to the end as fast as they can go. Then rapid reading skill will have been used purposefully and the desire to find out what happened will have been satisfied. The discussion which follows may reveal additional words which need to be clarified for meaning and perhaps analyzed for pronunciation. The interpretation of the story which brings out character traits, attitudes, and insights can be discussed as the story unfolds its details.

Skimming is an effective technique, but it does not replace more purposeful reading later.

SCANNING Scanning means to examine carefully, point by point. Sometimes this term is misused to mean the same as skimming. Be careful here! The child who reads a mathematics problem for the essential details is scanning carefully. He need to know first what the situation is in the problem. Once he has the mental image of the situation he must look more closely to see what he is to find out. Then he is ready to reread in detail to pick out the essential facts he will need in reaching a solution. Recognizing what he needs to know and identifying needed facts are essential steps in scanning the problem. Sometimes the facts are stated concisely and clearly. Sometimes they are implied but not definitely stated. Sometimes there are extraneous facts which the child must sift out in order to make use of only the ones needed in the immediate solution.

This kind of reading calls for looking closely into the content and examining carefully point by point. In reading mathematics the child is often given experiences in using these skills. In the cartoon in Plate 10 he is given too many facts. He does not need all the numbers. The cartoon helps him see the point about which facts are irrelevant to the problem.

In a problem such as, "Mary cut 9 inches from a yard of ribbon. How much did she have left?" the child must be led to discover for himself that he needs a fact not specifically stated in the problem. Then he must be able to call up from his background the needed fact, in this case the number of inches in a yard. If the child does not do this on his own, the teacher may need to guide his thinking by asking how long the original piece was, perhaps measuring off a 36-inch length of string and suggesting that the remaining piece is no longer a yard and that the length may have to be expressed in some other measurement. When the child has been led through such an experience, he will have discovered the hidden fact and will have used his scanning skills.

It is not enough to lead the child to make the application in the specific situation. He must eventually come up with his own conclusions that some material, mathematics problems for instance, must be read carefully and with infinite attention to detail. He won't always have a teacher by his side to remind him of needed facts, to question him about the facts he missed, and to direct his thinking through the solution of the problem. A reading program which teaches the child to think, then supplements that with helping him know when he has succeeded, is developing independence and maturity.

Scanning is a speed skill, not to see how fast you can go, but to know which speed is needed in a given situation. It is an example of the principle "fit speed to needs."

CURSORY VERSUS CAREFUL READING These topics were discussed at length in Chapter 8. Cursory reading can be done rapidly with occasional pauses to take in details which meet an immediate need, challenge a passing interest, or arrest the attention of the reader. It may be intermittently fast or deliberate. The speed will vary from time to time during the reading depending on the attention and the purpose of the reader. It is related to skimming. Careful reading is usually done more deliberately in order to accomplish a different purpose. It may be done step by step as directions are followed. It may require a second or third reading for needed facts or details. The cook may read a recipe in a cursory manner and clip it for future reference. The rereading will come when she makes the dish. This will be careful reading. She may not try to remember the details because she will reread the recipe when she uses it again. After repeated uses she may eventually remember the ingredients, the amounts, and the steps. The mastery comes as a result of repeated use rather than in preparation for the initial use.

The same principle applies to much of the reading the child does in the classroom. Much of his reading can be done in a rather superficial and cursory manner if he is led to see reading as meeting a personal need. Once he has skimmed over the material and decided for himself of what value it is to him, he will know where to find out what he wants to know. Then rereading is no longer a matter of doing it over again because it was not well done in the first place, but rather a matter of more detailed reading for a different purpose.

Then scanning becomes a tool he uses when he wants details, support for a point, directions for a project, or information to be used in a report. Whether he scans or skims will depend on whether he is doing cursory or careful reading.

PREVIEWING Quite young children can learn the useful tool of previewing. If the teacher is addicted to the theory that all reading must be done thoroughly, exactly, and correctly and that whatever is read must be remembered and tested, then she is not going to help children learn effective previewing skills. Just as good advertising and attractive displays stimulate sales, so effective previewing and inviting format stimulate reading.

Effective previewing techniques are demonstrated in the story entitled "How Living Things Help Themselves."[2] The children can preview the entire

[2]Byron H. VanRoekel and Mary Jean Kluwe, *From Fins to Feathers,* Basic Second Reader, Strand 2 (The Harper & Row Basic Reading Program), Evanston, Ill., Harper & Row, 1966, p. 47–72.

selection to find out from the subtitles what the living things are. The resulting list can be organized into two sublists: plants and animals. Some of this information will come from a quick glance at the reading matter itself, much can be inferred from the illustrations, and some will result from more detailed reading. The child who has previewed twenty-five pages in this manner before he starts to read for details is aware that both plants and animals are living things and are equipped to help themselves. Now he is ready for detailed reading, not to find the answers to fact questions, but to make inferences based on more basic questions such as: Why do living things need to help themselves? How are plants different from animals? What other plants and animals also help themselves? How are their methods similar to the ones we read about?

Previewing can tell the prospective reader what it is all about and can help him decide for himself whether or not he wants to or needs to read in greater detail. Sometimes it is just as valuable to find out through previewing that one does not want or need to read a certain selection as it is to find out that he does. He may get part of the information from the pictures, part of it from the subtitles, part of it from the reading matter, and part of it through inference in the discussion with his classmates. The important item is that he gets the information.

Previewing is a technique which utilizes speed not only in recognition, but also in selection of pertinent points. The child needs to see it as different from mastering basic skills of word recognition and correct articulation in oral reading. When he has learned to preview, he has learned that in adapting his speed to his needs he may read different materials at different rates, and he may read the same material at different times for different purposes, and thus employ different rates in the rereading.

DETAILED READING WITH NOTE TAKING Gleaning the important details and recording them for future reference involves detailed reading and note taking. Effective note taking is dependent on the setting of purposes for reading before the actual reading takes place. It follows previewing. When the reader knows he is looking for particular information, he will be on the alert for words or phrases which will yield a list leading to the answer to a specific question.

In the story of "The Cowboy's Work on the Winter Range"[3] the title helps set the purpose for reading. One can readily establish the point that this section is going to tell about kinds of work. It is obvious who is doing the work, where it is being done, and the time of year when it takes place. These questions do not even need asking. The one question that is not

[3]Daisy M. Jones and J. Louis Cooper, *From Actors to Astronauts,* Basic Fifth Reader, Strand 2 (The Harper & Row Basic Reading Program), Evanston, Ill., Harper & Row, 1964, pp. 136–139.

answered in the title is, "What are the kinds of work?" Now a purpose for reading has been established.

The introduction explains that each paragraph tells about one kind of work. By the simple expedient of counting the paragraphs the children can deduce that there are five kinds of work. Now the purpose for reading each paragraph is to find out what kind of work it is telling about. The paragraph may give some additional details about the work and perhaps even elaborate on some of the accompanying activities or reasons for the work, but the basic point to be gleaned from this first rapid reading will be the kind of work it is discussing. Now the child is ready to prepare his paper in outline form to take notes. It will look something like this:

Kinds of work on the winter range
A.
B.
C.
D.
E.

Now he knows there are five things to look for. There will be one kind of work named in each paragraph. He is ready to read and take notes. His rate of reading will depend on the skill with which he is able to locate the particular word or phrase naming the kind of work. He may skim rapidly over each paragraph picking out just the part that tells him what he wants to know. He will end up with a list which includes such phrases as riding over the area, keeping a lookout, cleaning the pipes, seeing that there is salt, and feeding the cattle. The note taking answers a specific question. It gives the reader an overview of the selection. It organizes his thinking. It prepares him for more detailed reading later to support or elaborate on his points answering such questions as "How?" and "Why?" Again the rate of reading will be determined by the purpose for the experience. Such material may justifiably be read more than once. It isn't always read at the same rate. The good reader learns to fit his speed to his needs.

REVIEWING The reader who knew why he read, knew what he was looking for, and who took effective notes has at his command organized information that is easy to review. Review techniques can be based on the structure and format of the printed material or on the notes taken during the previous study. The example about the work on the winter range will yield a list for a notebook. When it comes time to review the pupil may find it more helpful to review his notes than to reread the text.

A book which makes liberal use of side heads, paragraph headings, italics, topic sentences, and summaries provides the reader with the tools for reviewing as well as for previewing. Preview techniques are used to survey the material, predict what is coming, and establish a purpose for reading. Review techniques are used to recall, organize, and see relationships in what has been read.

Speed then is not so much a matter of how fast one can read as how fast one *should* read to accomplish the purpose.

SELECTING APPROPRIATE TYPE AND RATE OF READING

Maximum speed in oral reading is limited by the rate at which one can articulate the words, but that does not necessarily mean that that is the most desirable speed. Sometimes a quick pace and staccato style will express the meaning intended. Sometimes a slow deliberate pace and emphatic stress on certain words gives the desired effect.

Speed in silent reading is limited only by the rate at which one can take in the printed symbols and translate them into meanings. The rate of silent reading will be determined by the purpose for reading and by the type of material selected for attaining that purpose.

Skimming lets the reader move over the surface lightly picking up the high points. Scanning slows him down for details. Cursory reading is related to skimming and careful reading is related to scanning. Previewing is a technique which enables the reader to look over the material quickly to find out what it is all about and to set purposes for more careful reading on the second time around. Note taking concentrates attention on the established purposes for reading. This is a more deliberate procedure followed by rereading for supporting details. Reviewing can be rapid if well-established purposes have been set originally and if careful note taking has resulted in organized knowledge.

The accomplished reader is neither a slow reader nor a rapid reader. He is a reader who sees different purposes for reading, has mastered a wide variety of skills, is able to select that skill which fits his immediate purpose, and is able to fit his speed to his needs.

HOW TO DEVELOP SPEED

With all this background about what speed is and how it is related to reading processes we must not pass by the topic without saying something about the development of speed as a reading skill. Speed can be increased with conscious effort and with practice. One can learn to take in longer eye spans. The reader who knows his present stage of development is ready to start an improvement program. Mechanical devices have their place. Conscious effort is important. Knowledge of progress encourages the learner and convinces him he is getting some place. This in turn serves as a further motivating device.

MECHANICAL DEVICES

Devices such as flash cards and reading pacers are designed to help the student acquire speed and skill. They have their place and can make a contribution to the learner. They cannot guarantee results.

Flash cards are exactly what the name implies. A flash card is meant to be "flashed." The teacher who holds the flash card before the group for an indefinite period of time while they all study it has missed the point. The teacher who moves the flash card before the class in a semi-circular motion is giving the children a lengthy exposure and perhaps a blurred vision of motion rather than a quick perception of an image. Flash cards should be flashed. They are designed for a quick exposure and instant recognition. They are perhaps best used with a curtain card. If a flash card is placed in the direct line of vision of the viewers, then is quickly exposed by raising and lowering the curtain card, the view will be a quick exposure of a stationary image.

Reading pacers employ a similar principle. Various kinds are available. The pacer may be in the form of a moving light which leads the eye over the reading material. The pacer may raise and lower shutters over a series of phrases in a reading selection thus pulling the eye along over the reading matter at a rhythmical pace.

A reading pacer which uses shutters for exposure is a mechanical device based on the premise that the reader may have three or four eye fixations per line. Such a device measures the eye span by the inch or by the number of words rather than by the idea. This reduces the reading process to a mechanized performance rather than to a thinking process. Take the sentence below for example.

> All the children played in the house because it rained.

There are ten words. If the eye span is measured by the number of words, the sentence may be broken up for a two-word eyeful.

> All the / children played / in the / house because / it rained.

If a three-word unit is established, the divisions look like this.

> All the children / played in the / house because it / rained.

If an attempt were made to make the recognition units of equal length as measured by the inch, and if four fixations per line were established with the shutters, then the divisions would appear thus.

> All the child / ren played in / the house bec / ause it rained.

Actually none of these patterns fits the ideas. The efficient reader would read the sentence in one of the following ways.

All the children / played / in the house / because it rained.
All the children / played in the house / because it rained.

Speed exercises for a group set the same pace for all. This may actually slow down some readers and leave others confused because of their inability to conform. Speed exercises cannot teach word recognition or comprehension. They can only provide practice on skills which are already understood so that the reader becomes more efficient and thus more rapid in his performance.

CONSCIOUS EFFORT

Speed can be increased by conscious effort on the part of the learner. The mechanical device is merely a motivating technique, an external pressure to increase attention and effort. It tends to challenge the learner to play to win, to beat the system, to increase skill without necessarily getting any more meaning. By simply taking a 3 by 5 file card and pushing it down the page covering the part that has just been read the reader can get much the same effect. He is able to keep pushing himself. He covers what he has already read and thus prevents unnecessary regressions. He is conscious of slight pressure and is able at any point to adjust the pressure to his own ability. He is able to speed up or slow down as the need may be, that is, he sets the timing to coincide with his individual ability.

KNOWLEDGE OF PROGRESS

The reader who is working for increased speed is helped by a knowledge of his own progress. A short timed test at intervals, such as once or twice a week, will enable him to keep a record over a period of time and know whether or not he is gaining in speed.

TIMED TESTS The child can plan and execute his own regular speed checks alone or with a partner. Total class speed checks are possible but probably not as effective as individual checks. Teach the child to construct his own test. He may take a selection from any book he can read at his independent level and actually count the words; or he may arrive at an estimate of the number of words in the selection by counting the words in every fifth line and then multiplying by five. In longer selections estimates can be based on the number of words in every tenth line.

Once the number of words has been established the child is ready for the timed test. He may time his partner and then read while his partner times him. He may read for an established number of minutes, say three or four or as many as five, then check to see how many words he has read; or he may read a given selection noting the time elapsed. Computing the words per minute is a problem in simple arithmetic. Comprehension checks following speed checks are helpful. The partners may compose them for each other or the teacher may participate in this part of the exercise.

RECORD KEEPING The child can soon learn to keep his own record. This relieves the teacher of the task of keeping some twenty-five or thirty separate records and is much more effective motivation for the learner. A simple chart listing date of test, words per minute, selection read, and comprehension score can be kept to show the cumulative effect of the series of timed tests. A graph which shows fluctuation and, we hope, increase in speed is an interesting and an encouraging record. It also has the bonus value of teaching a bit about mathematics graphs.

PLANNED IMPROVEMENT Unless testing and record keeping are followed by a plan for improvement, they can become merely an accumulation of scores. If the child finds he is not gaining, he will be ready to ask why. Perhaps the material is too difficult. Perhaps he is not using efficient eye movements. Perhaps he is not establishing his purposes for reading before he starts. Perhaps he is permitting himself too much lip movement or subvocalization. Perhaps he is devoting too much time to detailed word analysis and struggling over words which he really knows. Once he has determined why he is not gaining momentum he is ready to apply measures that will correct the difficulty and help him toward success and growth. If he is gaining he will be encouraged by the record and will be stimulated to even greater efforts.

The child who sets his own goals and keeps his own records will make greater gains than the one who participates in group drills under the direction of the teacher.

Speed is an individual matter. Appropriate rate is more important than mere speed.

Part Three

USING READING SKILLS

or

Now That He Can Read, What Shall We Do About It?

Can you imagine a violinist spending ten or more years of his life practicing to perfect his skill, then when he graduates, placing the violin in its case and putting it on the shelf with the feeling that now he is through?

That is exactly what some children do with their reading skills. They start to school at the age of 6 or so, spend ten or twelve years in the pursuit of learnings, not the least of which is reading, then upon graduation literally toss the books over the banister and breathe a sigh of relief. The old rhyme, "No more school, no more books," is not all fiction. Many graduates really do feel that they are through with books. To them reading has been a necessary school experience, one which they needed to get behind them in order to get on with living.

What a tragedy! What a waste! What an indictment!

Reading skill is not acquired for the sake of the skill itself, not for a score, a record, and a promotion, not for the accumulation of credits. Reading is a skill which one needs and can and should use the rest of his life. The one who can and does read has at his command the tools necessary to be completely informed and entertained the rest of his life.

Reading skills are the means of finding out what the writer has to say. They are the means of locating needed information. They provide the reader with insight into learnings in the other disciplines. Reading not only arouses interest in a wide variety of subjects but it also satisfies many of those interests. Reading skills are highly individual and must be used to meet personal needs. And all children can use reading skills within the scope of their abilities whether those abilities be at one end or the other of the continuum.

It is not so much a matter of whether one **can** read but whether he **does** read. The reader who upon graduation shelves his ability to read is just like the musician who puts his fiddle in the case and snaps the lock after he gives his recital.

Reading skills grow rusty if not used. They grow more and more effective when used regularly. In Part Two we identified the reading skills and illustrated techniques for developing them. It is the purpose of Part Three to show how these skills can be used to comprehend the message, to locate needed information, to read in the content areas, to read about special interests, and to read independently. Further purposes of this section are to help the teacher understand how to meet the needs of individual differences of all children including the exceptional ones, and to provide needed remedial or corrective measures for those who didn't get it the first time.

10

COMPREHENSION

or What's the Idea?

If we want children to comprehend, we must teach for comprehension. This must begin at the very beginning. Mastery of mechanics and skill in word analysis will be the by-product of the goal of comprehension. They will be a means to an end and not an end in themselves.

Since the purpose of the lesson is to teach the child how to read, we must use our time to teach him rather than to check up on him to see if he can. After we teach him, then we should give him an opportunity to put into use that which he has just learned.

When children come to the upper grades as word callers and masters of mechanics with little or no thinking, we cannot excuse ourselves by saying they have been improperly taught. We can help them. But first we must put our own emphasis on comprehension. And I don't mean testing them to see if they can answer the questions. This merely aggravates the issue. I mean teaching them how and letting them succeed. This is quite different from having them read, then testing them to see if they have comprehended.

Children see just what they are looking for when they read. If they think the teacher wants them to read orally to prove that they have studied and know all the words, then they will concentrate on studying the words so they can read fast without making a mistake. If they think the teacher wants them to produce answers that can be marked right or wrong as a basis for arriving at a grade, they will spend their time searching for the right word to match up with the question or the blank in the exercise book. They are not thinking. They are merely following directions. The teacher or the author of the work exercise has already done the thinking and is merely telling the child what to think.

When we have established comprehension as an objective, then we are ready to help children develop concepts, utilize study skills effectively, and follow sequential steps leading to understandings.

A POINT OF VIEW

If your objective is to teach the use of the printed page as a means of comprehending the meaning of the author, then why start in the opposite direction? Why not start directly toward the goal? Let comprehension of meaning be the major objective at all times. Let mastery of mechanics be the by-product.

If your purpose is to teach, then why start out by testing? Why not use the time and the energy to teach the child how and give him an opportunity to practice that which he has learned? Let testing or checking be the measuring device that comes at the end, after the teaching and practicing have taken place.

Let us examine a few classroom situations to see which is means and which is end product—comprehension or mechanics. Let us reflect on lesson sequence to see if we are checking up, finding errors, and providing corrective measures or if we are presenting new concepts, providing for successful performance, and then measuring the end product. Your philosophy of education, what you believe to be your responsibility, will show up in the lesson sequence and in the point of emphasis.

MECHANICS OR MEANING?

Do you know what you believe? Where do you put the emphasis in your teaching? Examine the following statements. Do you believe:

- That you can't read till you know the words?
- That you get thought from the printed page?
- That reading is a mechanical process used in getting thought?
- That the printed page is the source of information?

If you believe these things, you belong to the school of thought that emphasizes mechanics. Your objective is the mastery of mechanical skill in the hope that comprehension of meaning will come later.

Now examine this set of beliefs. Do you believe:

- That you master words by using them in reading situations?
- That reading is a thought-getting process which is eventually reduced to a mechanical skill through usage?
- That you must bring thought to the printed page?
- That experience is the source of information and that the printed page is merely a means of stimulating the recall of meaningful associations?

If you believe these things, you belong to the school of thought that emphasizes meanings. Your objective is the comprehension of meaning and skill in mechanics becomes the by-product of your teaching. Oh, yes, it will come. It must come. But it is not the initial approach.

What you believe will show up in the typical expressions that creep into your daily lessons. It will be evident in the sequence and point of emphasis in the teaching of reading at any level. It will show up in the approach—the approach to beginning reading, the approach to a new story, or the approach to a new reading situation. It will show up in the place and purpose of drill on reading skills.

Yes, there will be drill in either case. It is not a matter of "to drill or not to drill," but a matter of when to drill, on what, and why. It will show up in the relation between silent and oral reading. It is not an either-or situation when it comes to silent and oral reading. It is a matter of purpose, relationship, and sequence. An examination of some typical classroom situations will make the meaning clear.

MECHANICS AS EMPHASIS

If you believe that mechanical skill is more important than meaning, your approach will be: Learn the words! Study your lesson! Get ready to read!

You will begin with a word list. You will tell the children the words and emphasize the importance of remembering them because they will need them in the new story. You will give them a lesson to study. Their purpose will be to get ready to recite. They will approach the recitation period hoping they have mastered all the things the teacher will ask in order that they may render a successful performance and get the coveted word of praise. The lesson period itself will be a mere check on the effectiveness of the child's attempt to study or learn independently.

When the lesson is in progress you will hear yourself using some of the following expressions:

- How many times did you read your lesson?
- Did you know every word?
- Did you look up the words you didn't know?
- Are you ready to read this morning, Amy?
- I liked the way Bobby read. He knew every word.
- Did anyone hear any mistakes?
- Maybe tomorrow you had better take your book home to practice.
- Good readers know every word.

Have you heard any of these expressions? Have you ever used any of them yourself? I wonder what the story was about, but comprehension of the story was not the objective because we were talking about the teacher who believes that mechanical skill is the major objective and that comprehension of meaning will come later.

The lesson sequence will begin with an assignment, which may come at the end of the recitation period with, "For tomorrow we will begin on page 97 and read over to page 101. I'll put some questions on the chalk board for you in the morning." There is no particular point to attacking the new assignment now, so the children put their books away. In the morning the questions appear and hands wave in the air. "Must we write out the answers?" It's a task to be done. How does the teacher want us to do it? Anything to please! Lessons are read. Answers are written. And time for recitation comes. Then what happens? This is the way the lesson goes:

- How many of you found all the answers?
- Let me see your papers.
- You may read first this morning, Mary.

Now the process of taking turns at oral reading begins. Mary is a good reader. She knows all the words. She gets through her paragraph or her page with few or no errors and we move on to the next victim. He is not so fortunate. When Billy reads the children look around. They wave their hands violently in the air wanting to tell him the words. They skip on ahead and lose the place. The teacher raises her eyebrows and taps her pencil on the edge of the grade book. She may even sigh with relief when Billy is through. His reading is constantly interrupted with such expressions as:

- Now look at that word. Don't you know it?
- We had it yesterday. How does it begin?
- No. Who can tell him?

In an attempt to improve reading you may resort to drill. You may drill on the "new words" as given in the word list in the back of the book. You may ask the children to say the list of words. You may do this before or after the reading. You may ask Billy to take a list home with him to have his mother hear him say them. But this does not keep him from saying *that* for *what* and *then* for *when* as he reads orally.

Then you resort to word analysis or phonic drill hoping to teach him how to tell the difference. Now he knows that one begins with *th* and the other begins with *wh* and he can tell them apart, but he can't remember which is which. We are no further along than we were.

MEANING AS EMPHASIS

If you believe that meaning is basic and that mechanics are the by-product, your approach will be:

- Let's see if we can find out what Mother said.
- In the first line on the next page you will find out whether Mother let the children go.
- There are just three people in this story. See how quickly you can find their names on the first page.
- Just one word will tell what Mike made. See how quickly you can find it. How many times did you find it on this page?
- The boys were talking about different kinds of *pens*. See if you can find out what they were and why it was a joke on them.

In this case you begin with the point to the story. You emphasize finding out. You meet new words head on and have a need for them. Perhaps the new word which tells what Mike is making is *boat*. You may say, "I won't need to help you with this new word because you can see it in the picture." That is a picture clue. The author put the pictures there for a real purpose and he meant for us to use them in teaching.

Perhaps the new word is *laughed*. You may say, "Mother thought it was funny and she did something. See if you can find out what it was. It is a new word but I don't think I will have to tell you. It begins like *look*. Did you find it?" That is a context clue supported by a phonic clue in the form of an initial consonant compared to a known word.

The lesson sequence will begin with a motive for reading the story, a curiosity for finding out, an eagerness to know what happened, pure joy in reading the story. If the children have handled the books over and over again, if they have been pulled through these same stories unsuccessfully on previous occasions, if they have sat idly by and listened to a more advanced group read the same stories over and over, then there is no point to reading the story. The materials need to be fresh and exciting to the readers. There must really be something new for them to find out.

As we approach the story we may discuss similar events within our own experiences; we may study the pictures for clues to the climax; we may decide what we would do under similar circumstances. Now we are ready to find out what really happened.

New words or bothersome words appear in context. We meet them in response to a question rather than in isolated and abstract testing situations. Our objective is to find out what happened. We read silently to get our answers.

Next comes the discussion of what we have learned from reading the story. In this discussion misconceptions will come to light, points will be cleared up, troublesome vocabulary will be revealed and clarified perhaps with chalk board presentation and the use of all possible clues from context, pictures, or phonic analysis and meaning.

Now we are ready for the oral reading. The child is not being tested to see if he knows all the words. He is sharing with others his interpretation of a passage that already has meaning for him. It may be to show how a character sounded, to describe a scene, to express excitement, or to prove a point. Of course the oral reading is successful. We have just taught him how to do it. Now the oral reading becomes a positive, satisfying experience for the child. It is a pleasure for the teacher because she has an opportunity to see the fruits of her efforts. The child practices good oral reading; therefore, that is the kind he learns to do.

Drill or practice may fit into this picture, too. If so, it is for the purpose of perfecting skills essential to good expression in oral reading. We examine *was* and *saw* to see how they are different. We read both of them in the same sentence to see which makes sense. We come to an inductive conclusion about the pronunciation. We may make lists of words that begin alike, end alike, or contain the same element in order that we can generalize on some basic facts that will give us independence in drawing similar conclusions when we meet other words in the future.

If you still believe that reading is a mechanical process and that it is your responsibility to teach words, then you may expect the children to puzzle over the hieroglyphics on the printed page and try to make associations of meaningless sounds with equally meaningless symbols. The outcome is bound to be a parrot-like memory process and a word-calling rendition in oral reading. It is true that some of the more brilliant children may some day see the connection and begin to associate meaning with the process, but by that time habits are formed and the children are bound to become adults who must go through life laboring with verbalization of all material read. If they do not actually verbalize through audible expression or through lip movement, they will at least read with tense vocal cords.

If you are convinced that the reading is a thought process, then you may expect children to read to find out needed information or to enjoy the sequence of the story. They will apply reasoning instead of memory to word attack. They will see silent reading as getting thought and oral reading as expression of thought. They will learn to blend context clues and phonic analysis in the word recognition process. They will gain skill through practice on material within their present level and grow through constant raising of sights.[1]

DEVELOPMENT OF CONCEPTS

Comprehensive reading is built on understanding. The child who has had experiences which yield meanings has background on which to build. If he has not had those experiences, it is part of the job of teaching to provide them. In addition to having background the child must also have the ability to identify the unit of thought in his reading. This means reading for total ideas as they are related to the rest of the content.

BUILDING BACKGROUND

The child who in reading orally stops at an unfamiliar word as if he had met a blank wall is the one who is saying the words instead of reading the ideas. Telling him the word will only result in his parroting it after the prompter and going on with the exercise. When he comes to the same word again in the next paragraph, the performance will be repeated. This is an indication that he did not get the idea in the first place. He only imitated the vocalization without understanding. He is not reading; he is performing a mechanical act. He is responding to an external stimulus in a prestructured manner. This is behavioristic learning. This is a conditioned response. This is based on the bond psychology of learning. It may involve little or no insight. The child can learn the response without necessarily understanding why the associations are made. He can learn to respond to the stimulus without comprehending the meaning back of the words or expression.

The child who reads in this manner is the one who can say all the words but cannot answer the questions. He may be able to pick out the right words to supply acceptable responses to fact questions or to fill blanks, but he will be unable to infer meanings, arrive at hidden meanings, or interpret in terms of his own experiences. This kind of learning reduces reading to a technical process based on mechanics. The behaviorist would say that such a definition of reading is satisfactory and that the teaching of thinking is necessary but is another skill above and beyond the mastery of mechanics. Regardless of which philosophy of reading you accept the reading act itself has limited value to the reader unless he also does the

[1]Daisy M. Jones, "Mechanics Versus Meaning—Teaching Versus Testing, A Plea for the Right Start in Comprehension," *The Reading Teacher*, January, 1953, pp. 15–22. Used by permission of International Reading Association.

thinking. Whether you teach thinking as a part of reading or in addition to reading it still must be taught. Personally, I prefer to think of reading as a cognitive process and begin with the thinking phase. This means that mastery of mechanics will be the by-product rather than the approach. It means that the skills will grow with use rather than be developed for use. This calls for building background for reading through meaningful experiences. Such backgrounds can be built through labeling, demonstrating, and experimenting with meaningful relationships.

LABELING OBJECTS In the classroom the child is helped to gain the concept that objects have names, that those names may be represented by symbols, and that there is a systematic plan in the use of the symbols to represent the sounds. The bulletin board which shows pictures or objects such as a ball, a box, a book, a banana, a balloon, a baby, a bird, a bug, a bell, and a bottle is helping the young learner associate names with objects and to recognize the symbols which give vocalization and picturization to the meanings which he can express through words. The bulletin board which groups such pictures and words into repeated patterns such as the initial *b* is leading the child to discover for himself the basic principle of the initial consonant and to see a systematic plan in such symbol-sound relationships.

DEMONSTRATING CONCEPTS Meanings need to be clarified. The teacher who uses a model to illustrate the principle of an island and develops the concept that an island is land surrounded by water is developing meaning before the term is introduced. She is introducing the concept and the vocal rendition of the term before the word itself is presented in printed form for either pronunciation or phonetic analysis. A model can also be used to develop other geographical concepts such as a peninsula or a strait. When the child sees a body of land that is almost an island, one that is surrounded on three sides by water, one that joins the main body of land in just one place, then he is ready to be introduced to the term peninsula. He hears it first as the teacher gives a name to the formation. As the teacher says the word she points out that part of the word includes the concept of an island. Now vocabulary is being enlarged in a meaningful setting. It is being used to identify or name a concept rather than for pronunciation followed by an attempt to find out what it means. The teacher may point out that the body of land is partly insular in shape. It is almost an island. It is called a peninsula. Now the children are better prepared to look at the word, find it in the book, and identify other peninsulas on the map.

In this sequence the idea was developed first, then the name was learned, and finally the form was recognized both in print and on the map.

This is an example of building background before introducing the term. It means that the child has learned the words to express his ideas rather than sought to find meanings for words.

EXPERIMENTING WITH RELATIONSHIPS Children can discover meanings. Let them experiment with eight pencils on the table. Have three removed. The question, "How many are left?" is readily answerable because the children can see the five pencils remaining on the table. The teacher may ask, "How many are remaining?" or she may make the statement that the ones left are the ones that remain. Now the word remain begins to take on meaning. The children may pick it up and use it. As they approach division problems they may discover that if they have seven pennies and want to divide them between two children each child will get three pennies and there will be one left over that cannot be divided. Again they have had a concrete experience with what it means to have something remain. They can be led to generalize that the part that is left over is what remains. Now the term remainder in mathematics becomes a name for a concept already understood rather than a word whose definition must be learned. Apply this idea to the discovery of other meanings such as the prefix *tri* in triangle, tripod, and tricycle or to the suffix *able* in answerable, manageable, and acceptable. Such scientific discoveries help to make vocabulary serve as a tool for expressing meanings and gradually make the reader more and more independent.

IDENTIFYING THE UNIT OF THOUGHT

When building meaningful backgrounds the idea is more important than the pronunciation. The child learns to look for the idea. An idea is seldom couched in an isolated symbol. Frequently isolated words give no idea or even a false idea. It usually takes the setting in context to give complete meaning.

THE ISOLATED SYMBOL Seldom does a symbol in isolation express an idea. Knowing the soft and hard sounds of *g* and when to expect to find each may even result in wrong pronunciation and consequently wrong meaning if the child follows the rule without taking context into consideration. The child who has learned the rule for soft *g* when it is followed by *e, i,* or *y* may pronounce *get* or *give* with the soft g sound and in his mispronunciation miss the meaning entirely. If he reads, "*Get* the book," as "*Jet* the book," or "*Give* the book to me as "*Jive* the book to me," he will have followed all the pronunciation rules accurately, yet will have distorted the meaning completely. The symbol only triggers the vocal response. It does not represent meaning.

THE WORD Sometimes a single word represents meaning and sometimes it does not. A word which represents a concrete idea may stand alone and convey meaning, but even that can be confusing. Nouns which name concrete objects that can be handled, labeled, or pictured can usually stand alone, but the child who has learned the following words through an association with picture vocabularies may be in trouble when he sees them in different context:

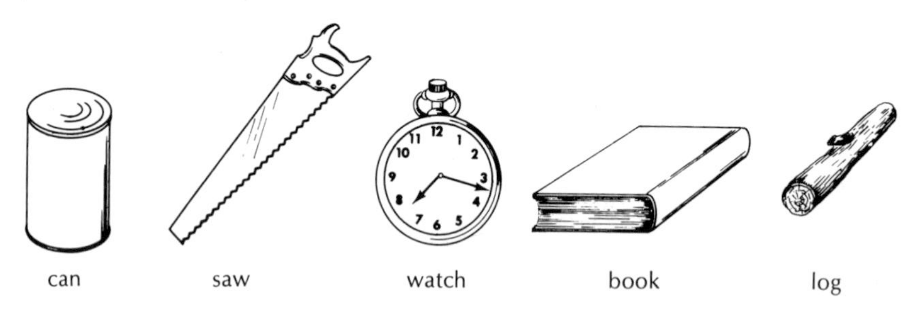

Consider these same words in the following sentences. The pictures are of no help; in fact, they are a hindrance to meaning.

> Billy *can* fly a kite.
> The children *saw* the airplane.
> He learned the *watch* word.
> I will *book* the meeting for Saturday.
> He kept a *log* of the journey.

Even action verbs, descriptive adjectives, and some adverbs are confusing. Figures of speech cause queer quirks in our language. It takes more than pronunciation of words or phonic analysis of sounds to understand the meaning of "a cold shoulder," "He was kept in the dark," "The rumor got a rise out of the crowd," "He was on his own," "up a tree," "behind the eight ball," and so on.

CONTEXT The entire phrase or clause is sometimes needed to convey the meaning. Sometimes it takes the whole sentence and occasionally an entire paragraph or more to get at the real meaning. The play on words that makes narrative writing intriguing sometimes calls for considerable insight before real meanings are evident. Unless the reader can identify the unit of thought and express it in a conversational tone his reading may be meaningless.

DEVELOPMENT OF STUDY SKILLS

Once the child has differentiated between the importance of mechanics and the getting of meaning and has learned to read for the idea his first major hurdle has been crossed. If he lacks understandings for the new ideas being presented, he needs the help of the teacher in developing that background. It takes quite a mature reader to know what he doesn't know and where and how to find out what he needs to know. This is where the help of the teacher is needed in developing effective study skills.

The child may possess the mechanical skills he needs but he doesn't always know which ones fit the situation. Without this kind of guidance he may end up passing tests and getting scores but unable to use reading skills to get information or to entertain himself.

IDENTIFYING THE SKILLS NEEDED

Some of the needed skills are mechanical in nature. Many of them are thinking skills of a higher order. Applying the rule is one thing. Making the judgment is still another.

MECHANICAL SKILLS The teacher is offering help in the use of mechanical skills when she asks questions or gives directions which direct the child toward the structure of the word.

- How does the word begin? (an initial consonant clue)
- Cover up the first two letters. That leaves a word you already know. (identifying word parts)
- Cover up the *ing* at the end and see if you know the first part of the word. (identifying root words)
- That's two words put together. See if you know each of them when you see them alone. (dividing compound words)
- That rhymes with a color word. Can you figure it out for yourself? (meaning clue plus phonic clue using ending phonogram)

THINKING SKILLS Sometimes the teacher will lead the child to use thinking skills in identifying an unfamiliar word.

- Look at the picture. What did Tommy make? (a picture clue)
- How do you know there were lots of children at the party? (recalling meanings and inferring ideas)
- Read on to the end of the sentence and see if you can figure out what makes sense in the story. (using a context clue)
- What would you do if you didn't have enough? Find *enough* in the sentence. (telling an unphonetic word in oral context)

BUILDING INDEPENDENCE

Lead the child to help himself. Merely telling him the words he does not know only encourages him to ask for more words. Recall the suggestions offered in Chapter 4 on what to do when a child comes to a word he doesn't know. If the situation calls for developing independence, guide his thinking toward helping himself. It is hoped that eventually he will decide that, "If I ask her for the word she won't tell me. She will just tell me what to do to help myself. I might as well help myself to begin with. Let's see! Now what shall I do to figure it out."

When the child gets to that stage he has gotten the point. He sees the teacher not as a source of information, but as a guide toward independence and self-help. In his desire to be mature, to be independent, he will eventually declare his independence and strike out on his own. The wise teacher will be the one who gives him the clues he needs to use his mechanical skills and his thinking skills so he can do it for himself.

SELECTING NEEDED SKILLS Sometimes the child doesn't know which of his skills to use to fit the occasion. Again that is where the teacher comes in. She notes the nature of the difficulty, the type of word, the ability of the child, then asks the guiding questions which will cause him to use the appropriate skill.

FITTING LEARNINGS TO ABILITIES The child who tackles a job too big for him needs a teacher at hand to give him the boost that will bring success. The child who hesitates on things he could do for himself needs the teacher at hand to encourage him and provide the little successes that grow into big successes.

These helps cannot be reduced to a set of rules which are guaranteed to work. They demand the attention of a sensitive teacher who watches growth day by day, who watches individuals, and who knows which ones are ready for next steps and which ones still need a supporting hand. Each step forward is evidence of growth. Each hesitation or step backward is a warning that there is danger ahead. The teacher who acts on the danger signals, supports the forward steps, and keeps children all moving in the right direction is succeeding. This is far more important than getting them all "up to norm" or sorting the successes from the failures.

STEPS IN COMPREHENSION

If the reader is to comprehend in his reading, he must set out with that as a goal. That point of view cannot wait till he has learned the ABC's or finished his workbook or memorized some rules or passed a test. From the very beginning he must get the idea that the purpose for reading is finding out what the symbols have to tell. He gets that impression when his mother reads him a story at bedtime. He is fostering that concept of reading when the nursery school or kindergarten teacher is sharing his favorite story book with the rest of the class. He is associating meaning with print when he sees the labels on objects about the room, his name on his own possessions, or the list of things on the bulletin board. He is being impressed with the importance of the printed symbol as a means of conveying a message when he carries a note from his mother to his teacher or from his teacher to his mother. The teacher or mother who explains to him what the note is about and how the message is conveyed is stimulating in him a feeling of need for mastering the techniques that will enable him to use reading as adults use it.

RECOGNIZING RELATIONSHIPS BETWEEN SYMBOLS AND IDEAS

As soon as the learner recognizes that there is a relationship between the symbols and the ideas, he is ready to start using them. Memorizing long lists of symbols can become a meaningless task. To tell the child he can't read till he knows them is like telling a 5-year-old to put his pennies in the bank so he will have money to go to college when he grows up. Young children are oriented to the here and the now. The young financier is much more interested in spending his money for the whistle, the ice cream cone, or the Saturday afternoon movie than he is in accumulating a bank account for the future.

Any attempt to stimulate interest through games, prizes, drill devices, rewards, and artificial sugar-coating only tricks the child into practice which he soon regards as school-oriented, teacher-dominated, reward-seeking behavior. That is what causes him to see reading as something outside his personal needs and interests, something he must do to please adults, to get grades, to pass, so that he can grow up and get through school and get it over with. When he sees reading in this light it becomes a chore. The goal is the reward, the grade, the promotion, and graduation. That is the reason he looks forward to the day when he can put his books aside and get on with the business of living as he sees it. To him reading is not a personal goal and a means to self-satisfaction because he has had "false gods" placed before him.

If we want the child to maintain his interest in reading, he must see his skills result in getting the story *now*.

ACCEPTING COMPREHENSION AS THE GOAL

Children right from the very beginning need to see reading as a means of getting the meaning. In order to do this they must have a purpose for reading. At first this needs to be established under careful teacher guidance. Eventually the child can do it for himself. The teacher is offering this kind of guidance when she says:

- Let me see what your mother said in her note.
- Did your mother read the story to you? Would you rather tell the boys and girls about it, or do you want me to read it to them?

• We'll put our toys on this shelf which says "Toys." Then we will know where to find them when we need them.

• The title of the story tells us what is going to happen. How do you know there is going to be a race? Let's read to see if we can find out who had a race and who won?

• Notice the story is divided into three parts. Read the titles of the parts. That will help us know what is going to happen.

• The questions at the end of the chapter will help us know what we are supposed to find out. Let's read them first.

• This section in our geography book has used heavier type to name the paragraphs. If we read them first, we will have an outline of the section before we start.

• The caption under the picture explains what the people are doing.

• The directions for the experiment list the materials we will need. Let's collect them first. Then we can read the rest of the directions a step at a time as we do them.

• The information you will need to plan your costumes for the play will be found in the story. Watch for it as you read.

• Why was the campaign a failure? As you read look for indications of poor judgment on the part of the leaders.

• How did you know from the very beginning that Paul was going to win the class election? What were his qualifications?

The child can't answer any of these questions or follow those directions by filling blanks with one word! These guide lines offered by the teacher help the reader see comprehension as the purpose for reading. They lead his thinking into the content rather than the mechanics. The helps with mechanics will be for the purpose of getting meaning rather than for accurate performance. The accuracy of performance will have to come, but the accuracy will no longer be for the acquiring of a score, for winning, for getting the most right, for passing. Now it will be for the purpose of getting right information, right impressions, right concepts as a basis for comprehension.

USING READING PURPOSEFULLY

Once the reader has recognized the relationship between symbols and meaning and has identified the problem, then the steps in comprehension in reading involve skills presented in Chapter 9.

RECOGNIZING THE PROBLEM The reader must establish a purpose for reading. Whether recognition of the problem comes as a result of teacher direction or eventually as an independent activity, it must come. The reader who opens a book and starts reading the first chapter just because it has been assigned to be read is reading purposelessly. The mature reader is the one who knows why he is reading. It might be to find out how to repair a car, to find out who committed the crime in the mystery story, to gather points for a debate, to plan a vacation, or to while away an idle evening. But unless the reader attacks the reading material with some kind of purpose in mind, he will lay aside the book for other pursuits.

PREVIEWING Do you ever turn the pages and look at the pictures before you start to read a book or magazine? You are previewing to find out what it is all about and to decide whether or not you want to pursue it. Do you ever look at all the chapter titles before you start a book? Knowing what is coming helps to set purposes for reading. Do you always read a magazine from front to back, or do you sometimes read the jokes, then read the articles that appeal to you, postponing the less interesting ones till later or sometimes forever? You are previewing. You are a selective reader. That's good!

Words were written to be read, but reading them just because they were written is sometimes a waste of time. Unless you want to know what they say there is no point in reading them. The discriminating reader knows why he is reading and what he expects to find out. It may sometimes be all right to read just to see what it is all about, but if all your reading is of that type you won't learn much and if you do it will be only incidental. Previewing is a comprehension technique as well as a speed technique.

CAREFUL OR CURSORY READING Cursory reading gives one a general idea of what it is all about. That has its place. Sometimes it is all you want to know about a subject. The discriminating reader and the well-informed person is the one who knows a little about many things and a great deal about his special interests. The astronaut may know more about space flight than the average citizen, but that is his business. The statistician may know more about the operation of a computer than the teacher, but that is his business. The teacher may know more about child development than the salesman, but that is her business. The fifth grade boys may know more about the rules for the baseball game than the girls, but that is their business. Cursory reading helps one know what is available. Careful reading comes about as a result of established purposes for reading. Each one is done for a different purpose and at a different rate. The accomplished reader knows how to do both, when to do each, and why he is doing it.

REREADING When the teacher says, "Read it again to find ——," she is not punishing the child for not having done it well in the first place. Too often the child gets the impression that he is supposed to get it all the first time he reads and that if he is asked to reread it, it's a sign that he did not do it well the first time. How many times have you heard a child say, "I've already read that"? The truly capable reader often rereads for a purpose, for example, to verify details, to get additional information, to enjoy a picturesque passage, or to identify major points. The reader who decides to reread and who knows why he is rereading is a better reader than the painstaking student who labors over an assignment trying to get it all the first time.

REVIEWING AND SUMMARIZING The reader who finds all the answers to the questions in the assignment and prepares a paper to hand in and be graded may think he is done. But the reader who sees the answers as a summary of facts he will use or sees the use for the facts as a reason for collecting them will approach the assignment with a different motive. When the identification of kinds of work done by the people in a given geographical setting is to be used as a basis for planning the mural, then the mere listing of facts will not be sufficient. When the study of the characters is for the purpose of planning a play based on the story, then the analysis of the character traits will take on a new meaning.

The reader who is able to state in a few short sentences the major things he has found out has made the information his own. The reader who is able to see miscellaneous facts in related groups which have a bearing on a problem is using review and summary to serve his own ends. These ends will be better served if the facts are useful and if they are organized. The reader who has recognized his problem has previewed and read purposefully. Then he will find reviewing and summarizing quick and easy.

ESTABLISHING SEQUENCES

The teacher who would guide children toward comprehension in reading will need to see the steps which lead to the story or the information rather than to the skills. Here are the steps: (1) introduction, (2) motivation, (3) silent reading, (4) discussion, and (5) oral reading. Let's examine them one at a time.

INTRODUCING THE STORY Building a background based on children's previous experiences provides a sound approach to a new lesson whether it be story or factual material. An introduction presupposes that the introducer knows the two elements being introduced. Obviously, Alice cannot introduce Marjorie to Ted unless she knows both Marjorie and Ted. The same applies when it comes to introducing a story to the children or introducing the children to a story. The assumption is that the teacher knows both the story and the children and that she is the intermediary who will get them together and help them get acquainted with one another. A good introduction must be based on something within the experience of the prospective reader and at the same time be relevant to the story being presented. Let's take some examples.

The story to be introduced is "The Three Pigs." The teacher says, "If you were going to build a house, what material might you use?" She is beginning on the assumption that children know something about the building of houses and that the use of materials is part of the point to the story.

The story to be introduced is "Hansel and Gretel." The teacher says, "If you were lost in the woods, how would you find your way out?" Again, she begins on a point in the story and assumes a background of experience in the life of the child that will give him a connection.

The lesson is a study of Greece. As the teacher pulls down the map she says, "If you were going to live in Greece, what kind of clothing would you need?" Again the teacher is assuming that clothing is of interest to the children and that they have enough background of information about the reading of maps to enable them to speculate about the possible kinds of weather they might find in Greece.

PROVIDING A MOTIVE Children should be looking for something definite when they start to read. And I mean something besides finding out if they know all the words. They should be looking for ideas, information, answers, and support for a point of view. In other words, they should be reading for comprehension. In the case of the introduction when Alice introduced Marjorie to Ted, she motivated the acquaintance by saying. "You'll enjoy each other because you both play golf." Immediately Marjorie and Ted have something in common. Pursuing the relationship is stimulated.

In the case of the story of "The Three Pigs" the introduction cited above could be followed by a motivating statement which suggests that in this story there were some pigs who built houses. "Read to find out what materials they used, which was best, and why?"

In the case of "Hansel and Gretel" the teacher may follow the introduction by suggesting that Hansel and Gretel were lost in the woods and met an old witch. "Think about what they did. Did they do the right thing? Might there have been a better way out of their predicament?"

In the case of the geography of Greece she might suggest that even though the country is in a mild region facing the Mediterranean Sea there may be other factors affecting the climate. "As you read try to find out what they are. Collect facts to support your contention about the need for a winter coat, overshoes, or summer clothes."

A motive for reading should grow out of the introduction and should give the children something to find out. In the case of an especially capable group of children the motive may be for a whole story. They are the ones who have established some independence with reading skills and have exhibited an attention span that will carry them through to the end. For some groups who are less mature the motives may have to be doled out paragraph by paragraph or section by section. For slower groups it may be necessary to "spoon feed" them sentence by sentence, literally leading them by hand through the reading, for example, "Read the next line to find out where they went," "The next line tells you who went with them," or "Now find out what they saw."

Sentence by sentence guidance can be gradually discontinued as the children gain independence. The more detailed guidance will be needed with the children who are slower to grasp the total significance of the reading act, with the ones who have more difficulty with mechanics, and with material that offers a greater challenge. The teacher will have to "feel her way along" to know how much guidance of this kind to offer. She should give enough to guarantee success, but not enough to make the child unnecessarily dependent. Only the teacher working with the child in the specific situation will be able to judge that fine line of differentiation between too much and too little.

GIVING CHILDREN TIME TO READ Silent reading for comprehension is a necessary step after the introduction and the motivation. Once the children know why they are going to read, they need time to do it for themselves. While the silent reading is going on the teacher is available to smooth out rough spots, help with mechanics, and encourage hesitant workers. This is the time to help quietly with words, touch a shoulder lightly to keep a wandering mind on the track, smile encouragement to one who looks discouraged, prod the inattentive with a gentle reminder, and supply additional challenge to those who finish first. In teaching, knowing when to keep still and wait is just as important as knowing when to guide and help.

PROVIDING FOR DISCUSSION If the motive is to be accomplished, discussion is necessary. Unless this step is taken the children will get the impression that the silent reading was merely for the purpose of practicing so they will know all the words and can read without making a mistake when they are called on to perform.

It is during the discussion that real checks on comprehension will be made. The teacher who lets the children tell what they found out, the reason for the race, the number of children at the meeting, the kinds of materials out of which the houses were built, the wicked tricks of the old witch, the kinds of climate in the mountains, the character traits of the hero, and the causes of the conflict between the nations will be inviting them to share their comprehension with the rest of the class. This involves more than remembering what was read. It extends into interpretation and analysis of information. During this discussion meanings of new words can be brought out. The children may discuss what the author meant by a challenge, a secret meeting, suitable materials, a misleading remark, a moderate climate, a trustworthy person, or a conspiracy for supremacy. These discussions will bring to light deeper meanings of words. Children will hear and use the new terms. Both meaning and pronunciation of such words will be assured before they are met in an oral reading situation. Then when the oral reading does take place it will not be a test to see if they know the words, but an exercise in the use of known and understood words to convey meanings.

CULMINATING WITH ORAL READING Finally, the oral reading will be the conclusion to the lesson rather than its introduction. It will be for the purpose of sharing information, proving a point, interpreting a descriptive passage, personifying a character, dramatizing a conversational part, or enjoying a beautiful selection. The oral reader will not be facing a test. He will be performing a feat which he has learned. The listener will not be listening for mistakes. He will be enjoying some one else's interpretation of a passage or gaining information he has not already obtained for himself.

A STUDY IN ALTERNATIVES

At the outset it was suggested that if we want children to comprehend we must teach for comprehension rather than for word recognition and perfection of mechanics. Throughout this chapter our thinking has been directed toward planning teaching to accomplish this goal. Mechanics have been kept in their proper setting. At no time has there been a denial of the importance of the perfection of mechanical skills, but they have been pictured as a by-product of good reading rather than as the approach to the establishment of good reading habits, skills, and attitudes.

Putting the emphasis on comprehension calls for an adequate background of understanding for the material to be read. That background must be built. For the younger child the teacher's experience and insight are invaluable because the child does not know what background to build or what experiences to call upon to relate to the reading material. As the child grows more sophisticated in his learnings, he will become more independent in searching for information and understandings basic to comprehension. As he masters the mechanical skills and can devote more of his attention to the thought of the written material, he will grow in his study skills. As he develops under teacher guidance the essential study skills for adequate comprehension and learns to select the techniques most appropriate to each situation, he will become more independent as a purposeful reader.

When he learns the relationship between symbols and meanings, he will apply those learnings to all reading experiences. When he recognizes the problem and learns to use previewing, cursory and careful reading, rereading, reviewing, and summarizing as comprehension skills, he will grow more and more independent not only in the reading class, but also in his personal reading activities. The establishment of these learnings is dependent upon the child's attitude and the teacher's skill.

In order to determine whether or not you are that effective teacher who is leading children toward maturity in reading comprehension check up on your beliefs and on your teaching procedures by asking yourself the following questions.

- Are you checking on him to see if he knows the words or are you teaching meanings so the words will come?
- Do you tell him to figure it out for himself or do you offer him the kind of help he needs?
- Do you have him read to you to see if he knows all the words or do you teach the idea and let him use the words to express it?
- Do you have him read orally to prove that he can do it without making a mistake or do you let him read to share an idea he has already assimilated?
- Do you listen to see if he makes mistakes or do you listen to see if he is conveying the idea?
- Are you using oral reading as the approach or is the oral reading the culmination—the expression of an idea?
- Do you correct his mistakes after he reads or do you prevent mistakes by teaching him how before he reads?
- Do you teach mechanics hoping comprehension will come or do you teach for comprehension recognizing mastery of mechanics as a by-product?
- Are you testing him or are you teaching him?

11

LOCATING INFORMATION

or They Want to Know. Where Will They Find Out?

There is quite a difference between teaching a child how to read and teaching him to use his reading skills as tools for learning. There are many adults who actually know how to read but who seldom or never use a dictionary, visit a library, refer to an encyclopedia, consult a table of contents, or look up needed information. Some do not know that these tools for satisfying curiosity exist and some ignore them because they have associated them with school learning and are not aware that they are available and useful for learnings beyond the classroom.

Before the learner can use reading as a means of getting desired information, he must first recognize the sources available. Then he must have considerable skill in using the sources to acquire the information. In this chapter consideration will be given mainly to the use of printed materials as a source of information. They certainly are not the only source.

SOURCES OF INFORMATION

When books were scarce sources of information were chiefly word of mouth and personal observation. With the mechanical production of books printed matter became more available, but the number of titles and the number of copies of each title were limited. As more materials were produced the variety increased. As knowledge expanded it became increasingly necessary to keep up to date. The modern expansion of mass media and technical devices for communication has in some cases replaced and in other cases expanded the need for printed matter. The informed person is the one who knows where to go for needed information whether he is in school or out. Let us examine some sources of information.

TEXTBOOKS

Textbooks have too often become just that, *text* books. The word text is often associated with the Bible. That gives it an authoritative connotation. It implies truth, the subject for a sermon, the basis for discussion, the Gospel. A textbook is usually used by a teacher and a class as a basis for study. As such it serves some useful purposes. But it can also lead to some dangerous practices.

In the days when published material was scarce it was a fortunate class that could find a book containing the information needed. Then perhaps only one title was a justifiable base for study. But in these days of a multitude of published books on every subject the possibilities for the use of textbook materials are different.

A textbook can provide an orderly plan. It can serve as a basic source of information. It can serve as a preview of the field to be covered. It can serve as a summary or review at the end. It can serve as a basic minimum for those pupils who lack the ability which comes with intelligence, maturity, or extended interests.

A single textbook cannot provide a complete survey of a topic. In these days of expanding knowledge, extensive publications, and varied points of view the person who reads only one source is narrowing his vision. He will be the one who reads to find out what to think rather than what to think about or how to think. He will be the one who collects the facts and accepts authority rather than the one who searches for truth. He will read the ads and the political speeches and be swayed by emotionalism. If he reads only one point of view, he will not learn to read with discrimination and to make decisions.

When a class uses a common basic text for everything there is the danger of turning the class period, the study period, and the recitation period into an assigning and testing situation instead of into a learning situation. What is the alternative? There are many sources of information about almost every conceivable subject. The class that uses a text to provide an organized approach to a topic will be stimulated to raise questions and seek answers on their own. This will lead to the exploration of other sources of information as a basis for comparison and discussion. Almost any topic may be discussed in various textbooks. Information collected from a variety of sources leads to the type of class activity in which the child who is contributing may be telling something the rest have not read. The others will be listening to him because he has something to say. He will speak with confidence if he knows the rest want to hear what he is saying.

Use of multiple texts in a classroom can serve more than one practical purpose. It can give different points of view on the same topic. It can add breadth, enrichment, and insight as a basis for constructing one's own impressions. It can provide for a wide span of abilities. The teacher who has a variety of materials available will be able to provide fruitful reading for the less capable pupils as well as challenge for the more capable.

Yes, textbooks as such are good sources of information for class study. Multiple copies of a single title in the hands of all are limiting. Multiple titles can provide breadth of information. They can also provide for differences in ability or levels of maturity. Textbooks should be sources of information and guides, not masters. The teacher who leads children to "cover the book" will permit them to view the final examination as the end of the course. The child who pursues the course by raising questions and searching for information will view the end of the term as an open door. He has learned where to find information and how to use it. He sees commencement as commencing instead of finishing.

REFERENCES

There are some sources of information which one consults only to get specific answers to specific questions. This type of reference, unlike a text, does not determine continuity or sequence in learning. Such sources include dictionaries, encyclopedias, and reference books.

DICTIONARIES Sometimes a dictionary is used to find out what a word means. Sometimes it is used to determine which of several meanings apply in a given situation. A dictionary can help determine correct spelling. A dictionary will indicate accepted pronunciation. Sometimes the reader may want such information as derivations of words, correct form for past tense, or perhaps a synonym. The same word may be looked up many times, each time for a different purpose.

The child who views dictionary practice as an assignment will be the one who looks up the words the teacher has had him mark and will copy whatever is there without thought as to the pertinence to the problem at hand. The child who learns to respect the dictionary as a useful tool is the one who will keep it handy and use it to answer his questions.

The dictionary may give more than one meaning for a word. In that case a judgment must be performed to decide which meaning fits the specific situation. Sometimes the context in which the word is used suggests a meaning which enables the reader to infer the probable meaning. In that case the dictionary becomes the source for the verification of a theory rather than the authority for formulation of an answer.

The dictionary may give more than one pronunciation for a word. It may be a matter of acceptance of more than one sound for a letter. Is *bade* pronounced with a long *a* or a short *a?* Is *route* pronounced with an *ou* diphthong or with a long double *oo* sound? It may be a matter of placement of the accent. Is the accent on the first or the second syllable in *illustrate?* Is *rebel* pronounced *reb′el* or *re bel′* or can it be either? And what is the difference? The dictionary may not give the answer, but it will furnish the information on which to base the decision.

The dictionary may be used to determine the correct spelling of a word. But as the little boy said, "How can I look up the word to find out how to spell it unless I already know how to spell it?" He was partly right, but he does have clues and with a bit of judgment he can follow his clues to an answer. If he wants to look up the word *match* and if he knows anything at all about initial consonant sounds, he can be fairly certain the word begins with an *m.* If he wants to look up the word *break* and he has learned to distinguish the auditory sound of the *br* cluster at the beginning of the word, he will have his first clue. His next clue may lead him to the *bra* combination and he may find the word *brake* which does not fit the meaning in his immediate situation. This will lead him to another step in search of a word that meets his need. This calls for more than following directions. It calls for the forming of judgments, the making of decisions, and the application of facts to situations.

Sometimes checking the spelling of a word may present a considerable challenge to the child. Let us suppose he has heard the word *ceramics* in his art class. He has used the word. He knows what it means. But he does not know how to spell it. When he has occasion to write it and his teacher tells him to look up the correct spelling, he is faced with a real problem.

First he has to decide, "How does it begin?" It might begin with an *s* or it could begin with a *c*. The only thing to do is to pursue both clues. Now he is acting like a detective. If one clue doesn't solve the mystery, he can always go back and follow up on the other lead.

Suppose he decides to follow the *s clue* first. Then what is the next letter? He reasons that it is probably a vowel because he does not hear a consonant cluster at the beginning of the word. But what vowel? It could be an e as in service or sermon. It could be an *i* as in sir. It could be a *y* as in syrup. It could be a *u* as in surface or surplus. It probably won't be an *a* or an *o*. He follows these leads and fails to find his word. He decides to abandon the *s* clue as a possibility.

Next he decides to try the *c* clue. If the *c* is the correct beginning, what would likely be the next letter? Again he reasons that it would probably be a vowel. The next question is, "Which vowel?" He reasons that it is probably not an *a, o,* or *u* because when *c* is followed by those vowels it usually has a hard sound, as in can, cold, and cut. By the process of elimination he decides the second letter must be either e or *i* or possibly *y* as in cent, city, or *cymbal*. He decides to follow the *c* clue with each of the vowels which present possibilities. He starts with the *ce* not necessarily because he thinks it is the most likely prospect but merely because in alphabetical sequence it comes first. He starts down the words in the dictionary beginning with ce and thinking *r* which is the next sound he hears. And there it is! Ceramics! Mission accomplished! What a thrill! He is a real detective. He has followed the various clues and has solved the mystery. He does not need to go on to the *ci* or the *cy* clue. He has learned how to use the dictionary to find out how to spell a word. Not all words will be that difficult, but when he has accomplished this feat he has become an independent learner.

The student who learns to use the pronunciation key in the dictionary has become an independent learner. This may be of more value to him than learning a diacritical marking system, because different dictionaries use different systems. He may need help at the outset but he must eventually cut the strings and glide on his own.

The student who learns the meanings of the marks which indicate hyphenation and syllabication has acquired a useful tool. The student who learns the meaning and the use of the accent mark through a study of its use in words he already knows how to pronounce is ready to apply it to words which are new to him. The student who learns how to utilize phonetic respellings is applying the phonics he learned earlier in a constructive manner. Now dictionary usage is no longer a classroom task. The dictionary has become a useful tool for the rest of the child's life.

The student who learns to use word origins as given in the dictionary is in a position to understand not only what a word means but how it came to be. He does not have to be a high school student studying Latin to learn that *aqua* means water and appears in such words as aquamarine, aquaplane, and aqueduct. He does not have to be a student of Greek to learn that *arch* comes from a Greek word meaning chief and appears in such words as architect (chief builder) and archway (chief or main way).

REFERENCE BOOKS Almanacs, atlases, encyclopedias, and other itemized materials are sources of information.

Encyclopedias, like dictionaries, are also reference tools. They are a source of needed information. Many of them are arranged in alphabetical order like a dictionary. Others are arranged in topical order with an index volume which provides an alphabetical listing to aid in locating information. In order to use an encyclopedia one must first have a question, a problem, a topic. Once the topic has been identified the child needs the mechanical skills that will guide him toward the location of the information. Mere location of information is not enough. There may be six or eight pages on the life of Thomas Jefferson, but all he wants to know at the moment is the dates of the Jeffersonian administration to enter on the chart of contemporaries he is building in history and literature.

Other references can also include books which might have been originally designed as textbooks. Even though the class may identify a given book on the history of the United States as a text for the course, they may have single copies or small sets of other United States history books available. The difference between these books and the text may be not so much in the design of the books as in the use that is made of them. When the books are used to look up additional information or different points of view, they become reference books.

The child who reads about Magellan in four different textbooks will have more insight than if he had read from only one source. He may find duplication. That may add weight to the facts. He may find additional information. That will add to his total store of knowledge. He may find different authors giving different emphasis to certain events. That may lead to the forming of a personal judgment about what is important. He may find conflicting information. That will lead him to be a discriminating reader. All of these findings will cause him to see the importance of weighing and evaluating everything he reads. Just because it is in print is no proof that it is so. Eventually he must come to the conclusion that ads, propaganda, slanted news stories, and sensational headlines must be read with a critical eye. Critical reading does not necessarily mean finding fault. It may mean evaluating and passing judgment before accepting.

LIBRARY CARD CATALOGUES Libraries are gold mines of information. The card catalogue is the student detective's most effective tool. The learner who establishes an acquaintanceship with the library early in his reading experience is laying for himself a foundation that will make all his school work profitable and all his lifetime learnings fruitful. He needs to know where the library is, what is in it, how to find it, and how to use it. These understandings don't just happen. They must be taught.

Not only must the child know when he needs more information, but he must also know where and how to find it. A sample of direct instruction in the use of the card catalogue at sixth grade level is given in Figure 18.

Using a Card Catalogue

A card catalogue is a kind of index. There are usually three cards made out for every book in a library. Any one of those three cards will tell you where to look for the book and several facts about the book. Study these cards and answer the questions.

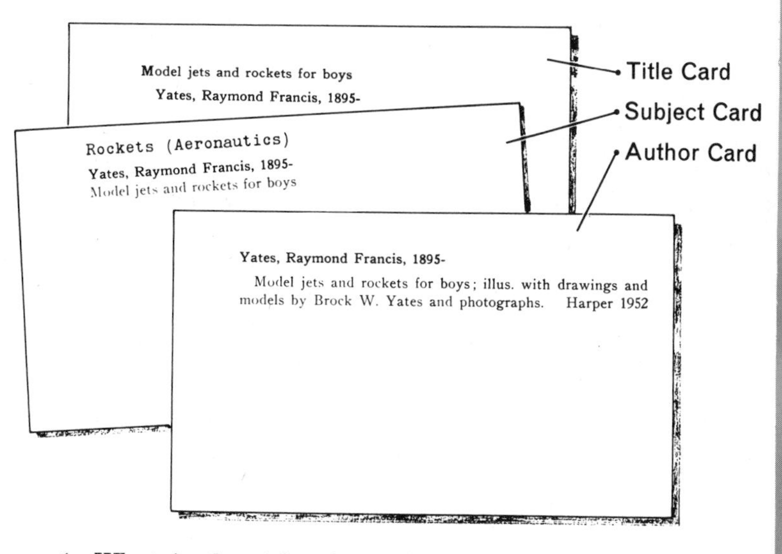

1. What is the title of the book?
2. What is the author's name?
3. What company published the book?
4. What is the date of publication?
5. Who is the illustrator of the book?
6. In what year was the author born?

169

Figure 18. Teaching the use of the card catalogue [Eldonna L. Evertts and Byron H. VanRoekel, *Seven Seas,* Basic Sixth Reader, Strand 1 (The Harper & Row Basic Reading Program), Evanston, Ill., Harper & Row, 1966, p. 169].

FICTION Much information in reference books will be in the form of factual material. A library also contains much fictional material which may have a basic purpose of recreational reading, but may also have a much broader use. A class studying the history of the West may benefit by reading a number of fictional stories based on the history and the people of the early West. Much of the story content may be imaginary and most of the characters may be fictional, but the intent of the author was to help the reader visualize the times, the places, and the people of a period in history. Fictional material can be a basis for forming vivid mental pictures, effective informational backgrounds, and broadened points of view. When used in this manner it, too, becomes reference material.

CURRENT PUBLICATIONS

Things are happening so fast these days that it is becoming increasingly necessary to have information as soon as it has been revealed. Current publications help to keep us abreast of what is happening.

PERIODICALS The monthly or weekly news magazines summarize important happenings. They also provide the reader with interpretations as viewed by the editor or the news analyst. Reading more than one such source of information does more than keep the reader informed. It helps him screen the wheat from the chaff and make his own judgments. Schools have been quick to recognize the value of such reading matter in the classroom.

Weekly news magazines have curricular advantages. They are relevant to what is happening in the world. They stimulate the reader to go beyond the limits of the textbook. They lead him to be open-minded. And most of all, they will always be "fresh." No child will be able to say, "I read that last year." Such reading will lead to a lifetime habit and to a continuation of learning beyond the classroom.

NEWSPAPERS Many teachers are finding that local or national newspapers have a place in the classroom. The children can learn to read the comics for themselves. There are usually puzzles, questions and answers or special columns geared to the younger readers. Starting with these portions of the newspaper the child turns the pages looking for his special interest and at the same time notices other features he will eventually learn to read.

A geography class can collect news stories about various parts of the world. A history class can skim the paper looking for facts related to the period they are studying. A current events class can study the analysis of news by commentators and interpret in terms of their personal ideas of democracy and freedom. The English class may study the editorials for style or content. The potential journalists may analyze the headlines for brevity of statements, slanting of news, and reader appeal. If the practice of reading a newspaper is established early, the reader is not only informed and alert but he is building a reading habit that will carry beyond the textbook and the classroom.

MASS MEDIA

Radio and television not only give us the news as soon as it happens, but in many cases as it happens. This is true when you listen to a political speech, watch an inauguration, or view the launching of a space rocket. These sources may at times seem to circumvent reading, but frequently they actually stimulate more reading.

OTHER SOURCES OF INFORMATION

There are sources of information that do not require reading. They are not to be overlooked, neglected, or discounted. Often the learner can find out what he wants to know simply by asking someone. He may have a personal interview with an older person who can give him details about something that happened long before he was born. He can often find out what he wants to know by observing for himself. He can watch the eggs in the jar as the tadpoles hatch. He doesn't need to read the newspaper for an account of the game he watched in person. He doesn't need to read the geography textbook for a description of Cape Cod if he spent his summer vacation there. But interestingly enough the child who is most interested in hunting up information about tadpoles in the encyclopedia is the one who watched them hatch. The sports fan who is most likely to read what the newspaper has to say about the game is the one who was there. The child most likely to enjoy and understand the description of Cape Cod is the one who has been there.

Other sources of information serve several purposes. (1) They provide background for comprehension. (2) They serve as a source of information for the child with a reading problem. (3) They give information perhaps not available in printed form. (4) They may supplement what has been read. (5) They may stimulate further reading.

STUDY SKILLS USED TO LOCATE INFORMATION IN PRINTED MATTER

It is not enough to know where to find out. This must be followed by knowing how to find out, how to select, how to evaluate, and how to apply what one learns from the vast abundance of sources available in today's world. Written materials use different organizational techniques, different forms of presentation, and different styles of writing. Each of these helps the reader find out and recognize the information he needs.

STUDY SKILLS BASED ON PARTS OF A BOOK

Did you ever see an adult thumb through a book trying to find some point he remembers reading and wants to refer to again? This indicates lack of knowledge of the structure of a book. The parts of the book should be taught to the child in a purposeful manner.

TABLE OF CONTENTS A quick look at the table of contents will tell the reader what is in the book and how it is organized. It serves as a preview. It helps the prospective reader know where he is going, or perhaps whether or not he really wants to go. The 11-year-old boy may read the chapter titles and decide, "This is girl talk. I don't want to read it." He should have a perfect right to lay the book aside and choose another. The 10-year-old researcher may look at the table of contents of a science book and decide that Section Three on Electricity is the one he wants to read. He may turn to it without so much as looking at the rest of the book.

The table of contents can serve as a valuable tool in referring to a book that has already been read. It may help to relocate needed information. It may serve as a good review in a brief and organized form. It may serve as a summary which highlights the main points. The use of a table of contents should begin with the first introduction to a book. The teacher who leads the children to look at the list of stories in the preprimer is helping them see that this book contains six stories. They are on numbered pages and we can quickly find the one we want by turning to the page number indicated. The subject-matter teacher can help children preview a book in the same manner. The geography text will take us to other parts of the world. The places we will visit in our imagination are named in the chapter titles and give us a preview of what we are to study. Yes, tables of contents serve as previews and reviews, summaries, sources of information, and organizers of ideas. The teacher who leads children to use the table of contents is helping them increase their competency in the use of books.

INDEX Some readers fail to distinguish between the purpose of a table of contents and an index. The index is usually in the back of the book and is an alphabetical listing. It is a means of locating all references to a given topic. For example, the science book may mention fungus growths in several different chapters throughout the book but may not have a chapter on the subject. In that case the topic would not appear in the table of contents but would be listed in the index. Such a listing might give several page numbers not necessarily in sequence. This would tell the reader where to look throughout the book. In his reading he might skim quickly over the indicated pages looking for the references to fungus growths, then pause to read carefully the important statements. This would involve skimming to locate and scanning to pick out needed details. It would lead to cursory reading to get the point and careful reading to get the facts. This is a reference use of a textbook.

There are different kinds of indexes. A general index at the back of the book is an alphabetical listing of topics. There may be an index of people mentioned in the text, an index of authors, an index of first lines as in the case of poetry, an index of geographical places, an index of foreign expressions, and so on. Knowing where the index is, what kind it is, and how it will help in locating the material makes it a useful tool. Such use will save time and give satisfaction in the quest for information.

GLOSSARY For the convenience of the reader many books include a glossary. A glossary is usually introduced in a reading textbook as an intermediary step between a picture dictionary and a regular dictionary. In Chapter 4 a sample page from *From Far Away Places* illustrated a glossary at third grade level. The glossary is limited to the words used in the text and the meanings employed in that particular book.

A glossary is usually placed in the back of the book. Attention should be called to it and instruction given as to how to use it so that it may function during the reading of the book. Many textbooks call attention to terms appearing in the glossary by a technique such as underlining. If the text does not make this provision, the teacher should call attention to the glossary and direct the use of it until the understanding is clear and the habit is established. This may need doing over and over again with different materials.

LISTS OF TABLES AND FIGURES In a book which makes liberal use of tables and figures one often finds a list printed in the front. This list is similar to the table of contents. By reading the titles of these tables and figures one can determine what points are presented graphically and on what pages they will be found. This should be called to the attention of the children learning to use a book.

APPENDIX Supplementary or explanatory material is often included in an appendix. It contains information that the writer did not feel should be included in the body of the manuscript, but which adds to or clarifies the text. The reader who previews a book before he reads it will discover the appendix before he starts. He will see this as a source of concise information which he can use to support or summarize his findings. Sometimes when he is using a book as a reference instead of as a text the information he is seeking may be more readily found in the appendix than in the context of the book itself.

FOOTNOTES Frequently an author wants to support his information or his point of view. He may further define a point or cite the source of his facts or the opinion of another in a footnote. What he is really saying when he adds a footnote is, "This is what I mean," or "Don't take my word for it. This is where I got my information," or "I'm not the only one who thinks so. Here are the names of others who agree or disagree with this point of view."

Footnotes also lead the reader down tangent paths which extend, enrich, and broaden his point of view. If he stopped to look up a footnote reference, he might find that the author did not interpret the quoted source in the way that the original author intended. The reader might discover that quoted statements lifted out of context can be made to give different meanings. This kind of discrimination in reading will help to make him a thinker rather than an imitator. This is truly critical reading.

STUDY SKILLS BASED ON SPECIAL FORMS USED IN PRINTED MATTER

The author of an article or a book usually has in mind some key points he wants to make, a basic outline of the ideas he wishes to present. If he is a skillful writer he leaves his reader with some generalizations. Pictures add concreteness. Graphic materials give information and show relationships. Punctuation and other typographical devices give to the reader the emphasis and interpretations he would like to convey through the use of voice and gesture.

PICTURES One of the most common means of adding insight and understanding to the reading material is through the use of pictures. The illustrations in the children's story books clarify the characters, the action, and the concepts. Pictures in most preprimers are used to carry much of the action of the story until the beginner acquires enough vocabulary to depend on the text and the symbols to discover the meanings for himself. Pictures are effectively used in beginning dictionaries. They serve to introduce new vocabulary and to clarify meanings. Pictures serve as background and as motivation.

In content areas pictures serve a vital purpose, that of providing accurate information. The picture in the geography text can do more to clarify the meaning of *plateau* or *prairie* than pages of description. The picture in the mathematics text which shows the children divided into three groups of six each has done far more to clarify the concept of division than can pages of explanation. Pictures are a real source of information. They should be used.

The reader must learn to use the pictures in previewing. He must read the captions under them before he starts to read the text. This will enable him to set his own goals and build his own background for reading. When he learns to do this on his own he is beginning to do for himself what the teacher formerly did when she introduced and motivated the lesson.

GRAPHIC MATERIALS Some concepts can be pictured graphically through the use of maps, charts, diagrams, graphs, tables, and figures.

A *map* is a kind of chart. Most maps are used to represent portions of the earth's surface. Reading a map is a skill which must be learned. An effective way to teach this is to help children construct their own maps before they attempt to read commercial maps. In this way they discover the need for a scale, a legend, and the use of color.

A *chart* is a type of map used to represent information through the use of lines or curves. Charts often show relative sizes, positions, sequences, or comparisons. The child who uses tally marks to represent the number of items counted is beginning the use of chart form to show relationships. This will give him a background for reading similar charts in textbooks, newspapers, and advertisements.

A *diagram* has much in common with a map. The chief difference is that diagrams depend more on straight lines and geometrical designs to show relativity in sizes or significance in ascending or descending order. The class that diagrams their group organization is laying a foundation for reading diagrams in printed materials.

A *graph* is a type of diagram used to represent relationships usually mathematical in nature. When children draw stick figures to represent symbols they are constructing a simple graph. Reading a graph is a skill which needs to be taught if it is to become useful in the interpretation of information.

A *table* is an arrangement of information in systematic order. It is usually presented in column form which is more easily interpreted than the same information itemized in a paragraph. Children make use of this idea when they make lists of animals, toys, cities, and products for example. This technique is widely used in business reports, recipes, and directions. The child who learns to read such tables is increasing not only his speed in acquiring information but also his depth of comprehension through the organization of knowledge.

A *figure* makes use of symbols and reduces information to a form that is more vivid. Figures help clarify concepts, relationships, and facts. Their forms vary with different types of subject matter.

PUNCTUATION AND OTHER TYPOGRAPHICAL DEVICES Punctuation is more than a set of mechanical puzzles designed to confuse the student of the English sentence. Punctuation really takes the place of gestures, pauses, inflection, and voice quality which the writer cannot impart to the reader directly. He uses the period to tell his reader when he has finished an idea. He uses the comma to indicate that he is at a temporary pause but that more is coming. The semicolon indicates a slightly greater break in thought but not quite the finality of a period. The question mark triggers a state of inquiry. The exclamation point indicates a heightened emotional tone such as surprise, fear, excitement, or caution. Quotation marks literally "fence off" what the speaker has to say. Capital letters set the mind to a new approach leading into a new thought at the beginning of the sentence or call attention to more important items such as the name of a person or a special place.

The child who learns to read the punctuation marks as well as the words is reading to comprehend the idea. The teacher who helps him with such interpretation from the very outset is paving the way not only for more effective and meaningful reading, but also for more precise and effective writing. The teacher who calls attention to the punctuation marks in the very first pages of the preprimer is adding both to comprehension and understanding. Preprimers use commas in direct address and in a series. They use periods, exclamation marks, and question marks as terminal signposts. They even introduce direct discourse with quotation marks.

The child will not get this for himself. He may not even notice the commas unless they are called to his attention. He will not know their significance unless he has guidance from the teacher in the interpretation. Without this guidance he may become a word caller instead of a reader. The child who hears punctuation marks called by their correct names, even though no direct attempt is made to teach them and even though he is not asked to use the terms himself, will gradually come to recognize them and use the terms in conversation. When he meets them as a new learning in language they will be familiar concepts in a new setting.

The beginning reader does not learn to utilize punctuation marks by being told to stop at periods, pause at commas, drop his voice at the end of a sentence, and raise it at a question mark. Such instructions are usually meaningless and result in his reading with a rising inflection as if to ask the teacher, "Is this what you mean?" He should be led to discover how the punctuation marks accompany meaning instead of being expected to use them to decipher meaning. The teacher helps him get the meaning, then points out the punctuation marks that accompany different meanings. Through repeated experiences he begins to generalize and apply his knowledge to new situations. Eventually he becomes independent in the application.

Other typographical devices are also used by the author to call attention to certain points he thinks are more important than others, that he wants the reader to be sure to notice and to remember. If he is speaking directly he may say them a little louder or on a higher or lower pitch of his voice; he may pound his fist on the table or repeat himself. In writing these approaches are lost. He must find some other means of calling attention to them. He may underline them, write them in italic or boldface type, or use all capitals to make them stand out.

The reader who learns to utilize the special forms used in printed matter is extending his reading skills. He goes much farther than mere word recognition. He transcends comprehension based on phrases and total sentences. He utilizes the principle of organization. These techniques enable him to reconstruct the whole and form generalizations based on patterns and principles. This kind of skill in reading helps him find out what he wants to know. Using this skill in locating and collecting information calls for more than mere vocalization of words. It involves insight, understanding, and interpretation.

STUDY SKILLS BASED ON STYLE OF WRITING

When one speaks he uses various devices to convey his ideas and his feelings to his listeners. He may use gestures, facial expression, tone of voice, tempo, emphasis, pauses, and phrasing. These devices all add color, meaning, and variety to the spoken word.

Much of this is lost when the message is reduced to the impersonal form of the printed page. The author who wants to relay his ideas and feelings more effectively to his reader has learned to make use of other devices to show what he thinks is important, how he would organize his ideas, and what he would leave with his reader. These include outlines, lists, headings, subheadings, side heads, topic sentences, previews or introductory statements, and summaries. The reader who learns to recognize and utilize these guide posts in written material is an effective reader.

EMPHASIS The author may adapt a style such as a numbered list, an outline, side heads, boldface type, or tabulation. These techniques are attention-getting devices. The skillful reader will pick them up in the previewing stage. He will notice them as he skims over the new material quickly for general impressions. He will also recall them in the review or summary stage.

The author who has five points to make about the importance of conservation may tell you in an introductory paragraph that there are five major methods of conserving natural resources. Then in the presentation he may devote one paragraph to the discussion of each. He may number the paragraphs. He may give each paragraph a title, a heading, a side head written into the margin, or a lead phrase which is printed in italics or in heavier type. These are all devices which enable the reader to pick out the five points by glancing at the format of the paragraphs. The use of emphasis in writing helps the reader become more efficient in getting the point. The teacher who calls attention to such devices is helping the reader establish purposes for reading and become more independent in both gathering and organizing information for more efficient retention and use.

TOPIC SENTENCES Some authors use topic sentences more consistently than others. Take a chapter from a well-written textbook and try reading just the first sentence in each paragraph through a section. Did you get the general idea? Did it make sense? This author has made use of topic sentences to provide the reader with an overview. Now go back and reread one of those first sentences, following with a more careful reading of the rest of the paragraph. Notice that many well-constructed paragraphs state the thesis in the opening sentence. The rest of the sentences are devoted to expanding, explaining, and illustrating the original point.

Identifying the topic sentence can be a useful technique in locating information. The reader who is able to pull out significant statements is getting more from one reading than the student who has read his lesson three times or the one who knows all the words or has found all the answers to fill the blanks.

PREVIEWS AND INTRODUCTORY STATEMENTS Some books entice the reader into the content by providing an introductory statement. The popular magazines have made good use of this technique to win an audience. The "teasers" at the beginning of a story are designed to make you want to read it.

> Life to Mary seemed dull and uninteresting until she spent the summer in a New York office. There she found new meaning in other people's problems and new purpose in life. What she did about it unravels into an exciting tale of adventure as only this author can spin it.

There! Wouldn't you really like to read it now? That was what the publisher intended. He knows how to sell magazines. Some school texts have been slow to capitalize on this idea. They have often presented the stories or the information and left the teacher with the responsibility for providing the incentive for reading. A book which gives the child a reason for reading and whets his appetite has helped to stimulate him to read.

The third chapter in the story of "The Mystery of the Gold Coins" is motivated in this manner:

> Chapter III introduces a new character. As you read you will discover how the boys felt about him. Why do they feel this way?
>
> In this chapter, also you will learn more about the characters of Tom, Allen,

and Louise. Try reading this chapter with a pencil and note paper handy and jot down words which describe the four characters.[1]

Such an introductory statement is planned to give a purpose for reading and to help the child set his goals in terms of meanings.

SUMMARIES The fact that a summary comes at the end of a chapter does not necessarily mean it must be read last. It may be read first as a preview. This is especially true in reading material on a familiar subject. Sometimes the subject is so familiar that the summary is all you may want to read. Sometimes the summary brings out new points and makes you want to go back and read the chapter to see how the author arrived at such a conclusion. Sometimes a summary will be read both first and last. The summary is another device the author uses to organize his ideas and to impress upon his reader the important points.

Developing study skills in finding information, in using parts of a book as locational tools, in recognizing and attending to special forms for organization, and in utilizing devices the author uses to tell in print the things he would have told in person are all ways of increasing comprehension. Comprehension will be increased when the student learns to use study skills which help him locate information, ferret out significant points, and assimilate the author's message. The experienced author utilizes these devices. The wise teacher teaches these devices. The effective reader masters these devices.

[1]Daisy M. Jones and J. Louis Cooper, *From Coins to Kings*, Basic Sixth Reader, Strand 2 (The Harper & Row Basic Reading Program), Evanston, Ill., Harper & Row, 1964, p. 55.

12

READING IN THE CONTENT AREAS

or This Is Not the Same as Reading a Story

Reading has one of its greatest uses in the pursuit of information in the content subjects. When we teach word analysis, speed, skimming, scanning, outlining, and gathering of facts and do not follow through to make the reader an independent and self-directed user of these skills in the content areas, we have not completed the task.

There has been debate over whether story content in reading should be based on children's everyday experiences or on stories of literary merit. Either point of view still leaves some textbooks used for the teaching of reading composed mostly of narrative material. Reading stories will teach children to read stories. Reading word lists will teach them to read word lists. But will either one teach them to expand the specialized skills necessary

for adequate reading and interpretation in the subject-matter areas—science, social studies, arithmetic, and various types of literature?

The reader needs a variety of skills of quite a different nature to read textbooks in other subjects as compared with the ones used in word drills or story reading. Since children vary in their interests and abilities, since skills vary in their applicability, and since content in the various areas differs in form and emphasis, the needs for teaching must vary.

This approach begins on the assumption that we are not all at the same place and do not all have the same needs. This applies to teachers as well as children. Therefore, if some of the suggestions offered in this chapter sound a bit formal or somewhat removed from the theory that you have heard elsewhere, it is because the answers are being presented not in terms of where the ideal teacher is or where all of us "ought to be," but rather in terms of where some of us are now and what steps will help us to move forward in the right direction. Let us start by identifying the problems, then follow with plans for teaching strategies.

IDENTIFYING THE PROBLEMS

Stating platitudes like teaching at the opportune moment, providing for individual differences, and helping each pupil feel successful often leaves the teacher with a feeling of frustration. That's what she thought she had tried to do. The first step is to recognize the problems. Consider these questions:

What is the point of view on which the reading activities are based in the content areas? That is a matter of *grammar*.

What are the kinds of reading the child must learn to do in the content areas? That is a matter of *purpose*.

Who should do the teaching that will help children use reading effectively in subject-matter areas? That is a matter of *responsibility*.

When should the teaching take place? That is a matter of *time*.

What kind of reading matter is needed for such teaching? That is a matter of *materials*.

How should the teaching be done? That is a matter of *method*.

POINT OF VIEW

The answer to the question about the nature of the activities required for successful reading in the content areas is a matter of grammar.

When subject-matter teachers complain, "But he can't read!" what they really mean is, "He can't read the material I am trying to teach with comprehension and understanding." This makes the verb *read* a transitive instead of an intransitive verb. The word *read* used as an intransitive verb, that is, without an object, leads to such statements as, "He can't read," or "He reads well." These are dangerous and inconclusive statements because one might read a story about a skating party with considerable pleasure and understanding and yet completely misunderstand the directions for performing a science experiment.

Read used as a transitive verb leads us to talk in terms of objectives. The child must learn to read historical facts, directions for experiments, story problems, graphic materials, questions, opposing points of view, conflicting information, and lyrical poetry. Now reading becomes specific. The question is no longer, "Can Suzie read?" but rather, "Can she read the biographical information? Can she distinguish fact from fiction?"

Read must be used as a transitive verb.

PURPOSE

The answer to the question about kinds of reading in the content areas is a matter of purpose. We must decide whether we will emphasize mechanics or meaning or whether we can balance the two.

EMPHASIS ON MECHANICS If we examine some of the comments coming from the self-appointed critics, some of the advertised cure-alls, and some of the materials designed for pupil use, we will find that much of the thinking is based on the philosophy of reading which assumes a mechanical process that can be mastered by any child who follows the directions, engages in the drills, and jumps the hurdles on time.

Some people seem to assume that reading is saying the words on the printed page and that the cues are the letters of which the words are composed. In some programs mechanics are so overemphasized that many of the learners develop into robots who know the words but miss the point.

EMPHASIS ON MEANING The swing to an emphasis on meaning was no doubt partially influenced by misinterpretations of some of the research and misquotations of statements by some of the authorities. In the early 1930s we often heard the statement that phonics not only failed to contribute to the child's success in reading but "that it was often a detriment to the getting of meaning." This statement was too often quoted in part and given the interpretation that "phonics was a detriment." Consequently, at one time some educators, some schools, and some programs neglected mechanics and as a result brought down upon our heads the criticism that we were bringing up a generation of children who lacked skills which lead to independence in the reading act.

Then the pendulum started to swing in the opposite direction and, possibly due to the much maligned Johnnies who can't read and to the unfavorable comparisons with the Ivans who supposedly can read, there was a rash of overemphasis on measurable skills which come from drill on techniques. I predict that within the next decade we are due for an about-face in criticism for bringing up a generation of puppets who can pronounce all the words but miss the point.

Carl Lefevre suggests that we must begin with meaning and employ "a synthesis which moves beyond the spelling and word attack and into reading processes at the sentence level even in beginning reading."[1] He criticizes the word-calling practices in the elementary school and makes a plea for the unity of the meaning-bearing pattern.

BALANCING THE PROGRAM What is really needed is a balanced program in the subject-matter areas. This includes maintenance of word recognition skills through a systematic development of special vocabulary needed for effective reading in these areas. Then there is need for follow-through in the organizing, relating, and thinking skills.

To attempt to teach ideas without skills with which to express them is futile. To attempt to teach skills without ideas on which to build them is meaningless and empty. The two phases must be developed side by side.

RESPONSIBILITY

Answering the question about who is going to do the teaching is a matter of responsibility. Should such skills as utilizing subtitles, italics, outlining, topic sentences, summaries, paragraph headings, and picture captions be taught in the reading class or in the subject-matter class? Will the learnings acquired in the reading class carry over to the subject-matter class? Will teaching the needed skills in the subject-matter class involve so much time that the subject itself is neglected?

IN THE SUBJECT-MATTER CLASS For years educators have been saying it is the job of the special subject teacher to develop the skills as needed. They have acted on the theory that the mathematics teacher will teach reading for detail, that the geography teacher will teach map reading, and that the science teacher will teach the reading of formulae. This theory has not yielded results.

As long as the child does his learning all under one teacher there is a good chance that these skills might be taught in their natural setting and that the teacher may help the child make the transfer. But when the work is departmentalized or when the intermediate grade child has a teacher who is subject-matter minded, who does not see the transfer of the skills, or who does not recognize the different skills needed, then the child does not get the help he needs in reading in the content areas.

Furthermore, the teacher who is involved in putting across the ideas in

[1]Carl A. Lefevre, "A Comprehensive Linguistic Approach to Reading," *Elementary English*, October, 1965, pp. 651–659.

the subject-matter area is likely to find her allegiance divided between the ends and the means to the end. She may feel that time taken from the content to clarify the techniques of obtaining the information will distract from the main goal. She may feel that the skills should have been developed elsewhere.

IN THE READING CLASS The crucial issue then revolves around classroom management. If the situation is a self-contained classroom, if the same teacher teaches both the reading skills and the content subject, and if the teacher sees the over-all problems deeply enough to plan the lessons to encompass both types of learning—all these are tremendous "if's"—then the answer has to be, "It really doesn't make much difference where the teaching is done or who is responsible for it."

But since these are such big "if's," it seems more practical to give an answer on the assumption that not all teachers have arrived at that mature state and that most of them need help in getting there. That being the case a practical answer seems to be that the reading skills needed in the content areas are reading learnings rather than science learnings or mathematics learnings or social studies learnings. Therefore, the logical answer is to make them a reading job and teach them in the reading class.

TIME

The question about when the teaching should be done involves scheduling. It is naïve to say that the time to teach a given skill is when it is needed. True as that may be, if the teacher does not recognize the time or the need, nothing happens. The question of time involves both the matter of sequence in the total curriculum and the time in the daily schedule.

IN THE TOTAL CURRICULUM Take first the matter of timing in relation to the total curriculum. Perhaps the intermediate grades represent the period of greatest emphasis. However, in the primary grades background must be built through the establishment of basic skills and the development of positive attitudes toward informational material.

When a child is introduced to subject-matter textbooks which demand a great deal from his reading skills, he must become more independent in the use of reference materials and research tools.

IN THE DAILY SCHEDULE Next take the matter of timing in the daily schedule. Deciding whether to do the teaching in the science class or the reading class has to be answered with, "It all depends." If we depend on teaching the essential interpretative skills in the subject-matter classes, there is grave danger that the job won't get done. It is like asking the teacher to serve two masters. If the emphasis in the mathematics class is put on how to read the problem, the problem itself may never get solved. If the emphasis in the social studies class is put on how to read the map, the facts may never get assembled and organized as a basis for seeing the relationships and solving the related social problem.

Assigning the teaching to the reading class fixes responsibility. Let us assume that the objective is to teach the children how to preview a section in the text to pick out the major points by using paragraph headings or topic sentences. In that particular lesson the skill of locating the points may be more significant than the points located. The application of that skill to reading may need to be pointed out. A lesson with that stated objective is a reading lesson rather than a science lesson and the teacher can direct the class activities toward the accomplishment of the stated purpose without experiencing guilt pangs about the covering of informational material.

MATERIALS

Identifying, selecting, and using materials to teach the skills needed in the reading to be done in the content areas involve the question, "Should such material come from the content area textbook or from a reading textbook?"

Selecting the material for teaching must always be based on the stated purpose for teaching. If the purpose is to teach the skill of previewing, the use of the glossary, outlining, inferring meaning, identifying character traits, or any one of a number of other reading skills needed for success in the content areas, the first requisite is availability of material that illustrates the point. It is easy enough to say that the books are full of examples—but where? The teacher who has to spend time hunting up the material may spend so much time locating the examples that there is no time left to plan, let alone to teach.

IN THE SUBJECT-MATTER TEXTS Let's begin with the problem of selecting material from the textbooks in the content areas where the skills will be applied. Then, shall we use the same text for all children regardless of ability or level of achievement? That sounds illogical on the face of it, yet how many teachers either are expected to do so, or at least think they are expected to do so, and consequently face this frustration day after day?

If the children are not all using the same material, where can we find a suitable variety? By this time the teacher is so bogged down in selection of material and management of the class that she has probably lost sight of the skills which were so neatly and concisely stated in the purposes when she started out to write the lesson plan.

It might be a good idea for the teacher to rewrite some of the content material making adaptations in terms of specific needs of the class. "That's a good idea," you say, "but when will I get it done?" That is a very practical question. It is about as logical to expect the teacher to write the material for teaching as to expect the doctor to make his own hypodermic needles or the carpenter to fashion his own saws and hammers. The professional worker has a right to expect to select his tools but not necessarily to make them.

The above points lead to the logical conclusion that the teaching of the reading skills to be used in reading in the content areas demands materials especially prepared for that purpose. They need to be designed to get the specific job done. When one selects a passage from a social studies textbook to teach the use of topic sentences and then finds to his dismay that the author has not been consistent in the use of this technique, he is only compounding the difficulty. In order to teach the use of topic sentences one needs material in which the point to be taught is stressed. This can be secured best by utilizing materials which have been prepared for that purpose. Once the child has established the skill he can be taught that it is a technique often practiced by good authors, one which he can look for in other reading material, and one which he can recognize and use in his independent reading.

When the teacher depends on the textbooks in the content areas for examples of maps and graphs, directions for experiments, mathematics problems, topical headings, paragraph summaries, and so on, her first job is locating the material. This assumption leaves the busy teacher with the responsibility for identifying the learnings, finding the materials, and providing the variety of books needed. If the teacher is working in a self-contained classroom where all the books related to subject matter areas are available, such an approach becomes possible, but certainly not very convenient. If the work is departmentalized, then inaccessibility of materials is added to the many other problems.

IN THE READING TEXTS In order to put in the hands of the teacher as well as the child the needed materials for effective teaching of reading skills in the content areas it seems sensible to prepare textbooks which will give the guidance and the materials to do the job. Begin with excerpts from books of the kinds of materials to be taught. Use them as examples. Put them in a reading textbook. Write into the text for the children the guides which will help them master the specific skills needed. Show them first what the skills are. Then help them identify the circumstances in which the skills are applicable. Give examples of situations where they will be used. Teach the children how to use them and let them know when they have succeeded.

Finally, the child must read something. Reading must be a matter of communication of an idea. If the objective is to be accomplished, the responsibility must be assumed as a reading job. Specific skills must be pointed out and taught directly. The teaching must be assigned to the reading period. And there is need for specifically prepared materials in order to facilitate the job of teaching the child how to use these reading skills for the reading tasks he must face in the content areas.

That leads to the final question of "How?"

PLANNING THE TEACHING STRATEGIES

The answer to the question about how to teach is a matter of method. The time-worn arguments about transfer of training might be examined here. A skill is transferred to a new situation only when the learner sees the similarities between the learned skills and the situations involved. The teacher who helps the child acquire the skill, apply it to a given situation, and recognize its need in a new situation has led him through the necessary steps to application.

We cannot assume that just because the child can pronounce all the words that he can read and get the author's meaning.

We cannot assume that just because the child can answer the questions at the end of the chapter, particularly if they happen to be all factual questions, that he can interpret the ideas in the light of present day problems.

We cannot assume that just because the child can locate the facts or define the words or follow the directions or quote the opinions of the author that he has recognized the problem and has drawn reasonable conclusions which he can defend in the light of the evidence.

We cannot assume that just because the child can itemize the topics that he can see the relationships and organize the information into cause and effect, into major issues and supporting evidence, and into the sequential patterns of events.

Yes, children must be taught to read a mathematics problem for an analysis of the question to be answered. They must be taught how to read and follow directions. They must be taught how to read factual information for sequence, relationships, and inferences. They must also be taught to select the reading skills needed in each different situation.

Mastery of vocabulary does not guarantee the development of these specific skills. And the development of the skills does not necessarily guarantee their application in the subject-matter areas. It is the job of the reading teacher to follow through and point out the skills, teach the techniques, and show the needed applications. This calls for planned developmental teaching.

MEETING THE NEEDS OF INDIVIDUALS

Now that the materials have been selected, the purposes have been established, the responsibility has been fixed, and the time has been set aside, the next question is, "How shall we go about teaching in order to meet the needs of the various individuals in the class group?"

There are two basic ways to adapt instruction to individual differences. One way is by varying the responses expected from the pupils. This presumes that all are using similar material, but all are not doing the same things with the material. The other way is by varying the material used by different individuals. This presumes that the materials will vary both in content and in level of difficulty.

VARYING THE USE OF MATERIAL The adaptation of instruction to individual differences by varying the use of material involves at least three factors: (1) all members of the class may be pursuing the same topics; (2) all may be using basically the same material, that is, the textbook; (3) different pupils may be doing different things with the same material. When points 1 and 2 pertain, then the question to be answered revolves around point 3, that is, what kinds of different things will the different pupils be doing? Some may be reading the text to organize information. Some may be seeking answers to specific questions. Some may be working with the teacher directly.

VARYING THE LEVEL OF MATERIAL USED The adaptation to individual differences by varying the material involves three different factors: (1) there may be a variety of materials in the classroom; (2) there may be extensive pupil and/or teacher preparation in anticipation of the proposed lesson; (3) the classroom management with different children doing different things takes on a new or different aspect when contrasted with a total class performance on a single topic with uniform materials. When points 1 and 2 pertain and the materials are in readiness, then the question to be answered revolves around point 3, that is, what kinds of organization and what types of activities will be going on in the classroom? Some of the activities will involve small group discussions, identification of problems, collecting of information from various sources, outlining or summarizing information which has been collected, and planning culminating activities designed to share the information with others.

USING A COMMON TEXT EFFECTIVELY

When the entire class is using common source material from a textbook in a content subject such as science or social studies and the teacher wishes to make adaptation to individual differences based on what the children do with the material, the problem becomes one of grouping and differentiation of assignments. The teacher who is facing thirty children must have a practical answer to where they are and what they are doing. If she allowed time for only a five-minute interview with each child, she would have to spend two and a half hours to talk to everyone in her class. Impractical, you say? Of course it is. Then a more practical solution is to give instruction in groups thus meeting the needs of several individuals at one time.

GROUPING There are two extremes in grouping—each individual working alone and the whole class working as a unit. Too often only these alternatives are considered as plans for classroom work, but there is a workable solution between the two poles. When a class is to be divided into groups the immediate question is, "How many groups and how shall the divisions be made?" Let us begin on the assumption that the teacher has never grouped children for work in the content areas and therefore doesn't know how to start.

Frequently the first thought is to divide them into two groups but I'd like to pose the thesis that three groups are easier to manage than two. The abilities of the children in a class can be represented by a line which is a continuum from low to high. If you divide the class in the middle to form two groups, the lower half of the class spreads from very low to average while the upper half spreads from average to very high.

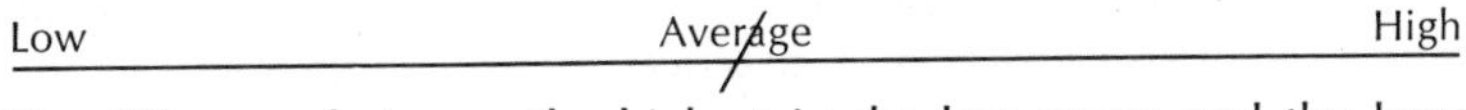

Low ———————— Average ———————— High

The difference between the highest in the low group and the lowest in the high group is a fine distinction. Deciding where to draw the line can be frustrating. Furthermore, when working with the lower half of the class you find yourself doing one of two things either of which is probably wrong. If you teach to the average, the slow ones act as a "dead weight" pulling down the momentum of the class. If you teach to the lower portion of the group, the average pupils are not challenged and are often wasting time waiting for the slow ones to perform. When working with the upper half of the class you will have the same problem. If you teach to the average pupils, the bright ones are bored with the routine work that they already know how to do and are wasting their time and talents. If you teach to the upper portion of the group, the average ones are often discouraged by a pace that is beyond them.

Let's take a look at what happens when you try three groups instead of two. Again start with a class represented by a line which is a continuum from low to high, but divide it into three groups.

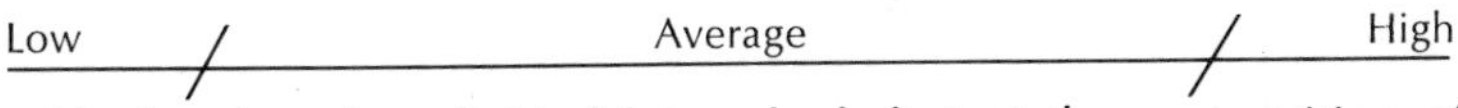

Low ——/—————— Average ——————/—— High

Now with the class thus divided let us look first at the composition of the groups before we consider what they will be doing. The lowest segment of the class is made up of those who often act as a deterrent to the learnings of the average or more capable. They no longer cause the total class to bog down and they are no longer ignored while the rest proceed. The upper segment of the class is made up of those capable pupils who have initiative, self-propulsion, and learning skills that enable them to go ahead with more material and at a faster pace. The middle section may represent as much as half the class. They will be able to do the assignments but will not be discouraged by the more rapid pace of the accelerated learners.

VARYING THE ACTIVITIES Let us look at each group separately to see what they can do with that common source material, the textbook.

Group I represents the more capable members of the class. They can read the basic material independently and compose questions to guide later discussion. They may also research available supplementary materials for additional information.

Group II represents the hypothetical average. They can read the basic text to find answers to planned questions. Such questions may be at the end of the chapter or on the chalk board. The children can outline the facts according to a specific assignment. They can work independently if they know exactly what to do and what is expected of them. True, this may not be the most creative of assignments, but I did not start out to tell you how to develop Utopia. I am trying to help you get started in grouping and differentiation of instruction in a practical classroom situation.

Group III represents the lowest section of the class. It is assumed that the work the rest are doing is beyond the realm of expectation and that some kind of adjustment must be made. The teacher can work with this group while the others are doing their assignments. The material in the textbook can be read "with" them, that is, through guided reading and individual response based on limited abilities. For example, the teacher may start the paragraph saying, "This tells about the products raised in this section of the country. Find the names of fruits and vegetables raised on the truck farms in this region." Perhaps these slower pupils can pick out the names of the products while they might not read the entire paragraph with total comprehension. After compiling a list, the teacher can then move on to the next paragraph which tells how big the farms are, what machinery the farmers need, in what cities they sell their products, etc. At the end of fifteen minutes these slower learners will not have covered the entire assignment and will not have worked independently to get all the answers, but they will have learned something and they will be ready to make a contribution to the total class later.

DIVIDING THE TIME Working with different groups engaged in various activities calls for management. Let us begin on the assumption that we have a period of one hour for this work. The teacher oriented toward subject matter will tend to see the hour as a total period in which to engage the whole class in a discussion. When she approaches her task that way, the teacher is not conducting a learning activity; she is merely checking to see whether or not the pupils have studied their lesson. She finds that the capable ones have done it but could have done much more if they had been challenged. The average ones have plodded along in a superficial manner and have "gotten by." The slow ones did not succeed. This pattern goes on day after day and the end result is A for some, C for others, and F for the stragglers. All that has really happened is to collect evidence to support the grading system. She has adjusted to individual differences by indicating which ones succeeded and which ones failed.

Let's try dividing the period in much the same manner as we divided the group. The first reaction of a teacher who has never divided the time into segments for differentiated instruction is to divide the period into two parts using the first half for supervised study and the second half for "recitation" which amounts to watching them do their "homework" and cutting in half the amount of time available for "checking up" on them. Little more has been accomplished here than in the former plan.

I challenge you, it is easier to manage a class period divided into three segments than into two. Consider about ten or fifteen minutes at the beginning as a planning period. Then allow about twenty or thirty minutes for an acivity period. That leaves about twenty or thirty minutes at the end for a discussion or sharing period. How will those allotments of time be used?

In the planning period indicate to Group I the topic, the sources, and their responsibilities. Indicate to Group II the specific assignment based on pages and questions. Then move with Group III to a secluded section of the room where you can work with them for ten or fifteen minutes in a teaching-learning situation described above.

Now consider the next fifteen or twenty minutes as an activity period. Give at least half of this time to the low group who need careful guidance in order to experience success. Sit down with them in a closed circle where you can have a one-to-one relationship with each individual guiding the reading, putting your finger under the exact place in the book, holding their undivided attention on a topic or an activity they can manage. Leave them with the responsibility for copying a list or illustrating a point in readiness for the total class discussion which is coming later.

This leaves you with ten or fifteen minutes for a check on the other two groups. See if the "middles" are finding answers. Challenge them to add information or interpretations of their own. Don't forget the best group. They may be independent, alert, and capable, but they may also need some guidance to make the best use of their abilities. See if they are utilizing all the supplementary materials available. See if their questions or topics or outlines will help the rest of the class move forward to deeper insights in the discussion which is to follow. Note special contributions which are ready so you will be able to lead the discussion and give them adequate introduction.

This brings us down to the last part of the class period. Now we are ready to call the entire class together for a common discussion on a topic based on a single text. Begin the discussion by letting the slower group make their contribution first. Now they are no longer trying to avoid the teacher and keep her from finding out that they are unprepared. They have something to contribute. They experience success and then are relaxed enough to listen to the contributions of the others and learn from the class discussion. They have literally been "taken off the hook" and freed to learn. For them the recitation period has been changed from one of frustration based on getting caught without the lesson to one of sharing in which they are contributors as well as learners.

Next proceed to the basic assignment pursued by the middle group. They will fill in the details, answer the basic questions, and complete the topic. Some of them may even contribute supplementary information, interpretations, or opinions.

The final step is the challenge presented by the independent workers. They will have additional information from other sources. They will be able to summarize and organize the facts. They will be able to interpret in the light of previous experience or related topics. They will be the ones who will raise issues and discuss implications. They will have an opportunity to use their superior abilities and in so doing will contribute to the learnings of the rest of the class who have already had their turn and are open to these further contributions.

All this leads to planning for the next day, the next week, the next unit. The organization of the class into three groups and the period into three segments will grow with experience. Once the mechanics are well established for both the neophyte teacher and the class there will be variations which will lead to that ultimate goal or Utopia which we mentioned earlier.

Perhaps this goal will involve the more mature approach to adaptation of instruction to individual differences based on differentiated activities when a variety of sources of materials are available. That is the second way we suggested for differentiation. Let us examine its possibilities.

USING A VARIETY OF MATERIALS EFFECTIVELY

Perhaps a more sophisticated approach to the problem of adapting instruction to individual differences in the classroom is that which provides different activities based on different sources and different materials depending on the nature of the subject, the needs of the learners, and the interests of the individuals. Then the problem involves organization of materials in addition to organization of the class and the time.

ORGANIZING THE MATERIALS You may have textbooks on the general subject, more than enough to supply each child, but there may not be more than eight or ten of any one title, and there may be only one copy in some cases such as encyclopedias, special reference books, and perhaps a more adult book or a more primary book which takes care of the needs of the extremes.

How can you get these materials organized so that what you want and need will be ready and available when the time comes? If the materials are not well organized, there can be a great deal of lost time and wasted motion in the classroom not to mention disorder, confusion, argument, and frustration on the part of the learners.

Use capable pupils to spot supplementary materials. About a week or two before you plan to launch a new unit plan a conference with two or three of the more independent workers. Explain to them the topic, the problems, the sources, and the needs. Ask them to go through all available material and spot references which will be useful. They may insert slips of paper in the books marking the pages. They may find it helpful to indicate on the end of each slip the topic which will be found in that place. They may decide to compile a formal bibliography, perhaps even with annotations. With a little experience they can become quite proficient in making such preliminary preparations for the approach to a new unit. This is not only helpful to the rest of the class, but also a constructive use for their time. They are increasing their research skills at the same time they are forwarding the work of the rest of the class.

ORGANIZING THE CLASS Once the materials are ready the next step is to organize the class into a workable group. Help each pupil to see his place in the total picture. Don't let him visualize himself as "just one of the mass" doing, or failing to do, what everyone else is doing. Each one should see something he personally can do to forward the total class project. It may be researching reference material, reading the text, copying in his neat handwriting the report prepared by someone else, lettering the poster, painting the model, sorting the pictures, arranging the bulletin board, drawing the drapes, or making the announcement.

Help each pupil feel responsible for making his contribution. If he knows that everyone else is doing it too and feels that some can do it much better than he, he will tend to relax and let the others do it. But if only he is responsible for seeing that the tickets are ready or the curtains are drawn or the lights are turned out for the movie, then he becomes more concerned not only about the job to be done, but also about the total job of the finished production.

Each child should feel a sense of accomplishment. If he is permitted to tackle something he can do and is helped to succeed, he will enjoy success. Such an experience makes him more willing to tackle another job in the future. Once he gains self-confidence he will keep on moving forward to more advanced tasks and thus will grow. But, if he is put in the position of competition with others who already have a head start on him, he will accept failure as his lot in life and will learn to live with stagnation. This does not encourage either learning or growth. And one doesn't have to be the "smartest" one in the class for some jobs. Sometimes the genius who can write the script couldn't possibly synchronize the production. And sometimes the one who has lots of good ideas may lack the social skills to get everyone else in on the act. From success comes encouragement. From encouragement comes the will to try again. From trying comes growth. From growth comes learning.

ORGANIZING THE ACTIVITIES Once the materials have been organized and the members of the class know what they are to do the activities can be planned in terms of purposes leading to learning. Too often the activities involved in teaching in the subject-matter areas are limited to situations based on an assigning-checking-evaluating point of view instead of on a stimulating-guiding-assimilating-organizing point of view. If the teacher perceives herself as an authority, a taskmaster, a policeman, a judge, and a dispenser of rewards and punishments, then she will assign the lessons, see that the children study, check up on them to see if they did, and keep the records as a basis for measuring out the scores and admitting them to the next higher level in the heavenly kingdom of academic achievement on their way to eventual liberation. On the other hand, if the teacher perceives herself as a guide, a source of help, a leader, an organizer, and an assistant in self-evaluation, then she will stimulate, supply materials, advise, help children keep their own records, and provide some of the know-how which leads to organization and sharing of knowledge on the way to deeper insights and eventual independence in the learning act.

In the reading class the objective may be to teach the children how to read, but not so in the social studies, science, or mathematics class. Here the objective is to get the information. Reading is only one of the ways, albeit a very important and useful way.

On test day the objective may be to measure the effectiveness of skills or the results of learning, but not every day is a test day. There are many more days devoted to learning than to checking up to see what has been learned.

This leads us to an analysis of the types of activities involved in the effective pursuit of material in the content areas. The first thing we must do is to recognize the objectives. Then we can plan for different types of activities to meet the objectives.

PLANNING FOR DIFFERENT TYPES OF ACTIVITIES

Let's take a look at five specific types of activities essential to the pursuit of a topic in a subject-matter area.

ACTIVITIES INVOLVED IN RECOGNIZING BACKGROUND INFORMATION In daily life most of us pursue an activity because something has called it to our attention and we are eager, or at least willing, to pursue it to see what it is all about. It might be that the curriculum outline has mandated the study of magnetism or the law of supply and demand or the Louisiana Purchase or kinds of triangles. The teacher may feel some compulsion to "cover the material" because "it's in the book." That doesn't necessarily give the child any particular reason for pursuing the topic. He might be uninterested and uninformed. That doesn't necessarily mean the topic is obnoxious or repulsive to him. It could mean that it has just never come to his attention and he doesn't know enough about it to be either interested or disinterested. It is the teacher's job to set the stage.

Setting the stage for a new topic helps the child either to recall experiences or to build necessary backgrounds so his approach will be meaningful. This can be done through discussion. The teacher who is planning to launch a study of the expedition of Lewis and Clark may start out by discussing with the children such questions as, "If you were going on a long journey where no one you know had ever been before, what preparation would you need to make? What equipment might you need to take with you? What records would you plan to keep?" The discussion will lead up to the statement that, "These were the problems faced by Lewis and Clark when they left from St. Louis on May 14, 1804, for their historic journey."

The approach can also be made through a survey or inventory. Children sometimes think they know all about a given subject and face it with an attitude of "What? That again!" Perhaps they are approaching the section in the history book which describes the voyages of Columbus. A quick pretest over some of the details may surprise them as well as the teacher about how little they really do know. Such a test does two things. First, it lets the children appraise their own past learnings so that they approach the new not with boredom at having to cover the same old territory, but as a challenge because there is so much they have missed on previous excursions down these same learning paths. This kind of preliminary survey can be either oral or written. It arouses curiosity and opens the door for exploration of familiar territory with a new point of view.

The teacher who knows whether or not background exists, knows what background is relevant, and makes sure the children not only have a suitable background but also know its relevance is the one who is laying the foundation for successful learnings and forward progress.

ACTIVITIES INVOLVED IN IDENTIFYING THE PROBLEM Awareness of the information needed and the possible sources tends to take the children along in the planning stage. This does not mean that the teacher will do no planning ahead of time. She will need to be ready to supply materials, offer suggestions, and guide thinking along constructive avenues avoiding fruitless tangents.

When the children are planning a display for the cafeteria showing nutritional foods and balanced diets, they may have all kinds of questions. They are going to use their information for a campaign on better eating habits and an analysis of food costs. They will raise such questions as:

What foods are needed for a balanced diet? (Health)
Where do these foods come from? (Geography)
How do they get to our local stores? (Transportation)
What determines the cost? (Economics)
Which ones are the best buys? (Economics)
How can nutritional values be conserved? (Chemistry)
How should they be served? (Home economics and etiquette)

As the children seek answers to the questions they will be looking for information to use in their plans rather than for answers to "hand in." The learner who helps identify the problem, decide what information is needed, and where he can find it will not have to be told how much to read and whether to write answers out or not. He is ready to assume that responsibility for his own learning.

ACTIVITIES INVOLVED IN COLLECTING INFORMATION When hunting answers for an assignment is the only activity in the pursuit of a topic, the children become collectors of information for the sake of passing the test. But when the activities involved in collecting the information are a means toward the other activities, then the collecting of information takes on a new aspect.

Reading the textbook is an excellent source of information, but too often it is the only source. Information collected from supplementary material at a more advanced level is a challenge for the capable pupils. Information collected from supplementary material at a lower comprehension level is an adaptation to the lesser abilities of the slower workers without having to insult them. Even the adult frequently reads a child's book if it has the information he wants or needs.

Information can also be collected from other sources. The truly discriminating research worker at any age level is the one who utilizes all sources at his command. A picture may have just the right information about a costume or the size of the covered wagon. Personal interviews often reveal information not available in print. Direct observation sometimes gives more authentic information than a reporter's account. The child who visits the local Red Cross and comes back with statistics about the number and kinds of help rendered is making a contribution. The child who watches for days to find out what happens to the bean sprout is making a more valuable contribution than the one who quotes "what the book says."

Merely collecting the information is not enough. The learner must have some use for the information other than to answer the teacher's questions if he is to make it his own.

ACTIVITIES INVOLVED IN ORGANIZING INFORMATION A list of important points can serve as a summary. Identifying the subpoints to support the main points will change a mere list into an outline. The summary which states briefly just the main points is valuable as a reference. Illustrations often serve as devices for organizing. The findings which conclude a study of the activities of pioneers in the local region lend themselves to an exhibit of real objects. A mural may bring together the facts in pictorial form and organize effectively the information gleaned about a historical period, a certain industry, or the sequential development of farm machinery. A diagram may organize information and summarize it concisely and effectively. This can be used in a study which relates the density of population to the value of the natural resources or which compares rainfall and the length of the growing seasons. Any statistical information can be reduced to graphic form. Any spatial relationship can be reduced to a map or diagram. When information is organized it takes on relative meaning. When the children do the organizing for themselves, they are acquiring a deeper understanding than when they merely read the facts from a textbook. Now they are ready to make use of the facts.

ACTIVITIES INVOLVED IN SHARING INFORMATION Seldom does one gather information merely for the sake of gathering it. Usually when one finds out something he either expects to use it or to impart it to others. When children see as the only end in gathering information the repeating of it on a test, they will either learn it in a rote manner or perhaps not learn it at all. But when they have use for it, they will add new zest and purpose to the activities which precede the sharing. Now the purpose is evident, the problem is identified, the children are collecting the information for a specified use, and the organization is designed to put it in a form to be shared.

The actual sharing of the information demands an interested audience. When the class has worked in smaller groups or committees and not everyone has gathered the same information, there is a ready-made audience in the rest of the class. When a broader audience seems desirable, there is always another class or the rest of the school in an assembly. Perhaps mothers have served this need more often than any other group. The "program" which is planned to show the mothers what we are learning at school is far better use for the children's time than the one which is developed by taking time out from school work to "practice." These sharing activities can take different forms.

Reporting is one of the simplest and most frequently used. This can be an effective use for oral reading or speaking skills. If not overdone or if not allowed to become routine and monotonous, it can be good for both the reporter and the audience.

Explaining an illustration is a form of reporting which capitalizes on the multimedia appeal to an audience. The child who is making a report and has the support of a picture, a model, or an exhibit to take his mind off himself and center it on his message is more self-confident. The audience with something to look at is thinking about the message rather than about the person giving the report and is probably learning more for both reasons.

Discussing the character traits of a hero may be more stimulating than a recital of opinion by one person. Panel discussions in which several have an opportunity to contribute are effective sharing techniques.

Role playing helps to personify ideas. A dramatization gives life to reports. Telling what happened on the Mayflower is one thing; dramatizing the scene of the signing of the Mayflower Compact is quite another. Telling how Tom Sawyer got the fence white washed is matter-of-fact, but dramatizing the scene adds reality and forcefulness to the incident.

Demonstrating while explaining adds reality and forcefulness to a report such as how to make a paper boat.

Even the child who is hesitant to appear before an audience has his part in sharing information if the activities are built around more than mere verbal interchange. There is always need for someone to operate the electrical switches, manipulate the charts, dress the puppets, greet the guests, and keep the properties in order. It takes all kinds of workers to make any production a success.

One kind of responsibility is not necessarily better or more important than another. Perhaps the child with the keen mind and the nimble tongue would be all butter fingers if he had to make the stage properties. Perhaps the child with the beautiful voice would never get all the parts together if there were not a stage manager to see that each incident followed in its right sequence.

The class which engages in these various types of activities to collect, organize, and share information is doing more than following directions and performing assignments. They are laying the groundwork for the use of their reading skills in situations beyond the classroom.

The teacher who is able to identify the crucial problems and to plan teaching strategies to meet the needs of individuals will be making reading in the content subjects serve its intended purpose. She may begin by using a common text for all. She may progress to a variety of activities and eventually to a variety of materials. She will lead children to do more than merely collect information. She will teach them to organize information for use both in school and throughout life.

13

ATTITUDE, INTEREST, AND INDEPENDENCE

or Why Should Johnny Read Anyway?

There have been volumes written about why Johnny *can't* read but very little about why he *doesn't* read. Perhaps the real reason he doesn't read is that he doesn't want to. He sees no reason for it. He doesn't enjoy it. He isn't very successful. And he can see that it serves no useful purpose for him. Oh, yes, it may please his teacher or gratify his mother or earn him an A or keep him from being retained, but other than that, well, he'd rather play baseball or watch TV.

DETERMINING WHY JOHNNY DOESN'T READ

In this case we are talking about the Johnnies who seemingly have near normal ability. Granted there may be mental defectives or children with such severe physical problems that the reading act is next to impossible. There are still plenty of children going through our schools who are branded as nonreaders. To say that they *can't* read is not quite accurate. I can play the piano but I don't. The same might be said for my bridge playing. Consequently when I am asked to play bridge, I usually say, "Oh! I *can't* play bridge." It might be more accurate to say, "I *don't* play bridge." Now I am not willing to admit that I lack the intelligence to learn to play the piano or to learn to play bridge. Therefore, the only logical conclusion I can reach is that I could but haven't bothered to put enough effort into it to learn.

Many children who *can't* read might be better identified as children who *don't* read. They have all the physical facilities—sight, hearing, vocalization, and coordination. They have the mentality as evidenced by their conversations, their handling of life situations, their general good judgment, yet they do not seem to master the reading act. From all indications they seem to be teachable, yet they do not succeed in reading. Why not? Could it be that they react to reading in the same way that I react to bridge? They possess the basic knowledge but they do not have the necessary drive or desire to pursue the learning to the point of skill.

The child who doesn't read well avoids the situation because he doesn't like to show up less capable than his peers. He feels inadequate. He is embarrassed. He soon learns that it is easier to get out of it than to try. There are lots of ways to evade the reading situation. He can be sick when reading time comes. He can drop his book or punch his neighbor or go to the pencil sharpener. He can distract the teacher's attention by talking about something irrelevant. He can pretend he doesn't care. He can bluff and make the teacher and the rest of the class believe he knows when he really doesn't. Each day that he avoids the reading situation he has added to his negative attitude and subtracted from his skill. Eventually he reaches the stage where he not only believes he can't, but he gives up.

ATTEMPTS TO FIX THE BLAME

All right. Then why doesn't Johnny read? We have tried all kinds of excuses. They can be boiled down to about five basic ones. Let's examine them one at a time.

LACK OF ABILITY This is a possibility in terms of physical facilities. He might be blind or deaf. He might be physically impaired to such an extent that normal procedures are impossible. If he lacks the native intelligence, which just might be the case, then perhaps we are asking for the impossible. If you have actually convinced yourself that he really does lack the ability to learn to read then perhaps it would be good judgment to direct your energies elsewhere. That might mean to those who can benefit from your efforts or with Johnny to other channels of communication besides reading. Caution! Don't be too quick to give up and check him off as incapable. And don't refuse to recognize real incapacity if it actually exists. Your decision may be partly determined by what is best for Johnny and partly by what is best for the other twenty-nine Suzies and Sammies in the room with Johnny. But the decision will have to be yours. And you will have to live with it. And Johnny may have to live with your decision the rest of his life.

LACK OF PRACTICE If he lacks skill merely because he does not read enough, how can you get him to practice? It is a platitude to say, "Create a desire." But how? The workbooks, the stores, the advertisements, the textbooks are full of suggestions. There are games that camouflage the drill and make the child think it is fun. There are exercises which hold up scores or grades or stars or promotions as rewards. They may "trick" the child into practicing. These may get results with some children. Then there are highly interesting stories which will intrigue him into reading to find out what happened.

The only way to become proficient at almost any skill is to spend considerable time perfecting it. What 16-year-old has to be made to learn to drive a car? No one ever has to say to him, "Come on now. It's time for your driving lesson. You must pass the test." The 16-year-old in today's society sees a car as a status symbol and learning to drive as a privilege. The motivation is built in. He will listen to the instructions. He will practice. He will ask for more time to practice. He will learn.

The learner who sees a need for reading, who is mature enough to master the necessary skills, who really wants to learn is teachable. The rest is easy. All the teacher has to do in a case like that is to provide him with the time, the materials, the helps, and the opportunities. He will seek out her teaching instead of waiting for her to attract his attention. He will be asking, "How am I doing?" instead of avoiding the teacher.

Once the child decides to learn to read nothing can stop him. Too often he is not allowed to make that decision for himself. The adults in his society have long ago made the decision for him and he is merely the victim of the circumstances of being 6 years old and in a society which demands that he attend school at that stage of his development.

UNSUITABLE METHOD Current research indicates that the teacher is more important than the method. Also what works with some children does not always work with others. The teacher who is familiar with a variety of materials and a variety of methods is equipped to try something else. First she must win the cooperation of the learner. The material may need to be packaged attractively. It may be presented so as to appeal to his sense of competition, his enthusiasm for games, his interest in stories, his desire for information, his need for success. But once he is on the road to learning he will proceed on his own momentum. It is not so much a matter of which is the right method or the best material, but rather what other methods are there to try and which will work for him?

INAPPROPRIATE MATERIALS Lack of success in reading is sometimes blamed on the materials. An attractive package does make a difference. The pictures in the magazines, the flashy blurbs challenging the prospective reader are only bait, but they work. If the child has not learned to read and has seen no need for learning, it may be helpful to bait the trap to get him started. Take a look at the materials of instruction. Are they attractive to this particular Johnny who doesn't want to learn to read?

LACK OF DESIRE If Johnny doesn't want to learn to read perhaps, instead of insisting that he must, it might be better to stop and ask why. His mother doesn't read. His father doesn't read. At home he sees adults using their time to watch TV, play golf, play cards, ride around in a car, gossip, just sit, or wander from one shopping center to another. He does not see reading as a desirable or profitable use of time. He just plain sees no point to it. All the school can do is create for him a situation in which reading is attractive, is possible, is successful, and is within his abilities. It is easy enough to figure out why he doesn't want to read. Putting him through the externally imposed practice exercises in the workbook, on the machine, in the class drill may result in some automatic responses that pass for success and result in scores, but they won't teach him to want to read. If he really wants to read, method will take care of itself.

IDENTIFICATION OF THE REAL DIFFICULTY

Determining the nature of the difficulty is not quite the same as fixing the blame. In the preceding section we implied that the real difficulty is lack of desire and that may grow out of an accumulation of factors such as lack of need, lack of initial success, and negative attitude.

LACK OF NEED The child can often find out what he wants to know without bothering to read. He is more interested in fishing or playing ball or milling around with the gang on the street than he is in reading. To him reading serves no immediate purpose. He may even come from a "privileged" environment where his father has a secretary, his mother leaves him with a maid while she pursues her professional career or her personal pleasures, or where more emphasis is given to the pursuit of material things than to the cultural aspects which accompaany reading. As he learns other ways of satisfying his wants reading becomes more and more remote and his needs for reading become fewer and fewer.

LACK OF INITIAL SUCCESS The child may feel that he tried once and it didn't work and he sees no need to try again. If he did not experience success in his initial attempts at reading, he may assume that he can't and not bother to try thereafter. There are many people who go through life on the assumption that there are certain things they cannot do. The businessman may say, "I can't type a decent letter." What he really is saying is that he tried once and the results were so poor it was easier to hire a secretary than to keep on trying so he didn't bother to try again. Then there is the youngster who cannot swim because his first attempt was based on the theory that you "just push him and let him sink or swim." Perhaps he didn't drown, but he had such a fright that he avoided the water ever after. Many times a child who thinks he can't read is in the same position as the learners described above. His initial attempts were unsuccessful, frustrating, and defeating. He finds it more expedient to avoid the situation than to face the consequences. I can't say that I blame him much. Maybe we were in error when we pushed him in over his head. Maybe we should have held his hand just a bit longer to ensure success with his first steps.

NEGATIVE ATTITUDE The child who assumes from the beginning that he is not going to like reading is the one who approaches learning with a negative attitude. Where did he get such an attitude? Perhaps his mother says in his presence, "I do hope he will get along in school better than I did. I never did like to read much myself." Or perhaps his older brother has said, "Just wait till you start school. The teacher will make you read that stuff whether you want to or not."

It doesn't do much good to fix the blame for Johnny's not reading. It helps a little if you can isolate the difficulty. The only thing that really does any good is to get him to want to and then make it possible for him to experience enough success that he will be encouraged to keep on trying. If you get over those two hurdles the rest will come. Oh, yes, you still will need to work at it and you will need some materials, but most methods and most materials will get results with most children, especially if they want to learn and they have an enthusiastic teacher who wants to help them.

REMEDYING THE SITUATION

Once we get the child started on the road to learning to read then we are ready to help him. The situation can be remedied if we take the right steps in the right order. This includes ensuring readiness, making success possible, and establishing self-direction.

ENSURING READINESS

We have already had a whole chapter on readiness. Here we are talking about a different kind of readiness—a readiness that goes far beyond initial success with mechanics. One might think of himself as ready to learn to walk, ready to stay at school all morning without mother, ready to cross the street alone, ready to drive a car, ready to take a position in industry, ready to perform an operation on a patient, ready to fly a spaceship to the moon. When we use the term readiness in this connotation, we are assuming a background of preparation, knowledge, attitude, and ability for attempting any new experience in life. It must encompass background for reading any new material at any level and an eagerness to approach reading with anticipation of success and satisfaction from now on.

INITIAL SUCCESS The first step is to make sure the learner has success with his first reading experience. Unless the beginner experiences such success he will be like the swimmer who nearly drowned. That first step must yield success if we want him to have the courage to take the next step. If we push him into reading while he is so immature that he must struggle against almost insurmountable obstacles, he will become discouraged and quit. If we encourage him to move forward a step at a time and see his own accomplishments as he goes along, he will be like the little engine who could. At first he will say,

> I think I can! I think I can! I think I can!

then after trying he will say,

> I thought I could! I thought I could! I thought I could!

and finally he will shout with glee,

> I knew I could! I knew I could! I knew I could!

READINESS FOR MATERIAL AT ANY LEVEL This involves more than mastery of mechanics. It involves background of meaningful experience on which to build new concepts expressed in the reading material. Readiness to read a mathematics problem presupposes a concept of number language. Readiness to read history presupposes a concept of time and the relation of the past to the present. Readiness to read about a foreign country presupposes the ability to use words to reconstruct mental images of things not seen. This may depend on comparisons with similar places within the immediate experience. It may depend on pictures. It may depend on person-to-person accounts which lend vividness to the imagery.

Readiness to read a map presupposes experiences with that type of graphic representation and instruction in the interpretation of the key. Readiness to read a chart, a diagram, a table presupposes experiences in reducing statistical or factual information to such a form and an understanding of the author's technique when he presented his material in that form. Readiness to use reference sources independently and effectively presupposes instruction in the use of a table of contents, an index, a dictionary, an encyclopedia, and so on. The learner who is plunged into any of these more advanced reading experiences without preparation may view them as puzzles beyond his comprehension and lay them aside as inconsequential or impossible.

Stimulating interest is perhaps the first step in building this kind of readiness. The lesson which begins with, "For tomorrow take pages 47 to 53," doesn't do much to establish interest. Even the lesson which begins with, "Next we will take up Chapter Nine. Read the chapter and write out the answers to the questions at the end" still leaves the learner cold. His only reason for tackling the assignment is that it has been assigned and he is supposed to earn credit. Stimulating interest calls for a background of concepts and a challenge to read. Let's look at some more positive approaches.

Building on what is already known employs the principles of introduction and motivation discussed in Chapter 10. Let's try a few approaches to illustrate the point. The lesson is a study of the effect of mechanization on life in the South during the reconstruction period. The teacher assumes the children are familiar with factory jobs and with people out of work. She begins with such questions as: "What would be the problems you might face if you were working at a job for which a big new machine had been invented which could do as much work in one day as you have been doing in ten days?" Now the children see the advantages to the plantation owner who can get more work done faster. They see the problem of expense in buying the machinery. They see the problems faced by families whose breadwinners are out of work. They see the problems of retraining workers for new kinds of jobs. This approach builds on what the children already know. It leads to new meanings they are going to face in their reading.

Developing concepts basic to learning becomes a necessary next step if children are to approach the new material in a state of readiness. Another example will further illustrate this point. Suppose the lesson is one in economics, the principle of the division of labor. The children might experiment with a class project such as producing thirty copies of a poetry collection so each child can have a copy. They might first have each member make his own. Then they might try the division of labor and find that the results are better and it is more efficient use of time thus permitting greater specialization of abilities and more satisfaction. This approach will help them understand the economics of a country which has developed assembly lines, mass production, and skilled technicians.

Providing challenge encourages the children to keep on reading. The teacher can provide the children with purpose for reading by raising such questions as: How did the industrial revolution change life in the South? In the North? How has mass production affected the people? the businessmen? the products? Interest thus stimulated will lead to reading for a purpose and toward independence in setting one's own purposes.

MAKING READING POPULAR Reading needs to be seen as something respectable and desirable. It needs to be made the popular thing to do. Sometimes it might be a good idea to have a library period in which everybody reads, even the teacher. The teacher might be having a greater influence on the children if they see her enjoying what she is reading. When a child sees others chuckling over a funny story or crying with a character who loses a favorite pet, he will want to share in the evident enjoyment. Reading is the road to satisfaction.

MAKING SUCCESS POSSIBLE

When the child is convinced that success is possible, he will be ready to give it his best efforts. There are things we can do to help.

ELIMINATING DISTRACTIONS We might try eliminating some of the distractions which get in his way such as the constant demands for his time. As long as there is someone standing by to urge him, "Hurry up and get ready for gym class," or "Put that away now and get out your workbook," he is going to feel pressured and his attention will be distracted from his reading. As long as he reads in a setting where the TV is blaring forth, where those around him are doing activity work in which he would like to participate, where someone is constantly reminding him of the position of his book or his posture, he will have his mind on those distractions instead of on what he is reading. As long as he is distracted by the mechanics, he will miss the point to the story. He needs a setting in which the story is the all-consuming reason for reading.

AVOIDING FRUSTRATIONS Learning is based on successes. The learner just has to begin with something he can do. For each learner there are different levels of learning which lead to success or failure. Frustration is created when the work is pitched at a level for which the child is not prepared and at which he has no hope of success. He will either avoid it altogether or perhaps try a time or two and give up. No learning takes place this way. This is particularly true in reading. After a paragraph or two, if the reader is not getting any meaning, either he will plod on saying the words he knows and skipping the rest in order to complete the assignment or, if he feels he has any choice in the matter, he will merely lay aside the book and quit.

DEVELOPMENTAL INSTRUCTION When the work is pitched at a level for which the teacher has built background and at which the child is able to work, he is teachable. He may need guidance in the form of the development of meanings for special vocabulary. He may need to be told what to look for. He may need help in selecting pertinent points. He may need direction in sensing relationships and in organizing. But he can do it with proper instructional help. This is the way he grows. He needs some experiences of this type in order to keep raising his sights. But if all his reading is of this kind he may come to think of reading as hard work, as a school-imposed chore, as something he must do whether he likes it or not.

DEVELOPMENT OF INDEPENDENCE Independence is established when the work is pitched at the level at which the child can do it without any outside help. Every reader has a right to this feeling of success and freedom which goes with independence. However, if he never reads anything except what is exactly at or below his level, he may grow up to be the adult who reads only the comics or the popular articles geared to about sixth-grade level. Reading instruction must recognize these levels and adapt to the needs and abilities of the child in order to avoid frustration, encourage growth, and develop independence.

If we take the steps just suggested in order to remedy the situation, perhaps we will get Johnny to read. But just wanting to isn't enough. Wanting to play the violin doesn't make one a musician. Wanting to skate doesn't make one an Olympic champion. Merely wanting to read won't make the learner into an accomplished and independent reader. If we are going to help him toward the twin goals of desire and independence, we will have to pave the way, capture his interest, lead him forward one step at a time, and push him from the nest as soon as he is ready for his solo flight.

BALANCE BETWEEN CHALLENGE AND FRUSTRATION The fine point between challenge and frustration is one which the teacher has to "play by ear." If the work is pitched at such a low level that the child is not challenged, there will not be much growth. If the work is pitched at such a high level that he has to keep his energies constantly stretched taut, the tension will eventually snap the strings. There is a fine point in between where he keeps pushing forward on the growing edge without snapping the strings or dulling the blade. Finding that balance makes teaching effective.

It is not the same for any two children in a group. Every child needs two experiences in reading going concurrently. He needs some practice with material so easy that he can read for speed, enjoyment, and the pure fun of reading. If he does only that kind of reading, he will not grow in his skills and insights. He also needs some practice which challenges him to stretch a bit and try new things, new words, new associations, new techniques, new ideas. But, if all of his reading is of that kind, he may see it as a chore and never really enjoy it. He must have some of both every day to provide balance.

RECORD OF ACCOMPLISHMENTS Sometimes a child is accomplishing more than he realizes. Keeping a record over a period of time gives him tangible evidence of his achievements. Children like to keep a record of the books they have read. Any kind of record-keeping device which enables the child to look back and see from whence he has come, how far he has traveled, and where he is now is convincing and encouraging. By the time a child gets to fourth or fifth grade the evidences of growth are not so easy to pinpoint even with objective tests. If he thinks he is just "running in place," he will feel no accomplishment. An analysis of the list will show how many biographies, how many animal stories, how many mystery stories, and so on. Variety on the list will give him a feeling of growth. A lack of variety may help to direct his future efforts. A look at the list of books read last year as compared with those read this year may give some indication of quality of reading, difficulty of material, and growth in ability.

A tape recording of oral reading filed for future use may provide a comparison that is quite convincing. The child who listens to a tape he made several months ago often looks surprised, giggles, and says, "Is that me?" He can see the growth. He doesn't need a report card or a score to know that he is making progress.

ESTABLISHING SELF-DIRECTION

The ultimate aim of the teaching of reading is to make the child a reader. When he reaches the stage where he sees reading as a source of information, as a means of personal satisfaction, as something he can do, as something he wants to do, then he will be independent. He will move on his own momentum. Such independence comes only after a long time, perhaps years of guidance. Complete independence may never be attained by some of the children. We can, however, give them a chance at independence so they can develop tastes, share their interests, and recognize independence when it comes.

SELF-SELECTION AND SELF-PACING Choosing one's own reading material is one of the first principles of independence. When the child is told what to read, he sees it as a duty, a responsibility, an assignment. When he is given a choice of which book he will read, at least he has taken the first step toward independence. When he can be given the choice of whether or not he will read, he is completely independent. When he chooses of his own volition not only what to read, but to read, he is truly an independent reader.

Self-pacing is the next step in independence. How much he reads, the level at which he reads, and how fast he reads are matters for him to decide. If he reads because it is the reading class period, if he reads because this is the library period set aside for that purpose, if he reads because the assignment says for him to put in so much time or cover so many pages, then he is being propelled by an external force. When he can select a book at a level which he believes he can manage, when he can spend as much or as little time with it as he chooses, and when he can relax and enjoy it without having to meet any standards or deadlines, then he is an independent reader impelled by an internal force.

DEVELOPMENT OF TASTES Discrimination in reading is another step toward independence. When a child reads a lesson or a book because the teacher says it will do him good, he is not being allowed to develop his own taste for reading. He needs to sample all kinds of reading material. He needs to find out for himself how it tastes. A bit of this and a taste of that may help to stimulate his appetite. If we are going to improve taste, we need to begin where students are, tantalize them with new materials, and keep them stretching. Sometimes reading a part of a book to them and putting it within reach is a good way to do this.

OPPORTUNITIES FOR SHARING People are by nature gregarious. If we enjoy a thing, we enjoy sharing it with our friends. A child who has truly enjoyed success in reading a story will be eager to share it. And he isn't interested in reading it to someone who will listen to see if he knows all the words. He may take the book home to share with his mother. He may get satisfaction from sharing it with his teacher or classmates. He may get good practice and personal satisfaction by sharing it with the children in another classroom, perhaps a room of children younger than himself. But share it he must.

RECOGNITION OF INDEPENDENCE The child who feels the pride of independence has it multiplied when that independence is recognized by his teacher or his parents or his classmates. The teacher who says, "Go ahead. You don't need me," is giving him the confidence he needs. The mother who says, "Why don't you go to the library this week without me?" is giving him the independence he needs. Once the reader sees himself as one who can read, as one who does read, as one who is independent in the selection of his reading material, he is ready to use his reading skills to become a lifetime learner.

Fixing the blame and identifying the difficulty will not build right attitudes, interest, or independence. The situation is remedied only when we ensure readiness for whatever is to be read, make success possible, and start the child on the road to self-direction.

14

INDEPENDENT ACTIVITIES

or When Children Work Alone

Why should the child work alone at times? This is a crucial question for both the child and the teacher. It is basic to learning to read on the part of the child and to managing the classroom on the part of the teacher. In most classrooms consisting of one teacher and thirty or so children there are times when the child works alone. If the teacher has the children divided into groups for instructional purposes and works with only part of them at a time, obviously the rest must be doing something and doing it without the direct supervision of the teacher.

REASONS FOR INDEPENDENT WORK

Some learning activities and assignments are performed in the classroom and some are performed in other settings such as in the study hall, in the library, or at home. Whenever the child works alone there must be some reason. That reason may perhaps be a practical one, but still inadequate in terms of educational objectives.

INADEQUATE REASONS FOR WORKING ALONE

Sometimes independent work activities are planned because classroom routine leaves time which must be utilized. The teacher must do something. She may not know what is best or she may not be able to manage time to do what she knows. As a result independent activities often serve no educational purpose. They may be scheduled:

- To fill up time.
- To keep children quiet while the teacher works with another group.
- To provide a basis for evaluating and rating the child.
- To produce evidence of work done to send home for inspection.

SOME GOOD REASONS FOR WORKING ALONE

One of the marks of growing up is the ability to provide for oneself and to become independent. This is just as true in reading as in providing for physical or social needs. The reader who becomes independent has matured. And he can't become independent unless he has the opportunity to "try his wings" and see what he can do on his own. There are some valid educational reasons for having the child work independently. Consider these:

- To encourage the child to make decisions about interests, activities, and next steps.
- To provide freedom for him to make choices for himself.
- To allow him to learn to plan and use his own time.
- To permit him to evaluate his own efforts.
- To allow time for thinking, reflecting, deciding, and planning.

ACTIVITIES FOR THE INDEPENDENT WORK PERIOD

Let us examine some of the kinds of activities and materials which will further educational objectives in independent work periods. Some activities may be assigned by the teacher, some may be planned by the group, and some may grow out of individual interests. Some may be routine and some may be creative. Some of the materials may be in the form of supplies and some may be equipment of a more permanent nature.

ORIGIN OF THE ACTIVITIES

ACTIVITIES ASSIGNED BY THE TEACHER Sometimes the activities in which the child engages will be assigned by the teacher. She may direct him to read certain pages, write out answers to certain questions, fill blanks in certain exercises, write his reactions to a story, a description of a scene, a summary of an incident, or a sketch of a character. If the work is directly assigned by the teacher the child must know exactly what he is expected to do and how to go about it; otherwise he will either waste time and effort in getting started or turn out a product that does not conform to expectations. Teacher assignments may occasionally be good use of time, but certainly all activities should not be thus directed because the ultimate goal is initiative and self-direction on the part of the child.

ACTIVITIES PLANNED BY THE CHILDREN Sometimes the children will participate in the planning of the independent activities following the reading of a story. They may decide to make a list of the characters together with traits describing each character. They may decide to look for incidents in the story to support the decisions about character traits. They may divide the task and have different children write about each character. They may assign to some members of the class the job of writing and to others the job of illustrating so they will have the necessary variety of material to present their conclusions. They may decide to dramatize the story. One committee may take on the task of listing the properties needed, another that of planning the settings, another that of listing the characters, and still another that of writing the dialogue.

In these cases the children will have decided what needs to be done, they will have had a part in deciding what each one individually will contribute, and they will have accepted the assignments. They will know what to do and how to do it. They will pass judgment on the acceptability of the completed task. They won't need to be evaluated or graded.

ACTIVITIES INITIATED BY THE INDIVIDUAL Sometimes the activities in the independent period will be initiated by each individual child for himself. When the child gets to the place where he does not have to be told what to do next, he is an independent worker. The child who says to his mother, "There's nothing to do!" or the child who says to his teacher, "I'm done. What must I do now?" is not an independent worker. He is not self-propelled.

The teacher who starts early to help children acquire skills and make decisions about their own work periods is helping them to become self-propelled and independent. The sooner she can cease saying, "Next you may do this," and start asking, "What do you plan to do next?" the better will be her teaching. This can start at an early age. Even first graders can be led to make their own decisions about their independent activities and report what they have accomplished. Let's look at some examples.

On the first day of school the teacher introduces a picture which she can label. It may be a simple line drawing of a cat, thus:

After the children have identified the object and have talked about it she may tell them that she can make the card tell what it is by writing the word *cat* under the picture. Then she is ready to start them on their first step in reading and following directions. As she writes on the chalk board she says, "This says, Draw a ———." and as she comes to the word *cat* she prints it and points to the name under the picture without saying it. Next she asks someone to come and do it. Then the children may be supplied with paper to follow the same directions. So much for the first day. The children have read and followed printed instructions. They have used a picture clue to identify a concrete word.

The next day the teacher may add another card to the picture dictionary. This time it may be a chair, a house, a ball, a bat, or whatever object seems appropriate to the current interest. When one new word card is added daily, in a couple of weeks the picture dictionary will have grown to ten words, each of which can be readily identified by reference to the pictures as needed. Directions can be expanded to include more than one act. For example, the teacher may say, "Today I am going to tell you two things to draw." Then she writes on the chalkboard, "Draw a cat. Draw a horse." The children can follow the directions without help. As the cards in the picture dictionary accumulate it may seem expedient to remove some of the earlier ones to make space for the new ones. Also, some of the earlier ones may become so familiar that reference is no longer necessary. They may be kept in a box or on a table where they can be used if needed.

The picture dictionary idea can also lead to independence in planning activities. Some day the teacher may say, "Here is a sheet of paper. You may draw two things. You decide what they will be. When you get done you may put their names under them or, if you need help, I'll write the names for you." Now when it comes time to share the results of the seatwork it is no longer necessary to check each one to see if the child has followed directions, to see if he has done what the teacher said, to see if his work is right or wrong. Now it is an opportunity for him to tell what he has done. He can show his picture and tell the rest, "I made a cat and a ball."

The picture dictionary can be supplemented by the addition of other concepts to lead the child toward even greater independence and a widely expanded set of activities. Concurrently with the introduction of the labeled pictures the teacher may plan during another time of the day to introduce the color names. The child will probably already be familiar with the colors and the verbal names, but he may not have seen the words in print. The elaborate color chart with the clown holding the balloons in all different colors each one labeled in attractive lettering is spectacular, but it may be confusing to the child who cannot take in so much at one time. A much simpler color chart, developed one step at a time, is more useful as a teaching technique. The teacher begins with a 9x12 sheet of tagboard and a quarter sheet of red construction paper. With the children she discusses the color. The children name things that are red such as an apple, Billy's sweater, Sally's socks, the new book, the rose in the vase, the buttons on the teacher's dress, the crayon in the box, the stripes in the flag, and so on. Then the teacher tells the children that they may need to know the word *red* and how it looks, so she will help them by putting the red paper on the card board and writing the word *red* under it. This can be expanded a color a day to develop a reference for independence. The cards are placed in a conspicuous place where they can be used as a reference.

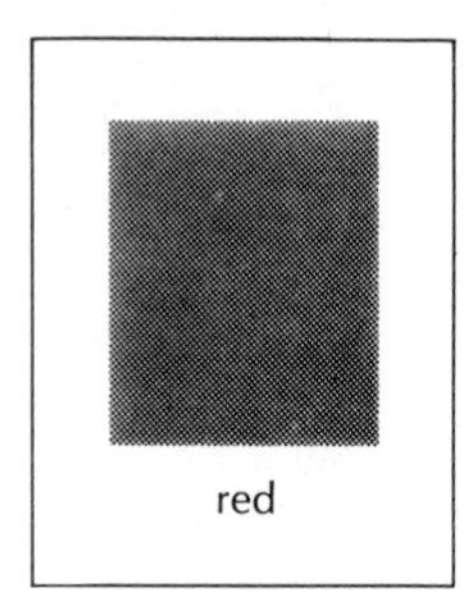

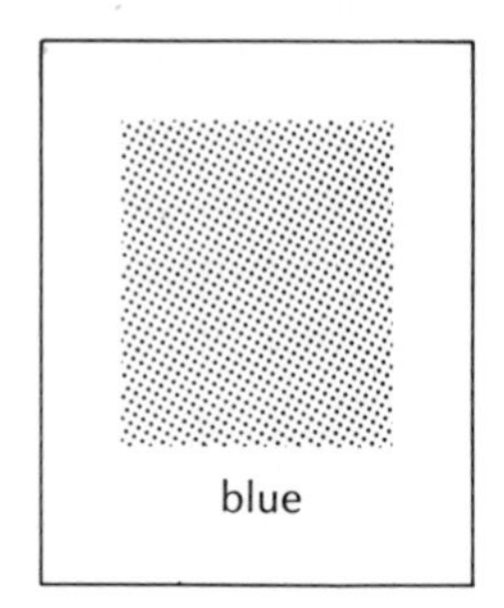

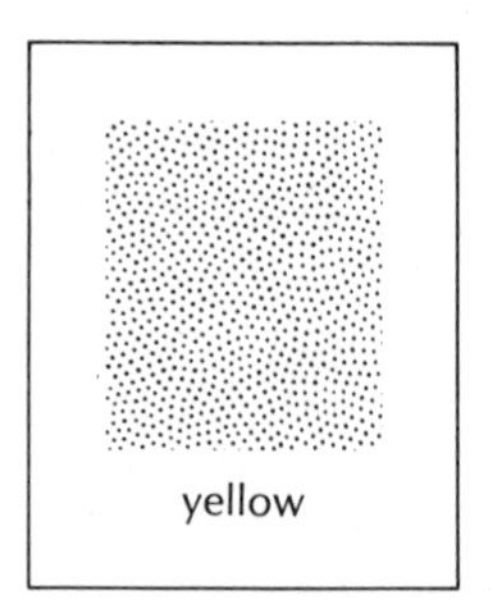

Now the children are ready to expand directions to read, "Draw a house. Color it red." As the teacher writes she says, "This says, Draw a ________. And this says, Color it ________." This type of exercise can be expanded almost indefinitely. As soon as the children know two picture dictionary words and two color words they can be given directions for four different pictures: a blue house, a red house, a blue ball, a red ball. As soon as they know three picture words and three color words they have the background for nine different pictures. Figure this out for yourself. Four of each will make sixteen pictures and five of each will make twenty-five pictures. The expansion multiplies rapidly as pictures and colors are added. If a new picture is added daily for two weeks and a new color is added daily for the same period of time, there will be 100 different possibilities. Now the children are ready to use their initiative in deciding what to draw and how to color it. This calls for creativity and self-propulsion. The sharing period is no longer a check on right and wrong responses, but an opportunity to use language to explain what has been done.

Simultaneously with the development of the picture dictionary and the color chart comes the development of a number chart. In the period set aside for number concepts the teacher may choose to help the children recognize the group of objects, the number symbol, and the word that expresses the idea. The elaborate number chart which has an assortment of brightly colored pictures in various number combinations can be attractive. When the teacher has made it at home and has brought it in as a finished product for display, the children will exclaim over it and and forget about it. They will not see it as a tool for establishing independence but rather as a decorative addition to the room. It is better to keep it simple and build it day by day with the children.

Simple 1-inch squares of colored paper, probably all the same color, make a good number chart. The first lesson may be a discussion of *one*. The teacher may place the square at the top of the 9 x 12 sheet of tagboard. As the children point out one chair, one book, one pencil, one window, one boy, they will get the concept of one as standing for a quantity. Then the teacher may introduce the numeral *1* and the word *one* and add them to the chart. The next day they may do a similar exercise with *two* and build a second card. If they devote ten minutes a day to this type of experience and if a new card is added to the collection daily, in two weeks the number chart will have grown to ten. The cards will look like this:

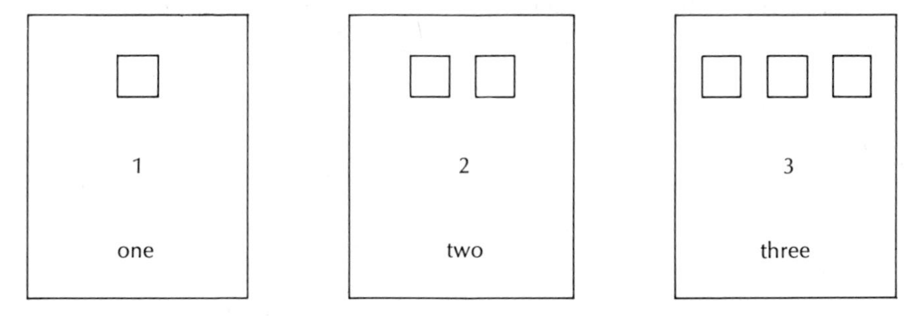

It is now possible to visualize a room where one bulletin board is devoted to a picture dictionary, the space above the chalkboard is devoted to a color chart, and a space in the rear of the room is devoted to a number chart. Whether all this gets done in two weeks or not will depend on the abilities of the children and the planning of the teacher as well as the other demands on their time. But when that much has been developed there will be possibilities for 10 x 10 x 10 different pictures. That makes 1000. The directions on the chalk board can be varied to include such ideas as:

Draw three balls. Color them blue.
Draw two houses. Color them green.

These can be further varied by giving such directions as:

Draw three balls.
Color one ball blue.
Color one ball red.
Color one ball green.

Still further variation can be provided by writing directions to read:

Draw a ball.
Color it red and blue.

Now one ball has two colors on it. This is increasing the complexity of the directions, varying the possibilities, and inviting creativity. Along with these directions the child may be given opportunities to decide for himself what he will draw and how he will color it. In the early stages he may tell the teacher what he wants written beneath his pictures. As soon as he feels the urge he may start labeling his own pictures. And he does not need to ask the teacher, "How do you spell *red?*" because it is on the bulletin board where he can help himself any time. He is now becoming independent and self-propelled.

These examples can be expanded to include other phases of the curriculum. A class studying the farm in social studies may collect pictures of farm animals, farm machinery, farm buildings, and farm products. The names of these objects will be available around the room as the pictures are collected, labeled, and added to the bulletin board or the mural. A child will not need to ask how to spell cow, garden, tractor, milking machine, barn, gate, or fence. They are all in evidence for his use. He is becoming independent. He can use them to label his drawings or to express his ideas in writing.

This type of independence grows as the child matures. As soon as he learns that he can work without being told what to do and how to do it he will start deciding for himself what he wants to do. Now the teacher will need to supply materials and offer encouragement. She will need to listen to his plans and his accomplishments. This is better use for her time than thinking up what to have him do and checking on him to see if he did it right. The child who learns to use the picture dictionary is adding another dimension to his independence. The more mature middle grader who learns to use textbooks in subject matter areas for information, graph paper for illustration of numerical relationships, art media for demonstrations of ideas, and words for the expression of his concepts is growing in independence. He does not need a list of questions to guide him in his independent activities. He does not need prepared material to direct his thinking. All he needs is the raw material, the sources of information, and a busy mind.

ACTIVITIES CREATED INDEPENDENTLY Activities which involve creative expression on the part of the learner are at a higher intellectual level than those directed by the teacher. Art work, writing, and dramatization come in this category.

Art work is an effective means of self-expression. The child who has an idea and wants to develop it by producing a picture, a clay model, a diorama, a mural, or an artistic production in any form is using what he has assimilated through reading to express his interpretation or his reaction to the information or the ideas. He does not need pictures to color or questions to answer. He has learned respect for his own ideas.

Writing is creative if it is unique. The child who wants to express his own ideas in written form is more creative than the one who answers the questions, fills the blanks, or copies from the chalk board. He may transpose a story from narrative form to dialogue form for dramatization. He may write another ending to the story. He may extend the story by having the characters perform some additional feats. He may create some new characters to add to the story or to develop a totally new story. The child who can use his time for creative writing no longer needs someone to tell him what to do and how to do it. All he needs is the material with which to work, a space in which to work, and enough help in answering his questions to keep him going.

Dramatization and reproduction are creative activities for independent work periods. The teacher who can manage a room where children are taking initiative and working without direct supervision is setting a stage for this kind of independent activity. This calls for careful planning with the children. Then, there are always the children who cannot take direction from another child, those who quarrel if they do not have their way, and those who have not yet learned how to work without creating confusion. The teaching skills required to solve these problems involve classroom management rather than reading techniques. The teacher who takes the time to work with the children so they understand how to proceed on their own is saving time in the long run. How will a committee ever learn to function without the teacher patrolling their work unless they are given help in planning, allowed to try, and guided in evaluating their own work to see how it can be improved?

MATERIALS FOR THE INDEPENDENT WORK PERIODS

The child must have something to work with. Many materials are prepared and sold commercially. These are designed to challenge the child and utilize his time. Why are they sold so widely? Because buyers believe they solve a classroom problem. What problem? Do they keep the child "busy" while the teacher works with another group? Do they provide him with practice on needed skills? Do they serve as a check on the effectiveness of teaching and learning? Do they provide a basis for evaluation and grading? Do they provide a link between home and school so the parents will be informed of the child's progress? Do they give the learner independence and self-direction? All these questions are valid and all these reasons are offered at times for the use of such materials.

Prepared materials wisely used make a contribution to learning. However, one must be careful not to become so dependent on ready made materials that the child has no opportunity for using his own ideas in creative expression. Let us examine some of them and their potentialities for learning.

SUPPLIES AND EQUIPMENT Anything which does not have to be prepared specifically for a given assignment comes under the heading of supplies and equipment. This includes blank paper of all kinds, crayons, paints, pencils, scissors, modeling clay, and so on. A child who has an idea usually needs some kind of supplies or equipment to carry it out. Such items should be available and he should know how to secure them.

GAMES AND DRILL DEVICES Many nonconsumable materials are planned for independent use by the child. They can be merely time consuming or they can be instructional when the child is able to follow the directions. Perhaps their greatest value is motivating the repetition of learnings that have been clarified but need reducing to skill and automatic response. The cards, the blocks, or the pictures for the game can be used and placed back in their original container for reuse from time to time. The same child can enjoy a word game with a set of cards over and over again.

Just as the bridge player repeats the performance of dealing, bidding, and taking tricks the child repeats the performance required by the game he is playing. This need not be meaningless repetition. The theory of the game is that each new experience presents new challenges and new learnings. No bridge player says, "I've already played that game." He is always challenged to try his skill again because he expects to meet a new situation, a new combination of cards, and another chance to win or at least to improve his skill. The same is true with games in the classroom. They furnish repeated practice which the learner accepts for the challenge of the game. Such devices do not yield records to be scored or answers to be checked right or wrong. They merely challenge the child to practice for the fun of the game. They yield a by-product in the form of a skill. They may be one legitimate means of inducing the child to practice.

DITTO SHEETS Whether the teacher makes up the master copy of a sheet for duplication to meet the needs of her particular class or accepts a commercial product made up in printed form for use on the school duplicator, she still has the opportunity to select in terms of children's needs. Such materials are flexible in adaptation to individual differences. When correctly used they can be an effective use of both time and materials. Record keeping and efficient filing are essential for good results.

WORKBOOKS Consumable workbook materials have been on the market for about a half a century. Their use has spread widely. Many teachers feel that they are valuable teaching tools. Many children enjoy using them. Most publishers of basic reading programs provide such materials and advocate them as an integral part of the total program. They do not solve all the problems but they do have their values. However, if a workbook is used as a test and if that is the only use that is made of it, then it has questionable value and there may be little learning involved.

The responses in the workbook can be marked when the exercise is finished. If the responses are all right, the child may be rewarded with a star. If they are mostly wrong, both he and the teacher find out that he did not know or could not do it. Sometimes the child may be required to go back and make corrections and sometimes he may not. However, without further instruction the child may not know how to correct his work. Thus the results the second time around may be no better than the first and the additional element of distaste for the whole thing will be added to the negativism toward the exercises themselves.

Of course, the workbook with an accumulation of poorly done pages may furnish some tangible evidence at the end of the grading period or the end of the year if the teacher finds it necessary to face the parent with an explanation of why the child got a low mark or why he is being asked to repeat a grade level assignment. These are questionable uses for workbooks. Perhaps the same amount of time might better have been spent in teaching him how rather than in finding out what was wrong with what he had already done.

A workbook can serve a constructive purpose when it is used as a teaching tool. The new concept will be worked out with the children. This makes sure they know what to do and how to do it. The marks in the workbook may even be made under the supervision of the teacher in the small group. In that case the responses will be right because the teacher working with the children has ensured understanding before the responses are placed on the workbook page in the form of lines or rings or blanks filled or questions answered. The workbook used in this manner does not need to be "graded" by the teacher in a laborious and time-consuming period after school because the responses are right in the first place. The child will have learned how and will have practiced correct responses. This use of the workbook does not solve the seatwork problem, but the experiences suggested above in which the child initiates his own activities can be used to meet that need. The workbook used as a teaching tool can be a valuable asset.

BOOKS FOR INDEPENDENT READING Reading is perhaps one of the most appropriate uses for independent periods. The child who always has a book in his desk which he can pick up is like the adult who always has a magazine or a book on the footstool in the living room to pick up whenever a moment permits time for reading. The reason for teaching reading is so the reader can read. Then what better follow-up activity could accompany the teaching of reading than more reading? The child who has chosen a book at his independent level on a subject that interests him doesn't have to ask, "What shall I do next?" and doesn't have to be reminded by the teacher to "Get busy."

RELATION OF THE INDEPENDENT WORK PERIOD TO THE READING PROGRAM

Sometimes the independent work is done in the classroom under the direct supervision of the teacher. Sometimes it is done at school but in some type of study hall, library, or monitored setting. Sometimes it must be carried home. It should always be used and evaluated.

ASSIGNMENTS

The lesson which ends with an assignment which says, "For tomorrow take the next chapter," provides no motive for reading the next chapter. If the recitation period is devoted to checking up on the children to see if they have read their lesson and have found the answers, then the tendency will be to postpone pursuing the assignment until just before class time the next day so the answers will be "fresh in mind."

The assignment which ends with, "What do you suppose they will do about it? The next chapter tells you," establishes a motive for reading the next chapter. When the enthusiasm is developed and suspense is stimulated, the children will want to find out what happened. Telling them to put away the story now and get out another lesson will only result in their reading the next chapter with the books in their laps to find out what happened. That's good! Perhaps they should use the period immediately following the class period for the assignment rather than postponing it till the next day.

An assignment should be an opportunity to put into practice that which has just been learned or a time to carry forward an experience or an activity which has been started and left for completion independently. When the motive is strong the learner will want to do it right now. He won't want to wait till some other time. The reason for action is there. Satisfying it immediately represents learning and growth.

HOMEWORK

Homework is a type of assignment. Should the child take his books home? This is a question which has been answered in different ways by different teachers. There are reasons for the various answers, some negative and some positive.

NEGATIVE REACTIONS Taking books, especially readers, home will be examined first. To begin with if the books belong to the school instead of to the individual child, there is always the problem of lost or damaged books and financial responsibility. It is easier to keep the books under lock and key than to fix responsibility or to retrieve lost books. Of course, no child ever learned to read or to enjoy reading a book that is locked up in a cupboard. Then, there is the matter of what is done with the book when it goes home. If the child takes his book home and his mother drills him on tomorrow's lesson so he can read without making a mistake when he is called on, then the enthusiasm for the story, the wonder of reading to find out, the eagerness to read on to the end has all been lost and the child sees the reading class as an exercise or a test of his ability to perform. In that case the mother did the teaching and the teacher merely heard the children recite, apparently to pass judgment and keep a record. A clerk could listen for mistakes and keep the record. Clerks command less remuneration than professional teachers.

POSITIVE REACTIONS Taking books home at night might provide sound educational objectives for homework. The children have just finished a book in class. They can take it home to share or to show how well they can read. Or suppose a new technique has just been learned at school and needs some more practice. The child who knows what to do and how to do it just needs some extra practice. He can work on his own and can find the time at home. Perhaps he will need a partner or a listener. The helper at home is not put in the position of teaching him how, but rather of supplying the interested adult attention needed to perfect the skill. The truly independent learner will eventually practice without adult attention, but that may have to await maturity and stronger personal motives for learning.

A homework assignment should never be for the purpose of getting someone else to do the teaching. It should never be for the purpose of figuring out new learnings independently. It should never be for the purpose of testing. It should never be for the purpose of filling up so much time or earning credit for hours spent.

Homework should be for the purpose of putting into practice what has just been learned, for perfecting skills which need additional repetition, for pursuing in greater depth an idea, a concept, or an activity which has been previously planned, motivated, and launched. Viewed in this perspective the task will be something for which the child is ready whether it is pursued at school or at home. He will be able to proceed on his own. He will not be so much concerned about whether it is right or wrong as how he will use it and whether it has value in his own planned activities.

The controversy over homework which has pressured our children into more effort too often suggests a concern about supremacy and standards rather than learning. Some teachers are opposed to homework and thus bring down upon themselves the criticisms of parents who feel that their children should be making greater gains. Some teachers are advocates of homework and bring upon themselves the criticisms of parents who feel that their family recreation, church life, or personal affairs are being imposed upon by such demands. Either answer creates problems.

In my opinion homework should always be made available but should never be made mandatory. No teacher is fully cognizant of the conditions at home. To demand home reading from a child who has no suitable lighting, no place that is quiet, or no time from family obligations is to create for that child a conflict he is unable to resolve. To refuse homework for the child who wants it or whose parents expect it is equally disastrous because the child is frustrated by the conflict between home and school and listens to the criticisms of one for the other. If homework is put in the light of showing the parents what we have accomplished or preparing for supplementary contributions to the class, then it becomes optional, is encouraged, provides for success, recognizes individual differences, and develops initiative. It avoids both of the criticisms cited above. This is not a "sitting-on-the-fence" attitude to evade criticism; it is merely recognition of reality. The wise teacher will face the issue and act accordingly.

CRITERIA FOR EVALUATING INDEPENDENT ACTIVITIES

Then what shall we have the child do when he works by himself? What is good use for time between classes? Is "seatwork" necessary? Can the child work independently? In order to answer these questions and to pass judgment on the kinds of materials used, the kinds of activities planned, and the use of time for independent assignments the teacher needs a set of criteria for evaluation. If each time she plans an assignment or suggests an independent activity she would ask herself the following questions, she would be evaluating the activities in terms of educational objectives:

- Is this effective use for time?
- Is this something the child can do without direct supervision?
- Are the materials ready?
- Are the materials suitable to the task and to the maturity of the learner?
- Is the child interested in pursuing the assignment?
- Will the exercise contribute to his needs?
- Will he be practicing correct responses?
- Does he have freedom of choice in deciding what to do, how to do it, and whether or not to do it?
- Has he been given any responsibility for preparing and planning for the use of his time or his materials?
- Can he check on himself to determine what has been accomplished or to judge the correctness or effectiveness of his work?

Not all independent activities will meet all these criteria. At times the teacher faced with a roomful of children and with the problem of getting all the work done may have to settle for something less than perfection, but if she can answer most of these questions with an affirmative response most of the time, she will be doing for her teaching exactly what we are asking her to do for the children's learning. She will be headed in the right direction. She will be making headway. She will be growing toward more effective use of time and more independence. That is the goal of all teaching and learning.

15

INDIVIDUAL DIFFERENCES

or No Two Alike, They're All Exceptional

There has been a great deal of talk about individual differences but actually very little has been done. Many educators and many technicians believe the advent of the computer, programed instruction, and ungraded classrooms show much promise of bringing the theory into reality.

Why haven't we done much about it? Well, to begin with we are reaping the results of a philosophy based on uniformity, conformity, and mass production. This leads to a certain amount of standardization which may have some advantages such as economy of time and materials when it comes to manufacturing as well as repairing mechanical equipment. There are times when it is advantageous to have human beings standardize certain phases of their behavior such as driving on the right side of the road and making all traffic signs uniform. But when we project this attitude to all phases of man's development we have lost sight of the individual.

We are all exceptional. Think of something you can do especially well. Then you are exceptional. You deviate from the norm in the positive direction. Now think of something you believe you could never do. Who says you couldn't do it? Perhaps it might be more accurate to say you haven't done it and you are not expecting to put the necessary time and effort into it to learn to do it with sufficient skill to make your performance acceptable or comparable with that of others who have succeeded. Then you deviate at the negative end of the scale. Some negative deviation may be real inability and some may be a matter of effort or desire.

There are various kinds of individual differences and various theories as to their causes. Some are positive and some are negative in their relation to school learning. Before the teacher is ready to do something about it she needs to take a careful look. An analysis of an individual or of a typical class group will provide her with background for making decisions about adjustments that can or should be made in the regular classroom and help her decide when special provision should be made for those cases which deviate from the norm to the point where the work of the group can no longer move forward.

CAUSES OF DIFFERENCES OR EXCEPTIONALITY

Was he born that way? Did his experiences make him that way? Can we do anything to develop him into a different kind of person than he now is? These are the questions which have been bothering educators for ages. And the way the teacher answers them will largely determine how she will handle the situation. Whether exceptionality is congenital or developmental is debatable. We are not going to attempt to settle the issue here. However, we might give the teacher a bit of advice about how she will meet it.

HEREDITY

If the teacher really believes the child was born that way, that his heredity has already established the limitations of his learnings, then she will tend to accept him with a fatalistic attitude and merely adjust her teaching to what she views as his potential or his limitations. Heredity does have some effect. There's no denying that. Nature has decreed that living things reproduce their kind. Cats have kittens and oak trees produce acorns which in turn produce more oak trees.

Don't let yourself be trapped, however, into believing that it is all based on heredity and there is nothing you can do about it. Accept the child as he is and keep trying to help him become better. Any gain is reward for the effort. You may be surprised what environment can do.

ENVIRONMENT

Surroundings influence the kind or quality of life that is reproduced. Science has proved that this is true of both plants and animals. The teacher who is fatalistic and accepts what is is not likely to push forward very many frontiers of learning, but the teacher who accepts what is as a challenge to see what she can do with it may help the learner go beyond what nature has seemingly decreed. Cultivating the young plant, feeding the hungry animal, or nourishing the receptive mind have been known to change nature.

If the teacher really believes she can change nature, then she will put forth every effort to create an environment rich with learning opportunities. She will surround the child with concrete objects, engage him in meaningful language experiences, and help him interpret his environment in terms of how he feels, what he thinks, and what it means. The teacher is in command of the environment which the child meets in the schoolroom. Whether it is arid or fertile depends on her.

On the other hand, don't let yourself be trapped into believing that heredity can be ignored. There are limits beyond which we cannot go no matter how hard we try. A child with small parents is not likely to become a giant. A child whose parents either have limited mentality or make little use of what mentality they have is not likely to surpass them too much. This may be due to lack of stimulation from the environment as well as lack of potential, but at least they do seem to go together. Don't try to settle the controversy. Merely recognize the situation as it exists and try to help each child become all that it is possible for him to become. Reading is a good place to start.

KINDS OF DIFFERENCES

No two alike is a truism. If we placed all things, all people, on a scale we would find that they would distribute themselves from one extreme to the other. This is graphically represented on what is commonly known as the normal curve. The great masses will fall in the middle ranges. We tend to see them as all alike. There are fewer cases at the extremes. These we refer to as the exceptions. This is more readily observable in physical factors than in social, intellectual, or emotional characteristics.

The differences which exist are differences of kind as well as of amount. Children come in all sizes. They have varied backgrounds. Some come from homes which are affluent while others have to struggle to pay for necessities. Some have traveled and have experienced contacts with technology, nature, or people while others have led a sheltered life either from lack of opportunity or from overprotection. Some have had all kinds of challenges which stimulate the mind while others may have had little or no contact with learnings related to school activities. Some have matured earlier than others.

Since all children are exceptional in some way and to some extent, consideration must be given to the effect of this exceptionality on school adjustments and especially on learning to read. When we view exceptionality as the extremes at either end of the scale as we move away from the norm, we find that such deviations encompass both the negative which interferes with learning and the positive which may foster accelerated learning or creativity.

Let us take a look at the various kinds of differences and how they affect the child in the process of learning to read.

PHYSICAL DIFFERENCES

DEGREES OF DIFFERENCE Exceptionality based on physical differences in size is rather obvious. Unless a person is a giant or a midget he usually finds himself fitting into the pattern of society without too much difficulty. Other kinds of physical differences which are negative in nature have to do with such handicaps as blindness, deafness, or crippling conditions. Let us not forget the existence of those physical differences which are positive in nature such as special talents, special ability in coordination, perfect voice pitch, keen vision, or unusual sensitivity with any one of the sensory organs. They range along a continuum from

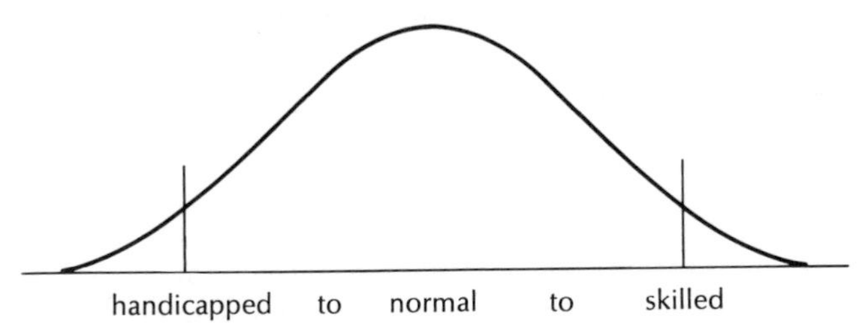

Physical differences show up in gross outer development. Ten children all the same age are obviously not all the same size. These gross differences are accepted without concern unless the deviation is so extreme as to make the child noticeable or to make it difficult for him to fit into his peer group.

EFFECT ON SCHOOL ADJUSTMENT Other physical differences which may affect reading are of greater concern to the teacher. These include vision, hearing, speech disorders, crippling conditions, and general physical development.

Visual difficulty can cause the child to experience frustration in attempting to read the printed page. It may be a mere maturation problem. It is an established fact that the shape of the eyeball makes the young child naturally farsighted. There are evidences that focusing at near point without undue strain comes sometime after the age of 6, perhaps as late as 7 or even 7½. Adjustment to that phase of development may call for a delay in reading small print, for the use of large type, or perhaps for the use of projected material in the early stages.[1]

Obviously, a blind child must make an adjustment to reading differently from the sighted child. It is the child with limited vision who is more likely to concern the teacher in the regular classroom. Some children with limited or faulty vision make the adjustment very well, but they may suffer undue fatigue in the reading act and may seem to have a short attention span or lack of interest. Other children may have difficulty in making the adjustments. They actually do not see accurately or clearly and as a consequence get wrong impressions. The teacher aware of these possibilities will follow up the eye checks to determine whether or not faulty or inadequate vision is the cause of seemingly negative exceptionality in the learning-to-read process.

Hearing, like vision, can be restricted or completely lacking. Again, it is obvious that the deaf child must make adjustments to the reading situation different from those of the child with normal hearing. However, it is the child with limited or impaired hearing who will be more likely to concern the teacher in the regular classroom.

Some children with limited hearing make the adjustment very well. They may learn to watch closely, turn the head to one side to catch the sounds, watch to see what others do, or put forth extra effort. A hearing loss may actually go undetected because the child is able to compensate so well, but he may also suffer undue fatigue from the extra effort he must put into hearing. There is danger that he may be branded as inattentive, listless, or disinterested.

Other children may have more difficulty in making adjustments to hearing impairment. When the hearing impairment is in given frequencies the child may experience difficulty in hearing accurately the sounds or the sequence of sounds. Since the auditory impressions he gets are basic to his reproduction of language, he must hear accurately before he can be expected to speak accurately. The child who misses the endings on words, misses certain basic sounds, or misinterprets what he hears may be the one who talks baby talk, drops endings, runs words together, or makes substitutions such as "wun" for "run," "dist" for "just," and "hep" for "help." He may also be the one who sees no connection between the phonics he is learning and the words he is using in his daily speech. He may be the one

[1]Arthur W. Heilman, *Teaching Reading,* Columbus, Ohio, Merrill, 1961, p. 51.

who experiences difficulty in spelling because what he hears does not correspond with what he sees.

The teacher must be aware of these differences and the ways in which they can affect the reading program. This calls for a careful follow up on the auditory testing in order to determine whether faulty or inadequate hearing is the cause of seemingly negative exceptionality in learning to read.

Speech disorders may be habitual or physical. The child who has all the physical mechanisms for making the sounds and has learned inappropriate speech patterns through imitation may have speech habits which can be corrected. Some of the corrections may come with maturity. The discerning teacher will note these speech deviations and will either work with them individually or refer the child to a specialist. A speech therapist may help with speech habits. The child who has a real speech impairment due to physical differences may need medical attention. Such physical deviations as cleft palate, harelip, or tongue-tie are problems that teaching will not solve.

The teacher who is aware of these possibilities will provide corrective measures before she attempts to force the reading program. If the child talks baby talk because he is mentally immature or has imitated that pattern, then accurate articulation may be a reading readiness exercise for him. If he fails to make some sounds or substitutes others such as *w* for *l* or *r,* then those in turn will give him inaccurate impressions which will affect both reading and spelling. The teacher should either determine the cause or seek professional help in diagnosing each case. She should gear the reading program to the needs for remediation in speech.

Crippling conditions often affect motor coordination, locomotion, and stability. Degrees of crippling vary from extreme to mild to sometimes hardly noticeable. Some crippled children were "born that way" and some are the victims of disease or accident. Whichever is the cause these children have a right to their places in society. Many of them can make reasonably good adjustments and most of them can learn to read although the process may have to be adjusted to their exceptional characteristics. The child who has crippled or paralyzed appendages may have more problems than difficulty in locomotion or handling a book. He may have the additional emotional reactions that cause him to hesitate to use even that ability which he has. He may need more than teaching. He may need the kind of emotional and moral support that comes from an understanding teacher.

The alert teacher will be in communication with the parent for information on the cause and the extent of the condition, will be able to establish rapport with the child to the point where he sees her as his friend and ally in the learning process, and will be informed about the school situation so that she can help make necessary adjustments to meet his special needs.

General physical development is related to reading. Simply being strong enough to meet the demands of a rugged and active day can make a difference. The child who sits passively while others engage in activities may be exhibiting lack of general physical efficiency. This may be due to malnutrition, to a frail body, or to an exhaustive schedule which does not provide him with sufficient rest. The wise teacher will look into this matter and try to identify causal factors. There are things which can be done. Perhaps a visit to the school nurse or the family physician will reveal the cause. Perhaps the awareness of a parent who cares can change the pattern. It just might be that the teacher or the school will need to adjust demands to the abilities of the individual child. There are such adjustments as larger print, corrective glasses, hearing aids, seating arrangements, rest periods, reduced schedules, and lesser demands which make it possible for the child to live within the limitations of his physical disabilities and yet learn what he can.

Exceptional physical development is observable in the child with robust health. He has fine coordination, physical balance, grace, and poise. He always seems to be alert, eager, and ready to learn. This is not all a matter of luck. He may have inherited a strong body, had excellent care, and learned to take responsibility for his own well being. In any case he is the child who will be susceptible to learning because he possesses good eyesight, has acute hearing, feels energetic, and is ready to meet each new challenge, including reading.

The teacher who would lead children to success in reading will be aware of these possibilities, will find out about them, and will do something about them to help the child make the necessary adjustments or else readjust school demands to fall within the abilities of the child.

SOCIOECONOMIC DIFFERENCES

DEGREES OF DIFFERENCE Exceptionality caused by socioeconomic differences has become a major consideration in today's schools. Many educators believe that the child's economic background and the resultant social position he attains has much to do with his self-concept, his mental development, and consequently with his success in learning to read. A drive through any city will reveal the differences in communities. A look at the children in a slum neighborhood as compared to those from well-to-do homes will reveal the differences. It shows in the houses they live in, the clothes they wear, the grooming they maintain, the games they play, and the very expressions on their faces. Socioeconomic differences cannot be lumped into general categories. Being without money is different from having insufficient money. Having an adequate amount is different from being so affluent that ones does not realize the value of material possessions. The children in our classrooms range along a continuum with the extremes being the exceptional ones. They range from the deprived to the affluent.

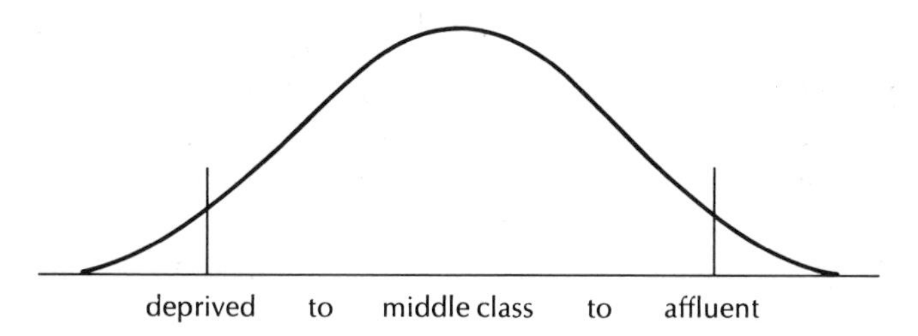

EFFECT ON SCHOOL ADJUSTMENT Adjustment to school is reflected in material things, personal experiences, language development, and social position.

Limited financial means may cause some children to come to school irregularly because they have no shoes or indisposed to learn because they are hungry. Some children may not be able to provide themselves with small learning tools such as crayons, paper, or perhaps books and if these are not furnished the child may find himself unable to participate in the school program. When money is not to be had or when it is unwisely spent, the child may feel inadequate. And, in addition, he may have to listen to constant haranguing about finances till he feels that money or the lack of it is the source of all his other inadequacies.

Effective use of material possessions might be exceptional. The child who comes from a home where books are provided but are not so numerous as to lose their value, where toys are available but are not heaped in unused piles, where clothing is plentiful but not a matter of exhibition, and where the home is adequate and comfortable without being a palatial status symbol is more exceptional than we sometimes realize. He is indeed fortunate to come from a background where thought can be devoted to cultural and mental development. He is going to view reading in a different light from the one who lacks these material possessions or the one who worships them.

The child who comes from a home where money is in short supply but where the parents have pride and management ability may have quite a different reaction. If the mother is skillful at managing the grocery money and keeps the family well fed without comment, he may never know that he is "poor." If the family sets standards that put higher value on reading, pleasant relationships, and wholesome entertainment, the child may grow up hearing old favorite stories, making his own music in family song fests, playing games created with little or no equipment, and learning to respect the dignity of self-sufficiency. He may be the child who is unharmed by economic lacks, not because they do not exist, but because they are not permitted to interfere with the things in life that money cannot buy. He has learned that you don't have to have money to enjoy a sunset, to be clean, to play a game, to read a good story, to carry on a lively conversation, to sing a song, to live on a schedule that provides adequate rest, or to love one another. Fortunate indeed is the child who lives in such a home. He may be better off than the one who comes from an affluent home where status-seeking adults always manage to be in debt no matter how great the income.

Limited personal experiences restrict some children. They may never have been to a zoo or a museum. They may never have ridden on a pony or a train. They may never have seen farm animals. They may never have talked with adults. These limitations may or may not be a result of lack of money. They could stem from lack of interest on the part of the parents or lack of concern because of outside influences. Perhaps there is no one who cares or has the intelligence and initiative to provide experiences for the child.

Language is also a social factor. The child who uses language effectively to communicate with his peers and with his teacher is the child who will be able to recognize language in printed forms. Until the child can be made to feel comfortable with language any attempt to teach him to read will result in rote repetition of sounds rather than in meaningful expression of ideas. Once he has formed that impression of reading he is likely to separate in his mind the whole idea of reading from meaning. He learns it as an exercise in mental gymnastics connected with classroom requirements. Adequacy in oral language must precede reading.

Social differences are perhaps more subtle but nevertheless very real. Children soon become conscious of such differences. They know all too soon who lives in the big house, who has a new dress, who goes to the nicest church, and who gets invited to the birthday parties. As soon as the child establishes his place on the social ladder he begins to accept it as reality and to behave accordingly. Often the one who is timid and seems to have nothing to say really wants very much to say something. As he says less and less his language skills deteriorate instead of developing. This all has its effect on learning to read. The teacher who would help the child build a suitable background for reading may find it helpful to give him a feeling of social acceptance with people. Sometimes the efforts need to be directed toward those who do the excluding rather than toward those who are excluded.

Children from better homes do not necessarily succeed in school just because they happen to live in nice houses. And children from deprived homes do not necessarily fail just because there is a short supply of things money will buy. Social and economic differences do have an effect on learning to read. The wise teacher will be aware and will either alter the conditions or adjust them to the child's advantage.

INTELLECTUAL DIFFERENCES

DEGREES OF DIFFERENCE Exceptionality as revealed by intellectual differences perhaps disturbs teachers more than the others chiefly because traditionally it is the intellectual development of the individual that is considered the goal of education. Many times the child with intellectual ability can succeed in school in spite of physical handicaps, emotional disturbances, or socioeconomic deprivation. In other cases limited intellectuality seems to be aggravated by physical, emotional, and socioeconomic lacks. The matter of which is cause and which is effect is subject to debate. Whichever is the case it is obvious that most classrooms have children whose abilities to use their mentality in such specific skills as learning to read range all the way from retarded to gifted.

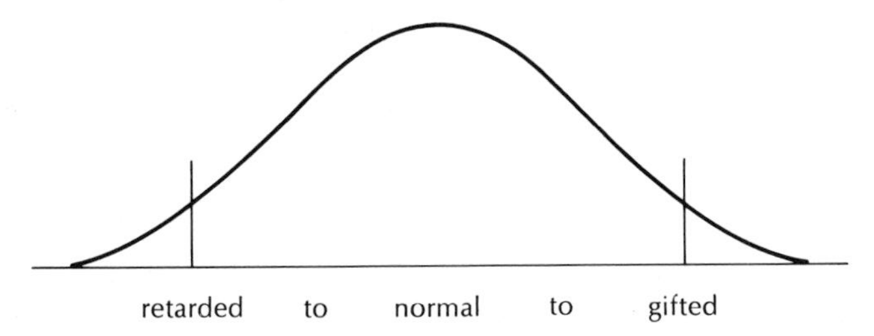

EFFECT ON SCHOOL ADJUSTMENT How the child uses his intelligence to make his adjustments to school expectancies will be influenced by his background of experiences, his level of maturation, his mental ability, his growth pattern, and by the teacher's expectations.

Experiential differences can be more significant than physical, social, or economic differences. The child who has had his attention called to the different kinds of flowers, the different materials from which houses are built, the different colors, sounds, tastes, smells, and feelings is richer for having had such experiences. He will be the one who has the vocabulary to distinguish between a rose, a daisy, a violet, and a lily. To him they won't all be "just flowers." He will know the difference and will be able to express it. He will not be limited to such terms as pretty, nice, bad, and awful. He will be able to express his ideas using much more meaningful and accurate terms such as fragrant, pleasant, interesting, juicy, etc. His ability to use language to express, as well as to perceive, ideas will stand him in good stead when he approaches reading.

Words describe experiences. Experiences give meaning to words. The experiences must come first. Oral speech precedes written form. The teacher can evoke experiences which already exist and utilize them in teaching; otherwise she will need to provide them before she can expect the child to read about them. A city child who has never seen a pony may find reading about one meaningless. A real pony is good. A ride on a pony might be even better. A vicarious experience through a movie or a flat picture is better than no experience.

Maturation comes from experience. To postpone reading waiting for maturity to happen will not help much. The teacher must know how to take inventory of children's backgrounds. Some will have a basis on which to build and may be ready to attack reading at once. Some may lack such backgrounds and to plunge them into the intricacies of reading too soon may be inviting failure and frustration, or at least verbalism without meaning. It may be necessary to build a background of experience before asking them to relate abstract symbols to sounds which express meaning. They may benefit by some trips such as to the supermarket, the airport, the post office, the local park, the variety store, or even to the woods to examine the trees, the flowers, and the birds. Such experiences accompanied by appropriate conversations give meaning to language. Effective experiences may be gained by collecting pictures to identify and name objects, by smelling different odors from flowers, foods, and spices, or by tasting different foods to introduce the terms sweet, sour, peppery, salty, or spicy. The children may benefit from a feeling board on which is mounted a piece of sandpaper, a scrap of velvet, a satin ribbon, a furry object, or a spongy piece of rubber. They may benefit from plunging their hands into soft putty, fluffy cotton, icy cold water, sand, flour, gravel, dry leaves, squishy mud, or thick molasses.

Some children have had limited intellectual stimulation which may not necessarily be the same as lack of mental ability. If the child has had no experiences which help him distinguish between funny and sad, huge and tiny, or tepid and cool, then he may lack these cognitive learnings even though he possesses the potential for achieving them. A child who lacks stimulation cannot be adequately measured by mental tests which presuppose experiences common to most children of his age.

Mental ability does make a difference. Some children are eager, alert, and receptive. Anything you plan or say or do is like sowing seed on fertile soil. They learn readily and expand rapidly. Some are dull, listless, and passive. Anything you plan or do or say is like sowing seed on barren rocks. They appear to look beyond you or around you. They may be sitting quietly with properly folded hands. They may be facing the right direction, but you cannot seem to establish eye-to-eye contact with them. You can tell by the vacant look on their faces that you just are not getting through to them. Whether that difference is native and inborn or a result of experience is beside the point. Any teacher knows readily which children she is communicating with and which ones are just not there.

Limited intellectual capacity is directly related to learning to read. Mental tests for advanced pupils are often based on the assumption that the child can read the directions. Even with the very young child where reading has not yet been taught, many of the same experiences which build background for reading also build background for effective performance on a mental test. Many authorities question the validity of intelligence tests for this very reason. The question might well be asked, "Does lack of intelligence cause inability to read, does lack of experience cause poor results on an intelligence test, or do they merely coexist?" Whatever the answers to this cause-and-effect question there is still evidence to support the theory that they do exist side by side.

Intellectual development varies in degree. Some children are merely slow learners. Given enough time and encouragement they may eventually attain satisfactory levels of performance. Some are mentally retarded. Even with time and encouragement there seems to be a limit to the level at which they can achieve. One of the most difficult tasks for the teacher is distinguishing between the slow learner and the mentally retarded. Once she has decided she still must be constantly alert for indications that her diagnosis could be wrong. To classify the slow learner as mentally retarded may result in setting sights too low and not using all his potential. To classify the mentally retarded as a slow or normal learner may result in undue pressures and in setting sights too high, thus developing frustrations for both the teacher and the child. The best solution is to accept the child as he is, try to keep him challenged, work for growth, and learn to accept his best efforts. This does not mean to give up or adopt a futile attitude. It only means to be positive, watch for growth, and utilize every spark of promise without overtaxing the child.

Measures of intelligence are helpful. They should be used, not to tell the teacher what to expect, but rather to support her observations. And even then the results should be considered only as indicative of the level at which the child is currently performing, not necessarily the level at which he might be capable of performing.

Growth patterns are affected by physical growth, social background, economic opportunity, and experience as well as by intellectual capacity. Some children mature more rapidly than others. Some mature earlier than others. A later maturing child may ultimately reach a higher level than his quicker companion. Physical growth patterns are easy to observe. Intellectual patterns are just as real but not as easily observed and certainly not as readily accepted.

The negative acceleration curve represented in Figure 19 shows the child who starts off with early rapid growth and levels off at an early age. Figure 20 shows the positive acceleration growth curve. It starts slowly but gains momentum as it progresses. Figure 21 shows the more irregular growth pattern typical of many children. It represents spurts of growth and plateaus along the way. Sometimes this curve is negative and sometimes

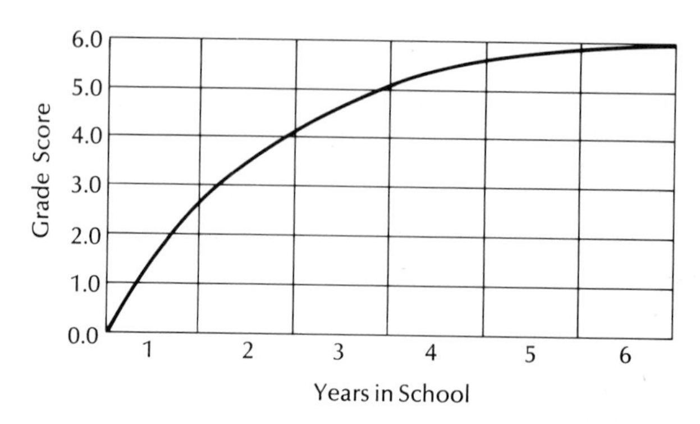

Figure 19. Negative acceleration curve in reading achievement.

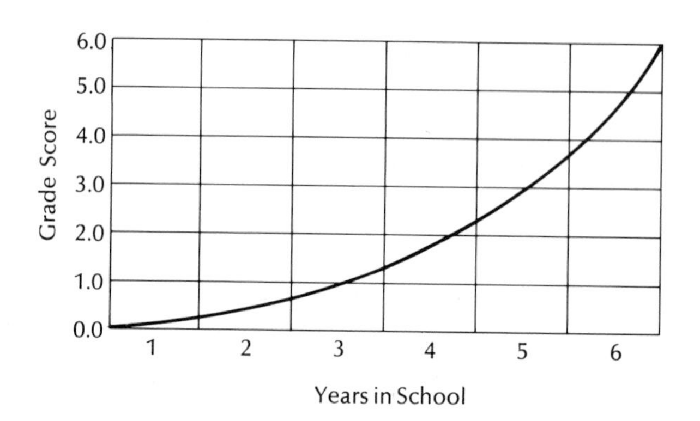

Figure 20. Positive acceleration curve in reading achievement.

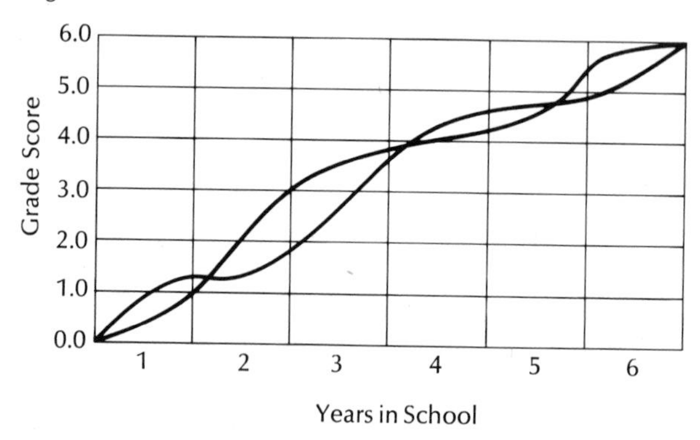

Figure 21. Irregular growth patterns showing spurts and plateaus.

positive depending on what segment is being viewed, but it is constantly upward. Physically it is not likely to go backward when the measurement is in terms of height, but it could go backward in terms of weight. Intellectually some children grow by spurts, go through plateaus when no progress seems apparent for a period of time, and actually seem to regress at times. Every teacher has witnessed the child who seems to know one day and has completely forgotten the next day.

Rates of maturation, patterns of maturation, and levels of maturation all affect learning to read. Adjustments to rates, levels, and patterns can facilitate learning. Rowing with the current gets better results than struggling against the rapids. The teacher who recognizes maturational differences and adjusts to them will get more growth out of the children than the teacher who assumes they all "ought to work up to grade level" and proceeds on the assumption that they shouldn't be in her room unless they can.

Teacher expectancy also seems to influence learning. It is too easy to say that the child is dull, that he has a low IQ, that he just can't learn. Such an approach is defeatism. The teacher who takes this attitude denies an opportunity to learn. There is evidence to support the theory that children perform much in the manner in which the teacher expects them to perform. Rosenthal and Jacobson conducted an experiment in a public elementary school telling teachers that certain children could be expected to be "growth spurters" based on the students' results on the Harvard Test of Inflected Acquisition. In point of fact, the test was nonexistent and those children designated as "spurters" were chosen at random. What Rosenthal and Jacobson hoped to determine by this experiment was the degree (if any) to which changes in teacher expectation produce changes in student achievement.[2] Many believe that the low expectations of the teachers for the children in the slum areas are basic causes of lack of accomplishment in such schools.

EMOTIONAL DIFFERENCES

DEGREES OF DIFFERENCE Exceptionality due to emotional differences is less easily identified but more troublesome when the differences exist as negative deviations. They are more likely to be ignored until they become definite problems. The positive deviations are more likely to go unobserved or be taken for granted. Some individuals become so negative in their reactions to their environment that they are recognized as problems to themselves and to society and become subjects for psychiatric treatment. Such problems do exist among school children and do relate themselves

[2]Robert W. Rosenthal and Lenore Jacobson, *Pygmalion in the Classroom,* New York, Holt, Rinehart and Winston, 1968, chap. 7.

to the problem of teaching of reading. Emotional deviations distribute themselves along the same continuum as other differences.

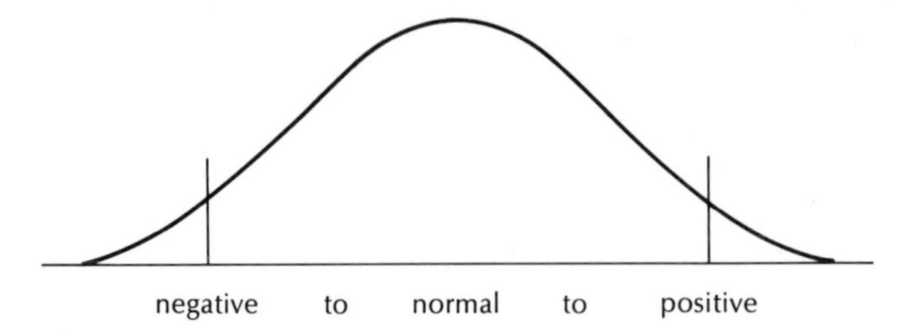

EFFECT ON SCHOOL ADJUSTMENT Emotional differences are even more subtle than social differences. Some children are deprived of emotional satisfactions. Perhaps Johnny has never had any one to cuddle him or tuck him into bed with a good night kiss. Perhaps he has never been made to feel that he is important to someone else. He may accept himself as a "nobody," a person for whom no one cares. Given the same physique, the same opportunity, and the same experiences two different children will react differently. No amount of record keeping, programing, routinizing, or demanding will make them all alike. The sensitive teacher who recognizes this is the one who will be able to establish a person-to-person relationship with each child and challenge him to grow in his own right. These children exhibit behavior which ranges from excessive aggression to extreme regression with the adequate personality between the extremes.

Excessive aggressiveness is revealed in the child who exhibits overt behavior to the point where he disturbs others as well as himself. He may be the one who marks up his classmate's workbook, knocks the reader out of another child's hands, pushes his own materials off his desk onto the floor with a clatter, stamps his feet when trying to read, loses his library book in a mud puddle, or willfully destroys school property. He may feel unequal to the task expected of him and may be expressing his emotional reactions along aggressive lines designed to "get even" or to distract attention from his real problems. He may be an emotional problem rather than a discipline or instructional problem. Restricting him or punishing him may only aggravate the situation. The wise teacher will ask why, then attempt to alleviate the situation instead of reprimanding the child. Perhaps he needs professional help with his personal problems before the reading situation is pressed.

Regressive or withdrawn behavior to the point where the child takes little or no part in classroom activities may be an even more serious problem to the child himself than overaggressiveness. He may think he can't. He may see himself as inadequate and undesirable. He may compensate for his self-imposed inadequacies by withdrawing from the situation. He may have learned long ago that it is easier to keep still than to create a scene. He will be the child who sits quietly, stares out the window, forgets to "watch his place," merely smiles and shakes his head, and never seems to get his work done. He puts forth very little effort and offers no resistance. He may be compensating for a situation outside of school with which he has no power to cope. The teacher who is sensitive to the needs of children will look for causes of such withdrawn behavior and apparent listlessness. She will attempt to provide some success each day no matter how small. She will recognize personal needs and use reading to draw him out instead of as a weapon to drive him farther and farther into his shell.

The adequate personality is the mark of the child who is emotionally mature. He is more approachable than the one who is emotionally immature or unstable. He says, "I think I can" or "I'll try," instead of "I can't." He reaches out his hand for the book, the flashcard, the picture, or the paper instead of hanging his head or putting his hands behind him. He is always ready and willing to help a classmate who is less fortunate. He will be able to succeed without having to excell. He sees his successes as accomplishments rather than as winning. He finds learning a positive experience. Reading will be just one more new experience for him. He will take it in his stride.

In school we tend to become more concerned with negative than with positive deviations from the norm. How different does a child have to be to be considered exceptional? How far does he have to deviate before his differences interfere with progress in the typical classroom in such learnings as reading?

Too often we tend to take for granted the positive deviations from the theoretical normal. If the child can "keep up," can do the assignments, can make good grades, can pass each year we seem to feel that he is "getting along all right." His superior abilities may go unnoticed or unchallenged. The teacher who is aware that there will be as many children who deviate from the norm in a positive direction as in a negative direction will be watching for superior children. They must not only be recognized but they must be challenged. And that does not mean that they must be pressured or exhibited or exploited. Their abilities must be used so that they can develop to their own fullest potential.

ANALYSIS OF DIFFERENCES

The first task of the teacher then is to "learn" the children before she can hope to "teach" them. She must learn about their special abilities, their individual problems, their unique combinations and characteristics, and their present levels of maturity. This applies to individuals as well as to groups.

IN THE INDIVIDUAL

A study of the individual may be based on ability or on the present level of achievement. These are not quite the same.

BASED ON ABILITY For each child the teacher will need to survey to determine his abilities. She can do this by familiarizing herself with his experiential background, his special talents or skills, his special abilities or limitations, and a measure of his intellectual ability.

The IQ alone can be misleading or even useless unless it is accompanied by a bit of good judgment. Two children with similar IQ's as measured by a group intelligence test may be quite dissimilar in most other ways. They may both have IQ's of 110 but one may be 6 years old and the other 8 years old. That immediately indicates an even wider spread in mental age than in chronological age. The extra two years of life may mean a decided difference in experiences. Two children may be the same chronological age but one may have traveled extensively with his parents and the other may have stayed with a nurse while his parents traveled without him. One may have a rich background of readiness for reading and may actually score higher on a formal test even though the less experienced child may have an equal potential which has not been stimulated.

Two children reared in the same family and with what seems to be similar experiences and equal opportunities may differ markedly. One may be a follower and the other a leader. One may have had the experience of being the younger brother with the older one held up as a model. He may never have learned to utilize his experiences in the same manner as his older sibling. All these differences must be noted by a sensitive teacher aware of individuals and their needs.

BASED ON LEVEL OF ACHIEVEMENT When planning the reading program for a child the teacher will need to take into consideration the level of material he can handle independently as well as that which he can manage in an instructional situation. She must also be aware of the level of material which causes frustration for him. With these factors in mind she will be able to avoid discouragement and failure and at the same time guide his reading experiences to provide pleasure and satisfaction as well as challenge and growth.

IN THE TYPICAL CLASS OR GROUP

Class groups need to be studied to determine not only the over-all problem but how each individual fits into the picture.

BASED ON ABILITY When the teacher surveys her class with an eye to expectations based on learning ability, she will tend to categorize them into slow, average, and capable learners. Dangerous as this may be it does have its merits. The very slow ones are easily identified. Similarly the very capable ones stand out. The gray area in between is where the difficulties lie. And drawing the line is almost impossible because somebody is always near the border and it is difficult to decide on which side of the line he belongs. Also children tend to vary within themselves. Perhaps John belongs in the upper group in terms of physical size and manual dexterity, but he may belong in the middle or lower group in terms of reading ability. Making some rough decisions about ability will help the teacher arrive at some expectations based on potential. She may decide that for some children the expectations are somewhat limited, for others they are normal (whatever that is), and for others they are almost boundless.

BASED ON LEVEL OF ACHIEVEMENT When the teacher surveys her class with level of achievement in reading as the factor, she will tend to categorize them into slow, average, and high based on whether they are presently reading below, at, or above the norm for the grade to which they have been assigned. Even then children tend to vary within themselves and also from time to time.

A GUIDE FOR APPRAISAL

Perhaps it will help if the teacher has some guides to structure her subjective judgment and personal observations. This can be done on an individual basis or for class groups.

APPRAISING THE INDIVIDUAL Sometimes we get an impression that a child is unusually capable because he does one thing well. That can lead us to setting unrealistic goals for him. Sometimes the reverse is true. We may see a child who meets a frustrating experience and sheds tears on the first day of school. From that one experience we may jump to the conclusion that he is immature or emotionally unstable and we may be blind to all the other evidences of maturity. Checking against such a list as the one offered in Table 19 guides the thinking of the teacher in seeing the child as a whole. This check list is not designed as a test with a score. It merely gives some tangible answers on which to base judgments. More "yes" answers than "no" answers may reveal something to the teacher. Many "no" answers in one group of questions may give a clue to where a weakness lies and consequently provide some guidance in planning instruction. The teacher who sees each child in this manner has analyzed the situation in relation to the problem.

Table 19. A SUGGESTED CHECK LIST FOR APPRAISING THE BACKGROUNDS OF INDIVIDUALS WITHIN A CLASS GROUP

Name ______________________________ Date __________

Date of birth ______________________________ Age __________

Directions: For each question below indicate "yes" or "no" as a basis for judging abilities or level of maturity.

Experiential Background	*No*	*Yes*
Has he been to school previously? (Nursery or Kg.)	______	______
Does he come to school alone, without adult guidance?	______	______
Has he been to a store alone to make a purchase?	______	______
Has he had the responsibility for the care of a pet?	______	______
Has he ridden on paid public transportation alone?	______	______
Does he assume responsibility for his own clothing?	______	______
Does he know where his possessions are kept?	______	______
Does he put materials away when he finishes with them?	______	______
Has he been to a zoo or a museum?	______	______
Has he mailed a letter or package at the post office?	______	______
Does he have his own banking or savings account?	______	______
Does he have a personal allowance to manage?	______	______
Background of Special Talents or Skills	*No*	*Yes*
Does he sing? Alone? In tune?	______	______
Does he play a musical instrument?	______	______
Does he express himself well with art media?	______	______
Does he exhibit grace and skill in body movement?	______	______
Is he adept at physical feats such as running, skipping, hopping, jumping, climbing, etc?	______	______
Special Disabilities or Limitations	*No*	*Yes*
Is his body free from deformities or abnormalities?	______	______
Does he have full use of all his organs of locomotion and manipulation?	______	______
Does he hear accurately and well?	______	______
Is his vision normal?	______	______
Is his speech free from impediment?	______	______
Are his speech habits socially acceptable?	______	______
Does he have general good health?	______	______
Intellectual Appraisal	*No*	*Yes*
Does a measure with an intelligence test indicate ability at least normal or above?	______	______
Does he show good judgment in meeting new situations and making decisions on his own?	______	______
Is he reasonably independent in his daily responsibilities commensurate with his age?	______	______
Does he show self-confidence in assuming responsibility for his own acts and his own time?	______	______
Is he willing to tackle new situations such as playing new games, going new places, and meeting new people?	______	______

APPRAISING THE CLASS GROUP Caution must be exercised lest the teacher fall into the rut of thinking of herself as a teacher of third grade, of slow learners, or even of bright children. The teacher who sees her teaching responsibilities as generalities to which most or all of the children conform is in grave danger of missing the individual. In a classroom where children are placed in groups of twenty-five or thirty, working with each child individually becomes impractical, if not impossible. Yet treating them all alike, having them all do the same things at the same time and at the same rate, and expecting the same results from all of them is equally impractical.

Comparing achievement with level of expectation will help the teacher see each child as an individual within the total group. When the teacher distributes the class on a simple scattergram similar to the one shown in Figure 22, she can see similarities and identify those children who might benefit by working together temporarily.

Achievement Level in Reading	Ability or Level of Expectation		
	Slow	Average	Capable
High	Betty	Paul Sammy	Sara Tom Edith Gregg
Average	Alan Mary	Pamela Ann	Harry
Slow	Ruth Bobby David	Frank	Martha

Figure 22. Analysis of achievement versus capacity.

Sara, Tom, Edith, Gregg, Harry, and Martha all have high IQ's as measured by the group intelligence test, but they certainly are not alike and cannot all be put in the same group and treated to the same instructional program. The first four seem to have considerable ability and seem to be doing quite well in reading. The chief danger for them is that they will not be allowed to use their extra ability because they are permitted to go along with average work and are unchallenged. The question here is not, "Are they up to norm?" but rather, "Are they growing at a pace commensurate with their abilities?"

Now Harry is a different problem. He seems to have plenty of ability. But he is plodding along at an average pace in reading. Perhaps he is not aware that he could do more. Then perhaps that just might be all right for him. Possibly he is a musician or a junior business executive and he hurries away from school to spend time with whatever it is that interests him. Must he give up these special interests in order to excell in academic work? It just might be all right for Harry with his keen mind to settle for ordinary school work and bend his efforts toward the genius he may someday become in his special field.

Martha is still a different problem. She seems to have exceptional ability, but she is not producing even at the mythical average in reading. Why? Does she have a physical problem such as hearing, vision, speech, or locomotion? Does she have a personal problem stemming from economic deprivation and social inadequacy? Perhaps she is learning more than she is exhibiting. She needs further study.

Now Betty, Alan, Mary, Ruth, Bobby, and David seem to have somewhat limited ability, at least as indicated by the group mental test, but the scores on the reading test do not coincide with this expectation. Perhaps Ruth, Bobby, and David are limited in intelligence. It just might be that they are doing all they can. They may fit that descriptive phrase, "working up to capacity." The first question to ask is, "How much have I a right to expect from them?" The next question is, "Are they growing?" If so, perhaps that is satisfactory until there is evidence that there is more ability than tests have shown to date.

But Alan and Mary are different. And Betty is still more different. Theoretically it seems as if they are achieving more than we have any right to expect. Why? Perhaps the mental test has underevaluated their abilities. It might be worth the effort to retest them. The teacher's observations and judgments are worth considering. If their abilities have been underestimated, they may be moved to the right into one of the other boxes. If their abilities still show limited capacity, take a look at their chronological ages. The very fact that they have lived an extra year or two could account for enough broader experience to give them some advantages in achievement. Another avenue to explore might be the motive for achievement. Have physical limitations caused them to spend an unusual amount of time in reading? Have they been pressured to achieve for status reasons? Are they more concerned about scores and winning than about reading for enjoyment?

Paul, Sammy, Pamela, Ann, and Frank fall into the category of the average student. But they do not all achieve the same! Even though Frank seems to have at least average ability he does not measure up in reading. Again we must look for a reason. Is he young for his group? Is he maturing at a slower pace? Is he on a plateau in his learning pattern at the present time? Does he have health limitations? Are there so many distractions in his life that reading seems irrelevant to him. It is just possible that Frank needs something besides more remedial reading.

Paul and Sammy are somewhat like Betty, Alan, and Mary. They seem to be achieving more than we had expected. That's encouraging and that's good, but it is a good idea to ask why. Have they been underestimated as to ability? Have they been pressured? Do they have special ability in reading?

Finally we come to Pamela and Ann. The teacher who thinks she is teaching fourth grade may teach the whole class as if they were all like Pamela and Ann. In actuality it is unusual to find more than two or three children in any classroom who fall in that center box.

This kind of analysis of a typical class won't answer all the questions. There won't be distinct lines separating the groups. But the teacher who sees them thus will be in a better position to plan the best possible program for each and still work within the limitations of a total class. Putting all the older ones together certainly isn't the answer. Putting all the bright ones together is no better answer. Assuming they are all average, or ought to be, only ignores the problem.

Figure 23 provides a basis for the analysis of any class group at any grade level. This can be done with actual test scores from standardized mental and achievement tests or it can be based on the teacher's subjective judgment after considerable experience with the children. The figure provides nine boxes in which to enter the names of the children. An analysis of the children whose names fall in the respective boxes as numbered in the table will lead to the following conclusions

1. These children show achievement far above level of expectancy. There is reason to question the validity of the mental test. Could they have had unexpected help on the reading test? Perhaps retesting will be appropriate.

2. These children show achievement above estimated capacity. Real effort and good work habits could lead to this result. On the other hand, their ability may have been underestimated or they may have been subjected to undue pressure.

3. These children have high ability and high achievement. Their deviations from capacity may actually be negative. They may benefit more from breadth of experience than from acceleration.

4. These children have less than average ability. Still they are achieving up to norm. They may be working hard. They may be over age.

5. These children have normal ability and normal achievement. They fit the theoretical average. Too many teachers teach as if they were all here.

6. These children have ability above normal but are doing average work. This often results from mass teaching, uniform standards, and lack of challenge. They may or may not need to be stimulated to a higher level.

7. These are low achievers apparently because of lack of ability. Some

CLASS ANALYSIS—ACHIEVEMENT VERSUS CAPACITY

Grade ________ Subject ______________________________ Date ________

School ______________________________ Teacher ____________________

Mental Test Used ______________________________ Date ________

Achievement Test Used ______________________________ Date ________

		Capacity or Estimated Level of Expectancy		
		Below Grade Level	At Grade Level	Above Grade Level
Results	Above Grade Level	1. Children who show Capacity half year or more *below* norm Achievement half year or more *above* norm	2. Children who show Capacity *within* half year of norm plus or minus Achievement half year or more *above* norm	3. Children who show Capacity half year or more *above* norm Achievement half year or more *above* norm
Test	At Grade Level	4. Children who show Capacity half year or more *below* norm Achievement *within* half year of norm plus or minus	5. Children who show Capacity *within* half year of norm plus or minus Achievement *within* half year of norm plus or minus	6. Children who show Capacity half year or more *above* norm Achievement *within* half year of norm plus or minus
Achievement	Below Grade Level	7. Children who show Capacity half year or more *below* norm Achievement half year or more *below* norm	8. Children who show Capacity *within* half year of norm plus or minus Achievement half year or more *below* norm	9. Children who show Capacity half year or more *above* norm Achievement half year or more *below* norm

Figure 23. Suggested form for class analysis.

of them may even show positive deviations from capacity. They may actually be "doing as well as can be expected."

8. These have average ability but seemingly are not achieving up to capacity. Look for possible causes. Help them to improve if possible. Avoid aggravating emotional or health problems which could be causal.

9. These are serious deviations. If the mental tests are indicative there must be a cause for low achievement. They are a major concern in the reading improvement program.

MEETING THE NEEDS OF INDIVIDUALS

The problem then is how to manage the total group without losing sight of the individuals. It is something like managing a family. The wise mother sees each member of her family as an individual within the total group. This does not divide the group, it only lets each individual see his place in the group. The teacher in the classroom will do much the same thing. Once the class has been analyzed so the teacher knows special abilities and disabilities, special interests and talents, various levels of attainment in different areas, and needs based on different backgrounds, she is ready to help the class plan so each may contribute to the group and all may learn. With this approach she will not need to pass judgment and determine who is best or who won. She will only need to keep a record and help each one decide what he has learned. Usually she will work with the group as assigned. Occasionally she may need to seek outside help for those who are unable to adjust to group instruction.

PROVISIONS IN THE REGULAR CLASSROOM

In many situations there is no place else to put the child who deviates from the norm and the teacher in the "regular" classroom has to keep him whether she wants him or not. He is there. He comes every day. He has to be lived with and dealt with. If he will sit quietly without bothering the others he may be tolerated and ignored. Only when he makes his presence felt in such a manner that he won't be ignored does he really bother the teacher. But since he is there the teacher in the regular classroom must make a decision about what she is going to do with him. She cannot evade the decision by ignoring the situation because by simply ignoring him she has made a decision to do nothing about it. Recognizing the needs of the individuals as well as the group comes first. Then in planning for the work in the classroom the teacher will sometimes deal with the class as a total group. Sometimes she will divide the class into smaller groups based on needs or interests. And sometimes each individual will be working independently.

RECOGNIZING THE NEEDS Then perhaps it would stand her in stead to know some of the sources of help which are available. Sometimes the help for the child is actually as much help to the teacher in the management of the classroom and to the rest of the children who are exposed to the abnormal situation as it is to the deviant child himself. There are at least five things the teacher can do.

Learn to know the children and thus know which ones to refer to special agencies or special personnel for help. In many communities there are service clubs whose members are eager for worthwhile projects to help children. Some school systems employ special personnel to do special testing or counseling and to provide special instruction or therapy. The teacher should acquaint herself with all the services available and how to obtain them. Then she should put together what she knows about the needs of her children and the services available in order to refer each case to a source of help. Many times correcting a difficulty will clear up a major classroom problem. Many times recognizing a difficulty and finding out that it is one of those "stumps you just have to plow around" will prevent unnecessary agitation. This job then is twofold: recognizing what kind of help children need and finding out where to get the help.

Provide some kind of success for each child each day. This sounds so simple that it hardly seems worth stating but it is often neglected. The slow learner can do something. To put him in competition with others who can do better and let him face defeat and failure day after day merely teaches him that he can't, that he is no good, that he is inferior, that he is a failure. He can succeed at something, though. It may be listening to a younger child read, carrying the message to the office, or sorting the puzzle pieces. When he is made to feel that the job is worthwhile, that he can do it well, and that others are depending on him, he will experience success which will help him to change his whole attitude toward himself, toward school, and toward learning. Any teacher can do this and she does not need extra time, special materials, a special room, or an assistant to get it done. The same might be said for those children at the other end of the scale, for example, the one with the beautiful singing voice, the one who reads well, or the one who has had the privilege of traveling to other parts of the world. Even the superior children sometimes feel that school is so routine that they are not accomplishing any great successes.

Recognize the limitations of each child. Insisting that they all keep up, all conform, all get done on time is putting the lid on some and stretching the rubber band to the breaking point with others. They all have their potentialities and their limitations. The teacher who sets the same goals for all the children and expects all to conform is failing to recognize this. The child who decides for himself what he will do or how much he can accomplish is doing two things. First he is assuming the responsibility for setting his own goals, and second he is facing attainable goals. If he succeeds, he will be willing to set higher goals. If he fails, he will see failure in terms of his own estimate of his potential rather than as frustration in an attempt to live up to an external expectation set by the teacher. The child can be led to see his accomplishments in terms of progress rather than in terms of winning. If he is doing more or better than he did yesterday or last week, that is enough to chalk up success and build a launching pad for further successes.

Develop tolerance for others. In a classroom where a uniform standard of achievement is set for all and where records are kept to find out who succeeded and who failed or to determine who won, the children develop a competitive spirit that is destructive of personal morale and of group feeling. Even the very dull child in the classroom will be accepted in the same manner in which the teacher accepts him. If the teacher feels she must call on him to read, her attitude will show in the tone of her voice and in the expression on her face as well as in her very bodily posture. The children will sense her attitude and will look disgusted when he is called on and sigh with relief when he has finished. They learned their intolerance for him from the example before them. When the tasks differ the children can be led to appreciate the achievements of their classmates providing that achievement does not in any way downgrade their own accomplishments.

Help each one recognize his own potentials. This means recognizing his strengths as well as his weaknesses. Many of us, not just children, can do things we do not realize we can do just because we have never been challenged or have never actually tried. Moreover, many of us spend time and energy trying to do things that we should have judgment enough to by-pass and use our time for more profitable ventures. Sometimes the learner even at the elementary level needs to find out that there are some things he can do well and some things he might better leave for others to do. The first step is to accept what one cannot change. If Billy is in a wheel chair he isn't likely to be on the baseball team. Struggling to get on or lamenting the fact that he can't won't help much. Accepting it is the first step toward facing reality. The second step is to capitalize on what he can do rather than to agitate about what he cannot do. They don't all have to do the same things. Learning to be unique is a laudable trait. It is one that is too often forgotten in a society which emphasizes conformity.

PROVIDING FOR TOTAL CLASS ACTIVITIES Total class activities will occupy part of the time. When all the children are interested in a common topic they may discuss, share, and learn from each other. Some activities such as games, listening to poetry, singing, and library reading do not call for differentiation of abilities and can be engaged in together or simultaneously without anyone feeling that his contribution is necessarily better or worse than others.

PROVIDING FOR GROUP ACTIVITIES Grouping may be necessary or helpful for other activities. Sometimes a group will be formed on the basis of special interests. Sometimes groups will be organized around instructional needs. At other times the level of attainment of selected children may be the factor that determines the makeup of the group.

Interest is the basis for grouping when one group is planning a dramatization. Another group may spend a week or so concentrating on horse stories. A group may be collecting information for the costumes to dress the figures for the diorama to show how life was in feudal days. As long as the common interest prevails the group will stay intact. When the interest wanes the group will disintegrate.

Instructional needs determine grouping when children are selected for help in specific areas. If the reading which has been done during the last few days has revealed that Betty, Paul, Sammy, Harry, and Martha have not yet mastered the principle of initial blends in the pronunciation of words, they may be grouped for some developmental teaching to clear up the difficulty. When the purpose has been accomplished the group will dissolve. Perhaps Betty, Alan, Mary, Paul, and Gregg are scoring well on reading tests, but observation reveals that while they know the words and can answer the questions they are not doing so well in expressive oral reading. They may be drawn out from the group for some special help in this category.

Level of reading sometimes dictates temporary groupings. Maybe Ruth, Bobby, David, Frank, and Martha are all at a level in reading below the norm for the grade. Perhaps this is a fifth grade classroom but they need material at second or third grade reading level for some instructional help in order to avoid frustration. The teacher who plans such a grouping will do it fully aware that if the teaching is effective both Martha and Frank may outstrip the others and move out of the group in a little while. Thus grouping based on level of attainment does not guarantee a permanent grouping. Even though they are all at the same level at the outset, they may have different potentials and may be moving at different rates and thus do not stay together indefinitely.

PROVIDING FOR INDIVIDUAL ACTIVITIES Individual activities constitute another means of meeting the needs of the individuals within the group. Perhaps Betty is the only one who is going to the first grade room to read a story to the younger children. Perhaps Alan is the only one who is preparing a report on his favorite hero. Perhaps Tom is the only one interested in reading *Treasure Island* at the moment. There will be times when each child in the room will be reading material he has selected for himself. Then such individual reading should be on his independent level and within his range of interest. The important point is not whether he is doing what the rest are doing, keeping up, conforming, and passing, but rather is he reading and is he enjoying it and is he succeeding?

The teacher who identifies the differences in the children in the total group and studies each individual in order to know not only how he is different but why is in a position to help each one learn. The teacher who analyzes her class in terms of ability and level of maturity and sees similarities and differences among the children as a basis for forming compatible groups who can work together to their mutual benefit will be managing the situation. The teacher who recognizes appropriate times for total group activities, effective techniques for small group work, and possibilities for individual activities will be providing enough variety to help each one grow. The method of teaching reading then is not so important as the recognition of the needs of the learners and the management of the situation. The teacher is the manager of the situation.

PROVISIONS IN SPECIAL CLASSROOMS

It is lamentable, but too often true, that children who deviate from the norm are either ignored or rejected. Rejection is particularly true of those who deviate in the negative direction, but those who deviate in the positive direction are also unnoticed.

The ones who deviate in the positive direction, that is, the ones who have unusual ability, special talents, or high intelligence, are often welcomed in the classroom so long as they are submissive and do not try to use their abilities along lines which are so creative that they interfere with the established routine. If the brighter than normal child will just come to school, sit still, listen, do what he is told, finish all his assignments on time, turn in neat correct papers, and respond with right answers, he is a joy to the teacher who is addicted to getting them all up to norm and maintaining high scholastic averages in her room. She will classify him as a delightful student, a good worker, a scholar, when in actuality much of his high potential is going to waste in the name of conformity and standards. His ability is actually unnoticed or, if noticed, is being ignored. The teacher doesn't have to worry about what he is going to do to the average, about his promotion, about what to tell his mother, about what to do about his assignments, because he conforms, he meets the requirements, he makes A's, and he spends his extra abilities doing things outside the influence of the school.

Whenever a child deviates negatively from the norm physically, emotionally, socially, or intellectually to the point where he cannot make the needed adjustments and still keep on learning, then perhaps it is time to start looking for a special classroom for him. Too often we give up too soon and tend to expect them all to be normal or get out.

A teacher may say, "Oh, no, I don't reject him. I just don't know what to do with him." If pressed for an answer too often the reply is, "I don't know where he belongs but he certainly doesn't belong in my room—or in a regular classroom." Further pressing for a specific answer will often bring the reply, "There ought to be a special room to take care of him."

What the teacher is actually saying is, "I don't know what to do with him. I have more to do now than I can get done. And I don't want to be bothered with him." She'll deny it, but it is sometimes true nevertheless. Examine your own motives. Do you really want special help for him? Or do you merely want to get him off your hands? There are two situations which justify providing special facilities for deviant children.

CHILDREN WHO CANNOT PROFIT FROM REGULAR CLASSROOM ACTIVITIES Sometimes it may be necessary to assign a child to a special classroom. Of course, that decision must be based on an evaluation of the activities going on in the classroom. If the teacher teaches to the average and expects them all to do fourth grade work because this is a fourth grade classroom, then perhaps all but one or two of them should be removed from that particular classroom and be "put somewhere else," but where? But if the teacher makes every attempt to provide for the wide span of abilities and interests and is still not able to reach some child because his deviation is so extreme that time and facilities are just not available, then perhaps he does need to go to a special classroom. Perhaps a child who is totally blind should go to the school for the blind; however, blind children have been known to make satisfactory adjustments in regular classrooms. Perhaps the child with a total hearing loss should go to the school for the deaf, but many children have learned compensations such as lip reading and have been able to live adequately in a hearing world. Perhaps the child with paralysis should go to the special room for the physically handicapped, but such children have won the cooperation and assistance of the more fortunate classmates and have been able to make necessary adjustments and still learn to read. Perhaps the intellectually superior child should be assigned to a special room, but there is more than one point of view on this also.

CHILDREN WHO ARE A DETRIMENT TO OTHERS Sometimes a child's deviation may be so far removed from normal that his presence interferes with or is an actual detriment to the learning of the other children. Then it is not so much a matter of whether he is benefiting from the regular classroom as whether or not all children are being given the best possible learning experiences.

If Frank is an emotional problem and vents his emotions through crying or screaming all day to the point where the teacher cannot sit down with a reading group and help them enjoy a story, then no matter how much Frank would benefit by being with other children, perhaps a different decision must be made because the rights of the other children must be considered. They have a right to their share of the teacher's time and attention. They have a right to enjoy their reading without an emotional disturbance which destroys the story and distracts the attention of all. They have a right to a calm atmosphere and peace of mind. If Frank is taking away their rights, then perhaps a special assignment may become necessary, not because it is best for Frank, but because it is best for the majority.

Special classrooms do have their place, but they should never be allowed to become a "dumping ground" for all those children the teacher doesn't know what to do with. They should be a source of extra help or extra challenge for those who deviate so far that their needs cannot be met in a larger group, and they should be a protection for the majority who can conform to society in groups.

Exceptionality is a matter of degree. Causes may be congenital or developmental. Some exceptionality may interfere with school learning and some may foster learning. Some provision for such children can be made in the regular classroom and sometimes special classrooms are a more desirable solution to the problem.

16

REMEDIAL AND CORRECTIVE READING

or So They Didn't All Get It! What Shall I Do About It?

The availability of money for special programs and for equipment and materials in education has accelerated interest in and emphasis on special programs designed to correct, remedy, or provide for unusual problems. This emphasis has led to increased publications, inventions, and developments designed to meet the needs and to capture a share of the consumer's money. As a result many schools have introduced special programs for remedial or corrective reading. They have employed reading specialists, set up reading laboratories, introduced diagnostic testing programs, and established clinics for the treatment of reading disabilities.

When we prescribe remedial measures we are admitting that there is something wrong with the initial treatment. Such an admission of failure or, if you want to put it more mildly, inadequacy in the initial instruction is saying, "We didn't do a good job in the first place and we must provide special facilities and special treatment to correct our mistakes." No matter how hard we try we cannot expect to bat 1000 every time; there are bound to be some children who do not succeed as well as we would like and some materials which do not always provide the types of learnings we expect with all the children. It is almost inevitable that there will be some correction needed in any program. However, it seems more important to give consideration to causes of difficulties in reading and attention to the prevention of the problems rather than to continue as tradition dictates and then have to devote our time, energy, money, and facilities to correcting our errors. Even so, any book on the teaching of reading would not be facing reality today if it did not have a chapter on corrective and remedial techniques in reading. We shall begin by identifying the terms, then outline the work of the clinic and show its relation to the total reading program.

IDENTIFICATION OF TERMS

The terms remedial reading and corrective reading have been used to mean different things. Diagnosis does not mean the same to all. Likewise clinics are pictured differently. Some have tried to refine the terms in order to avoid undesirable connotations and to make a distinction in meaning. The terms diagnosis, remediation, and correction are often associated with clinical procedures.

REMEDIAL READING

The dictionary says the word *remedy* comes from a Latin origin and means to heal again. It implies treatment which cures, relieves, or corrects an evil. When we use the term in its adjective form, as in the expression "remedial reading," the logical question is, "What is the evil we are trying to remove or correct?" That interpretation is not very flattering for the program of initial instruction in reading. The dictionary says further that to remedy is to give relief or to correct, to cure, to repair, to make right. It gives as synonyms restorative or corrective.

CORRECTIVE READING

The dictionary says the word *correct* is of Latin origin and means to make straight, exact, accurate, free from error. The adjective form implies measuring up to or meeting standards. The verb form means to set right or straight by changing what is wrong. Further definition implies bringing up to standard, curing, or remedying. Still another meaning implies counteracting or neutralizing. A final meaning attributed to correcting is associated with punishing. If we apply these meanings to reading, the interpretations are not very complimentary to what we have been doing.

If we are talking about "corrective reading" in the dictionary sense, what are we trying to make accurate or free from error? And why didn't we do it right in the first place? If we are using it as meaning to measure up to standard, what standard are we setting? Is the standard in terms of language structure or growth of the learner? If we are using it in terms of counteracting or neutralizing, why did we introduce an element which requires such treatment into the learning situation in the first place? If we are using it in terms of punishment, are we punishing the child for not having learned, for having learned incorrectly, or perhaps for not having the ability?

DIAGNOSIS

The word *diagnose* comes from a Greek origin meaning to recognize, to determine the nature of, to study the symptoms based on an examination of the facts. The application to diagnosis in reading is readily observable.

CLINIC

The word *clinic* also comes from a Greek origin. It is related to bed patients. Now a clinical case in reading is not actually a bed patient in the medical sense of the word, but he does come to a special place devoted to the study of and often to the treatment of clinical cases.

All this suggests an inadequacy in original teaching which I find difficult to admit. But since we have admitted that we can't hope to be successful with all our pupils, then perhaps we had better keep our clinics and maintain our corrective programs until we reach perfection in the prevention of errors and in the program of initial instruction in reading. We may never reach it, but we might come closer than we now are. In the meantime the diagnostic and remedial programs still have a place and clinics will probably continue to flourish. Therefore, it might be well to look at such measures in a positive light and see where they fit into the total program and what they have to offer to improve the reading program.

THE WORK OF THE CLINIC

The work of the clinic is divided into two parts, diagnosis and treatment. Diagnosis without treatment is futile. Treatment without adequate diagnosis is a waste of time and energy. The first would be like going to the doctor, then refusing to follow his advice. The second would be like administering the same treatment to all the children hoping some of it might do somebody some good. Let's look at both phases of the program to see what they have to offer.

DIAGNOSIS

The diagnostician has to know what to look for and how to find out. A good diagnosis can reveal the facts and give enough insight into apparent causes to justify recommendations for corrective procedures. A good diagnostician should study the child, use tests, analyze background, and develop a theory on which to base a prescription for treatment.

STUDY OF THE CHILD The first step in a good diagnosis lies in a study of the child himself. Find out who he is, what he is, what he thinks about reading, about school, about himself. Talk with him. He may give some basic clues as to his difficulties. After all, he knows more about himself than anyone else. Attempting to find out his difficulty without consulting him would be futile. The diagnostician cannot study only the records without looking at the child or listening to his own description of what bothers him.

USE OF TESTS Tests are important, but they do not tell the cause of the difficulty; they only reveal the facts which enable the diagnostician to view the learner and his difficulties with a bit more insight. The test may tell the level at which the child can read, the kinds of errors he makes, the rate at which he can read, the degree of comprehension he is able to maintain, and perhaps a bit about his reading habits.

Tests of vision, hearing, and general health are revealing. Faulty vision, defective hearing, or ill health can lead to fatigue. Fatigue leads to inattention. Inattention leads to inaccuracies and wrong impressions. Wrong impressions lead to wrong responses. Wrong responses lead to defeat and failure. Defeat and failure lead to resistance. Resistance adds to inattention. The less one attends to the task the poorer he becomes and the greater the effort required to pursue it. This, in turn, compounds the fatigue factor. It is not so simple as to say, "Get him glasses and he can read," "Make him pay attention and he will learn," or "Correct his errors and he will get it right."

ANALYSIS OF THE BACKGROUND Study materials, habits, attitudes, and relationships. The materials may reveal much about how the child acquired his habits and attitudes toward reading. The situation may tell much about his vision, hearing, personal attitude, peer relations, and rapport with parents and teachers. The good diagnostician leaves no stone unturned to find out as much as possible about the learner and his background. One never knows which facts are going to serve as possible clues. Difficulties are usually complex. Seldom does one ever put his finger on a single cause. The diagnostician must collect all the evidence available. Every clue must be examined. The clues may be in the child, in the reading act, in the materials of instruction, or in the situation.

DEVELOPING A THEORY It is the job of the diagnostician to make some associations, some judgments, and some decisions. From what he knows about reading problems, about the reading act itself, about the structure of the language, about the types of materials, about how children learn, and about techniques used in teaching he will attempt to put together the factual evidence and make associations based on possible cause and effect. These associations may be merely the playing of hunches. They may be based on previous experiences with similar cases. All the diagnostician can do is to arrive at a reasonable conjecture about the nature of the diffculty and the probable causes. This will give a basis for planning a program. It may be necessary to try a remedy and later, if it does not work, to abandon it in favor of another. The more experienced and the better trained the diagnostician the more likely he will be to make a correct diagnosis and effective recommendation the first time.

A test may help guide in deciding what the child is capable of doing. It is seldom that a test will tell why he cannot do it. If the diagnosis is right, the correct remedy is prescribed and the learner improves. If it is faulty and the remedy does not work, then there must be an open and honest evaluation of the problem and a willingness to try again.

TREATMENT

Once the diagnosis has been made the next step is to do something about it. The first step is determining the kind of remedial work needed, then taking the necessary steps to provide it. Specific difficulties require specific remedies.

TYPES OF REMEDIAL WORK Some children may be so inaccurate in their mechanical approach to reading that an attack on that problem is an evident need. Others may be seemingly adept at mechanics but may not get the point to what they read and thus indicate a need for attention to comprehension. Some may need both approaches simultaneously.

Mechanical needs show up in inability to recognize words and lack of skills in analyzing words for pronunciation or meaning. Obviously, if the child does not know the words, he cannot read them. And if he does not know how to work out the words, he will merely look at the printed symbols blankly with no reaction and wait to be told. Any attempt to teach reading while ignoring this problem would be like giving the sick child medicine while he slowly starves to death.

Mechanical needs show up also in lack of ability to utilize phrasing, punctuation, and linguistic expression through appropriate emphasis, pauses, and inflections. The reader who says the words and misses the point may have one kind of mechanical skill without the complementary ability of putting the parts together into meaningful wholes.

Comprehension needs show up in the learner's reaction to the material read. Does he get the idea? Can he interpret the meaning of the selection? Does he merely say the words or does he express an idea? Does his participation in a discussion reveal insight into the situation, the nature of the character in the story, the relationship between cause and effect? Is he able to apply what he has read to similar situations? For example, does he see the directions for painting a boat as applicable to painting a table? Does he see the triumph of right over wrong in a hero story as suggestive for his own life patterns? Only when he gets the idea and interprets it with insight so that he can use it independently has he truly comprehended.

SEQUENTIAL STEPS What to do about it is the hardest problem of all. Anyone can give tests and keep records. Armchair practitioners can theorize about cases and perhaps even prescribe remedies, but putting the suggestions into action is the measure of effectiveness. Whether the treatment should take place in the clinic, in the classroom, or in the home is a matter of opinion, but that something must be done about it is unquestionable.

The details about how to set up a clinic, diagnose all kinds of cases, and provide treatments to meet the various problems would fill a whole book. This chapter did not start out to exhaust the subject or to serve as a manual for running a clinic. It intended only to help the practitioner at the classroom level see how the remedial or corrective program fits into the total picture. Therefore, the following steps are merely outlined without detailed instructions. Much of what is offered here will fit just as well in a classroom as in a clinic. If one expects to help a problem case in reading either physical or intellectual, he needs to take these steps.

Establish the level of achievement that has already been attained. You can't go on from where you aren't any more than you can come back from where you haven't been.

Indicate specific learnings already mastered. Too often we generalize by saying, "He can't read." Sometimes there are some very specific things he can do. Finding out what they are and listing them is helpful to both the teacher and the learner. If he can already identify the letters of the alphabet, then we know we don't have to teach that. He may really think he can't read, but experimentation with preprimers or primers may reveal that, if he works at a level pitched low enough, he really can do it well.

Itemize the learnings not yet mastered. List them under skills and understandings. Arrange them in descending order as to difficulty or importance. Such a listing will be helpful when you pick out a place to begin, something definite to work on, and as a basis for checking them off as they are accomplished.

Indicate the direction of attack. Sometimes we make the mistake of looking at all the problems at once. They may look so overwhelming that we get a feeling of futility and lack the courage to begin. Decide where to begin and what to do first, then go to work. If we know what we are trying to teach and emphasize it specifically, we stand some chance of getting results. Otherwise, we may end up dabbling at a lot of things and doing nothing thoroughly. If we put our emphasis on one problem till it has been somewhat alleviated, then we can move on to another problem. This has a two-fold effect on both the teacher and the learner. It gives them a feeling of success because one thing has been checked off. It gives them a feeling of encouragement because the list gets shorter and it looks less forbidding and more possible of attainment.

Set attainable goals. This was discussed in the chapter on individual differences. If both the teacher and the child see the goal as impossible, they will probably see no need to start. The first step is to look realistically at where we are now and decide how much we have a right to expect. These goals should be set within the realm of possibility for the individual and should be in keeping with the needs for reading in the present situation.

Plan the details of the attack. Goals too far distant tend to become vague and to seem impossible. It is much more realistic to ask ourselves each day, "What am I going to try to get done today?" Then at the end of the day both the teacher and the pupil will benefit by answering for themselves the question, "What did we accomplish today?" Then, "What can I plan to get done tomorrow?" Actually jotting down such details serves two purposes. It gives a target toward which to shoot and it provides convincing evidence of goals accomplished. This is good for learning as well as for morale. Long-range goals have their place. The more mature the learner the farther into the future the goals can be projected and the more capable the learner the more he can assume responsibility for his own projected learnings.

Keep records of attainments. The child who is assigned to a remedial program has already failed in his own eyes as well as in the eyes of the teacher. He is so convinced that he can't that sometimes negative attitude is more of a deterrent to reading success than actual inability or faulty habits. A record that proves accomplishments is convincing. Keep records of materials used. List the books, the stories, the pages, the skills. Refer to them from time to time. Comment on how much has been accomplished. Keep a record of activities engaged in, stories read to others, workbook exercises completed, dramatizations, questions, papers, recordings, and so on. Keep a record of the direction of progress. Is it toward greater speed in silent reading, more accurate pronunciation in oral reading, more correct responses to comprehension exercises, or a higher level with more difficult material?

The child who sees that he can do more or harder or better work than he did a week ago, a month ago, or a year ago is convinced that his effort has been worthwhile. It is not enough to know what you have done and in what direction you are headed; you also need to know how much you have accomplished. Records of accomplishment can be kept in the form of anecdotal accounts, tape recordings, test scores, or itemized lists. Regardless of the type of record kept the child who can say, "Last month I could read 150 words per minute and now I can read 170 words per minute," is convinced he is getting someplace. The child who sees a score of 2.7 on a standardized test last year and a score of 3.9 this year is convinced he is making good progress. This is much more helpful for his morale than to say at the end of fourth grade he was over two years below standard and at the end of the fifth he was still almost two years below standard. One is a negative report on accomplishments in terms of unrealistic expectations and the other is a positive report of accomplishments in terms of realistic goals based on growth in the interval.

SUGGESTED REMEDIES FOR SPECIFIC DIFFICULTIES Table 20 offers some specific techniques which can be used either in the classroom or in a clinic. They are designed to pinpoint the remedy in terms of the difficulty and to provide the teacher with something tangible to try. The suggestions are divided into five categories: (1) visual, (2) auditory, (3) vocal, (4) muscular, and (5) comprehensive. The teacher making use of these ideas will want to keep the chart handy and perhaps add her own notations from time to time.

Table 20. READING DIFFICULTIES AND SUGGESTED REMEDIES

Types of Difficulties	*Suggested Remedies*
Visual Difficulties	
Poor vision due to external factors	Adjust lighting and seating. Adjust books and size of print.
Poor vision due to eye defects	Recommend medical attention. Adjust to the child's handicap.
Failure to distinguish forms with striking differences	Point out specific differences. Provide practice in matching.

Table 20. (Cont.)

Types of Difficulties	*Suggested Remedies*
Visual of Difficulties (Cont.)	
Failure to distinguish words similar in appearance (can, car; pat, bat)	Begin with smaller perceptional unit. Point out specified differences. Have child trace or reproduce forms. Compare and contrast forms.
Failure to distinguish position or orientation of patterns (reversals; no, on; left, felt)	Slide marker along under material to guide the eye from left to right. Give intrinsic drill which requires accurate discrimination. (He sits [near–neat] the door.) Check on comprehension.
Line skipping	Use material with one line on a page. Provide wider spaced material. Use a line marker. Permit child to run his index finger down the left-hand margin.
Word skipping	Provide wider spaced material. Reduce emphasis on speed. Stress accuracy.
Losing place	Use a line marker. Let child underline as he reads. Have child watch his book as the teacher reads aloud.
Short eye span	Provide easier material. Demonstrate reading by phrases. Ask questions which require a phrase for an answer. Provide material separated into phrases by wider spaces or slant mark.
Long eye pauses	Pace the eye movements by swinging the hand along under the line of print. Have child follow as teacher reads orally. Give rapid phrase card drill.
Many and irregular fixations per line	Give speed exercises on easy material. Reread same material for a different purpose. Use phrase drill.
Irregular and unrhythmical eye movements	Use marker to guide the eyes. Use material with wide spacing. Pace the eye movements. Have child practice orally after he has heard the teacher read.
Short eye-voice span	Provide easier material. Work for longer eye span. Teach when and where to pause. Give specific demonstrations on how to do it.

Table 20. (Cont.)

Types of Difficulties	*Suggested Remedies*
Auditory Difficulties	
Poor hearing due to external factors	Remove as much interference as possible. Adjust seating. Teach children to adjust to environmental interferences.
Defective hearing	Recommend medical attention. Seat child advantageously. Teach him to be a careful listener. Encourage children to speak clearly and distinctly.
Failure to distinguish similar sounds (bit, bat, bet; meal, mill)	Emphasize motor components of speech. Provide phonetic drills with sounds in their settings in whole words. Use words in meaningful settings. Practice oral reading at reduced rate with emphasis on articulation.
Failure to perceive sequence of sounds to blend into words	Exaggerate emphasis on initial sound, vowel sound, and ending. Do not isolate individual letter sounds. Repeat alliteration exercises. Practice rhymes.
Inaccurate auditory perception	Provide accurate pattern. Have child practice reading what he has just heard another read.
Short auditory perception span	Practice dictation exercises to be repeated orally or written. Gradually increase length of unit. Keep meaning attached so comprehension will aid auditory span.
Vocal Difficulties	
Speech defects	Consult a speech therapist. Avoid emphasis on oral reading until defects are corrected. Encourage and recognize improvement.
Baby talk	Provide a good example. Accept only the child's best. Never allow ridicule from classmates. Illustrate use of speech organs. Provide practice on difficult forms.
Inaccurate speech resulting in gross errors in meaning	Provide background of meaningful experience in conversation. Explain pronunciations and meanings of new words before reading.
Reading in inaudible voice	Make child conscious of audience.

Table 20. (Cont.)

Types of Difficulties	*Suggested Remedies*
Vocal Difficulties (Cont.)	
	Begin with small audience and gradually extend size and distance. Stand farther from the child. Use dramatization and puppetry. Use tape recordings.
Reading in high pitched, loud, or stilted voice	Emphasize meaning. Reduce emphasis on mechanics. Provide purpose for reading. Relieve any embarrassment.
Word calling	Provide a good example. Provide silent reading for meaning before oral reading. Ask thought-provoking questions requiring phrase answers. Emphasize responsibility to audience. Use informal dramatization. Reduce emphasis on mechanics. Work to lengthen eye span.
Lack of breath control resulting in stilted and expressionless reading	Relieve embarrassment. Use phrase drill. Use informal dramatization. Give vocal exercises.
Poor enunciation and careless articulation	Provide a good example. Reduce rate of reading. Provide practice on needed forms. Exaggerate examples for accurate impression.
Stuttering and stammering	Consult a speech therapist. Let child begin over again. Provide rhythmic exercises. Reduce emphasis on oral reading. Permit child to hold something. Work to build self-confidence.
Muscular Difficulties	
Difficulty in holding and managing a book	Provide a book rest. Let child read sitting at a table. Demonstrate effective means of holding a book and turning pages. Help child hold the book temporarily.
Head or body movement during reading	Allow child to sit while reading. Keep him reminded by placing hand on shoulder or book during reading. Provide easy material. Relieve embarrassment.

Table 20. (Cont.)

Types of Difficulties	*Suggested Remedies*
Muscular Difficulties (Cont.)	
Left-handedness or ambidexterity	Adjust to the child's individual difference.
Lack of muscular coordination	Develop one skill at a time blending new ones as mastered. Practice bouncing a ball or other large muscular actions. Provide rhythmical exercises to music.
Finger pointing	Point out limitations of such practice. Provide a marker as needed. Encourage speed in easy silent reading. Emphasize thought getting rather than word recognition. Use phrase flash card drills. Provide practice in reading from chalk board or chart.
Excessive lip movement	Show advantages of eliminating habit. Reduce amount of oral reading. Provide material with repetition. Provide external reminders such as holding finger over lips during silent reading.
Nervous habits	Avoid emphasis on speed. Use easy interesting material. Place firm steady hand on child or on his book.
Comprehension Difficulties	
Based on attitudes	
Overconsciousness of mechanics	Read for thought. Reduce emphasis on mechanical drills.
Excessive imagination	Provide exercises in which absolute accuracy is the aim. Ask specific fact questions. Distinguish between quoting and creating. Provide other outlets for imagination.
Inferiority complex and lack of self-confidence	Make success possible by providing easy material. Recognize success when it occurs.
Lack of interest and inattention	Find out what the child is interested in and capitalize on it. Provide strong motives. Gradually increase length of period as interest and attention grow.

Table 20. (Cont.)

Types of Difficulties	*Suggested Remedies*
Comprehension Difficulties (Cont.)	
Overdependence on others	Give individual assignment. Provide copy-proof seat work. Commend success. Put child in position of leadership.
Worry, nervousness, and fear	Find out and remove cause of fear. Make completion of assignment possible. Reassure child.
Overconfidence and overaggressiveness	Reduce praise for the time being. Increase the assignment. Place on committee where cooperation is essential. Challenge ability by harder material.
Based on habits	
Substitutions and insertions	Point out specific difficulties and importance of accuracy. Give specific questions to guide silent reading. Provide practice requiring accurate shades of meaning. Have child formulate questions based on his own silent reading.
Repetitions and regressive eye movements	Provide easier material. Have child read silently for meaning before reading orally. Eliminate word difficulties before oral reading. Cover what has already been read.
Lack of sufficient attention to detail	Assign specific directions to be carried out. Provide practice where differences in words change the meaning.
Guessing at meaning	Use intrinsic exercises demanding accurate word discrimination. Provide exercises with unexpected content or ending. Eliminate true-false, yes-no, or other checks which permit guessing.
Too much speed to the detriment of comprehension	Eliminate time pressures. Give specific points to look for. Stress thought getting.
Carelessness and waste of time	Give individual responsibility. Point out necessity for careful work. Limit time for specific tasks. Stay with him while he works. Appoint a partner to stay with him.

Table 20. (Cont.)

Types of Difficulties	Suggested Remedies
Based on skills	
Difficulty in recognition of words previously encountered	Use context clues. Provide picture dictionary reference. Teach phonetic analysis and syllabication. Use same word in different setting.
Inability to analyze words into natural recognition and pronunciation parts	Group words phonetically. Divide compound words. Listen for little words in big words.
Inability to attack new words independently	Develop visual aids, phonetic analysis, and context and picture clues.
Lack of recognition of abstract words in isolation	Use words in context. Keep meaning attached.
Lack of sufficient speed to make mental fusion possible	Reduce amount of oral reading. Give speed drills on easy material. Reread the same selection for a different purpose. Keep time charts as evidence of growth. Teach skimming to get general impression or gain a single point.
Inability to profit by punctuation	Teach meanings and uses of punctuation marks in printed material. Show examples where punctuation makes a difference in meaning. Practice oral reading with emphasis on expression of meaning as indicated by punctuation marks.
Inexpressive oral reading	Get meaning through silent reading first. Change directions from "Read it" to "Tell us what it says." Make child aware of his responsibility for imparting meaning to an audience. Remove copies of material from audience. Use dramatization. Interpret character by tone of voice. Show child both good and bad examples for comparison.
Misplaced emphasis	Reread the same material in response to different questions. Work for accurate shades of meaning. Use spontaneous dramatization.
Based on meanings	
Small meaning vocabulary in oral speech	Develop meanings through experiences and conversations. Transform language into one the child can understand.

Table 20. (Cont.)

Types of Difficulties	*Suggested Remedies*
Comprehension Difficulties (Cont.)	
	Teach vocabulary based on specific subject-matter areas.
	Teach affixes as related to meanings.
	Practice on antonyms, synonyms, action words, name words, descriptive words.
Inability to derive meanings from context	Provide concrete experiences with unfamiliar ideas.
	Include new words in meaningful conversations and explain meanings before they are met in context.
	Dramatize or picture word meanings.
	Provide meaningful dictionary study.
Inability to derive meaning from apparently known words	Identify descriptive words, name words, action words, etc.
	Provide concrete experiences.
Inability to recognize thought units	Find phrases in content to answer specific questions.
	Provide material with phrases or thought units marked or spaced.
Failure to comprehend long complex sentences because of short perception span	Combine two or more simple sentences into compound or complex sentences.
	Gradually increase perception span.
	Reread for a different meaning.
	Reread to the child and carry the thought unit through for him.
Failure to comprehend because of difficulty of material	Adjust material to level of ability.
	Help him decipher the meaning.
Failure to comprehend paragraph or story continuity	Provide a definite purpose for reading.
	Reproduce orally, pictorially, or in writing what has been read.
	Arouse interest by raising questions, starting a story, and leaving the child to finish it alone.
	Gradually increase length of assignment.
Inability to relate reading to previous experiences and to think independently	Ask thought-provoking questions.
	Locate descriptions, humorous passages, character sketches, etc.
	Read to verify a fact or prove a point.
Inability to think logically	Begin with a simple question and gradually increase difficulty.
	Use series of related sequential questions.
Inability to organize material read	Put items of a kind together.
	List events in order of occurrence.
	List items in order of importance.
	Identify cause and effect relationships.

RELATION OF THE CLINIC TO THE TOTAL READING PROGRAM

Yes, we will need our remedial reading programs until we have reached perfection in developmental instruction. That may be indefinitely because perfection is a pretty idealistic expectation. Then our major question is, "What is the relation of the clinic to the total reading program?" And a second question is, "How does the individual classroom teacher fit into the picture?" The clinic can offer three types of programs, namely, analysis, special help, and prevention.

ANALYSIS OF TYPES OF DIFFICULTIES AND COMMON CAUSES

The clinician may serve as a source of help for the classroom teacher who wants to work with the children. He can help her analyze the types of difficulties which are evident and help in accumulating the factual data on which to predict the possible causes of difficulty. Once the teacher has this information she may be able to meet the difficulties of the learner by adjusting what he does rather than by removing him from the group. This service is one which extends the influence of the clinic much beyond the case load. As the teacher becomes more independent in analyzing cases she will not only refer fewer cases to the clinic for diagnosis, but will also apply what she has learned about prevention in the classroom program so that there may actually be fewer cases needing remediation.

SPECIAL HELP FOR PROBLEM CASES

The clinician can give special help for problem cases. The clinic serves as a place for the child who cannot fit into the group processes practiced in the regular classroom. It may be a source of help for the child who has met difficulties due to health, mobility, emotional disturbances, or personal problems. The clinician may diagnose his case and help the classroom teacher plan the remedial program. Or he may follow through and provide remedial instruction. This will depend on the extent of the clinical facilities, the nature of the difficulties, and the type of service planned in the organization of the clinic itself.

PREVENTION OF FURTHER DIFFICULTIES

Perhaps the most important service a clinician can render to a good school reading program is that of prevention. The clinician who has identified some of the common types of difficulties in a given school program can familiarize the staff with his findings. This may lead to a concerted effort to prevent similar difficulties in the future. The clinician is able to point out common causes of difficulties and may be able to counsel with teachers and administrators to purchase materials, plan procedures, and use methods which will be preventative.

Actually a good reading clinic should be trying to work itself out of a job. The more effective the clinic the fewer cases will be coming to it in ensuing years.

Part Four

EVALUATION

or

Checking Up

Knowing where you are and when you have arrived is about as important as knowing where you are going and how to get there. Unfortunately, there are some people who just keep going but never actually arrive at the point where they can say, "There! That's done!"

In Part One we tried to set a backdrop against which to view the teaching of reading by reviewing trends and history. In Part Two we directed our attention to the mastering of the mechanical skills. In Part Three we considered the importance of using reading skills to find out what the print says. Parts Two and Three cannot be separated one from the other. Skills and their application must be developed side by side, each supporting and supplementing the other as the child grows in his reading.

Now we are ready for Part Four. It is designed to give us a backward look. It will help us review where we have been, take another look at the goals, and appraise the degree of success.

A chapter on evaluating achievement is designed to answer for the child the question, "How am I doing?" and for the teacher the question, "What have we accomplished?" This kind of evaluation avoids the question, "How much is it worth?"

Then the teacher needs to take a careful look at the materials of instruction, the methods used, and the classroom organization in order to evaluate each in terms of the immediate situation. Finally she might well take a careful look at the teaching act itself because, after all, the teacher is what really makes the difference in any classroom setting and with any instructional program.

Not until the learner can face reading with self-confidence, attack self-appointed tasks, and finish with the ability to evaluate his own performance has he become a mature reader. Learning to be on his own and recognizing when he can assume that responsibility are the ultimate goals of learning to read.

The teacher who sees the total program in perspective and balances the reading diet for the child is the one who will have succeeded in teaching him to read.

17

EVALUATING THE ACHIEVEMENT

or How Are They Doing?

When Tommy says, "Look, Daddy!" he wants his father to see how he is doing. It may be to get approval on his acrobatic skill or his accomplishments as a fisherman. When Freda comes in with a book and says, "Listen, Mother," she is not willing for her mother to continue preparing the evening meal while she listens. She wants her mother to give undivided attention to her performance whether it be reading a story, saying multiplication tables, or practicing her spelling. What she really wants is help in passing judgment on her ability to perform. Perhaps even more than that she wants to succeed and wants approval.

Evaluation in terms of "How am I doing?" puts the emphasis on personal accomplishment, growth, and progress toward a goal. This kind of evaluation is welcomed by all learners. Whenever evaluation is made in terms of good or bad, passing or failing, winning or losing, the child begins to see it not as an evaluation of his performance but of himself as a person. When he feels unequal to the demands, inadequate for the task, or less than competent in comparison with others, he begins to shrink from evaluation, to dread tests, to try to "pad the score," instead of to get an honest evaluation of the learning. When the goals are self-imposed and the measure is in terms of progress, the learner solicits evaluation. When the goals are imposed by another and the measure is in terms of an artificial standard which he may have no hopes of attaining, then the learner evades the situation. He thinks tests make him nervous. He says he goes all to pieces on a timed test. He says, "I know but I just can't tell it." What he is really trying to say is that, "This wasn't my objective. I don't think I can measure up. It isn't fair. I don't want to be measured by your standards. I'm afraid I can't. I'd rather not face the issue."

The teacher who knows why she evaluates has at her command some techniques for evaluation. The teacher who knows how to use evaluation as a basis for setting attainable goals, analyzing achievement, and reporting progress is ready to apply the results of evaluation by following through on a program to its conclusion and application.

PURPOSES FOR EVALUATION

There are some good reasons for evaluation. Appraisal of learning does not have to be negative. It can be to diagnose, to assess present level, or to measure growth.

DIAGNOSIS

Diagnosis is probably one of the best reasons for checking up on ourselves. A test which gives some concrete and objective evidence about what a child can read, the level at which he can read, the degree of independence he possesses in reading, his skill in word recognition, articulation, and phrasing, and the accuracy with which he comprehends is helpful. The evidence can be used to determine the level at which to work with the child, the type of material most suited to his needs, and perhaps some of the special learnings which need to be strengthened. Diagnosis is a legitimate reason for testing. It should be done early in the school year in order to permit time to do something with the findings.

ASSESSMENT AT A GIVEN POINT

Sometimes there is need to stop and make an assessment of the attainments in reading at a certain point such as at the end of the year, at the conclu-

sion of a unit, or at the point of transition from one level to the next. Such an assessment is exactly that and little more. It may be more a measure of the effectiveness of the school program, the teacher's efforts, or the value of the materials being used than of the growth or achievement of the individual. This type of testing is not being ruled out, but it should be used infrequently, with caution, and with full awareness of the purpose.

COMPARISON WITH ESTABLISHED NORMS Sometimes there is reason to measure a total group and reduce the scores to some kind of measure of central tendency such as a mean, a median, or a mode. There is a legitimate use for such measures of central tendency. They may help the teacher view the over-all results of teaching. They may guide her in seeing the accomplishments of her class when compared with similar groups in other rooms, other schools, and other parts of the country.

EVALUATION IN TERMS OF CAPACITY It must be kept in mind that seldom does an individual fit the theoretical patterns established by norms. Measures of mental ability suggest approximate levels of expectancy. Comparing achievement with the level of expectancy helps to answer the question about the extent to which the individual is working up to his ability. Statistics derived from such measures have their values, but they must not be confused with evaluation of progress.

MEASUREMENT OF GROWTH

A test repeated after an interval tells how much progress has been made. It may be the same test or a different form of the same test designed to measure the same things. The test may be composed by the teacher or it may be a commercial publication. Such a measurement will tell the amount of growth which has taken place. When studied intensively it can tell much more than that. It can tell which items not known a year ago are known now. Therefore, testing at intervals indicates both the amount of growth and the direction or nature of the growth. This helps in evaluating both the learning and the teaching.

TECHNIQUES FOR EVALUATION

We are constantly evaluating everything we do. When we hold up a picture for inspection, we are thinking about how well it illustrates the point intended. When the child reads and repeats himself, it is because he thinks he can improve the performance by going back and trying again. There are many ways of evaluating what we have done. In reading the teacher utilizes a variety of techniques, some formal and some informal, some consciously and some unconsciously. She may simply observe the child at work. She may keep a record of what she has noted. She may test to produce an objective record. The test may be one she has made or it may be a commercial test furnished by the school system.

OBSERVATION

No doubt daily observation is one of the most frequently used techniques of evaluation. The teacher listens as the children seek to improve their reading performance. She makes a mental note of Susan's lisp, Tom's nervous clutching of the book, Billy's hesitation to tackle a long word, Alan's reluctance to read before the class, Thelma's eagerness to read more than her share, Patty's scarcely audible voice, and Pam's halting word-by-word expression. As she notices these characteristics she is evaluating, diagnosing, and thinking about how she might help each one improve. This type of evaluation is enhanced when the teacher keeps a few written notes to supplement her memory.

RECORD KEEPING

Well-kept records provide concrete evidence of subjective observation. If the teacher gets the impression that Sandra is a slow reader, she may carry that impression through other experiences which belie the generalization. A record of what happens ensures accurate information and serves as a reference for comparison later. Such a record may be a diary account or a summary of statistical facts.

ANECDOTAL RECORDS When the teacher keeps a page in a notebook for each child and jots down some notes from time to time, a record accumulates. This provides tangible evidence of growth or lack of growth. Such notes may seem fruitless if they are based on subjective judgments repeated day after day, such as: "seems inattentive," "likes to read," or "doesn't pay attention." On the other hand, when the notes consist of definite statements of facts about what happened, she has something tangible with which to work. The following notes are much more helpful:

> Read the whole page without an error today.
> Asked to read to the class the part that told about ——.
> Voluntarily asked for help on a word meaning today.
> Missed three words on this page, all ending in *ed*.

If the same errors keep reappearing, there is evidence of need for teaching. If errors which were obvious a month ago no longer crop up, there is evidence of improvement. If the degree of difficulty of self-selected reading material is increasing, there is evidence of another kind of growth.

OBJECTIVE MEASURES Test results are more exact records. These may be scores from standardized tests reduced to stanines or grade scores or they may be raw scores merely indicating the number right. Lists of books read, pages covered, words learned, or skills perfected are also objective records.

TESTING

Tests which are used as techniques for evaluation may be informal or standardized. They may be teacher made or commercial.

INFORMAL TESTS Tests which fit the specific situation represent a closer relationship between the teacher and the learner and a better identification of the learner with the subject. They have the disadvantage of not being comparable from one test to another and not yielding scores which are objective.

STANDARDIZED TESTS On the other hand, tests which are scientifically constructed provide for progression in difficulty and comparison with established norms. They have their place if properly used and if not overused. Expense may be a factor. Teacher time in test construction and scoring may be saved. Machine scoring techniques may reveal little about the learners except their scores. Unless the test tells more than that, much may be lost in the overuse of standardized tests.

USES FOR EVALUATION

Evaluation is a continuous process. It takes place incidentally and informally as well as on schedule and with standardized measures. It serves many purposes among which are (1) a basis for setting attainable goals, (2) an analysis of achievement, and (3) a record for progress reporting. These uses all have their place and call for different procedures, different measuring instruments, different uses of the results, and different points of view. Each one, if used in proper perspective, can make a contribution. Any one used in isolation from the total reading program can be fruitless. It is the use that is made of the records or tests that determines the value.

SETTING ATTAINABLE GOALS

It's all right to hitch your wagon to a star, but it can be mighty discouraging to the plodder who sees no prospect of ever reaching the stars. Both the teacher and the child need to appraise the present situation, see where they are, and set their sights on something they are confident they can attain within the foreseeable future. Otherwise, they are doomed to disappointment which may turn out to be the alibi for quitting. And when one becomes so discouraged he stops trying, he is sure to stop growing. The question, then, is how to appraise the present situation and decide on attainable goals.

CHARTING PROGRESS When one sees where he came from, how much progress he has made, and where he is now, he has a basis for setting his sights for the future. Before we can justify the charting of growth over a period of time we need to take a realistic look at mental testing to see what it has to offer us.

The significance of the IQ has been questioned and as a consequence some educators and many laymen have lost faith in mental tests as measures of capacity and as predictors of learning. Some of the recent studies in readiness, notably those by Ames and Ilg and by de Hirsch have found other factors more indicative for predictions in reading readiness than IQ alone.[1] Even so there is evidence to support the relationship between measured intelligence and ultimate success in reading. Which one is cause and which one is effect may be debatable. However, that need not deter the teacher in her attempts to teach children to read. A careful look at what such tests do tell may guide us in setting goals. Goals set too low will not challenge potential ability. Goals set too high invite defeat, frustration, and failure.

Just what does an intelligence test measure? As such tests are currently constructed most of them measure responses to situations or experiences which the test maker assumes to be common to most children of the age level and background on which the tests were standardized. Critics claim they are slanted toward the middle-class urban child. If so, a child from a different background might respond less well, not because he has less ability, but because he has not had the experiences assumed by the test questions.

Imagine for a moment a child who has been kept shut up in a single room for the first seven years of his life. Also assume that the room is well lighted and comfortable and that the child has all the physical facilities for developing a strong body. At the same time consider his situation if he has no challenge from books, pictures, or playmates. All his care has been scientific but impersonal. He has never seen a pet, a train, an automobile, an airplane, or even a picture of one. Extend this theoretical situation in your imagination to the point where you conceive of a child who is physically mature but who lacks emotional, social, and intellectual stimulation for the first seven years of his life. Then administer one of our school-oriented intelligence tests to him. No doubt he would show up a moron. Does that

[1]Frances L. Ilg and Louise Bates Ames, *School Readiness,* New York, Harper & Row, 1964; Katrina De Hirsch, *Predicting Reading Failure,* New York, Harper & Row, 1966.

mean he lacks native capacity or does it mean that he has not had the experiences necessary to perform adequately on that test?

The children in our schools do not reach this extreme in their experiential backgrounds, but many do have certain lacks which affect their performance on such tests. Recognizing that possibility gives the teacher a basis for viewing the test results realistically. It might be said that each child possesses two IQ's. Let us call one the "potential IQ " and the other the "functional IQ."

The potential IQ is the theoretical level at which the individual might be expected to perform if he had all the opportunities and if he gave all he had to offer in the testing situation. Let's face it, few of us ever perform up to our maximum potential. We might not find it practical to press ourselves to function up to this theoretical peak along some lines. Running "as fast as we can" might exhaust us to the point where we would not have sufficient strength to perform other equally worthwhile feats. Perhaps we should ask ourselves, "What is the ultimate potential for this child in reading? What is the price? Is it worth what it costs in time, energy, effort, and attitude?"

The functional IQ is a more realistic look at the situation as it is. Simply stated, it is merely the level at which the child is functioning at the time he takes the test. If it is a group test and he is upset or distracted, if he is embarrassed or confused, then he may perform at a low level, not because he actually could not have done the exercises, but because he did not do them under those circumstances. The same conflicts which caused him not to perform on the test will also be affecting his reactions in the reading class and, as a consequence, will cause him to perform poorly there, too.

Perhaps he does have the potential to perform at a higher level, but the test did reveal the level at which he was functioning under those circumstances. Since he will usually function under similar circumstances in the reading class, the same deterrents to his success in learning to read exist there. Whether low performance on the IQ test causes failure to succeed in reading or whether inability to learn to read causes the poor performance on the IQ test is not the problem. The point is that they do tend to coexist and recognizing this fact provides guidance for the teacher of reading.

Unless something can be done about the child's work habits, his attitude toward school, his distractions, and his experiences, neither his measured intelligence nor his reading skill is likely to improve. If a child has been subjected to several mental tests, both group and individual, there may be some deviation in the results. If they are all consistently low, you may not know for sure which is "right," but you can be reasonably certain that he has limited capacity for the reading task at the moment. If the results are all consistently high, you may not know for sure whether he is very bright or almost a genius but you can be reasonably sure that, if he has the necessary physical facilities such as speech, sight, and hearing, he will probably learn to read. If he does not do so, you will have to look for other causes than mere lack of ability. If we accept these practical attitudes toward the relationship between intelligence and reading, then we can look at some theoretical statistics as a basis for giving us perspective on child growth as a background for predicting future success in learning to read.

Analysis of a class group will give us perspective. Let us begin with a typical classroom assuming that the children must be 6 years old on or before the 31st of December in the year in which they enter first grade. Then the youngest child in the room on September 1 will have a chronological age (CA) of 5–8. The oldest child in the room will begin school having already passed his sixth birthday on January 1st. He is 6–8 chronologically. The oldest child lacks one day of being one year older than the youngest child. All the rest range on either side of the midpoint which is 6–2. Unlike the characteristics which follow a normal curve of distribution, birth dates tend to fall throughout the year and the range is more evenly distributed.

To this spread of chronological ages let us add a range of mental abilities as accepted from the intelligence testing by assuming that the dullest child has a measured IQ of 75, the brightest 125, and the middle range about 100 which is considered average. Now the possibilities are compounded because not all the old ones are bright and not all the young ones are dull.

How can we use IQ or mental age (MA) to help predict the level at which a child may be expected to achieve in reading? Cleland gives the following formula for computing estimated reading level (ERL).[2]

$$\text{ERL} = \text{yrs. in school} \times \frac{\text{IQ}}{100} + 1$$

Here is an example computed for a beginning fifth grader who has just completed four years in school and who has an IQ of 120.

$$\text{ERL} = 4 \times \frac{120}{100} + 1 = 4 \times 1.2 + 1 = 4.8 + 1 = 5.8$$

Here is an example computed for a beginning fifth grader with an IQ of 90.

$$\text{ERL} = 4 \times \frac{90}{100} + 1 = 4 \times .9 + 1 = 3.6 + 1 = 4.6$$

Both of these examples are computed as of the beginning of the year. If one wished to apply the formula at the end of the year, he would need

[2]Donald L. Cleland, "Clinical Materials for Appraising Disabilities in Reading," *The Reading Teacher, 17,* no. 6 (March, 1964), 428–434.

to adjust the figure for the years in school, that is, at the end of the year a fifth grader has completed five years in school.

Adams and Torgerson point out that "the employment of mental age alone in estimating levels of educational accomplishment in any area of learning has a tendency to show that bright children achieve below expectancy and dull children above mental age."[3]

Gabriel M. Della-Piana gives a much simpler formula for estimating reading potential: "Simply subtract 5 from the mental age."[4] Thus, a child with a mental age of 6–0 is assumed to have the capacity to perform at 1.0 level in reading; 7–0 is equivalent to 2.0. Accepting this simpler formula to illustrate the point we can survey a class group to get a perspective on range of CA, IQ, and MA and then arrive at a figure we can call anticipated achievement (AA).

Figure 24 shows these distributions for nine typical children at the beginning of first grade. Accompanying each mental age is a figure designated as AA which stands for anticipated achievement. This is expressed in terms of grade scores and indicates the approximate grade level of work that could be anticipated from each child with the given mental age.

Chronological Age	Estimated Level of Ability		
	Dull (IQ 75)	*Average (IQ 100)*	*Bright (IQ 125)*
Old (6-8)	Alice MA 5-0 AA 0.0	Bobby MA 6-8 AA 1.8	Carl MA 8-4 AA 3.4
Average (6-2)	Donald MA 4-7 AA 0.0	Erma MA 6-2 AA 1.2	Fred MA 7-8 AA 2.8
Young (5-8)	Grace MA 4-3 AA 0.0	Helen MA 5-8 AA 0.8	Irene MA 7-1 AA 2.1

Figure 24. Analysis of chronological age (CA), mental age (MA), and anticipated achievement (AA) for nine typical cases at beginning of first grade.

Now let's look at each of these nine children as individuals.

Grace is young and dull. She has a mental age of 4–3 and probably the capacity to be in nursery school.

Helen is also young but has normal intelligence. According to the one

[3]Georgia Sacke Adams and Theodore Torgerson, *Measurement and Evaluation*, New York, Dryden, 1957, p. 74.

[4]Gabriel M. Della-Piana, *Reading Diagnosis and Prescription*, New York, Holt, Rinehart and Winston, 1968, p. 41.

criterion of mental age she is still at an immature stage for beginning reading. She may move into reading during the year.

Irene is also young, but since she is very bright she might be reading before she starts to school, particularly if she has been in a stimulating reading environment.

Donald is average for the grade but the tests indicate that he is dull. He probably is not mature enough to expect a successful attack on beginning reading yet.

Erma falls in that middle block. She is average for her grade and has average intelligence. She may be ready to attack beginning reading. Much will depend on her physical condition and experiential background. She is one to whom too often all the teaching is directed.

Fred is average age but very bright. He is more than ready and, like Irene, may already be reading.

Alice is older than the average but still dull. In spite of her extra year she may still lack the mental maturity needed to attack beginning reading with zest.

Bobby also is old for his grade and has average ability. He will probably succeed because he is ready for the task.

Carl is both older and brighter than the rest. He probably could have succeeded in reading last year, but because his birthday fell on the first day of January we made him wait another year.

Table 21 summarizes the range in IQ, CA, MA, and AA for these nine typical cases. This is not an unusual situation. Most typical classrooms will have representatives of each of these nine children with all the variations in between to fill up the twenty-five or thirty seats in the room. The spread may be even wider if there are any children duller or younger than Grace or brighter and older than Carl.

Table 21. RANGE IN IQ, CA, MA, AND AA FOR NINE TYPICAL CASES AT BEGINNING OF FIRST GRADE

	Range			
	Low	*Median*	*High*	*Spread*
IQ	75	100	125	50 points
CA	5-8	6-2	6-8	1 year
MA	4-3	6-2	8-4	4 years
AA	0.0	1.0	3.4	3.4+

The teacher who faces a roomful of children like this and asks them all to open the workbook to page 4 to do the same exercise together is ignoring reality and inviting trouble. The first trouble she faces is boredom for Carl and Fred and possibly even Irene. The second difficulty she faces is frustration and maybe even rebellion from Grace and Donald. Even Helen and Alice may feel some measure of defeat and uncertainty, Helen because she is young and Alice because she is dull. Bobby and Erma are the only ones who seem well equipped to do the task demanded of them and to keep pace, and even Erma may be a bit slow until she gets the idea.

PREDICTING ACHIEVEMENT Any teacher who thinks time will correct these discrepancies is only fooling herself. Education, if well administered, does not reduce or eliminate individual differences; it compounds or increases them. Take a look at these same children four years later when they enter fifth grade. A study of Figure 25 will give a vivid picture of these differences

Chronological Age	Estimated Level of Ability		
	Dull (IQ 75)	*Average (IQ 100)*	*Bright (IQ 125)*
Old (10-8)	Alice MA 8-0 AA 3.0	Bobby MA 10-8 AA 5.8	Carl MA 13-4 AA 8.4
Average (10-2)	Donald MA 7-7 AA 2.7	Erma MA 10-2 AA 5.2	Fred MA 12-8 AA 7.8
Young (9-8)	Grace MA 7-3 AA 2.3	Helen MA 9-8 AA 4.8	Irene MA 12-1 AA 7.1

Figure 25. Analysis of CA, MA, and AA for nine typical cases at beginning of fifth grade.

Table 22. RANGE IN IQ, CA, MA, AND AA FOR NINE TYPICAL CASES AT BEGINNING OF FIFTH GRADE

	Range			
	Low	*Median*	*High*	*Spread*
IQ	75	100	125	50 points
CA	9-8	10-2	10-8	1 year
MA	7-3	10-2	13-4	6 years
AA	2.3	4.9	8.4	6 years

in level of ability and anticipated achievement. Table 22 summarizes the range and spread of ability. Now they are chronologically 9–8 to 10–8, but look at what has happened to their mental ages. Instead of a spread of four years they now spread over six years.

By fifth grade someone along the way will undoubtedly have tried to reduce the gap by practicing a little retention and possibly even some double promotion. With the spread of chronological ages widened to two or three years and the intelligence factor remaining the same the spread gets wider and wider with the passing of time.

Growth patterns are also significant. It helps to take a long range view of the growth of an individual. Let's see what happens over a period of six years, from the beginning of the first grade to the beginning of the seventh grade, as we watch Donald, Erma, and Fred go through school. Table 23 summarizes the statistics of CA, MA, and AA for these three children representing low, average, and high ability.

Table 23. ANALYSIS OF GROWTH PATTERNS FOR THREE TYPICAL CHILDREN (DULL, AVERAGE, AND SUPERIOR) OVER A SIX-YEAR PERIOD AS INDICATED AT THE BEGINNING OF THE YEAR IN GRADES 1 THROUGH 7

	Donald (IQ 75)			*Erma (IQ 100)*			*Fred (IQ 125)*		
Grade	*CA*	*MA*	*AA*	*CA*	*MA*	*AA*	*CA*	*MA*	*AA*
1	6-2	4-7	0.0	6-2	6-2	1.2	6-2	7-8	2.8
2	7-2	5-4	0.4	7-2	7-2	2.2	7-2	8-11	4.0
3	8-2	6-1	1.1	8-2	8-2	3.2	8-2	10-2	5.2
4	9-2	6-10	1.9	9-2	9-2	4.2	9-2	11-5	6.5
5	10-2	7-7	2.7	10-2	10-2	5.2	10-2	12-8	7.8
6	11-2	8-4	3.4	11-2	11-2	6.2	11-2	13-11	9.0
7	12-2	9-1	4.1	12-2	12-2	7.2	12-2	15-2	10.2
Growth	6 yrs.	4-6	4.1	6 yrs.	6-0	6.0	6 yrs.	7-6	7.4

A study of this table indicates that each of these three children gained one year of chronological age for each year as he progressed through the six years in the elementary school. The calendar determined that and there is nothing we can do about it. But what of their mental ages and the corresponding anticipated achievement based on the grade equivalent of mental ages?

Donald is growing mentally at a rate three-fourths as fast as the normal child and therefore gains nine months of mental age for each year of his chronological age. The spread gets wider and wider.

Erma is growing at a normal rate and gains one year of mental age for each year of chronological age.

Fred is growing mentally at a rate one and one-quarter times as fast as the normal child and therefore gains a year and a quarter or fifteen months of mental age for each year of chronological age. The spread gets wider and wider.

The teacher who sets the same goals for Donald and Fred is headed for disappointment for herself and frustration for Donald, not to mention waste of time for Fred. When she sets out to bring Donald up to 5.9 on the reading test by the end of the year because he is in fifth grade, she is asking him to reach for the stars. He knows he can't, so he doesn't bother to try. Then the teacher says he is lazy or contrary. In actuality he has more sense than to struggle with something he knows he can't do. When she makes him hold a fifth grade textbook day after day and take his turn at failing when he is called on to read, she is only compounding the difficulty. At the end of the semester or the end of the year he will be no farther along than when he started. The only thing he will have learned is that he can't and possibly some effective ways of getting out of it. He is waiting till he is sixteen.

The fifth grade teacher who uses that same time to help Donald read something he can read at a level he finds possible instructionally may not get him up to that 5.9 she seemed to think was so desirable, but if she has helped him grow from second grade level material to third grade level material at least he has made progress. He has learned. He has taken that step which will make it possible for him to take the next one. She has helped him set a goal which was attainable and has helped him see his own progress. That is learning.

The teacher who is satisfied with a score of 5.9 for all the children in the room at the end of the fifth grade is accepting mediocre performance from Fred. He could do much more. But he can make A's without any effort and his promotion has never been in jeopardy. Setting attainable goals for him is just as important as for Donald.

Predicting achievement must be recognized as only a theoretical supposition, but it does have its place. If the goal is set too high, the teacher may find it necessary to watch developments and modify expectations in terms of the situation. If the goal is set too low, the teacher may find it necessary to keep herself informed of accomplishments and expand the expectations. That doesn't necessarily mean there was no use to have a goal. It only means the goal has served as a guide. Circumstances may cause alteration of the goals as the work progresses.

ANALYZING ACHIEVEMENT

Test results can be just figures for the records or they can be very useful. When the results are studied and analyzed they can tell much about an individual's performance. They can tell the teacher many valuable bits of information to guide her in her work with the children in taking their next steps in reading. Let's look first at the story they tell about the individual, then later what they tell about the class group.

WHAT TESTS TELL ABOUT THE INDIVIDUAL In the fall of the year Miss Anderson's fifth grade class was administered the California Reading Test and the California Test of Mental Maturity.[5] The tests were machine scored and the results were returned on a summary sheet. Miss Anderson studied them carefully. Tommy, Helen, Juanita, and Gregg were interesting cases. The results for these four children on both tests are summarized in Table 24.

Table 24. ANALYSIS OF TEST RESULTS FOR FOUR FIFTH GRADE CHILDREN BASED ON THE CALIFORNIA READING TEST AND THE CALIFORNIA TEST OF MENTAL MATURITY ADMINISTERED AT THE BEGINNING OF THE YEAR

	Name of Pupil			
	Tommy	*Helen*	*Juanita*	*Gregg*
CA	10-0	11-5	10-10	10-5
IQ	125	92	75	93
MA	12-6	10-6	8-1	9-8
AA	7.6	5.6	3.1	4.8
Norm	5.0	5.0	5.0	5.0
Reading Achievement				
Vocabulary	7.7	2.4	3.9	6.2
Comprehension	7.3	3.5	3.1	4.1
Average	7.5	3.0	3.5	5.2
Deviations				
From Norm	+2.5	−2.0	−1.5	+0.2
From AA	−0.1	−2.6	+0.4	+0.4

Tommy has an IQ of 125. The reading test indicated that he scored at 7.5 grade equivalent. Pretty good you say! Let's look more deeply into the matter. Here is what we can glean about Tommy from the cumulative record and these test results. He is a fifth grader with superior ability. He is capable of reading beyond his assigned grade level and his test indicated that he does. His vocabulary score is slightly higher than his comprehension score. A mental age of 12–6 indicates an anticipated achievement of 7.6 as computed by Della-Piana's simple formula. Tommy is no problem. Should he be double promoted? Or should he be challenged where he is? That depends on what kinds of challenges are offered. Classification is not our concern at the moment. We are merely studying what tests can tell us about the child.

Now let's look at Helen. She, too, is a fifth grader. She is older than most of the other children in the room. The cumulative record indicates that she repeated third grade. Her IQ is within the range of normal. When she was in first grade she couldn't keep up with the group but the family objected to having her retained. When she was in second grade the teacher

[5]Ernest Tiegs and Willis W. Clark, *California Reading Test*, Elementary, Monterey, Calif., California Test Bureau, 1963; Elizabeth T. Sullivan, Willis W. Clark, and Ernest W. Tiegs, *California Short-Form Test of Mental Maturity*, Elementary, Monterey, Calif., California Test Bureau, 1963.

suggested retention but the family protested on the grounds that she got along all right and passed last year. In the end the teacher gave up and passed her along to third grade against her own better judgment. In the third grade she had a teacher who attempted to adjust the work to her level. By the end of the year she was still working with a first reader and the teacher insisted that she be reclassified as a third grader for the following year. By this time Helen was convinced that she couldn't read and there was no use to try. For the next two years she put in time and avoided as many of the unpleasant situations in reading as possible. At the beginning of fifth grade the statistics suggested that she "ought to be able to do fifth grade work" because of her near normal ability and her extra year of age, but she wasn't doing it. When Miss Anderson administered the test she noted that on the comprehension part Helen got the idea that she was to underline one word in each box. She went through it quickly and marked the right number of words at random finishing in about half the time allotted. Miss Anderson's opinion was that the 3.5 on the comprehension part of the test was not truly indicative of her ability.

Juanita was in that same fifth grade. Her test results showed an average achievement of 3.5 as compared with an anticipated achievement of 3.1, even though the norm for beginning fifth grade was 5.0. Actually, if the mental test is any indication of her ability, Juanita was doing as much or more than we have any right to expect. Measuring her by these standards and pressuring her to get her marks up to grade standard would be about like urging a person of small stature to eat more to make himself taller.

Gregg is still a different picture. The average grade score of 5.2 as compared with the anticipated achievement of 4.8 looks good. When compared with the norm for beginning fifth grade it looks as if he were "right on target." When we look at the average grade we may conclude that he is doing all right, but when we look at the two separate scores we see a very interesting discrepancy. On vocabulary he scored 6.2 which is well above either grade placement or anticipated achievement. On comprehension he scored 4.1 which is not only below grade placement, but also below anticipated achievement. Miss Anderson knows much about Gregg that the tests do not tell. She knows that he is eager to please both his teacher and his mother. He works hard at memorizing what he is told to learn. He can say lists of words and utilize mechanical tools in deciphering pronunciations. He seems to have only a hazy notion of the content of what he is reading. She concludes that the scores on the test tell a fairly accurate story which supports her observations.

When tests are administered by some person other than the teacher and are machine scored, only the scores are available for analysis. When the tests are administered by the teacher herself and she has an opportunity to observe the children as they work, she knows much more about them. When she scores the tests by hand and observes the kinds of errors each child makes, she has a much deeper insight into their abilities and needs.

If you want only a final score for group analysis, then perhaps a monitored test will provide the data needed. But if you want a diagnosis and study of the individuals as a basis for further teaching, then perhaps the time and energy used by the classroom teacher to administer her own tests and to hand score them will be more than repaid in the extra insight into the needs and abilities of the children. What the test does not tell is why the child has the specific difficulties.

Part of the reasons for difficulties may be hidden in an accumulation of past experiences and part may be a direct result of the immediate situation. The teacher will not find this answer "in the back of the book." She

Table 25. ANTICIPATED ACHIEVEMENT AND READING GRADE SCORES FOR FIFTH GRADE CLASS IN SEPTEMBER AS MEASURED BY CALIFORNIA TEST OF MENTAL MATURITY AND CALIFORNIA READING TEST

		Reading Grade Scores		
Pupil	*AA*	*Vocabulary*	*Comprehension*	*Average*
Alan	5.5	5.8	6.6	6.2
Ann	7.0	7.2	6.6	6.9
Barbara	6.5	7.0	7.1	7.1
Bettie	6.5	7.3	5.5	6.4
Billy	7.0	6.8	5.2	6.0
Byron	6.0	7.1	7.2	7.2
Cathy	4.5	4.2	2.3	3.3
Charles	6.0	5.6	6.0	5.8
Clifford	5.6	6.4	5.7	6.1
Douglas	6.2	6.7	6.2	6.5
Dorothy	4.3	3.9	3.5	3.7
Erma	4.4	3.4	2.5	3.0
Florence	4.3	4.2	3.2	3.7
Frank	6.9	7.8	6.1	7.0
Fred	5.8	5.8	4.6	5.2
Grace	4.7	4.5	4.6	4.6
Gregg	4.8	6.2	4.1	5.2
Helen	5.6	2.4	3.5	3.0
Juanita	3.1	3.9	3.1	3.5
Margaret	3.2	3.8	2.6	3.2
Max	6.4	6.1	5.9	6.0
Mike	6.2	5.7	6.8	6.3
Perry	6.1	6.5	6.3	6.4
Roberta	5.6	5.3	6.1	5.7
Sara	5.8	4.9	3.8	4.4
Tommy	7.6	7.7	7.3	7.5
William	5.1	5.6	4.6	5.1

may speculate as to causal factors utilizing what she knows about the children, about reading, and about each individual child, but even with lots of experience she will still be speculating and occasionally she may make an inaccurate diagnosis. She should be alert to evaluate her own diagnoses regularly and note whether or not the prescribed treatments are getting the desired results. She should always be open and receptive to change whenever conditions indicate the need.

WHAT TESTS TELL ABOUT THE CLASS GROUP When Miss Anderson studied test results for the class as a group she had two purposes in mind. One was to identify strengths and weaknesses to determine where emphasis should be placed to round out the program of instruction. The other was to get an over-all picture of the class to compare with national norms.

Tommy, Helen, Juanita, and Gregg are just four of the twenty-seven children in the class whose test results are listed in Table 25. It is difficult to look at such a table and conclude anything about individuals or about class trends. Miss Anderson decided to study them and see what she could find out.

First she studied the scores in vocabulary as compared with the anticipated achievement. She placed each child on a scattergram as shown in Figure 26. This told her several things about the class. Any child whose name fell on the diagonal line was working at capacity as measured by the mental test. This did not necessarily mean he was working up to norm. Any child whose name fell above the diagonal line was working at a higher level than she had anticipated. Any child whose name was below the diagonal line was working at a lower level than she had anticipated. From the scattergram she drew these conclusions.

Seven were doing about what could be expected. They were Tommy, Ann, Max, Alan, Fred, Grace, and Florence.

Eleven were working above anticipation. They were Frank, Barbara, Bettie, Byron, Douglas, Perry, Clifford, William, Gregg, Juanita, and Margaret.

Nine were not working up to expectancy. They were Billy, Charles, Mike, Roberta, Sara, Helen, Cathy, Dorothy, and Erma.

Strange as it may seem no one fell in the center of the scattergram with both capacity and achievement at norm.

Sara and Helen were working below capacity and indications were that they might have been expected to work at or above fifth grade level or norm.

Roberta, Charles, Mike, and Billy were not doing quite as well as the mental test indicated, but they were working up to grade level or above and the deviations were relatively slight.

Cathy, Dorothy, and Erma were not working up to either norm or

Vocabulary Score	Anticipated Achievement											
	2.0-2.4	2.5-2.9	3.0-3.4	3.5-3.9	4.0-4.4	4.5-4.9	5.0-5.4	5.5-5.9	6.0-6.4	6.5-6.9	7.0-7.4	7.5-7.9
7.5-7.9										Frank		Tommy
7.0-7.4									Byron	Barbara Bettie	Ann	
6.5-6.9									Douglas Perry		Billy	
6.0-6.4						Gregg		Clifford	Max			
5.5-5.9							William	Alan Fred	Charles Mike			
5.0-5.4								Roberta				
4.5-4.9						Grace		Sara				
4.0-4.4					Florence	Cathy						
3.5-3.9			Juanita Margaret		Dorothy							
3.0-3.4					Erma							
2.5-2.9												
2.0-2.4								Helen				

Figure 26. Reading achievement in vocabulary compared to anticipated achievement as indicated by California Test of Mental Maturity for twenty-seven fifth grade children tested in September.

capacity, but the deviations were small in the cases of Dorothy and Cathy. Perhaps they could improve, but expecting them to "catch up" seems an unlikely goal.

Seven of those who were apparently working above capacity were also working above grade placement. They were Frank, Barbara, Bettie, Byron, Douglas, Perry, and Clifford. William with normal ability tested slightly above norm. Gregg was noticeable in the extent of his deviation. Juanita and Margaret were working at late third grade level and even that was more than the mental test indicated we had any right to expect.

Next Miss Anderson compared the scores on the comprehension part of the test with anticipated achievement. Again she placed each child on a scattergram as shown in Figure 27.

This time she found only five of them working above anticipation. They were Barbara, Byron, Mike, Alan, and Roberta. Compare this to the eleven in vocabulary. Only Barbara and Byron were working at this high level in both vocabulary and comprehension.

Six of them fell on the diagonal. They were Charles, Douglas, Perry, Clifford, Grace, and Juanita. The other sixteen were working below anticipation in comprehension. Immediately Miss Anderson concluded that as a class they were not doing as well in comprehension as in vocabulary. And again no one fell in that center square.

Again Sara and Helen fell below anticipation and below grade level. Roberta, Charles, and Mike moved up to equal or exceed anticipated achievement in comprehension, but Billy still fell below expectation and even lower on comprehension than on vocabulary. Cathy, Dorothy, and Erma maintained their same positions below grade level and below expectation. Fred, William, Gregg, Florence, and Margaret joined them with scores below both grade level and anticipation.

Frank and Bettie were working above anticipation in vocabulary but fell below in comprehension. No one with capacity below the norm for the grade exceeded the norm in comprehension.

A third study Miss Anderson made resulted in another scattergram comparing the scores on vocabulary with the scores on comprehension. The results are shown in Figure 28. An analysis of this scattergram showed that eighteen of the children scored at a higher level on vocabulary than on comprehension, four of them fell on the diagonal, and only five scored higher on comprehension than on vocabulary. This substantiated her earlier observation that the class appeared better on word recognition than on comprehension.

Thirteen children out of the twenty-seven made scores on both comprehension and vocabulary above the norm. Out of these thirteen eight did better on vocabulary than on comprehension. They were Tommy, Ann, Frank, Douglas, Perry, Bettie, Clifford, and Max. Two did as well on one

Comp. Score	Anticipated Achievement											
	2.0-2.4	2.5-2.9	3.0-3.4	3.5-3.9	4.0-4.4	4.5-4.9	5.0-5.4	5.5-5.9	6.0-6.4	6.5-6.9	7.0-7.4	7.5-7.9
7.5-7.9												
7.0-7.4									Byron	Barbara		Tommy
6.5-6.9								Alan	Mike		Ann	
6.0-6.4								Roberta	Charles Douglas Perry	Frank		
5.5-5.9								Clifford	Max	Bettie		
5.0-5.4											Billy	
4.5-4.9						Grace	William	Fred				
4.0-4.4						Gregg						
3.5-3.9					Dorothy			Helen Sara				
3.0-3.4			Juanita		Florence							
2.5-2.9			Margaret		Erma							
2.0-2.4						Cathy						

Figure 27. Reading achievement in comprehension compared to anticipated achievement as indicated by California Test of Mental Maturity for twenty-seven fifth grade children tested in September.

Vocabulary Score	Comprehension Scores											
	2.0-2.4	2.5-2.9	3.0-3.4	3.5-3.9	4.0-4.4	4.5-4.9	5.0-5.4	5.5-5.9	6.0-6.4	6.5-6.9	7.0-7.4	7.5-7.9
7.5-7.9									Frank		Tommy	
7.0-7.4								Bettie		Ann	Barbara Byron	
6.5-6.9							Billy		Douglas Perry			
6.0-6.4					Gregg			Clifford Max				
5.5-5.9						Fred William			Charles	Alan Mike		
5.0-5.4									Roberta			
4.5-4.9				Sara		Grace						
4.0-4.4	Cathy		Florence									
3.5-3.9		Margaret	Juanita	Dorothy								
3.0-3.4		Erma										
2.5-2.9												
2.0-2.4				Helen								

Figure 28. Reading achievement in comprehension compared to vocabulary as indicated by California Reading Test for twenty-seven fifth grade children tested in September.

as the other. They were Barbara and Byron. Only Charles, Alan, and Mike did better on comprehension than on vocabulary.

Billy was the only one that scored within the first half of fifth grade on comprehension and he scored well above that on vocabulary. Roberta was the only one that scored within the first half of fifth grade on vocabulary and she scored well above that on comprehension.

William, Fred, and Gregg scored above grade level on vocabulary but below on comprehension.

Nine of the children showed scores on both comprehension and vocabulary below fifth grade level. Out of these nine there were six who did better on vocabulary than on comprehension. They were Sara, Florence, Juanita, Margaret, Erma, and Cathy. Both Dorothy and Grace showed consistency. Only Helen in this group did better on comprehension than on vocabulary and we discussed her individual case earlier.

Miss Anderson stopped to analyze what these scattergrams told her. From them she drew the following conclusions.

• Since the tests were administered in the early fall in the fifth grade the norm was 5.0.

• The median anticipated achievement of 5.8 was more than half a grade above the norm.

• The median achievement of 5.8 in vocabulary was more than half a grade above the norm and equal to the anticipation.

• The median achievement of 5.5 in comprehension was a half grade above norm but slightly below anticipation.

• Achievement was at a higher level in vocabulary than in comprehension.

• Fourteen children had abilities above norm and were achieving above grade placement in both vocabulary and comprehension.

• Seven children had abilities below grade placement and were achieving below norm in both vocabulary and comprehension.

• Only one, William, had a capacity comparable to his present grade placement and he scored above norm on vocabulary but below norm on comprehension.

• Only six seemed to deviate from expectancy in such a manner that indicated need for further study. They were Billy and Fred who were both above grade placement in anticipated achievement and in vocabulary but not in comprehension; Roberta who was above grade in anticipated achievement and in comprehension but not in vocabulary; Sara and Helen with indicated capacity above grade placement but achievement below norm in both vocabulary and comprehension.

• No one fell in the middle square on any of the scattergrams!

• Roberta was the only one at norm in vocabulary.

• Billy was the only one at norm in comprehension.

• William was the only one at grade level in anticipated achievement and he was above norm on one part of the test and below norm on the other.

• Those who fell in the upper right-hand corner of the scattergrams might be said to be doing very well. In some cases they might be stimulated to do a little better, but there is room for question as to whether their time might be better spent in broadening their reading experiences rather than in accelerating their pace.

• Those who fell in the lower left-hand corner of the scattergrams might be said to be "doing as well as could be expected." In some cases they might be stimulated to do a little better, but it is doubtful if "bringing them up to norm" would be a reasonable goal. In some cases they are already doing more than one might expect.

- Only three different names appeared in the upper left-hand quadrant of the scattergrams. Gregg appeared there twice and Fred and William once each. The latter two were so close to the norm that their deviation could not be considered exceptional. Perhaps Gregg's ability had been underestimated although his comprehension score did not bear out this conclusion. He will bear watching.
- Only three different names appeared in the lower right-hand quadrant of the scattergrams. Sara and Helen appeared there consistently indicating that their capacities were greater than their achievements. Fred appeared there only once and he was so close to the norm that the deviation could not be considered exceptional. It is possible that the abilities of Sara and Helen had been overestimated.

Based on these conclusions Miss Anderson planned to do the following things in her instructional program.

- Ask for a retest on Gregg who seems to do better than expected.
- Ask for a recheck on the mental ability of Sara and Helen who do not seem to do as well as could be expected.
- Plan a different program in reading for the fourteen children in the upper right-hand quadrants of the scattergrams. The aim will be to challenge their abilities. This might be done with content books or with trade books in a self-selection individualized program.
- Plan an adjusted program for the seven children in the lower left-hand quadrant of the scattergrams adjusting the work to their instructional levels and pitching the pace at a rate they can manage.
- Keep careful records for the next six or eight weeks to find out whether subjective observation substantiates the above conclusions and to provide evidence of growth or change in any individual.

This kind of an analysis of a class group helped Miss Anderson pinpoint the problem cases and identify the types of difficulty. Too often the tendency is to see only a miscellaneous listing of scores as given in Table 25 and to discount their reliability because the individual cases whose scores are doubtful have not been spotted with reasons for the doubt. Wholesale retesting of the entire class is a waste of both tests and time for both pupils and teacher. Unless the retesting leads to a careful analysis the retest will only support the original skepticism. Careful analysis of the tests will help the teacher decide what measures to take in a developmental program. And unless she notes the types of difficulties she still has a further diagnosis to make.

REPORTING PROGRESS

Evaluation can be used as a basis for progress reporting. While a personal conference will tell the parent much about how a child is getting along, something about his work habits, and a reaction to his attitudes toward school, this can be highly subjective. Such evaluation is often couched in such expressions as, "He is a delightful child," "It is a pleasure to have him in the class," "He always tries to do his best," "You have every right to be proud of him," "He is often a disturbing element in the room," and "I think he could do better." These statements either encourage or discourage the parents without telling them anything. When the parent says he wants to know what the child is doing, how he compares, what the score is, what he really means is that he wants something concrete as evidence of accomplishment. There are several questions which can be answered: How much is it worth? What has been accomplished? What does the score tell?

HOW MUCH IS IT WORTH? This is a question which calls for placing a value on the learning and sometimes on the pupil himself. Providing him with an A or a C does not answer that question. All such a mark does is place the child on a scale. The basis for comparison varies with the judgment of the person doing the comparing. The C might mean that he stands at the middle of the class—a poor grade if he is capable of doing much better, a good grade if he is less capable. An A might mean that he is doing all that is asked, but maybe not much was asked and therefore nearly everybody got A's. Or if a great deal was expected very few got A's. Then the value of the A fluctuates. What might be considered worth a mark of A by one teacher might not meet the high standards set by another teacher. To some teachers an F is never justified if the child is doing the best he can. To other teachers an F means he is not doing the work outlined for the grade. Other reporting devices which attempt to compare children by ranking them are: superior, average, poor; 1, 2, 3, 4, and 5; plus, check, minus; or excellent, above average, acceptable, below average, and failing. These evaluation techniques are all designed to answer the question, "How much is it worth?" or perhaps more specifically, "How much is Sammy worth?"

WHAT HAS BEEN ACCOMPLISHED? This is a question which leads to a record of achievements that can be reported objectively. A test score can be merely a raw score which tells the number of right responses, a grade score which shows performance in terms of established norms, or a stanine or percentile which places the child on a scale so he can see where he stands. This ignores ability level and assumes that he ought to do what others are doing.

Perhaps even better than the scores is a breakdown to show what he can do and what he still needs to do. A report which tells the parent that he attempted 14 out of 18 exercises in the allotted time and got all 14 right is quite different from a report which tells that he tried all 18 of the exercises, finished before the end of the allotted time, and got 14 of them right. In these two cases the 14 right for the two children yields the same grade score, but the report is quite different. A listing of skills including a check on whether or not they have been attained is even more specific.

WHAT DOES THE SCORE TELL? Interpreting the score on standardized tests is something both parents and children can learn to do. When they see the scores as measures of progress rather than as hurdles crossed, the scores become an answer to the question, "How am I doing?" A report which is cumulative from year to year has much to offer. Table 26 summarizes such a series of reports for two representative children.

Table 26. CUMULATIVE REPORT OF SCORES IN READING FOR TWO TYPICAL CASES AT ONE-YEAR INTERVALS

	Grade Score in Reading	
Grade Level	*Mary*	*Tom*
3rd	2.8	2.8
4th	3.9	3.6
5th	5.2	4.4
6th	6.8	5.1
Growth	4.0	2.3

The report for Mary shows progress, growth, and accelerated pace. This is gratifying. A check with her ability may lead to the conclusion that such progress was to be expected. The report for Tom shows more limited progress, slow growth, and a slackening pace. This is cause for investigation. Perhaps he has normal ability and some other cause for lack of satisfactory progress must be identified. Or perhaps he has limited ability and such progress is in keeping with his capacity. Neither case can be judged good or bad on the figures alone. The figures tell only what happened, not why. The teacher must use them as a basis for further interpretation.

The child can be led to chart his own progress and to interpret the results for himself. When he participates in the evaluation, understands the test results, and helps to keep his own record, he will be able to explain his progress to his parents. This is one of the best types of reporting.

What about promotion? Should test results be used as a basis for promotion to the next higher level? That depends on so many things. If that is the only use for test results, then they are probably costing too much in money and time for the value received. If that is the only basis for determining the promotion, then perhaps the evidence is weak. Sometimes, however, the objectivity of the test scores serves as a valuable support for teacher judgment and even for convincing evidence when a parent must be faced with a decision he does not like.

APPLYING THE RESULTS OF EVALUATION

Unless subjective records and test results are used to further learning they have done little good. Records and scores which are merely filed away only accumulate evidence and dust. Before administering any test the teacher should give thought to what has been taught, what the goal is, and what she wants to find out. Then the test should be selected to fit the situation.

If for a short period of time, say ten or fifteen weeks, one group is drilled on word recognition techniques while another is taught with the initial approach based on meaning, and then both groups are given a test on mechanics, obviously the group which is tested on what they have been taught will outscore the other group. If testing is done after an even shorter drill period, perhaps six weeks, the situation is magnified. The question to be raised is not so much which group scored higher but which group has formed habits, attitudes, understandings, and learnings which will carry through to maturity in reading?

IMPORTANCE OF FOLLOW-THROUGH

Before we can decide what method is best, what materials are best, which teachers are best, what time is best to teach reading skills, and all the other questions related to reading, we need to take a longitudinal view of the whole situation. Since learning to read is not accomplished in six weeks or one semester or one year or even in the primary grades but is a long-term process with continuous growth, the testing done from time to time must be considered only check points along the way.

A reading program must cover not one school year, not just the elementary grades, but a whole lifetime. Too many of the research projects, too many of the testing programs which lead to conclusions stated with finality, and too many of the programs of instruction are built on short-term panaceas. Such an approach allows the learner to check out before he is finished.

Follow-through on any program is a first essential. The child who is introduced to first steps in phonics through the recognition of initial consonant sounds but is never taught any of the more advanced learnings about word structure is being allowed to quit before the job is done. The child who is introduced to reading as comprehension but is never given any insight into the structure of our language is getting only a part of the program. The child who learns a few of the fundamentals but is turned loose to read on his own without adequate guidance may stumble along with faulty and ineffective habits and may never reach maturity. Any program must be followed through to completion over a period of years and to application in all areas. Otherwise the learner is going to die on third base, or maybe second base; in fact, some of them may never even get to first base.

IMPORTANCE OF APPLICATION

In like manner the learner must be able to apply his reading skills to all reading situations. A test which proves that a child knows the words or even that he can read is not sufficient. The real evaluation of the program in the teaching of reading lies in whether or not he reads, what he reads, and how he uses the results of his reading. Perhaps the matter of application can be evaluated by asking the proper questions.

Does he read? *not* Can he read?

Does he use his reading skills independently? *not* Can he pass objective tests on word recognition and answer marking?

Does he use the facts gleaned through reading to interpret information and arrive at conclusions? *not* Can he find the facts?

Does he attack it with enthusiasm as a privilege and a pleasure? *not* Does he view reading as a chore and an assignment?

Evaluation can be for diagnosis, assessment, or measurement of growth. Effective techniques include observation, record keeping, and testing. Evaluation can be used as a guide in setting goals, in analyzing achievement, in reporting progress, and sometimes as evidence to support conclusions about classification or promotion. In applying the results of evaluation to the total learning-to-read process one must see that process as a long-term growth with follow-through and application of the utmost importance.

18

EVALUATING THE MATERIALS

or What Do We Have That Mark Hopkins Didn't Have?

It is true that you can't make something out of nothing. It is equally true that you can't make a silk purse out of a sow's ear. Or can you? What with modern science and man's ingenuity it almost seems that the old saying is no longer true. Perhaps!

Anyway, Mark Hopkins on his end of the log and the eager student on the opposite end might have resulted in considerable learning. But let's make learning a transitive verb. What was the student learning? Attitudes? Skills? Understandings? Ideas? The tradition doesn't say. But even Mark Hopkins might have done better with some of our modern, attractive materials. The question is, "What part do materials of instruction play in the teaching-learning process?"

TYPES OF MATERIALS AVAILABLE

Materials have changed over the years. Let us review these changes in order to see present-day materials in proper perspective. We might look at other things besides books, for instance, other types of printed materials, reading aids, and even technology.

BOOKS

When one says, "Read," he automatically thinks, "Books." It is true that one also reads magazines, sign boards, newspapers, musical scores, gestures, expressions on faces, tones in voices, and a multiplicity of other communications, but our traditional schools are based on the assumption that the printed word is the way to salvation, so let's stick to that as a basis for analysis of materials of instruction in reading.

Books may be considered under different categories. Textbooks include both the basal readers and the texts in other school subjects. Then there are reference books and trade books. They have all found their way into the modern classroom in increasing quantities and, we hope, with improving quality.

TEXTBOOKS There was the day when the textbook was the source of all learning. Often there was only one book for a subject, and sometimes there was only one copy of that book. Such a shortage was caused, first, by a lack of available printed materials and, second, by a lack of funds to provide more material or more copies of the same materials. When there was only one book and only one copy of the book, the teacher seemed to have little or no choice of method except to read or tell the child what was in the book, then check on him to see if he had learned it. When there was only one book but it came in multiple copies, one in the hands of each child, the teacher still seemed limited in the scope of teaching. The resulting procedure often turned out to be assigning the same lesson to every one, then checking to see if all had learned. Sometimes this procedure took on the pattern of utilizing class time to do the learning on the theory that "reading the lesson out loud" by taking turns around the class would give exposure that brought about learning.

BASAL READERS The development of readers, one for each grade, came as a result of the grading of the schools. The content was determined by the author who had his own opinions about what children could do and what was good for them. As a consequence many of the early reading textbooks were filled with moralistic stories, literature, and exercises in elocution. Changes came about in the content of readers as pressures were put on the schools to teach skills. Then came the readers with drill exercises, word lists, and rules. These were presented on the theory that mastering the mechanics would result in transfer to other types of reading. The study of child development led to a different emphasis which introduced content based on children's experiences and skills based on psychological rather than logical development. An examination of readers published at intervals over a period of a century or more will show this pattern.

At the same time that the content of basal readers was evolving the format was going through developmental changes. The size of the print was originally determined by the mechanical reproduction process available or the amount the author wanted to put on a page. A study of the child's physical development, his muscular coordination, his eye muscle development, and his attention span led to changes in the size of type used and the amount of printed material on a page or in a line. Pictures came to play an increasing part in the context of a child's book. At first the pictures were introduced to make the book more attractive, then the opportunity to make the pictures enhance the learning was seen. As pictures carried more of the message they came in for their fair share of criticism on the theory that they were supplementing the child's mastery of the printed form and were thus interfering with learning.

At the same time the publishers, in their eagerness to please more people and hence to sell more books, continued to compete with one another to produce more attractive printed materials. The modern textbook in reading is a far cry from the once revered *Blue Backed Spellers* or the *McGuffey Readers*. Those who look back with nostalgia on the good old days haven't actually tried to teach from some of that material with modern children accustomed to present-day advertising and the spectaculars of TV, billboards, and color magazines. For a comparison of readers over the years see Plate II.

TEXTS IN OTHER SCHOOL SUBJECTS Not only basal readers but also texts in other school subjects have changed a great deal. There was the time when the geography text was considered good if it was big enough to provide space for a double-spread map and if it contained factual information and descriptions of the regions presented. History was supposed to present the facts. A science textbook had a responsibility only for accuracy of information. A mathematics text needed only space for examples and drill exercises. A speller was made up of word lists.

Today's basal texts in the subject matter areas other than reading are greatly changed. Today a geography text must present more than facts. It must acquaint the child with a way of life and a reason for certain adaptations. The history book attempts to present more than one side and to influence attitudes as well as knowledge. This invites controversy. Mathematics texts, spelling texts, and science texts are seeking to guide the thinking of the learner as well as his skills and to help him become a lifetime learner instead of a living encyclopedia.

Not only have these subject matter texts changed in format, in content, and in purpose, but they have changed in quantity and in variety. When the learner has only one text and it is the sole authority available, then great care must be exercised to make sure the facts are indisputable. But indisputable facts are almost impossible to come by and are frequently deadening to the learner. If the child is to become a thinking learner, he needs to study facts from more than one view point and to be aware that many of the facts can be disputed even among authorities. Some are disputable because there is more than one point of view. Some become disputable because there is more new evidence which changes truth. The availability of multiple sources of information makes it possible for the learner to read widely and to find out for himself what is truth. This approach to reading and learning changes the content of books, the purchasing plans of schools, and consequently the procedures in the classrooms.

REFERENCE BOOKS Some books are used for reference to supplement the texts. These include such tools as encyclopedias, dictionaries, and atlases. The use of these books calls for a different approach to reading and a different type of classroom management. This point was discussed in greater detail in Chapter 11 which is devoted to using reading skills to locate information.

TRADE BOOKS Most modern schools are equipped with libraries of some type. Whether that library should be a room library, a central library, or a combination of the two is not the issue at this point. The issue is that the child today has access to literally thousands of sources of reading material. He gets books for his own personal library as gifts from friends and relatives. He picks up inexpensive books at the supermarket or local drugstore. He finds books of all kinds in his classroom. He probably has access to a public library of some kind. It may be a big building with a forbidding façade, it may be a low, rambling building with an inviting window, or it may even be a big bus fitted with library shelves which travels from one community to another.

What these books contain is another matter. Trade books are available in quantities, and it is the rare child who doesn't have access to some of them, good or bad, even comic books. The ones who do not make use of available books may spend equal amounts of time or money before TV, in the local movie house, or with useless toys. Access to books is no longer the problem; it is now more a matter of interest and choice, either on the part of the child or the adults.

OTHER PRINTED MATERIALS

Children today are literally surrounded by a sea of print. Newspapers, periodicals, advertisements, and circulars come into the home. All these plus workbooks, duplicated materials, and tests permeate the schools. The child is constantly being bombarded with printed materials. Whether he can or does read them is often a matter of more concern to the adults than to the child himself. Sometimes he is put in the position of reacting to the printed material in much the same manner as the child reacts to food when he is forced to eat.

NEWSPAPERS AND PERIODICALS There are perhaps more people with access to newspapers who do not bother to read them than there are people who would read them but do not have them. Even yesterday's newspaper which has been discarded by the neighbors is better than no newspaper. Discarded magazines of all kinds are piled high in the junk heaps. Anyone who really wants to see the printed word can find it to read. Inaccessibility through poverty, deprivation, or immobility is the exception rather than the rule. The child who would read can find, or can be helped to find, printed material to read. The quality of what he reads is another matter, but if he learns to read and to enjoy reading, the road to improved tastes and higher quality is available.

WORKBOOKS AND DUPLICATED MATERIALS Technology which made printing relatively inexpensive and the testing movement and scientific research which made objectivity popular led to the extensive use of consumable materials. Both workbooks and duplicated materials have waxed and waned in popularity. Some teachers believe that printed material in the form of hand-outs meets the need for "seat work" or between-class activities or something for the child to do while the teacher works with another group. These materials are neither good nor bad in themselves. It is the use that is made of them that might be judged good or bad. This was discussed in greater detail in Chapter 14.

READING AIDS

There's nothing like an epidemic to reveal sure-cure recommendations, and if you have an ailment all your friends and acquaintances have remedies to prescribe. The same is true of reading ailments. Everybody has a remedy for every problem. It is the diagnostician's responsibility to identify the specific problem and to prescribe the appropriate remedy. No remedy solves all problems, and no problem responds to all remedies. Nevertheless, the interest in devices to meet the needs has led to an abundance of materials on the market to improve the teaching of reading.

GAMES AND DEVICES Drill is intended to fix responses. The game or device serves as a motivator. It is supposed to intrigue the learner and "trick" him into practicing for the sake of the game. In doing so he is supposed to learn the response required for playing the game. The by-product of the game is the skill. The question might well be asked, "Is the skill of sufficient value and interest to induce the learner to practice without camouflaging or sugar coating?" Refer to Chapter 14 for further discussion and elaboration.

CHARTS, DIAGRAMS, AND MAPS Organization of learnings is based on the theory that the structure of knowledge is significant and that the child who sees order in what he learns is better educated than the one who learns only miscellaneous facts and stores them in memory chambers for retrieval as needed. There are all kinds of word charts, phonogram charts, sentence charts, sound charts, and language charts for sale.

In the same category with charts and diagrams are maps which are devices for organizing information and presenting it in a form that stresses relationships. Reading maps calls for both organizational skill and reading skill. Commercial companies have vied with one another to see who can produce the most attractive, the most unusual, the most effective materials of this type to get the message across to the reader. They all help. None will do the job alone.

PROJECTED MATERIALS Reading material projected for class use has certain advantages. It meets the need of the very young with immature eye development and far vision, thus circumventing the problem of focus at near point. In a class situation it provides a common center of attention for all. The teacher can be sure the children all "have the place" and can point out detail for all at once. Projection which involves motion adds reality to concepts. Children are stimulated by the novelty of the projected image. Such devices do not replace or substitute for the printed page. They are effective supplements.

SYMBOLS The reading process itself is based on the use of symbols. The ABC's diacritical marks, and phonetically regular alphabets are illustrations of symbolic representation of ideas.

The *alphabet* is the basic set of symbols traditionally used for learning to read and eventually as a tool for writing. Since the English language is not internally consistent in the relationship of sound and symbol because of its origin and evolution from other languages, it presents many difficulties for the beginner. There have been many attempts to provide the beginner in reading with some kind of symbol system on which he can depend.

Diacritical marks are used in most dictionaries. They range from the simple use of long and short markings for vowels to an elaborate plan which provides markings for various shades of sound for the different letters. Some dictionaries may provide a specific mark to indicate the difference in the sound of the letter *a* in each of the following words: bad, came, far, tall, and said. The more recent trend is toward phonetic respelling and the use of fewer such marks. Refer to Chapter 5 for a more complete discussion.

Phonetically regular alphabets such as i.t.a. are attempts to produce a one-to-one relationship between sound and symbol. They have sometimes been offered as panaceas for reading problems. The proponents of i.t.a. both in England and in the United States claim results in using it for beginning reading. Some skeptics may feel that just as good results can be obtained by other techniques if the teacher has equal zeal and skill.

When all is said and done, no device, no technique, no aid will give the learner either intelligence or desire. The most that can be hoped for is that these aids will make the task easy enough and attractive enough so that the learner will have enough success to make him willing to pursue the exercise. Even then there are critics who firmly believe that to be of value learning must be hard. In that case they would probably object to the use of any gadget or device that is meant to smooth the pathway and make learning painless.

TECHNOLOGY

Technology has made its contribution to education. If refrigerators can be turned out on the assembly line, if communications can be made automatically, if ovens can be operated by pressing the proper buttons, then, reasons the technologist, why can't learning be made an automatic response controlled by wires or levers or buttons?

That brings us to the teaching machines, the instruments, the "hardware." The theory is based on a behavioristic psychology and automatic response. The exercises are built on the principle of alternates. Each response is either right or wrong. The child is rewarded or praised for right responses and chastised or has the reward withheld in case of wrong responses. For learnings which are definitely right or wrong and for responses that need fixing without thinking this technique may make its contribution. But students of child development and humanistic psychology tend to question whether or not this is real learning and certainly whether it is enough. As yet no machine has been developed to determine attitudes, understandings, and interpretations. These are not subject to right or wrong alternatives. They are not subject to final answers. The machine, at best, can only feed the exercises to the learner in an automatic pattern. Its value is dependent on the program that is fed into the machine, in other words, the "software." The machine does challenge the learner. But it serves only as a motivating device and a monitor. It will work only so long as the child makes it work.

CHANGES IN MATERIALS

Yes, materials have changed. A look at how and why they have changed reveals the influences of both scarcity and abundance as well as of research. The cycles through which the changes have gone have affected format, content, and teaching procedures.

HOW AND WHY MATERIALS OF INSTRUCTION HAVE CHANGED

Change is evident. What materials are used may be determined by the scarcity or abundance of a product. The nature or direction of change may be influenced by research and study.

THE INFLUENCE OF SCARCITY AND ABUNDANCE When materials were scarce they were often inferior and expensive. The advent of the printing press and the development of mass production changed all this. No longer is it necessary to be content with a hand-written book, a poorly printed book, an inadequate or poorly bound book with material printed on low grade paper, or with dog-eared and weather-beaten materials.

Abundance creates competition. The producer must develop good materials if he expects to sell them. Otherwise, his competitor will capture the market and his inferior materials will remain unsold on the shelves. Abundance may complicate the problem of selection, but it does create competition which tends to improve the product. The chief danger from overabundance is waste and mental indigestion. At present more of our schools are concerned about what to select rather than whether or not to buy.

THE INFLUENCE OF RESEARCH Since an abundance of materials, mass production, and competition for the school's dollar have created the problem of what to buy, the emphasis has been placed on improving the product. Some of the improvements have been based on quality of the material, some on attractiveness of packaging, and some on content. These factors have been subjects of research studies.

The salesman who is "drumming up trade" for his product is constantly looking for research evidence to prove that his material is of higher quality, that it is more attractive to the consumer, and that its content is more effective as a learning medium. The teacher who is trying to influence learning in the classroom is looking for the same answers from research. Similarly, the administrator, the educational leader, and the specialist are looking for answers. They must beware lest they succumb to the temptation to accept "wrong" or "right" answers, "poor" and "good" materials, and "yes" and "no" responses to specific questions.

All research questions are relative. Right for what? Good for what? Unless the total picture is viewed, unless the entire learning sequence is observed, unless all children are considered, we run the risk of taking a prescription because it is good for one thing without recognizing that it may be bad for something else.

CYCLES OF CHANGE

We must view the cycles of change in the use of materials not as better or worse than what came before, but as steps in progress toward a saner, more balanced perspective on learning. This is true of changes which have come about in the format of books, in the content of books, in phonics programs, and in the area of controlled vocabularies.

THE FORMAT OF BOOKS Books have gone full cycle from miniature, fine print, unillustrated productions to elaborate, large, profusely illustrated works designed to attract the attention of the reader. There is even some trend to return to what was.

CONTENT OF BOOKS Content of books has experienced a similar cycle. Moralistic stories gave way to realistic stories. They in turn gave way to actual experiences common to childhood. Activities in which the children created their own reading material followed. There are those today who would advocate the abandonment of all books, especially the basal reading type, and let the children learn to read from self-created materials. On the other hand, there are those who would advocate a return to the "good old days" when children read stories with moralistic influence with "real literary quality." Some would even conclude with, "and the moral to this story is. . . ."

PHONICS PROGRAMS Phonics, too, has gone the rounds. From an over-emphasis on mechanics we rebelled and practically threw out the entire idea. No sooner had we reaped the results of our actions than we felt a clamor for a return to skills. It is not so much a matter of "phonics or no phonics," but rather a matter of how much, when, why, and how. There are those who firmly believe phonics will solve all our reading problems and those who believe there is no value in the study of phonics. I am convinced they are both in error. Phonics has its place. Refer to Chapter 5 for a further treatment of the subject.

CONTROLLED VOCABULARY Controlled vocabulary is another facet of the reading program which has had its ins and outs. Many can remember the first books which claimed to have a controlled vocabulary. When teachers first heard of the idea of controlling the rate at which new vocabulary was introduced, they thought the reading problems had all been solved. They reasoned, "Now I won't be faced with a dozen or more new words on a single page, words that have little or no relevancy to the child's background. If he can learn a few new words at a time and master them as he goes along, he will learn to read without difficulty."

How wrong they were! Their faith in the control over vocabulary proved to be just one more disappointment as they tried to rely on materials rather than on learning and teaching as a road to success.

There was a time when the publisher who could claim the fewest new words per page, the most regular repetition of words which had been introduced, and the lightest total vocabulary load was the one who captured the attention of the educationist. At that time the concern was for making learning easy, pleasant, and successful.

Then along came Sputnik! And our concern for quality, scholarship, and competition! Almost overnight we switched our objectives. Both parents and educators started to demand that learning be "hard" on the assumption that such an approach would create scholars, or at least rugged competitors, who could win or beat the other fellow or achieve. Then the books with controlled vocabulary became subject to much criticism as being soft, an insult to the intelligence of our superior children who were described as "bored" with school. Again it was the content of the material that was given the blame or the credit for learning or the lack of learning.

INFLUENCE OF MATERIALS ON LEARNING

I am convinced that most materials will work providing the teachers work and, even more, providing the learner works. As long as the learner is passive very little learning will take place. I am sure the results obtained from any method or any material are highly dependent on the skill of a creative teacher. Give me all creative teachers and I'll guarantee results with almost any method and any material.

The trouble with too many of the research findings is that they are based on the work of a highly stimulated and creative teacher. She does an inspired piece of work and shows outstanding results. Then the materials are given the credit. The assumption seems to be that if you will just use *this* method or buy *these* materials all your problems will be solved.

Neither the materials nor the method can do the teaching. Neither can they do the learning. It takes an inspired leader to really teach. And it takes genuine effort and self-motivation on the part of the learner to get learning. If we place our faith in materials and methods, important as they are, we are destined to play a losing game.

I like materials. I like methods. I am fascinated by teaching machines. I enjoy working with tests. But I am convinced they are only the means to help the teacher teach and the learner learn. They won't do the work while we sit and wait. They only serve as motivating devices to stimulate teachers to teach better and learners to learn more efficiently.

Of course, an efficient machine is better than an inefficient one, but a good mechanic will keep the inefficient machine running, while the poor mechanic will wind up waiting for someone to help him out. The analogy is obvious. The poor teacher will end up waiting at the desk for someone to come along with a remedy guaranteed to teach all her students to read, while the good teacher will get results with almost any method or any material. The bright pupil will learn more than the dull pupil because the slower learner will wait passively for someone else to do something about it or to tell him what to do while the bright pupil will seek out the answers and learn for himself.

19

EVALUATING THE METHODS

or That's Not the Way They Used to Do It

How does a child, or anyone for that matter, learn anything? Does learning proceed from the specific to the general or from the general to the specific?

And how does one teach another to read? Which comes first, mechanics or meaning? Why have so many different methods come and gone? What must be included in a reading program? How have the different facets emerged? What must one learn in order to be able to read? How can research help in the pursuit of answers to these questions? Exploring the significance of these questions will help us see why there have been so many different methods tried over the years.

LEARNING AND TEACHING

Before one can teach he needs a thorough knowledge of how learning takes place. This is especially important in the teaching of reading. The question about sequence from specific to general versus general to specific is directly related to the question of mechanics as a route to meaning versus meaning as a route to mechanics. These alternates are the basis for most of the variations in methodology.

HOW ONE LEARNS

How does one learn to talk, to type, to play a musical instrument, to drive a car, to skate, to speak a foreign language, and on and on and on? Does one start by analyzing the process, memorizing the parts, perfecting the separate skills, and then putting them together? Or does one simply "plunge in" and see what happens? Does the learner attempt to prevent error by anticipating the problems, the difficulties, and the separate skills needed or does he correct error as it occurs?

FROM THE SPECIFIC TO THE GENERAL Let's take learning to drive a car for example. One could study the manual till he could identify all the parts of the car, but that would not ensure his ability to drive. One could memorize all the rules of the road and pass the paper-and-pencil driver's examination, but that would not make him an expert driver. One could dismantle and reassemble the motor or the transmission of the car until he was an expert at the job, but that would not make him a driver. He could practice the separate skills of steering the car, shifting the gears, operating the switches, and applying the brakes, but that still would not make him a driver.

Let's take learning to read for comparison. One could chant the ABC's endlessly, but that would not guarantee reading. One could memorize the rules for the vowel sounds, blends, digraphs, diphthongs, syllabication, and accent, but that would not necessarily guarantee correct pronunciation, let alone meaning or interest. One could practice the separate skills of articulation, pronunciation, phrasing, and vocalization, but that still would not be reading in the sense of interpretation of meaning.

FROM THE GENERAL TO THE SPECIFIC Not until the driver is able to put all the driving skills together simultaneously and coordinate them into a whole pattern of synthesized movements can he really be expert at driving the car. Which does he learn first? When does he practice the separate skills? Anyone who has learned to drive a car will readily tell you that he does them all at once. It takes continued practice on the total operational pattern to perfect the skills. Each movement in isolation lacks value or purpose until it is blended with all the rest into a total pattern. Shifting gears cannot be done in isolation. It must be done while the hand is on the steering wheel, the foot is on the clutch, and the eye is on the traffic pattern. Steering the car is not sufficient unless it is coordinated with the appropriate pressure on the gasoline feed or the brake pedal as the need may be.

Likewise, learning to read calls for a coordination of activities blended into a whole. No one process isolated for independent learning will have real value until it becomes a part of the total pattern. The eyes, the ears, the hands, the mind must all work in unison. The mind must blend mechanical knowledge, skill in use, interpretation of meaning, judgment about apppropriate skills, and total configuration into a well-oiled process that eventually results in an automatic use of skills as a means of communicating with the author of the printed word.

Reading is not an easy process to master. It cannot be isolated in a single period in life such as a school grade. It is a gradually unfolding process which begins with the first audible sound or spoken word and expands continuously throughout life. As each new insight is gained it fits into previously established patterns of learning, always expanding and deepening the skills and the understandings. This may seem confusing to the novice but that is just the reason it takes more than a pattern, a method, a recipe to become an accomplished teacher of reading.

HOW READING IS TAUGHT

It is this dilemma over what to teach, when to teach it, and how to teach it that has been the root of the controversy over method in the teaching of reading for generations. Only when the teacher sees the total learning situation and the individual in his present position in the total learning process will she be able to help him take that next step. Trying to decide the sequence based on logical organization of subject matter fails to take into account the child's learning pattern. Trying to structure teaching around children's developmental sequences and ignoring structure of the knowledge results in a "hodgepodge" which leaves the learner with a lot of information but little or no insight. The teacher must know both the structure of the language and the developmental sequences of the learner. Trusting either one to the exclusion of the other leads to disaster. And that is the reason for controversy over methods in teaching reading.

This leads to the question: Shall we have the child master the mechanics as a route to reading or shall we have him read as a route to the mastery of mechanics? The answer is "Both."

Consider these two sequences for instance:

alphabet	ideas
sounds	meanings
phonograms	sentences
words	phrases
phrases	words
sentences	phonograms
meanings	sounds
ideas	alphabet

It will be noted that these two lists include the same elements. The difference lies in the sequence in which they are presented and in the methods used for teaching them. They represent two opposing points of view about methodology in the teaching of reading. Let's examine them.

MASTERY OF MECHANICS AS A ROUTE TO READING The first list begins with the abstract symbols. The learner studies the sounds they represent, blends the sounds together to make phonograms and eventually words, puts the words into phrases and sentences in the hope that meaning will come. Ideas are the ultimate goal.

In this case the instruction is based on rote memory and the piecing together of the parts. The principle is the same as memorizing the driver's manual on the route to learning to drive. It assumes that one must know the parts before he can recognize the whole. It is built on the theory that a child must know the letters and must be able to spell the word before he can read it. It is based on the assumption that knowing each word in isolation precedes reading and contributes to understanding.

READING AS A ROUTE TO MASTERY OF MECHANICS The second list begins with the ideas. The learner is helped to see that meanings are involved and then is shown how the meanings look when they are recorded in print. These meanings in the form of sentences are broken down into phrases and ultimately into words to observe repetition of pattern and to compare those of similar construction. Eventually words are broken down into their parts in order that the learner may discover a relationship between sound and symbol and arrive at association of letters with phonograms and sounds. The alphabet is the final step. Recognition of the various letters and their names as they are used in words precedes the alphabet in sequence. The sequential pattern of the ABC's both forward and in reverse is needed when the child arranges words in alphabetical order or uses a dictionary, telephone directory, or encyclopedia.

In this case teaching is based on total configuration, meaning, and analysis to discover the parts and their relationships to each other. The child starts with the idea. He notices similarities and differences in the patterns that are used to record the ideas. If he is precocious or if he lives in a rich reading environment, he may notice these similarities and differences on his own and seem to pick up his reading skills without actual teaching. Some children may need to have these similarities and differences called to their attention by a skillful teacher. Some may be slow to comprehend these patterns even with considerable urging on the part of the teacher.

I am convinced that children can learn to read by either approach, particularly if they have a dedicated teacher who firmly believes in what she is doing. I am also convinced that each approach does have an ultimate effect on mature reading skills and habits. Perhaps no teacher or no method uses one approach to the exclusion of the other, but the contrast influences the philosophy upon which teaching and learning are based.

READING PROGRAMS AND RESEARCH EVIDENCE

A reading program cannot be based on a single element. It calls for insight into both the language pattern and the learning processes. Research cannot isolate single elements. It must encompass not only methods and materials, but also the teacher as an influential factor.

ESSENTIAL ELEMENTS IN AN EFFECTIVE READING PROGRAM

We have tried various methods and materials in teaching reading. What is the "right" method? We must ask ourselves, "Right for whom?" and "Right for what?" In order to answer these questions we need to consider what the teacher must know before she can decide what to teach and to whom. It seems obvious that she must know what she is going to teach, that is, she must master the content of the subject matter. The teacher must also have a keen insight into the nature of the learning process itself before she can help the learner learn.

INSIGHT INTO THE STRUCTURE OF THE DISCIPLINE In the past many people believed that anyone could teach little children and that all the teacher needed was knowledge of the subject matter to be taught. As a consequence the less well-educated teachers were assigned to teach the younger children. This kind of teaching assignment brought forth techniques built on telling them what to do and listening to them recite to see if they did. As a result children learned to parrot right answers and teachers learned to listen and correct errors.

The *code system* on which the language is based must be understood by the teachers. They need to know much more than the alphabet and the words in order to teach children to read. They need to know much more about the structure of the English language than they will ever relay to the young learners. They need a keen insight into the pattern and organization of the system.

There are various methods for learning and consequently for teaching the code system. Many of them have been tried and discarded. Some of them have been discarded and then resurrected on the theory that a return to what was is a good solution to recurring problems.

Understanding *the structure of language* will enable teachers to make wise decisions as problems are faced. They will know which word patterns are dependable enough to justify pointing them out to the children as generalizations. They will know which words are irregular enough that it might be more expedient to tell the child than to belabor the situation. They will know which words to have the children attack as generalizations and which ones to develop through context. They will know why some learnings are more difficult than others. They will know when to emphasize form and when to encourage independence.

Teachers need knowledge of the structure of the language itself. Such knowledge is lamentably vague in the background of too many teachers. They need to know about our language and how it came to be. They need to know about the sound-symbol relationship and why the patterns exist. They need to know about the sentence patterns and the linguistic backgrounds of language. They need to know about the syntax of language.

Such knowledge will put the teacher in the position to know why difficulties exist for the immature learner. It will make it easier for her to make judgments about which patterns to call attention to and which ones to pass by casually without belaboring a point the child could not understand at the time. It will help her to know what backgrounds to build in order for the learner to be ready to cope with new concepts.

INSIGHT INTO THE LEARNING PROCESS The teacher who would meet the needs of all learners must have more than insight into the content of the subject matter. She must also understand the learner and the learning situation.

Stages of development of the learner must be understood. Study of child development leads to knowledge of the physical, emotional, and intellectual changes that are typical of given chronological ages, but this knowledge is not enough if it leads the teacher only to conclusions about what a child "ought to do" in "my grade." Perhaps, according to the books, a child *ought* to do certain things at certain grade levels or with a given measured intelligence, but the fact that he does not is still the matter for concern. Perhaps a child ought to weigh so much by the time he is one year old or ought to have so many words in his vocabulary at a given time or ought to be able to tie his own shoes by the time he starts to school or ought to be willing to stay in kindergarten without crying for his mother, but the fact that he does not do any one or all of these things changes the picture for him.

The child who does not weigh as much as he should may have been premature, he may be undernourished, he may have been subjected to disease or accident, or he may have a different growth pattern. The question is not how much ought he to weigh, but how much does he weigh and is he growing? Whether or not he talks at a given age is not so much the question as whether or not he has the facility and the background and is making progress. Perhaps he has never had shoes that have ties, or maybe even never had shoes at all. Perhaps he has never been away from his mother for one full hour in sequence. What he *ought* to do must be related to his individual nature and his own personal background.

The *learning situation* is equally important. An effective reading program cannot be outlined in terms of materials, methods, or sequences. It must be developed in terms of the learner and how he learns. Children don't all react to the same materials in the same manner. They don't all respond to the same methods the same way. They don't all develop in the same sequence. Only when the teacher has insight into the specific situation can she plan effective learning experiences. She needs to see a particular child in a particular situation in relation to specific learnings, materials, and methods. Only then can she succeed in blending the structure of the discipline with the developmental pattern of the child in order to come up with a prescription for learning.

That is the reason teaching is difficult, demanding, and exacting. That is the reason there is no panacea. That is the reason we can't put all our faith in materials or methods. The teacher is truly the doctor. And methods will continue to change as long as children continue to vary in their experiential backgrounds and in their responses to learning situations.

ESSENTIAL ELEMENTS IN EFFECTIVE RESEARCH

And, finally, we cannot draw any conclusions about the best method until we get perspective on the whole situation. The question, "Which is the best apple?" is answered by another question, "Do you want to eat it, bake a pie, or make cider?" To answer the question about which is the best method of teaching one must know the answers to many other questions: Who is the child? What is his level of attainment? Who is the teacher? What kind of person is she? What materials are available? How much time have we?

Much scientific research is designed to eliminate or control all the variables but two and come up with measurable comparisons. In the course of an experiment children cannot be isolated from all external influences. Neither can their responses be altered in a short period of time. Comparing one method with another even with thousands of children and large numbers of teachers and classrooms ignores the personal factors. Figure 29 illustrates this point. Three different programs are being compared. They are tried out

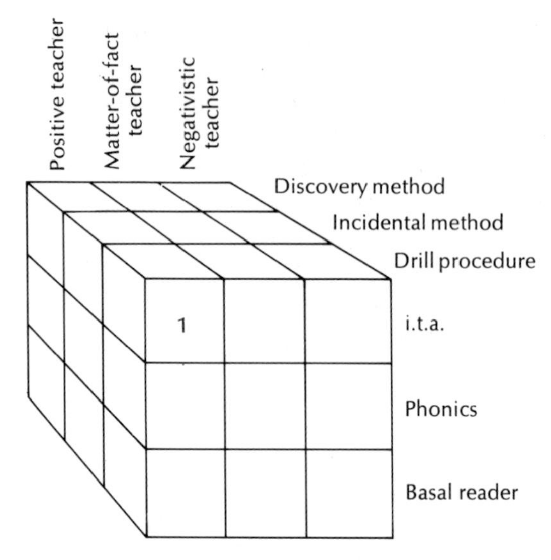

Figure 29. Three sets of materials used by three different types of teachers employing three different methods. There are twenty-seven different basic combinations in this schematic representation, for example, the teacher in Block 1 uses i.t.a. with a positive approach through drill techniques.

in twenty-seven different classrooms, nine for each program. They take the median achievement of the nine classrooms using a purely phonic approach and compare it with the nine classrooms using the i.t.a. program, and those in turn with the nine classes using a basal reader. This ignores the other variables which can and do occur and which are not or cannot be controlled.

THE TEACHER For example, take the teacher element. The teacher is important, perhaps the most important element in the learning process. If we were to divide all teachers roughly into three types of personalities, not necessarily equally distributed, we might come up with those in Group A who are warm and responsive with a positive approach to children. In Group C we find the teachers who are cold and resistant, dominating and impersonal. They create negativism toward learning. They may be intellectual but not necessarily stimulating. They may know plenty of facts but their appeal to children builds resistance. Then in Group B we might find the in-between sort of person, the matter-of-fact type of teacher who is colorless and bland. These teachers mark time and cover the assignment. They neither win the children nor antagonize them.

THE METHOD Next take the matter of method. It is possible for any one of the teachers described above to teach any one of the programs prescribed for the experiment by any of many different methods. Let's take just three methods for contrast. Suppose part of the teachers approach the material on the assumption that children must experience situations and discover principles. They insist on inductive thinking and insight. Another group of teachers falls into the category which believes that learning must be structured, that rules must be presented, and that rote repetition to the point of perfection is necessary before application. Still another group of teachers follows no particular method. They may be the laissez-faire type. They merely take the next page and listen to the children recite, meanwhile hoping that they will learn something.

THE MATERIALS Next come the materials to be used for teaching. Even though each teacher in the experiment has been given carefully prepared materials covering the comparisons to be made, there is little or no control over the other materials in the classroom. One teacher may supplement profusely with her own pictures, concrete objects, bulletin boards, and exhibits and also with numerous graded books for free reading. Another teacher may have a barren classroom; still another may use prescribed materials conscientiously without supplement.

Teachers find it extremely difficult to adhere rigidly to a program, a method, a book no matter how hard they try. Their individual personalities and their convictions about how children learn are bound to influence what they do in the teaching situation. By their own admission teachers in experimental programs do "bootleg" their own ideas into the classroom to supplement the prescription. The factors are just not all controlled.

Then we conclude that: Given only three sets of materials, three possible methods, and three types of teachers, we come up with not three factors to compare in drawing conclusions, but twenty-seven different combinations. Who is to say that the nine rooms all using the phonics workbooks are learning more or less because of the materials they are using? And all this still does not take into consideration the shades of variations among the typical examples cited.

And finally, the teacher who understands how learning takes place, how methods and materials are related to the reading process, and how different facets of the total program fit together is in a position to help the learner learn.

CHANGES AND EMERGING PROGRAMS

Changes in reading instruction have come about gradually. Many methods have been tried. Different facets of the program have emerged to meet newly recognized needs. An overview of this evolutionary process will give us perspective.

HOW METHODS HAVE CHANGED

In our chapter on the history of reading instruction we referred to the emphasis on rote learning, memory, and drill growing out of the scarcity of printed materials and the organizational patterns of the schools. In our summary of child development we referred to the differences between the learning of wholes versus the mastery of the separate parts. The discovery of basic principles as an approach to insight and learning presents another point of view. All these influences have brought about changes in methodology.

ROTE LEARNING, MEMORY, AND DRILL Methods based on rote learning and memory are an outgrowth of two factors. The first is the concept of how children learn and the second is the concept of the structure of knowledge.

The advocates of the rote memory approach believe that children must be "conditioned" to respond to a given stimulus in a given way and as a consequence become adult-like in their reactions to their environment. The assumption is that the adult knows what the child should learn and how he should learn it. Education becomes a process of "pouring in" needed knowledge and practicing needed skills.

The advocates of this approach also believe that learning must take place from the parts to the whole and that a logical organization of skills is the place to begin. The child is told to learn the alphabet because it is believed he must know it before he can read. He is drilled on the sounds of the letters because they are considered essential to the recognition and pronunciation of words. He is asked to learn the words because he will need them when he is reading.

WHOLES VERSUS PARTS Those who would proceed from the general to the specific see the learning pattern of the young child in a different light. They believe that memory for details is an outgrowth of recognition of a total configuration and that the child arrives at organization and structure as a result of observation of meaningful wholes. For example, he can recognize his own house on the street without knowing how many doors and windows it has. His recognition is based on location, general configuration, and familiarity with distinguishing details that are strikingly different.

Such reasoning is based on the assumption that recognition of words comes about in this same manner. The child will recognize a word because of its general location in relation to a picture or in a total sentence pattern. He will recognize its general configuration because it is outstandingly different from other words. For example, the word *cat* just doesn't look like the word *elephant*. Of course he can tell them apart! It is not until he meets two words that are more similar in appearance such as *cat* and *can* that he needs more detail to break them down. Now he must look at more than general configuration to tell them apart. These two words begin alike. The difference lies in the final letter. He must look with greater care and recognize not only the difference in the terminal letters but in the sounds they represent. Even then he may have to utilize context clues to help him distinguish between the two. In sentences such as

> I see a cat.
> I see a can.

the context is not very helpful, but in the following sentences he has a bit more help from meaning clues:

> My pet cat has soft fur.
> The can has soup in it.

Things get more complicated when the letters look alike. For example, telling the difference between *can* and *car*, especially if they are in manuscript writing and the minute difference is in the ending stroke of the final letter, requires the use of careful visual discrimination, knowledge of sound, and context. Which is the key to word recognition? All of them! The child who has learned to make his skills function automatically will not stop to think about which one he is using. He will read and, if it makes sense, he will go on. If it does not make sense, he will hesitate, correct his impression, and proceed. Only in the learning stages does he stop to think about which approach he is applying. And only in the learning stages does the teacher stop him to suggest techniques for word analysis.

DISCOVERY LEARNING This interpretation of the learning pattern has led to a critical look at rote learnings and memory for details, to the emphasis on drill, and to the excessive use of flash cards and drill and test exercises. This, in turn, has led to a point of view which suggests that the experiences and activities of the child are the place to begin and the child should be introduced to the printed form in order to show him how ideas look when they are recorded. Then he eventually analyzes the symbols and discovers the mechanics for himself.

This approach proceeds from the whole to the parts. It calls attention to obvious principles and patterns in known words. As the child's experiences expand he discovers new principles, new patterns, new insights. As his learnings unfold he becomes the master of his language and the tools that contribute to its usefulness as a medium of communication. His encoding skills are developed alongside his decoding skills. Some of his insights will be learned in connection with writing and spelling. Some of them will be learned in connection with listening and reading. All of them will be woven together into a harmonious and synchronized pattern that is meaningful and useful. And thus he has learned to read by discovering for himself the wonders of language.

While educators, research workers, and critics are debating the merits of the various approaches to the learning-to-read process the controversy continues between mechanics and meaning, wholes versus parts, memory versus insight, drill versus experience, group versus individual, and acceptance of fact versus discovery of principles. Perhaps the wonder is that children learn to read at all!

HOW FACETS OF THE READING PROGRAM HAVE EMERGED

The reading program itself must be subjected to the same critical analysis as the steps the child takes in learning to read. No one phase of the program can be effectively viewed in isolation. It must be seen in relation to the total learning pattern. The total pattern must include both the developmental sequences of the learner and a logical organization of the material to be learned. These points of view involve readiness, developmental reading, corrective measures, and the establishment of skills which lead to eventual independence. Let's look at them one at a time and fit them together into a "bird's eye view" of the total process.

READINESS While readiness has been dealt with in more detail in Chapter 3 it will be treated here as a concept and as a part of the total process. The experiences the child has before he approaches the printed page for the expressed purpose of reading are of great significance. It takes some physical and mental maturity to attack reading skills but these are not enough. The child who has never seen a book is not even curious about books. The child who has never seen animals except stray dogs and cats in the neighborhood is not ready to read about zoo animals or pets. The child who has not experienced snow or merry-go-rounds or airplanes or sandy beaches or kites or teddy bears or grassy yards or, or, or a multiplicity of other concepts included in stories in readers is not ready to utilize those concepts in reading, no matter how familiar he may be with the mechanics.

The child who has not experienced excitement, anticipation, glee, satisfaction, love, and other emotional reactions is not ready to read about them in the activities of the characters. The child who has not felt heat and cold, rough and smooth, pleasant and unpleasant, kind and cruel and who has not had these concepts expressed in words is not ready to read about them or to recognize the printed forms that represent them.

Experiential background to give meaning to vocabulary is absolutely essential as a readiness for reading. Whether that background precedes or accompanies school activities, it must come. There is just as much importance to such background in teaching the meaning of an acute angle to the geometry student as in teaching the meaning of the word *soft* to a 4-year-old.

DEVELOPMENTAL READING Developmental reading is the facet of the reading program which has come in for the most lively discussion, the most research on materials and methods, the most controversy about when, what, and how. It all centers around whether to master the sound-symbol relationships first and then utilize them in reading or to associate printed form with meaning and then analyze it for details and organizational pattern.

Developmental reading is a term which has come to be applied to the presentation of new learnings at any level. It is frequently used in connection with the teaching of more mature reading skills at advanced levels. Whenever a child is developing learnings to which he has not been previously exposed, he is experiencing developmental reading instruction. This is applied to word analysis, question and answer exercises, use of study skills and interpretation.

CORRECTIVE MEASURES Obviously everyone cannot be perfect in everything. We must learn to accept degrees of success along the way. If all children were equally capable, if the perfect method were discovered, and if the ideal material were provided, then there would be no need for corrective measures. While medicine has come a long way in prevention and in developing the well-rounded physical body, there is still plenty of need for the doctor. The same is true in teaching the young to read. We have many good materials on the market. We have many dedicated and knowledgeable teachers. We have many capable children. And many of them *are* learning to read. But we also have some who are not succeeding at the task set for them.

This is the point at which corrective measures become necessary. The teacher who can survey the situation and diagnose the case is the one who is in a position to apply remediation. But let us not forget that remediation is an admission of lack of success in the first attempt. It would have been better to have anticipated the problem and to have prevented it. But since this is not always possible, remediation becomes a necessary part of the total reading program.

Diagnosis means finding out not only what is wrong, but why. It is not enough to know that a child does not know the sounds represented by the letters, that he seems to reverse letter forms and word forms, that he can pronounce the words but seems to get no meaning from what he reads, that he confuses similar forms, that he is a word caller, that he points with his finger and thus slows down his processes, that he loses his place, that he is inattentive, that he resists reading, and that any one of a dozen other difficulties affects his reading. Knowing *what* his difficulty is is only the first step. The true diagnosis is based on *why* he has the difficulty. One child might confuse words which are similar in appearance because of faulty vision, another because of lack of understanding of the difference, and another because of lack of intelligence to make the generalization. Knowing why the child experiences the difficulty gives the clue as to what to do about it.

Remediation is like medicine. Prevention may be more desirable than cure, but once a condition exists it is essential to find the cure. And, for each patient and each condition the cure is likely to be different. Many remedial techniques are available to help remove reading difficulties. A child may be fitted with glasses or a hearing aid. Another may be given a concrete experience to establish meanings. Another may have the structure of the words analyzed and explained to him. Another may have the work pitched at a level with which he can cope. You cannot apply the same remedy to all children who interchange *was* and *saw*.

INDEPENDENCE There is a great deal of difference between the child who *can* read and the child who *does* read. It is doubtful if the difference is truly recognized. There are many adults who really can read if by read you mean the ability to pronounce the minimum of words, recognize their own names, identify the items on the grocery list, understand the comics, or follow the line of print as another reads. But many of these same adults actually do not bother to read in their daily lives. They avoid both practical and recreational reading. They substitute picture magazines, news broadcasts, and movies for reading situations. They seem to get along very well in life. Yet they grow up to be the very parents who agitate about it if their own children do not succeed in reading when they go to school.

The reader who develops skills enjoys reading. As his enjoyment increases he spends more time reading. As he spends more time he gains more skill. As his skills increase he gains more insight into the structure of the language and the style of the writer. This in turn develops taste. The truly independent reader is the one who can establish his own goals, select his own materials, and use reading as a means of satisfying his personal needs whether they be factual or recreational. Indeed, for him reading makes a full life. This is the ultimate goal of the teaching of reading. Recognition must be given to the fact that these goals cannot be measured at the end of a given grade or with an objective test that identifies tangible skills, number of words, or correct responses to fact questions. Maturity and independence are more than test scores.

20

EVALUATING THE ORGANIZATION

or Managing to Get It All Done

A backward look will convince us that organization has always been a part of the learning situation. The curriculum must be organized. The classroom must be organized. The schedule must be organized. The children must be organized. Unless there is organization in the mind of the worker, clear direction in the minds of both teacher and learner, and objectives in view, learning is in danger of being haphazard. Organization adds clarity of purpose, directness of action, and evidence of attainment.

PATTERNS OF SCHOOL ORGANIZATION

Traditionally organizational patterns have varied from the teacher-pupil relationship of the private tutorial system to mass instruction growing out of the demands of expanding populations. These have in turn led to certain grouping practices which have often created as many problems as they have solved.

INDIVIDUAL INSTRUCTION

Ancient philosophers taught with their followers at their feet. Early teachers guided the learnings of the young by taking them by the hand. Private tutors were the pattern of learning for the privileged classes. The little girl who learned cooking, sewing, and other household tasks at her mother's side was indeed privileged. The boy who learned agricultural practices or industrial skills as an apprentice was experiencing a one-to-one relationship between teacher and learner.

The increase in numbers of children to be taught and the growing demand for more education for more children brought about the practice of teaching in groups. Perhaps some dame schools and the original one-room schools were merely extensions of private tutoring with an attempt to tutor more than one child at a time.

TOTAL GROUP INSTRUCTION

Not until the numbers became great enough so that there was some need for separating children into groups with similar ages, similar backgrounds, or similar needs was group instruction really practiced. Mass instruction and the introduction of multiple copies of materials developed with the advent of the graded school. Out of this came lecture procedures, unison responses, and common goals for all regardless of abilities or interests. Such plans were designed to solve the problems of numbers, but experience has taught us that such economy of time, energy, and materials only created new problems. Alas! All the children were not alike; even if they were caught at a similar period in their development, they did not stay alike because some of them grew at different rates and branched off on tangents with different talents and different interests.

After trying to force children to fit a pattern many educators changed their tactics and tried to develop patterns to allow for individual differences. This led to the emergence of innovations in patterns of organization in the nation's classrooms.

EMERGING PRACTICES

Earlier changes were directed toward making adjustments in the sequence more often in order to eliminate the waste of time and effort caused by repetition of an entire year's work. This led to the twice-a-year admissions and subsequent midyear promotions. This plan caused the schools to reorganize twice a year. Many children had two different teachers each year, one for each half grade. Likewise, many teachers had two different groups of children each year, one for each semester. This plan lacked continuity for the child. It encouraged the teacher to become a "specialist" at a given level, usually quite narrow in concept. The child might take most of the semester to become adjusted to a new setting, a new teacher, and a new set of expectations. The teacher might become an authority on what is expected of children in the first half of the third grade, but woe unto the child who did not fit the expectations!

Later changes were therefore directed toward making adjustments in the program rather than in the administrative organization. This was designed to help the child move on from one level to the next without the constant interruptions in his adjustments and without expectations based on uniform standards. In order to make these adjustments it was considered necessary for the teacher to know more about the child as well as more about the content to be taught. In order to do this she needed to live with the child over a longer period of time and to see his progress from one level to the next. These adjustments led to practices which involved one teacher sometimes moving with a group of children from one level to the next over a longer period of time—perhaps two or more years. This also reduced the need for reorganization at half-year intervals and led to the gradual elimination of the mid-year promotion plan.

A broader view of child development opened up the possibilities of multi-age grouping and a gradual flow through the school situation as opposed to wholesale disruption and reorganization once a year or at stated intervals. Now with the emphasis on the child and what he was ready to learn rather than on the grade level and what was expected of him, a whole new point of view emerged. Out of all this came the return to individualized instruction with emphasis on self-selection of learning materials, personal record keeping, programed materials for teaching and learning, and continuous progress.

ELEMENTS TO BE ORGANIZED

Today administrators as well as classroom teachers are faced with organizational problems. They must organize the reading curriculum so that growth is assured and reading skills are applied in the total learning pattern. The classroom must be organized so that it creates an effective environment for learning and using reading skills. The schedule must be organized so that children will have effective experiences in reading both as a developmental process and as a useful tool in other areas. The learners themselves must be organized for effective work in the classroom. All this involves needs, interests, levels of achievement, and individual abilities in reading.

ORGANIZING THE READING CURRICULUM

There are at least two facets of organization in the curricular content of reading which must be considered. One has to do with the various phases of reading. The other has to do with the relation of reading to the rest of the curriculum.

PHASES OF THE READING PROGRAM Curriculum workers must give careful consideration to the phases of the reading program and the stages of development of the learners. These include readiness, development of new concepts, corrective measures as needed, and the establishment of ultimate independence in the use of reading as a lifetime skill.

Readiness is important. Chapter 3 presented the topic of readiness in detail. At this point we will merely define it as that stage at which the child is receptive to the new learning. This may be the initial approach to association of sound and symbol, meaning and abstraction, or the more advanced stages when the learner has sufficient background to understand the quantitative relationships in reading an arithmetic problem, the social relationships in reading about international conflicts, or the experiential background to interpret the meaning expressed in science journals.

Developmental reading constitutes the basic instructional program. Part Two presents developmental reading as it pertains to mastery of skills and Part Three as it pertains to the use of those skills involving comprehension and interpretation. It is defined as that stage of learning when the child is growing and maturing, reaching out, acquiring new skills and new concepts. If he is motivated, if his growth is continuous, if he is progressing, then he is developing toward maturity in reading.

Corrective reading is sometimes necessary. If the child has been through the process of learning to read and has formed some wrong impressions, some ineffective techniques, or some inefficient habits, then corrective measures are needed. This topic is dealt with in greater detail in Chapter 16.

Independence is the ultimate goal. Maturity comes with independence. This is the stage toward which the whole program is working. When the child has become so efficient in his skills that he applies automatically the tool that fits the situation and proceeds smoothly without interrupting his thought pattern, he has reached independence. When the child has become so motivated in the reading process that he accepts reading as a way of life, as a part of his daily pattern of living, and uses it as a means of getting information, as a means of self-satisfaction, as a means of communicating with the author, then he has matured as an independent reader.

READING IN THE TOTAL SCHOOL PROGRAM Curriculum workers need to keep these phases of the reading program in mind if they are to make curriculum content assigned to grade levels through textbooks meaningful and useful to the learners.

The *rest of the curriculum* is intimately related to reading. Using reading as a tool in the other subjects is of utmost importance. In order to meet this requirement in curriculum construction the reading process must be viewed as a part of the total school program. Reading must be seen as a process involving a coordination of physical and mental skills. Reading must be seen in perspective as it relates to the total language skills program which also includes speaking, listening, and writing. Reading skills must be seen in relation to other skills which involve muscular coordination, physical activity, mental association, and memory techniques. Reading must be seen as a tool useful in pursuing content in other areas of the curriculum where one follows directions, gains information, assimilates ideas, performs judgments, and draws conclusions. Reading is more than a skill. Reading is a thinking process.

Continuity and follow-through are essential. Not only must the reading process be viewed in relation to other areas on a horizontal basis, but it must also be viewed vertically. It is not enough to consider the approach to beginning reading. Unless there is follow-through in each new phase of the process there is danger that the learner will bog down along the way. The curriculum must be planned for broad coverage and also for continuous follow-through at each level.

ORGANIZING THE CLASSROOM

While good physical conditions do not guarantee learning, poor facilities can certainly impede learning. The same might be said for the use of the materials of instruction and for the learning activities which take place within the physical setting.

PHYSICAL FACILITIES The classroom with hard benches, forbidding atmosphere, threats of punishment and ridicule, and rigid requirements for posture was once thought to be conducive to learning. Perhaps all this did was to make the learner afraid not to learn. At any rate most modern classrooms are set up on the assumption that more learning takes place when the learner is comfortable. This includes comfortable seating, adequate lighting, and pleasant atmosphere. Of course, it is possible to get the atmosphere so pleasant and relaxed that there is no challenge and the learner goes to sleep or checks out. Nevertheless, the classroom should be inviting and challenging.

MATERIALS OF INSTRUCTION Appropriate materials of instruction are the right of the young in a society based on free universal education for all. The child who lacks the tools for learning is faced with a compulsory program for which he is unprepared. The kinds and quantities of books and other equipment that are needed are the responsibility of the taxpayers, the curriculum planners, and the school staff. These should all be organized for the child before he is asked to learn to read. The child should no more be asked to work in an ill-equipped classroom than the factory worker should be expected to assemble refrigerators in a plant where the parts and the tools are not forthcoming.

LEARNING ACTIVITIES The worker who is constantly impeded in his work because he finds it difficult, if not impossible, to get where he wants to go or to find what he needs will eventually give up the struggle. The learner needs to be in a classroom where there is sufficient room for his activities and where he has access to the materials he needs when he needs them. These are responsibilities of the school, the administration, and the teacher. The learner has a right to expect these things to be provided for him. This includes movable seating, adequate storage space, appropriate work areas, large audience settings, and a secluded spot for quiet study.

ORGANIZING THE SCHEDULE

Time is a commodity. Schedules follow time units. Time can be used effectively only when there is careful planning. In order to avoid waste of time the teacher must engage in careful planning, both long range and day-to-day.

PLANNING LONG-TERM SEQUENCES Planning sequences for the long term ensures reaching objectives or goals and gives perspective to the school program. The teacher who sees the yearly program in perspective at the beginning and keeps her eye on the ultimate goal is in a position to lead the learners toward maturity. Sometimes the remote goal is so far in the future that one has trouble keeping it in mind. It may be necessary to set up intermediary steps and check them off one at a time. This involves unit planning to meet subgoals. As each one is checked off it lays a foundation for the next one.

PLANNING THE SCHOOL DAY Even though the teacher may know where she is headed and may have ambitious plans for the units of study, she is still faced each morning with a roomful of children and must daily answer the question, "What am I going to do today?" "What's next?" "What shall I do now?" These pressing questions should be faced squarely, but they should not crowd out vision for the future. The daily plans in reading involve working with the class as a whole, working with subgroups organized for basic instruction, working with individuals, and developing initiative and independence on the part of the learners.

ORGANIZING THE LEARNERS

The organization of a school is complex. Each child must be considered in terms of the total school setting and special instructional groups. When the child arrives at school, he must be placed in an appropriate group determined by the administrative policy of the school. Once he is in the classroom he still must be given some place to sit, some kind of routine to follow, and some subgroup within the total group with which to identify in order that he may know who he is, where he belongs, and what he is supposed to do. This type of organization oils the machinery, reduces the friction, gives the child a sense of security, and facilitates learning. Organization is not the goal of education, but it is certainly a very important side issue which must be taken care of before the important business of teaching and learning can proceed.

IN THE TOTAL SCHOOL SETTING The sheer impact of numbers forces us to deal with children in groups. Getting them all placed in groups so they can be classified and accounted for on the records is an administrative problem. By the time the "system" gets around to the individual child he is sometimes lost in the shuffle. He becomes a number on a list, a dot on a chart, or a peg to fill a notch. If learners are to be organized so that reading work can be effective, some thought must be given to how this organization is going to take place.

It's the first day of school. In spite of all the care and attention given to preregistration and personal conferences in most public schools, when the children arrive en masse simply getting them down the hall and into classrooms where someone has time to say, "Good morning, Ellen," is a major undertaking. Various plans have been tried. Most of them can be identified under one of two categories. First it is necessary to decide where to put Jimmie *now*. This involves horizontal organization. Then, at the end of the semester or the end of the year, it again becomes necessary to decide what to do with him *next,* that is, where to put him, what to call him, and whether to promote him. This involves vertical organization.

Horizontal organization refers to assignment of children to instructional groups at a given time. All schools subscribe to some philosophy for the organization of their pupils whether by design or by default. If they have a basic theory and attempt to shuffle children to fit the theory, they have organized what they consider "teachable" or "manageable" groups and have assigned them to teachers where they will remain for a designated period of time. If they have no basic theory and merely accept the children as they come and put them in classrooms wherever there is available space, they have still subscribed to a philosophy even if it is by default. They have, in a sense, said, "It makes no difference how the children are organized so long as they have a teacher who is willing to help them learn." Or perhaps they have said, "We don't know, or we don't care."

These two approaches have resulted in some established patterns of horizontal organization. The most common are homogeneous grouping, heterogeneous grouping, and multilevel grouping. Other plans are variations of these patterns and many of the same principles apply. Each has its advantages and disadvantages. It is not a matter of which is right or best. It is a matter of the strengths and weaknesses of each and the adaptations which need to be made in either case. Let's compare them.

Homogeneous grouping is defined as an attempt to put together groups of individuals with like backgrounds or needs. A group may be homogeneous in one respect but quite heterogeneous in other respects. A group made up of all girls is homogeneous according to sex, but the girls may be of different ages, different abilities, and different backgrounds. A group of 6-year-olds is homogeneous according to chronological age, but it may be made up of both boys and girls, of both bright and dull, of both affluent and disadvantaged, and so on, thus making it quite heterogeneous when measured by other standards. A group may be made up of all high IQ's, but again they may be both boys and girls, they may have assorted talents or interests, they may be healthy or fragile, they may be highly emotional or relatively secure. Putting together children of common intellectual abilities does not guarantee that they will become a cohesive group. Most attempts at homogeneous grouping are based on the assumption that if children are at a common level of achievement and have comparable abilities they will form a teachable group. This plan has some advantages and some disadvantages which are summarized and compared in Table 27.

Heterogeneous grouping is defined as an attempt to put together groups of individuals with varying backgrounds and/or needs on the assumption that they will complement each other, will gain from the varied contributions of others, and will be permitted to adjust as individuals rather than as cogs in a wheel. There are various patterns which have posed as heterogeneity.

Some administrators merely take the names, arrange them in alphabetical order, and sort them into groups by some arbitrary method, such as taking every third name on the list. Some simply let them go to the room they wish as long as there is space to accommodate them. Calling this heterogeneous grouping is probably a misnomer. Perhaps random grouping would be more descriptive because there is no assurance that groups thus allowed to materialize will have the varying backgrounds implied by the term heterogeneous.

Table 27. HOMOGENEOUS GROUPING

Advantages	*Disadvantages*
Simplifies and reduces preparation of subject matter for the teacher	Leads to false assumption that same learnings will do for all
Provides "fair competition" for the learner	Reduces challenge for fast worker because he can equal or exceed goals of the group
Develops unity and cohesion within the group	Eliminates extra challenge for slow worker because he never sees a higher level of performance
Unifies goals in terms of subject matter	Reduces emphasis on development of the individual
Places emphasis on group attainment and conformity	Leads to waste of time and materials when used with individuals for whom program is inappropriate
Makes for economy of time and funds in management and buying of materials of instruction	Expects child to fit predetermined pattern and meet preestablished goals
Makes objective testing and record keeping systematic and uniform	Invites comparison based on standards outside the child and his stage of development
Provides a basis for comparison based on standards and common goals	

Table 28. HETEROGENEOUS GROUPING

Advantages	*Disadvantages*
Encourages the teacher to see each child as an individual within the total group	Increases and differentiates preparation on the part of the teacher
Provides challenges for all, even the most capable	May lead to "unfair" competition if slower learner is expected to keep up with his peers in all areas
Gives slower learner a higher goal and an opportunity to learn from others who may make a contribution to his meager background.	May divide rather than unify the group
Puts emphasis on individual rather than on total group	Makes for variety, duplicity, and sometime waste in buying of materials
Encourages use of time and materials in terms of needs	Makes objective testing, measurement in terms of standards, and evaluation in terms of attainments difficult
Encourages planning in terms of individuals	Demands a teacher as well as an administrator who is oriented to a child development approach rather than to a standards approach
Invites growth rather than competition and comparison	Demands an open mind toward children
Eliminates need for excessive emphasis on grades and awards	Is often misunderstood by parents and laymen who believe in standards, honor rolls, and awards
Puts emphasis on growth and learning	
Allows child to proceed at his own pace	

A program which plans to provide for heterogeneity in a group takes just as careful thought as homogeneous grouping. A truly heterogeneous group should be balanced between the sexes, should have an assortment of ability levels, should recognize various creeds, ethnic backgrounds, and social status, and should include different talents and different interests. If we say we want the child to experience a heterogeneous society and learn to live with all kinds of people, then we must put some thought into providing him with true heterogenity. A heterogeneous grouping plan has both advantages and disadvantages which are set forth in Table 28.

Multilevel grouping has reentered the picture within the past decade or two. It is an attempt to meet the objections to both homogeneous and heterogeneous grouping and to put the emphasis on learning and growth. In a sense it is a throwback to the one-room school with some modifications. It is a type of heterogeneous grouping with a plan. As usually conceived multilevel grouping refers to the organization of learners into a total group which encompasses more than one learning level and usually more than one age level. In order to visualize what happens in a given classroom over a period of three or four years study Table 29. Note how the personnel of the classroom flows through from year to year without a complete turnover at any one time. Most of the children will stay in the same room for three years. Some may need to stay four years. An occasional one may move on after only two years.

Notice how a child's position changes in relation to the total group each year. Let us suppose that Sally is both young and immature. In a room of all 6-year-olds she would be in the position of being the "tail-ender" in nearly everything the group does because she is small, young, and slow. She would soon learn to accept an image of herself as one who can't. If, at the end of the year, she were promoted with the entire class to the next grade, she would still be the youngest and the most immature member of her group. The only way she could get out of that position would be to go through the traumatic experience of being "retained" or "failed." Her image of herself as a "failure" would be reinforced, and she would then also have to go through the experience of adjusting to a new group and making all new friends.

On the other hand, in a multilevel group as described in Table 29 Sally changes her position in relation to the total group each year. The first year she may be the youngest and most immature member of the youngest group in the room. But in the second year she is in a group which includes some children who are younger and more immature than she is without having to lose her status with her original group. The third year she sees herself as one of the older and more mature members of the total group. In the meantime if she has found it more comfortable to read with some of the younger children during her second or third year, she

Table 29. PROGRESSION OF CHILDREN THROUGH A CLASSROOM OVER A SPAN OF FOUR YEARS BASED ON A MULTILEVEL SCHEME OF ORGANIZATION

FIRST YEAR	SECOND YEAR	THIRD YEAR	FOURTH YEAR
6-yr.-olds	*6-yr.-olds*	*6-yr.-olds*	*6-yr.-olds*
Sally	Barbara	Margaret	Beth
Jimmie	Cathy	Nancy	Carla
Alice	Donald	Phil	Bobbie
Mary	Eddie	Ruth	Frank
Fred	Howard	Steve	George
Billy	Kenneth	Virgil	Jan
Thelma	Louise	Walter	Marcia
7-yr.-olds	*7-yr.-olds*	*7-yr.-olds*	*7-yr.-olds*
Emma	Sally	Barbara	Margaret
Bob	Jimmie	Cathy	Nancy
Amy	Alice	Donald	Phil
Gregg	Mary	Eddie	Ruth
Susan	Fred	Howard	Steve
Helen	Billy	Kenneth	Virgil
Paul	Thelma	Louise	Walter
8-yr.-olds	*8-yr.-olds*	*8-yr.-olds*	*8-yr.-olds*
Wanda	Emma	Sally	Barbara
Anna	Bob	Jimmie	Cathy
Wilma	Amy	Alice	Donald
Gary	Gregg	Mary	Eddie
Betty	Susan	Fred	Howard
Alan	Helen	Billy	Kenneth
Sam	Paul		Louise
			Sally (9 yrs. old)

may have made sufficient adjustment so that she won't seem to notice when Alice and Mary go on to the next room and she remains with Cathy and Barbara for the next year.

A different adjustment may happen to Thelma. Perhaps she is one of those children with a birthday which caused her to just miss the entrance date the fall she was 6. That means she is nearly 7 when she starts and perhaps a full year older than Sally. At the same time she turns out to be very bright. If she were placed in a classroom of all 6-year-olds or first graders she wouldn't seem to fit. She is more mature. She can probably already read. She finds much of the work a waste of time. Yet she has not "covered the territory" and the teacher questions the wisdom of letting her "skip a grade," which seems to be the only way Thelma can get out of this situation. Otherwise she seems destined to go through school unchallenged if she has a teacher who adheres to grade level oriented curriculum. In that case she may form habits which will fail to meet her needs when she becomes an independent student.

On the other hand, in the multilevel classroom Thelma would immediately face the challenge of children older and more mature than herself. She might even work with the second graders on some occasions. If at the end of two full years in this room Thelma has done the work and has learned to work more comfortably with Amy and Emma than with Alice and Mary, she may move on to the intermediate level at the end of two years without actually having skipped anything. As for the rest of the children, most of them will not remember which year she started and with which group she was originally identified.

The multilevel plan has certain advantages and certain disadvantages. It will no more solve all the organizational problems nor teach all the children to read with ease and fluency than will any of the other plans. Both the advantages and the disadvantages are pointed out in Table 30.

TABLE 30. MULTILEVEL GROUPING

Advantages	*Disadvantages*
Makes for better adjustment of individuals	Challenges management abilities of the teacher
Provides natural flow of children through a group without a complete reorganization at any one time	Creates problems when children move from one school to another
Puts emphasis on the individual rather than on the group	Increases preparation in terms of subject matter and materials
Is more like the manner in which children move through a family group	Complicates problems of objective measurement, evaluation in terms of uniform goals, and grading
Enables teacher to work with an individual child over a longer period of time, thus knowing him as a person	Calls for reorientation of thinking on the part of traditional teachers and parents
Gives child a better self-image and a greater feeling of security	Could create problems in case of personality conflicts
	Upsets planned sequence when teacher turnover is heavy
	Complicates record-keeping in terms of who has read what

No matter which pattern or variation of patterns of horizontal organization is used, the real adjustment still has to be made in terms of the teacher-pupil relationships. All plans have advantages which will be enhanced by the "good" teacher. All plans have disadvantages which will be aggravated by the "poor" teacher. After all is said and done, I am convinced that it is not so important what group a child is in as what happens to him after he gets into the group.

Homogeneous grouping is only one step toward providing enough similarity to make mass teaching practical. Heterogeneous grouping is only one step toward providing enough variety to encourage recognition of individuals. Multilevel grouping is yet another step in the direction of individualizing the learning program by giving the child different perspectives of himself.

Vertical organization refers to the plan of moving children through the school program for the purpose of classification and promotion from year to year. A long-range view is concerned with what to do with the child at the end of the year, whether to promote him or retain him, whether to move him from one room to another, whether to continue with the same teacher or place him with a different teacher, whether to have him move through the graded structure year by year, or to vary from that pattern by moving at his own pace. This administrative problem calls for more than a classroom teacher's decisions. It must include administrative leadership, cooperative planning, and a long-range view of the total growth pattern of the child and the organizational structure of the school.

Classification of children by grade levels requires that a decision be made about where to put the child. This involves first a determination of grade classification, then a room assignment. If the groups are random, it may be a matter of where there is space for another child. If the groups are organized with some attempt at homogeneity or planned heterogeneity, then the decision will have to be based on the child's individual accomplishments and his personal potential. Once he is classified the problem is still not solved permanently. Progress during the semester or the year must be observed as a basis for deciding what to do with him at the end of another year.

Promotion is a perennial problem for classroom teachers. There are those who would promote all the children on the theory that repetition does not enhance learning. There are others with the opposite view which says we should uphold standards and if the child cannot do the work assigned to the grade he should be penalized or made to repeat till he has mastered the required learnings. The proponents of continuous promotion base their arguments on the theory that it is the responsibility of the teacher to meet the learner where he is and keep him progressing. This is based on the child-centered curriculum. The proponents of standards and retentions base their arguments on the theory that the child should meet the requirements, the school should uphold standards, and the teacher should enforce the regulations. This is based on a subject-centered curriculum.

Regardless of which theory is accepted the child grows continuously. The only way he can get to be 7 years old is to spend a year being 6 years old. The same is true of learning to read. The child who is pulled through a second reader at a pace too fast for his learnings finds himself out of breath and falling by the wayside. He can no more go back and do it over again than he can go back and be 6 years old again. The only sensible way for him to learn is to build each new learning on past experiences and keep on growing continuously.

IN THE CLASSROOM Once the children are organized in the total school setting and placed in the classrooms the teacher is faced with a further organizational problem. The activities and the curriculum content create situations which involve some total class activities, some grouping plans, and some individual learning experiences.

Total class activities include those times when the whole class engages in common experiences. Whether the children are grouped homogeneously or heterogeneously, the mere fact that they have all been assigned to a common place for instructional purposes and will be seeing each other daily in the same setting tends to make of them a group. Such groups develop cohesion. The child learns the names of the others in the room. He learns to expect to see the same faces daily. He makes adjustments to certain personalities and selects from his daily contacts those with whom he will form more intimate relationships. Circumstances have placed them together. There are certain things they will all do together merely because they happen to be in the same place at the same time. There are other things they will have in common as a result of the planning and management of the teacher.

Grouping within the class subdivides the group for certain experiences. The teacher may find herself organizing subgroups to meet varying needs such as practice on word structure or oral reading for expression. Groups may be based on common interests, for example, those children interested in dog stories, spaceships, famous heroes, or fairy stories may work together because of the similarity of their current concerns. Groups will be flexible so that when a need or an interest has been satisfied or when abilities fluctuate the necessary reorganization will take place.

Individual learnings often take place within the framework of the total group. Individuals do not always fit into groups. There will be times in every classroom when each individual will be working on his own at a task that is uniquely suited to him. There will be times when certain individuals are working independently while the majority of the children are working in a group situation.

BASIS FOR GROUPING

Grouping has long been a controversial subject in education. There is no one answer that assures uniformity, satisfactory progress for all, and ready-made answers. Woe to the administrator or the teacher who puts all his faith in a grouping plan to alleviate the ills of the classroom. Scores on tests help, but they do not solve the problem. Intelligence level and mental ability are worthy of note, but that is not enough. Level of achievement reveals something about the learner, but since children do not all "stay in place" in the race this also leaves something to be desired as a single factor in establishing groups. Even though children as well as adults tend to seek their own age groups there is more to age than how many birthdays one has had. The person who puts all his faith in grouping and seeks a single factor as the criterion is destined to disappointment. Remember the fable of the blind men and the elephant and the Reading Fable parody in Chapter 1? Let's apply similar ideas to grouping. If John G. Saxe will accept one more apology here is another parody, this time on grouping.

A GROUPING FABLE

It was six marms of school room fame
To learning much inclined,
Who sought to solve the grouping riddle
(Though each of them was blind)
That each by observation
Might satisfy her mind.

The first observed the mental tests,
And happening to be faced
With marks and ranks and median scores,
Cried, "This is where I'm placed.
God bless me! But the grouping riddle
Is surely IQ based."

The second seeing the mental ages
Cried, "Yes, I know 'tis so,
IQ may tell how fast you learn,
And where you hope to go;
But mental age tells where you are,
And what you really know."

The third observed achievement tests
And happening to note
The range of scores about the norm
Was heard at once to quote,
"Grouping is a simple skill,
Grade scores will get my vote."

The fourth observed the boys and girls
And found to her delight,
What most they want is age and size
To make the group just right.
"That's it," she said, "I'll use CA
And group with all my might."

The fifth who chanced to watch the friends
They chose from day to day,
Vowed she saw no need to fret
Or go too far astray.
The mystery of the grouping game
Is simply social play.

The sixth no sooner had begun
About the room some swings,
Than seeing boats and airplanes,
And houses, pets, and things,
Concluded that to group the bunch
You note what interest brings.

And so these marms of school room fame
Disputed loud and long,
Each in her own opinion
Exceeding stiff and strong.
Though each was partly in the right,
And all were in the wrong.

So oft administrative wars
Raise disputes most keen,
And lead to wide discrepancy
In what the others mean,
And cause them to condemn the plan
They may have never seen.

21

EVALUATING THE TEACHING

or You're What Makes the Difference

There is no one best way to teach reading. This is the conclusion reached by the experts who were responsible for the twenty-seven studies and research projects sponsored by the United States Office of Education beginning in 1965. Both research and common sense have led to that conclusion.

WHAT DO RESEARCH AND COMMON SENSE TELL US?

Both research and common sense can tell us much about the teacher as the important factor in the learning process. Research workers have studied methods, materials, and administrative procedures. They have done somewhat less with the qualities of the teacher. Common sense and observation have always been accepted as guides to children and how they learn, to teachers and how they affect the learning situation, and to the effectiveness of the varied approaches to reading.

WHAT RESEARCH HAS TOLD US

Everyone seems to preface what he has to say about the teaching of reading with the expression, "Research says . . ." and then quotes from assorted sources to support points of view about methods, materials, and administrative organization, as well as about the teacher.

METHODS Research talks about methods. Many methods have been tried in many different settings and with many different children. All have claimed success with some children in some situations. Some have been tried, acclaimed, later condemned and abandoned, then resurrected as proposed panaceas in an attempt to return to "good old-fashioned teaching."

In Part Two of the Sixty-Seventh Yearbook of the *National Society for the Study of Education* it is stated that,

> The twenty-seven cooperative studies of first grade reading supported by the United States Office of Education in 1964–1965 showed, with almost complete unanimity, that differences in results were far greater among the classes of teachers using the same method than were the differences between the averages resulting from contrasting methods of instruction. This dramatically shows how powerful an effect teachers have on the progress of beginning readers. It follows that many a poor reader might have done much better if he had been luckier in his first- and second-grade teachers.[1]

MATERIALS Research also talks about materials. The market is supplied with all kinds of gadgets and devices not to mention sets of books built around basic reading programs. Each one is based on the premise that the materials make the difference; yet children through the ages have learned to read with all kinds of materials, for example, the Bible, the Hornbook, the cathechism, moralistic tales, fairy tales, real life stories, charts, experience stories, word lists, phonogram cards, and so on and on and on. Materials have varied from small print on poor quality of paper to large attractive full-color pages. Content has varied from comics, to the big-little books, the ABC picture books, factual material, imaginative stories, and so-called literature. And yet children have learned to read.

And—some did not learn. Some failed to learn to read in colonial times. They dropped by the wayside and never did appear in the higher

[1]National Society for the Study of Education, *Innovation and Change in Beginning Reading Instruction* (67th Yearbook, Part II), Chicago, Ill., University of Chicago Press, 1968.

schools or universities as nonreaders, but instead found their places behind a saw or a plow where skill in reading the printed word was unnecessary or lack of skill was unnoticed. Some failed to learn to read a century ago, but they did not enroll in our rapidly developing high school system and nobody seemed to notice. Yes, some failed to learn to read within the memory of most of today's adults. Those who say that "in the good old days" everybody learned to read either have poor memories or are deluding themselves. If you think they could all read well, just listen to an older adult Sunday School class reading a verse until the text for the day's lesson has been covered. Or ask the first twenty adults over fifty years of age that you meet on the street to read to you at sight a representative paragraph from the editorial page of the local paper. The results will be revealing.

ADMINISTRATIVE ORGANIZATION Then research talks about the administrative organization of children. This, too, has come in for its share of experimentation in order to come up with a sure cure for reading ills as well as other learning problems. Reflect briefly on the history of our schools. The colonial children met in the summer kitchen and recited their ABC's at the knee of the dame who churned the butter or darned the socks while she listened. This was truly individualized instruction and rote learning. As communities grew this plan gave way to the village school with the itinerant schoolmaster who kept a session in the community as long as there were enough children with parents able to support him. This was the origin of the one-room school where children of all ages and abilities met to learn their sums and the alphabet. Rote learning was the most common practice, not so much because any research had proved it to be best, but merely because a lack of printed materials precluded any other practical approach.

As soon as a community grew to the point where there were more children than one teacher could handle conveniently, new approaches were explored. As towns grew and more teachers were added the idea of the "graded school" came into existence led by Horace Mann in 1847 in Quincey, Massachusetts. The grading of the schools led to the grading of the materials and thus developed the graded readers. This grading was predicated on one false assumption, that is, that children grow in a set pattern. This plan resulted in frustrations for the children, developed defeatist attitudes and rebellion against school, and did much to create the social problems resulting from misfits in the classroom. Since failing children and having them repeat a full year of work created so many problems, the experiment in mid-year promotions was developed. It was argued that promotion at the end of each half year would save time.

While all these administrative reorganizations were going on the "good" teachers were going quietly about their business of trying to help children learn to read. The good teachers knew what to teach and how to teach. The problem was what to call the children and where to put them. In other words the problem was not instructional but administrative. Variations of organizational patterns have been tried including ability grouping, streaming, readiness programs, adjustment rooms, special education, and remedial instruction. All these are simply attempts to fit children into the system. One of the more recent innovations has been multilevel grouping. Perhaps the only truly individualized program based on continuous growth is the private tutor working with one child.

TEACHER All this controversy about methods, materials, and administrative organizations boils down to one conclusion; it is the teacher who makes the difference. Research has not yet told us much about the teacher. The little research that has been done recognizes the teacher as an important variable, but what the qualities or characteristics are that make the difference has not been reduced to objective measurement. Massive research based on methods, materials, and administrative organization has consistently admitted that the teacher variable is one which is difficult to control and one which does affect results either adversely or positively.

True the teacher needs some ideas about how to go about teaching the child to read. She needs some materials with which to work. But teachers are individuals, too. Almost any method works with some teachers. And most teachers can get a measure of success with some methods. Almost any materials will work with some teachers and most teachers have more success with some materials than with others. Similarly almost any administrative organization can be accepted and used effectively by some teachers and most teachers work better under one organizational pattern than another.

The point to the whole thing is that if the teacher believes in the method, likes the material, and is convinced that the organizational pattern is effective, she will make it work. By the same token, if she is forced to use a method or material she does not believe in or to work in an administrative organization that she does not approve of, she can probably prove that it won't work.

Yes, it is the teacher who makes the difference!

WHAT COMMON SENSE TELLS US

Since the teacher makes the difference what does she need to know? She needs to know something about children and how they learn. She needs to know something about how she as a teacher is going to affect the learner. She needs to know something about the various materials and methods that provide approaches to learning to read. Then with all that knowledge at her command she is the doctor. She views each case as a separate problem. She surveys the situation, appraises the problem, diagnoses the difficulty, and prescribes the treatment. This prescription is a trial balloon on a daily basis. If it gets results and Johnny succeeds, she keeps on going. If Suzie does not respond to the formula, she tries something else. She varies the treatment as needed.

HOW CHILDREN LEARN Common sense tells us much about how children learn. If it were possible to prescribe one dose in equal amounts at the same time for all children, we could put teaching on the assembly line basis, program it on tape, and dispense with the one most expensive item on the educational budget, that is, the salary of the teacher. But since each child is a custom job and no two react alike, it takes individual diagnosis and treatment.

HOW TEACHING AFFECTS LEARNING Common sense tells us even more about the teacher and how what she does affects the learning situation. That is the reason the teacher must be informed and versatile both in child development and in reading materials and techniques. Then, given the freedom to teach, she has a better than average chance to succeed with each child at his level and in his own good time.

HOW ORGANIZATION AFFECTS LEARNING The most important thing common sense tells us about administrative arrangements is that they only facilitate organization and routine. They do not guarantee learning. The teacher who is put in the position of trying to mold the children into predetermined expectations in terms of materials, methods, and standards is doomed to frustration and failure.

HOW APPROACHES AFFECT LEARNING Common sense also tells us about varied approaches to reading which have worked and will work for different teachers and for different children. Children learn what they accept as worthy of their time and energy. Teaching is a person-to-person experience in which the challenger meets the challenged to the end that changed behavior is effected. There is no one approach that works with all—all teachers or all children. Therefore, the teacher must see herself as a professional facing daily issues and making many decisions for which she is capable and willing to assume the responsibility. All this leads to an examination of her philosophy of teaching.

TWO POINTS OF VIEW

The teacher must first examine her philosophy of teaching. Once she has decided what she believes and where she fits into the total learning pattern, she is in a position to chart her course. Let us examine two philosophies.

In one case the teacher sees her responsibility as that of assigning and checking the pupil's performance, then correcting and giving remedial instruction to eliminate his errors. In the other case she sees herself as responsible for teaching him how to perform a task, then letting him practice until growth has been achieved.

ASSIGNING, CHECKING, CORRECTING, AND REMEDYING If the philosophy of the teacher is based on the assumption that it is the role of the teacher to assign the task for the learner, see that he does it, and check on him to see that he did, then the next step in the sequence will have to be correcting his mistakes and remedying the situation. The teacher becomes the taskmaster, the judge, and the keeper of the records on which the rewards and punishments are based. This approach to teaching leads to some logical consequences.

- It leads to a poor performance based on lack of understanding prior to attacking the assignment.
- It leads to correction rather than prevention of errors.
- It permits the child to practice and fix wrong responses.
- It leads to performance for the purpose of showing the teacher what he can, or cannot do.
- It leads to concern for the rightness or wrongness of answers, for what the teacher thinks, and for marks and rewards.
- It leads the teacher to see herself as a taskmaster, assigning tasks and checking up on pupils. In that case teaching becomes a series of remedial measures instead of developmental steps.
- It leads the child to dread the new because of often repeated unpleasant experiences with situations for which he was ill prepared.

TEACHING, PERFORMING, PRACTICING, AND GROWING If the philosophy of teaching is based on the assumption that it is the role of the teacher to teach the child how and let him perform, then the next steps in the sequence will logically be correct practice and recording of progress. Now the teacher becomes the guide toward a series of logical steps in learning to read.

- The child renders a good performance because it is based on previous learning and understanding.
- He practices and fixes right responses because he learned how before he was asked to perform.
- His purpose for performance is to put into practice what he has just learned how to do.
- His purpose for practice is to perfect needed skills.
- The teacher sees herself as a guide and a helper as the child attacks each new problem.
- The child welcomes the challenge of the new because of the thrill of

mastering something and seeing himself doing it with a measurable degree of success.

CONSEQUENCES OF THESE TWO POINTS OF VIEW In either case, if the child is at the instructional level which challenges him for growth, we have to do some developmental teaching. If the teaching follows the unsuccessful performance, it is based on the assumption that he should have known. Should he, if the material is at his instructional level? Or should he be taught before he is asked to perform? When the teaching precedes the performance, it is based on the assumption that the child is ready to learn.

The child who comes through six years of elementary schooling based on a philosophy of test and remedy may emerge concerned only about mechanics and quality of performance. He may dread new situations, avoid learning, do anything to get it over with, and use evasive techniques such as guessing, bluffing, and perhaps cheating to attain the goal of marks and promotions. He bluffs or guesses because if he can make the teacher think he knows he can get by; making her think he knows is his objective because he has been conditioned for years to think that is the goal of education.

When he comes through six years of schooling based on developmental instruction and successful practice the opposite is true. Then he is concerned with meaning, with accomplishment, with enthusiasm for the new, with aggressive approaches to content, with a desire to continue, with a frontal attack on learning, with reasoned theorizing about solutions to problems, with open and frank questions, and with recognition of the teacher as a help and a guide in his development.

What do we want? Assigning, checking, correcting, and remedying? Or teaching, performing, practicing, and growing?

ARE YOU A TEACHER OR A TESTER?

Ask yourself, "Am I a teacher or a tester?" How can you tell? What do you believe about children? And about teaching? Examine your philosophy. It is revealed in what you say, what you do, what the children say, what the children do, and in the techniques you use and the children accept to evaluate the finished product. Let's take a look at some specific classroom situations illustrating these two points of view.

WHAT IS TEACHING? TWO POINTS OF VIEW

The word *teach* implies that somebody learns. Anything the teacher does which does not result in learning cannot rightfully be called teaching. Whenever the teacher gets the pupil to do something which results in learning then teaching has taken place. Is the pupil learning while he is listening? Maybe, and maybe not. Is he learning while he is struggling with an assignment which he does not understand? It is doubtful. He may be learning only that he does not know how or cannot do it. Is he learning while he is practicing wrong responses? Perhaps so, but what? Wrong answers, of course! What then is teaching? Think about this definition:

> Teaching is stimulating and directing the mental, physical, or emotional activity of the pupil to the end that learning takes place.

This definition begins on the assumption that no teaching has taken place unless some learning has also taken place. Physics tells us that if you ring a bell and no ear is within range you have only air vibrations. Similarly, if the teacher performs and no one learns she may be merely fanning air. Furthermore, the definition assumes that the learner must be active mentally, physically, and/or emotionally. It is unlikely that much learning takes place so long as the learner remains passive, even though in a receptive state. What then is the role of the teacher? The teacher stimulates the learner to action, then directs the course of that action toward the content or the skill to be learned.

What is the task of the teacher? Is it her purpose to help the children learn or to check up on them to see if they know? Is she responsible for helping them practice right responses or for evaluating and passing judgment on the responses they produce? Does the teacher teach? Or does she test? The complicated and lengthy definition given above can be stated very simply thus:

> Teaching is helping someone learn.

Put that little statement on a card and stand it on your desk where you can see it daily. It will help you keep yourself on the right track.

How can you tell whether you are a teacher or a tester? It shows up in your beliefs and in your actions. So why don't you . . .

CHECK UP ON YOUR BELIEFS

What do you believe? What do you believe about your job? About the purpose for the study period? About recitation periods? About marking pupil's work? What you believe determines whether you are teaching children or testing them.

Let's begin with a look at your job. Why are you teaching? Why did the community hire you? Are you there to tell the children what to do, then to check up on them to see if they did? Are you there to reward with praise, stars, or A's the children who comply and to penalize with reprimands, black marks, and D's the children who don't or can't carry out your instructions? Or are you there to help them learn? How can you tell? It shows up in everything you say and do, in your comments, your facial expression, your tone of voice, your routine procedures. What you believe speaks so loudly the children often cannot hear what you say, so perhaps you'd better . . .

EXAMINE YOUR PHILOSOPHY—IT IS SHOWING

You don't have to tell the children what you believe; they know. It isn't necessary to announce your beliefs to the parents; they can read between the children's reactions. A sermonette on beliefs to a visitor will be as superfluous as the announcement, "We are having boiled cabbage for dinner." One or two sniffs and even a stranger can tell what's cooking. What you believe shows up in everything you say and do. It shows up in everything the children say and do. In the final accounting it is obvious what you think the goal of education is.

WHAT YOU SAY Your philosophy shows in what you say. Take note of how you word your questions, your assignments, even your complaints. They all shout your philosophy.

Listen to your *questions*. Let's tune in on this room.

> What's the name of our story, Tom?
> Where is Newark?
> How much are six and five?
> What is manufactured in Boston?

Who wants to know the answers to those questions? The teacher surely doesn't. She already knows, or at least she should. Then why did she ask? There can be only one reason. She asked because she wanted to find out if Tom and Alice knew. She wasn't teaching them, she was testing them. If Tom and Alice knew, their replies steered them safely through the test. If they didn't know, there was nothing in the exercise that resulted in learning. Those who already knew probably didn't listen to the answers, or, if they did, it was for the purpose of catching someone in a mistake. Those who did not know busied themselves in distractions to avoid the situation and to keep the teacher from finding out they didn't know.

Questions can be a teaching technique. Listen to these.

> Why is "A Matter of Courage" a good title for this story?
> You may get the chairs, Alice. How many will we need?
> The text mentioned Newark. Let's find it on the map.
> Boston would be a good place to live because there is so much manufacturing there and you probably could get a job. Let's make a list of the kinds of factories in which we might apply.

Of course you see the difference. Now the teacher is stimulating and directing thinking. As the children respond they are collecting and organizing information. That is learning.

Listen to your *assignments*. Here are a couple for contrast.

> For tomorrow read Chapter Twelve and I shall ask you some questions.
>
> Chapter Twelve helps identify three kinds of simple machines. Tomorrow we shall see if we can classify some household tools under each. Bring in other examples if you can.

Now is the pupil reading to pass a test or to gather information to help him engage in a group project? Is the teacher testing him to see if he has studied his lesson or is she helping him use the information he has gathered?

Listen to your *directions*. Do you command, dictate, and dominate? Or do you guide, direct, and help the pupil make decisions? Here are some examples.

> I want you to look up the answers to these questions. Write them out in complete sentences. I won't accept any papers written in pencil or without a margin.
>
> That will make another good summary for our booklet on explorers. Do you think you can write it in ink the first time, or had you better practice in pencil first? I'll be glad to help you proofread your copy before you put it in final form. Don't forget your margin. Remember, when we punch our notebooks we need that space on the left.

Both teachers end up with the children writing a page in ink with margin and complete sentences. One tested. One taught. Which do you do?

Listen to your *pronouns* for a day or two. They reveal much about your philosophy. Do they sound like this?

> For tomorrow *I* want you to work all the . . .
> Will you do this for *me?*
> *I* won't take that paper till you correct the mistakes.
> If you are going to be in *my* room you will have to . . .
> *I* don't let *my* pupils . . .

And so on. If you sound like this, then it is *your* room, *your* class, *your* job, *your* responsibility, *your* decision and the pupils are merely puppets doing your bidding, or maybe trying to get out of as much work as possible and still get by.

The real teacher, the leader of boys and girls, the one who helps them learn sounds more like this.

> There are some examples of *our* new kind of exercise on page 17. Do *you* think *you* know how now? Then *you* may try them for tomorrow. How many do *you* think *you* can do? Suppose *we* all do the first four. Faster workers may finish the page if there is time.

Is that *your* best work? Are *you* satisfied to save it for *your* booklet the way it is, or do *you* think *you* had better recopy it once more?

Do *you* like that kind of work?

Is that the kind of action *we* can be proud of in *our* room?

The boys and girls in *our* room have decided to . . .

You see the difference. Now it is the responsibility of the learner and the teacher is the guide and the helper.

Listen to your *complaints*. Have you ever used these expressions?

That's all right in theory, but it won't work in practice.

That's a good idea, but it will never work with my children.

I'd like to do some activity work, but I have too many pupils.

That might work with bright children, but I have a dreadfully slow bunch this year.

Yes, I believe in some pupil responsibility, but our principal expects us to . . .

Those things are nice, but we don't have time. We are expected to cover so much by the end of the year.

It would be nice, but my room doesn't have that kind of furniture.

You couldn't use visual aids in our school. We don't have any way to darken the room.

Our community would never stand for that.

Those are all excuses, not reasons. If you really believe in something and want to see it work badly enough, you will convince others of the idea and make it work.

The real teacher sounds more like this.

That's a good idea. I wonder how much of it we could make work in our room.

With a larger number of children I find I must adapt activity work to one group at a time.

My children are slower than usual so I find new experiences take more preparation and explanation to put them across.

I think I will discuss that with the principal and see if he will help me work it out.

Perhaps we could adjust some of the required work to fit into some of these activities.

Let's see, we don't have a low table, but maybe we could work standing around a tall one if we don't work too long at a time.

We watch for cloudy days and draw the shades. Then our projected pictures show up pretty well. These days don't always come at the most appropriate time but the children understand and we manage.

That seems to be a new idea in this community, but maybe I can get one or two of the mothers to help me. If it works they'll have more influence on the rest of the community than I will.

WHAT YOU DO Your philosophy shows in what you do. Notice the materials you select. Even observe the room arrangement and the activities you plan. These seem like little things but they tell much about your philosophy of education.

Examine your *instructional materials* first. Do you prefer the same book in the hands of each child? Do you try to keep all the children on the same page? Do you feel that is easier to manage? If so, you are probably dictating what they shall learn and checking up on them to see if they have done the work. Do you avoid activities because the children are too noisy? Do the children look on a work period as an opportunity to "fiddle around"? If so, they are more concerned about what the teacher "allows" than about the job they are doing.

If the topic is "Kinds of Clouds," need everyone read identically the same text? Many books illustrate, describe, and identify clouds. Some might give more information than others. Some reading matter might be simpler for the less capable pupils. Some might be a real challenge for the extra alert. What if there should be a seeming discrepancy in the context of two references? Now, if your purpose is to test, there may be some difficulty in determining the accepted answer and justifying the mark, but if the purpose is to teach, then perhaps the reasoning involved in interchange of information and reconciliation of seeming conflicts will be a genuine learning situation. Do you welcome an experiment to see what happens? Do your children construct models with a determination to clarify a concept or display a new learning? Is so, materials will be tools for learning and will vary with the needs or talents of the children.

Look at the *physical setting* of the classroom itself. Did you ever survey a classroom when there was no one there—no children, no teacher, no visitors? There is as much difference between a testing room and a teaching room as there is between a furniture store window and a living room where a family works and plays and lives. Have you established the one best way for your furniture? Do you keep it that way all the time? Is it spaced so the children cannot communicate or look at one another? Is it "teacher centered"? Does the teacher's desk dominate the front of the room? Do all the children face the teacher? Does the teacher face all the children? Are the chalk boards, walls, bulletin boards, tables, and shelves neat, orderly, empty, and uncluttered? If so, then this is a room where the children are doing what they are told, striving to please the teacher—or aggravate her, perhaps—a room where they are being directed, tested, measured, and judged. They won't need anything but the text because the answers to the questions on which they will be tested are all there. They won't need to communicate with one another because they are all supposed to learn the same things and the only need for communication is with the teacher.

Take note of the *activities* you plan. If all the children are working on a common problem, they will need to share information, make models, plan activities, and seek teacher help. That will make necessary the grouping of furniture and frequent change in arrangement to meet different situations. Talking with a neighbor is no longer an infraction of a rule, a thing to be practiced behind a cupped palm or an adroitly held book, but rather a means of accomplishing a purpose. There is a time for communication among small groups and a time for total group discussion. Conduct is determined by the activity at hand and the polite thing to do or say under the circumstances rather than by what the teacher will or will not tolerate.

WHAT THE CHILDREN SAY Your philosophy shows in what the children say. What you believe shows up even when you are silent. The children will tell you. You can hear your philosophy echoed in their questions and in their responses.

Listen to the *children's questions.* Do they sound like this?

How far do we have to read?
Must we write them out?
Do you count off for spelling?
Are you going to take up the papers?

Questions like these imply that the children are doing the work to please the teacher, because she demands it or to earn a mark. So far as the children are concerned it is the teacher who wants the work done. It is her job. Either they resist, fail to contorm, and get a low mark; or they accept the inevitable, accommodate the teacher, and give her whatever she wants. If they get anything out of it, it is the reward, the commendation, or the passing mark. What did they learn? Possibly nothing or very little. Or if they did learn something, it was only incidental to the real objective of pleasing the teacher, getting the mark, and passing.

Children who are being taught instead of tested may ask such questions as these.

Is this the right way to start my letter?
Where can I find out what kind of leaf this is?
How does this work?
Why . . . ?
Where . . . ?

They really want to know. They are concerned about the teacher's evaluation only as it helps them to find out, to achieve, to perfect a needed skill.

Listen to the *children's responses.* Children are little mirrors. They reflect the philosophy of the teacher. Does Sally wave her hand wildly trying to attract attention and answer all the questions? Is she an honor-roll-seeker or a star-gatherer? Does Fred prop his geography textbook on his desk, hide behind it, or use other means of evading the teacher's glance in order to avoid being called on for response to a question to which he does not know the answer? Does Sam always come up with a rambling response, often a bit irrelevant and obviously designed to conceal the fact that he doesn't know? Have you noticed how Lillian always needs to sharpen her pencil or go to the restroom or see about a book just at recitation time? These are effective distraction devices until the teacher gets enough of them or catches on to the technique and curbs them. These children all show that their chief concern is connected with the teacher and how she reacts to them. If they expect to be measured and judged, they must have a tester instead of a teacher.

What are they studying? You certainly cannot tell by their attitudes or evidence of concern. That is only incidental to their real objective of making a good impression and earning rewards in the form of prizes, stars, and good grades. Sometimes the objective is negative and that is even worse. They may be trying to avoid a sharp remark, a low grade, or punishment.

How do children react when they are being taught instead of tested? They exchange ideas. They bring in new information about the current interest, be it butterflies, ancient Egyptians, or practical uses for percentage. They volunteer for extra assignments. They ask permission to rewrite an important letter. They hurry in from play to get started. They may disregard the dismissal bell and say, "Wait till I finish this." Their concern is for the task at hand. To them a job is something to do, not something to evade.

WHAT THE CHILDREN DO Your philosophy shows in what the children do. There are many good opportunities for reading children's actions. Observe the recitation period. Notice the lesson sequence. Take a look at how they use the study period.

Let's tune in on a *recitation period.*

"All right! Time's up. Close your books. How many of you found all the answers? You may take up the papers, Larry. Take the first question."

Pause. Hands are waving. The teacher's eye lights on Billy whose hand isn't up and who is avoiding her gaze.

"Billy!"

No response.

"Billy."

Still no response.

"Billy, stand up."

Billy shuffles to his feet.

"Did you find the answer to the first question?" (Now that was a useless question. Obviously Billy would have had his hand up and would have answered if he had known.)

"No."

"Why not?"

"I don't know." (And he really doesn't know why.)

"That's a pretty poor excuse. You'd better make better use of your time tomorrow. Tell him, Sandra."

"Thirteen."

"That's right. Take the next question, Erma."

Wait a minute! What was the first question about? Thirteen what? But that doesn't matter. The purpose of the recitation was not to do anything with the content. The purpose was to get the children to recite the facts which they had been directed to gather in order that the teacher might find out if they had performed as directed and how well in order that she might in turn pass judgment, evaluate, and arrive at a grade.

Now take this class period.

"Perhaps we had better go on to the geography lesson. Yesterday Jean asked why the people in the rural areas of the Philippines build their houses so high off the ground. What did you find out?"

Mary has a picture to show. Phillip has an old issue of the *National Geographic*. Amy has an encyclopedia she brought from the library. Thelma has a clipping from the daily paper. Several children have put slips into one or two of the geography books available. Bob is ready to tell what his big brother who has been there has told him. Information comes thick and fast. Each one has something to contribute. Some talk. Some read. Some show. All listen because each one is telling something the rest have not read out of the book.

Now the teacher attempts to lead the learning activity and direct it so that it will be profitable to all.

"These are such good ideas that perhaps we had better get some of them down. I'll write on the chalk board. Perhaps you'll want to make some notes on your paper, too. Let's begin with a list of materials the houses are made of."

Result: shared information, organized facts, pupil activity, teacher leadership, learning. Who found all the answers? What grades did the children get? Who cares? They found out what they wanted to know, didn't they?

Consider the *sequence of the lesson*. Do you hear the children recite, then make an assignment for the next day at the last minute? Do the children put their books away until tomorrow? In that case you have checked up on them to see how well they have mastered the assignment made yesterday and have told them what they will be tested on tomorrow.

Perhaps the sequence should be reversed. Try using a class period to develop something new and let the assignment be an opportunity to practice what has just been learned. Consider this example of questionable procedure.

"Tomorrow we are going to take up a new kind of sentence. Study the example and the explanation on page 87. Try the exercises at the bottom of the page. Perhaps you'd better take your book home tonight."

At 3:30 there is a gentle reminder. "I'd like to see some books going home tonight."

The next morning at study time Willie is bothering his neighbors. There is a sharp reprimand.

"Willie, get busy! Did you do all those sentences?"

"Yes."

"Then find something else to do or look over your paper."

Then at class time, "How many of you got all the exercises?"

Hands go up.

"What's the matter with you, Frank?"

"I don't know."

"Did you take your book home?"

"Yes."

"Did you study it?"

"No."

"Why not?"

"We went to church."

At this point the teacher looks irritated, sighs, and lets the matter go.

"You may exchange papers to grade. I'll read the correct answers. It's quicker that way. Count off five for each one missed and return the papers. When I call your name give me your grade."

Roll call.

"Put the first one on the board, John, the second one, Eva, and so on."

Now who puts the answers on the board? The children who got them, of course. What are they learning? Probably nothing. They already know or they are copying from the paper Mother helped them do last night. If they know how, they were either clever enough to figure it out on their own or else Mother did the teaching. If they don't know, it is doubtful that they will know at the end of this class period. And if they should, any teaching which takes place will be a matter of remedying faulty procedure rather than effective developmental instruction.

How much better it would be to reverse the sequence of the lesson. The teacher says, "Today we are going to take up a new kind of sentence. Open your books to page 87. Let's study the examples at the top of the page together."

Then the class period is used to develop the understanding. At the end of the period the logical question is, "Do you think you know how to do it? Then if you will look at the bottom of the page you will find some more practice exercises. Let's see if we can do them."

Notice that the emphasis is on knowing how rather than on the right answer or how many right answers each child got. If the lesson has been well developed, if the children know how, and if they really want to practice what they have learned, they will want to do it right then.

This brings us up to the *study period* which reflects the philosophy of the teacher. The way the children use the study period indicates whether they are getting ready to be tested or are applying something they have learned. When they study is one indication. What they do is another.

If they put off studying till the next day using just the fifteen or twenty minutes before the class period, they may just look at the lesson only to have it fresh in mind. In this case they are probably expecting the class period to be a test of their memory for what they have studied.

When they study immediately after the lesson period, more than likely they are plunging zestfully into something they have just learned how to do or something they have planned together. For example, they may be doing some drill on the exercises on a new kind of sentence, finishing a story started in class, or perhaps organizing an outline for a history dramatization they have just planned. No doubt their study period will result in effective performance because they know what to do and how to do it.

TECHNIQUES OF EVALUATION Most of all your philosophy shows in the techniques you use in evaluation. The teacher exhibits her philosophy of education in the way she marks the children's papers and in the emphasis she puts on the recording of results.

How do you *mark the children's papers?* Do you emphasize how much the children missed or how much they learned? Do you make corrections or do you require the children to do so and hand in the work again so you can reopen the case, sit in judgment once more, and perhaps hand out a benevolent pardon? Did you every try wielding a good eraser for the young learner neatly eradicating his errors for him? Then you can suggest the correct form so he can have the satisfaction of a piece of work well done without the disfiguring red marks which he glances at distastefully and chucks into the wastebasket.

Do you always *place a value on all written work* by trying to say how much it is worth? Do you write something at the top? Perhaps you write a minus 2 indicating that the child missed two of whatever it is. Why not a plus 38 to indicate that he got 38 of the 40 exercises correct? Do you write 90 or B at the top of the paper? If so, you have sat in judgment and arrived at a value or awarded a prize. That procedure encourages the pupil to work for the 100 or the A. If that is the goal, he may use questionable methods of attaining it. Sometimes it is easier to copy than to learn, and, if the A is the goal, either method gets results. When the teacher puts the A on the paper and says, "What did you get?" she is indicating that she has accepted that goal. No wonder the child does, too.

Where do you *place the emphasis?* Try asking the child, "Do you know how to do these examples?" The A won't answer that question. Try writing on his paper such comments as "Good work," "Neat paper," "You are doing much better," or "You need some help. See me a minute at recess and I'll show you how."

When the children do the work immediately after class with emphasis on knowing how instead of getting a grade and when they experience success and a feeling of achievement, they will not be so concerned about being "the best," "at the head of the class," or "beating the other fellow." If being the best in the class is the objective, then only one child can attain the goal and the other twenty-five or thirty are doomed to failure. True, several different ones may succeed at different times, but what of the fifteen or twenty Sammies and Suzies who never attain the goal?

When learning how is the goal it is perfectly possible for each one to succeed. Does it make a better worker out of Tommy to know that he has beaten his classmate and best friend? Couldn't he be just as good a worker if both he and Sam were working to achieve the same speed and comprehension and if both succeeded?

RESOLVE TO BE A TEACHER INSTEAD OF A TESTER

If you have followed this far, you are ready to summarize and draw some conclusions. Have you decided yet what you believe? Did you see your philosophy showing through the thin veneer of your classroom procedures? Did you like what you saw? Then why not resolve to:

- Teach the pupils how, let them do it, and enjoy success.
- Help them learn new processes. Then give them an opportunity to practice correct responses.
- Help them plan constructive tasks and guide them to more and more successful performances.
- Be a teacher instead of a tester.

Each day as the last pupil goes out of the door take stock. Ask yourself, "What have I taught today? What did the children learn?"

Can you say:

They know how to number an outline now.
They have learned the significance of the Louisiana Purchase.
They experimented with sound and discovered what makes a telephone work.
I did direct their responses in such a manner that they were active, sometimes physically, sometimes mentally, and sometimes emotionally.
I think I helped them learn.

If you can truthfully say these things, you are a teacher. Keep up the good work![2]

TEACHER COMPETENCY AND PUPIL ACHIEVEMENT

If we could put all teachers into three categories, inadequate, routine, and creative, and if we could put all pupils into three categories, dull, average, and superior, we would come up with at least nine combinations

[2]Daisy M. Jones, *Are You a Teacher or a Tester?* (Monograph No. 85), Evanston, Ill., Harper & Row, 1957.

		Teacher Competency		
		Inadequate	*Routine*	*Creative*
Pupil Capacity	Superior	Limited prospects Child may learn in spite of the teacher on his own initiative and from his environment	Good prospects Child will furnish much of his own stimulus Results will be commendable with mediocre effort on the part of the teacher	Good prospects High degree of learning can be expected There should be superior results in all skill areas
	Average	Very limited prospects Teacher will provide little or no stimulation Pupil is capable of only limited initiative Limited learning will occur	Fair prospects Child will achieve routine learning through rote memory to be able to pass tests and get by	Good prospects Child will probably achieve to capacity Teacher may be inspired to bring out his best points
	Dull	Very limited prospects Teacher will probably resent the child, reject him, discourage him, and let him regress instead of advance	Limited prospects Teacher will probably accept the child, perhaps with passivity She will do little to challenge him, letting him sit and put in time	Good prospects Teacher will accept the child for what he is She will challenge him for all she can get from him She will build on his ego to gain small successes She will help him grow and develop

Figure 30. School achievement, teacher competency, and pupil capacity.

of pupil-teacher relationships which would affect learning. If you can accept the assumption that teacher competency does affect pupil learning and if you can accept the assumption that pupil capacity does have an effect on his learning, then we can look somewhat realistically at the consequent relationships in the teaching-learning situation.

EFFECT OF TEACHER COMPETENCY ON PUPIL LEARNING

The inadequate teacher fails to see the challenge of learning. The dull learners may become even duller. The average ones merely put in time. The superior ones are in danger of losing the spark.

The routine teacher tends to accept the learners in a matter-of-fact way. The dull ones will probably do little except put in time. The average ones will plod along. The superior ones will exercise their own initiative and perhaps challenge her.

But the creative teacher tends to draw forth from each learner the best he has to offer. She leads the slower ones to a full life within their limited abilities. From the average pupils she draws a satisfactory performance with occasional spurts of unexpected attainment. From the superior pupils she draws a high level of performance with occasional bursts of genius.

EFFECT OF PUPIL CAPACITY ON LEARNING

Dull pupils are a vital challenge. Routine or inadequate teachers tend to become discouraged with them and too often get limited results. It takes a creative teacher to see their possibilities, make the necessary adjustments, and work for growth.

Average pupils tend to follow a routine path. Colorless or dull teachers will let them die on the vine for want of cultivation. Not much may happen unless they are challenged by an inspired teacher who brings out the better threads in their personalities.

Superior pupils will probably learn in spite of the teacher. However, if they are thwarted by a less than inspired teacher, they may lose some of the spark which they have. A routine teacher may permit them to learn, but they will be more challenged by a creative teacher.

Figure 30 points out the relationships between teacher competency and pupil capacity.

22

RECOGNIZING MATURITY

or They're on Their Own Now

This chapter is aimed for those individuals, including myself, who just must put things away and close the door. Unless the package is neatly wrapped and tied up with a string it just doesn't seem quite finished. I just don't like a sermon without a summary and conclusion. That is called closure. If you need closure, this final chapter will enable you to back up and take a total look at the learning-to-read process and its correlative, the teaching-of-reading, which we have tried to describe.

While this book has referred to the historical development of the teaching of reading, it has not been an attempt to give you history in detail. While it has referred to some research in the field of reading to support some of the points made, it has not been an attempt to compile, summarize, and interpret all the scientific research as a basis for proving anything.

What this book has tried to do is to give the classroom teacher who is facing a roomful of learners a point of view that will be helpful and practical. She can read the history, but that doesn't answer her questiton about what to do today with Samuel and Anthony or with Juan and Julia. She can read the research and find out what the statistics prove and with what degree of reliability as interpreted by such measures as standard deviations, degrees of freedom, level of reliability, and significance of difference, but then she still asks, "What shall I do about it?" She can read the case studies that suggest what to do with the individual who deviates from expectancy to the point where she is concerned about him, but her big question is not so much what is the trouble with Sara and what should be done about her, but rather what will she do with the other twenty-nine who won't be still and wait.

If this book has accomplished these purposes, it will provide the teacher with a guide to the development of mature readers who can meet the situation. It has attempted to show the total reading program by answering such questions as: Why read? How can reading be made a growing experience? What uses will the learner have for reading the rest of his life? And what should be included in a reading program to ensure the learner a balanced diet?

SEEING THE TOTAL READING PROGRAM

In order to see reading in its totality one must recognize the real purpose and make reading a growing experience so that the learner will continue to use reading throughout the rest of his life.

RECOGNIZING PURPOSES FOR READING

The reading act is a matter of communication. That means we must eliminate such practices as saying the words, taking turns, and testing as reasons for reading. When all is said and done there are only a few reasons for reading throughout life. All of these should apply to the classroom and to the established purposes for teaching reading. Specifically they are to get information and to enjoy communication with the author and with others.

TO GET INFORMATION If no information is forthcoming, if one knows the words but misses the point, if one misunderstands or misinterprets the information, then perhaps it might have been better if he had not attempted to read at all. One reads to get information.

TO ENJOY COMMUNICATION WITH THE AUTHOR The author has used the printed word either to preserve or to transmit his message regardless of place and time. Since he is depending on that means of transmittal, he is dependent on the reader in the same way that the speaker is dependent on the listener to complete the cycle of communication. All recreational and inspirational reading is based on the assumption that the reader wants to know what the author has to say, what he thinks, how he feels, and what he is trying to tell. Unless the reader does his part, unless he enjoys the communion with the author, unless he reacts to what he is reading, then most of the intent for both writing and reading has been lost. One reads to enjoy the experience of communicating with the author.

TO COMMUNICATE WITH OTHERS Sometimes one reads to communicate with others. This implies oral reading. Now a third dimension enters the picture in interpreting the reading act. The author wrote his stories, his ideas, his information to communicate with the reader. The reader reads silently to find out what the author has to say. Once he has found out he may have need to transmit his findings to others. That calls for the listener who becomes the third party in this three way communication. The reader has a double responsibility—first, to get the point himself and, second, to express the idea so that a third party can also get the information without actually reading it for himself.

Unless reading results in transmittal of information either to the reader pursuing the printed page silently and independently or to a listener who is depending on the spoken word, then true reading has not taken place. Therefore, we are going to answer the question "Why read?" by saying that the only real reason for reading is to find out what the author has to say.

MAKING READING A GROWING EXPERIENCE

Reading is more than a mechanical process. It is a set of skills and understandings which must be developed and expanded throughout life. The earliest steps are taken when the infant responds to the spoken word. As he acquires language he is laying a foundation for utilizing that medium when he encounters it in the printed symbol. As he learns the mechanics which help him interpret abstract symbols into ideas he is gaining mastery over a tool that will make him independent in reading for the rest of his life. In order to become that mature and independent reader which will make him a lifetime learner he must develop tastes, establish independence, expand his interests, and keep on keeping on.

DEVELOPING TASTES The reader needs to develop tastes which will give him an appetite for reading. This is done gradually. The development of tastes in foods is dependent on sampling different kinds, adjusting to different needs of the body, and becoming acquainted with customs, habits, and concerns of people in all parts of the world. The same is true in reading tastes.

The truly mature and discriminating reader is the one who has sampled widely and has been able to choose a variety of types of reading material to suit his various needs and moods. He will read the editorials, the advertisements, and the factual reports of daily events. He will read the jokes, the words of wisdom, the philosophical articles, the how-to-do-it sections in the magazines. He will read light entertaining narrative, heavy historical fiction, and biography. His tastes will be not only highly refined, but varied.

DEVELOPING INDEPENDENCE The mature reader must develop independence. This means being able to help himself, being independent of the teacher. He will know how to attack vocabulary, how to use a dictionary, how to find the information he wants, how to use the parts of a book, how to skim or scan, how to preview or review, how to read for details, or how to speed over a passage for a general impression. He will know not only how to do all these things, but also when to do them and why. He will long since have passed the stage where he has to ask someone else how to pronounce a word or where to find information. He is independent.

EXPANDING INTERESTS The independent reader must develop a variety of interests so that he is ready to read on his own. He can always pick up a book or a magazine and find something of interest and value. He can always visit a library and select reading matter for his personal use. He can always stop at a magazine stand or a book shelf and find profitable reading matter. He is never without something to do. He becomes a stimulating conversationalist as well as an informed citizen because he has learned to use reading as a means of making himself a more mature and a better informed person.

KEEPING ON KEEPING ON Perhaps the most important thing a learner does in the process of learning to read and in using his reading skills independently to become that interesting and informed person is to keep on keeping on. There is no merit in knowing how to read unless one reads. There is little merit in reading if one waits to be told what to read. There is doubtful merit in reading what one is told to read if he makes no application of his ideas acquired through reading. One never gets done. Tomorrow there is always a craving for more ideas to fill the void created by the passing of yesterday's ideas.

READING THROUGHOUT LIFE

What use does one have for reading the rest of his life? After school days are over reading is a part of one's total personality, one's very existence. All the rest of his life the person who has learned to read will use the skill and the habit to enrich his life. The reading he does will most of it fall into one of two basic categories. Some reading will be practical; some reading will be recreatory.

PRACTICAL READING Some reading is strictly for practical purposes. It will give the reader the information he needs such as the price of milk, the place of the special sale, the location of a historical site, the price of stocks, the names of the political candidates, the new inventions, and so on. It is true that other media in today's world give us much of our information, but, even so, the printed word serves as a record and a ready reference. You may hear the announcement but unless you jot it down you may find yourself referring to the daily paper or the information on the printed ticket to find out where the meeting is to be held or what time the performance is scheduled to begin. Yes, reading is a vital source of information. It is a practical skill without which today's citizen is greatly handicapped. It is more than a school subject, more than a tool to use in pursuit of an education. It is a basic skill which is both practical and useful.

RECREATIONAL READING Some reading is meant to be strictly entertainng. The person who can use reading as a source of entertainment for himself is never without something to do. Even if he reads only the jokes or the comics he is using his time for self-entertainment. When he learns to enjoy and appreciate literary selections and to use his reading skills to add to that enjoyment, he is a mature reader. He no longer needs to be told what to read or what to find out. All he needs is an opportunity, which means the materials and the time. He may have to steal the time from his bridge club or the TV set, but a truly mature reader will suffer no pangs of conscience in the theft of time. He may have to depend on the public library or the discarded magazines in the trash heap for the materials, but a truly mature reader will find something to read. Reading is like a chronic disease or a barbituate. Once infected or addicted he will find a way.

BALANCING THE READING DIET

Since we want to develop children into adults who know why they are reading, who are growing constantly in their reading skills, who are always refining their tastes, and who will use reading the rest of their lives, we must plan from the very beginning to give them a balanced diet.

THE INGREDIENTS

READINESS Such a diet must begin on the assumption that the child is ready for each new learning that is presented so that he will approach it with eagerness, zeal, and self-confidence. If that readiness does not already exist, it must be built.

MOTIVATION Such a diet must whet the appetite so that the learner will not only think he can, but will want to do it. This applies to both skills and content. He must see a value to the skills and must feel challenged to master them because they are not only useful, but intriguing. He must see a purpose for the content and study it because he wants to know what it has to offer him.

BASIC PROGRAM Such a diet must include a basic program planned so that he has all the necessary ingredients. It cannot be left to mere chance. If he is allowed to read at random without direction he may manage to pick up a few skills and some interesting ideas, but he may lack the balance and maturity that make him an efficient and a discriminating reader. The program must be so planned that he is introduced to a variety of skills to meet different needs and to a variety of materials to provide for different interests and demands.

INTEREST Such a diet must make sure that he is attracted to the reading program through his personal interests. Such interests come from within and cannot be superimposed. All the teacher or the program can do is to provide the setting and encourage the application. The diet which is based on interests must be applied by the learner through his own efforts. The teacher cannot do the learning for him.

PERSISTENCE Such a diet must be persistent. You cannot store up enough Vitamin A to do you the rest of your life. It must be restored each day as long as you live. Unless the reading program has built into it that quality of keeping on it may miss the target.

THE MENU

What then is included in a balanced reading diet? I would like to submit for your consideration the menu on the following page.

A BALANCED READING DIET

The Appetizer

A thorough readiness program

The Salad Course

Something light, appetizing, and easily digested

The Main Dish

A sound basic reading program including
- Meat—Worthwhile information and good content
- Vegetables—Factual information and interesting stories
- Side dishes—Skill in word analysis
  - Independence in word attack
  - Adequate perception span
  - Long eye-voice span
  - Accurate return sweep
  - Rhythmic eye movements without regressions
  - Speed suited to the purpose and the material
  - Ability to skim for general impressions
  - Study skills—including ability to
    - Use index and table of contents
    - Read figures, graphs, maps, etc.
- Vitamins and other basic food elements including
  - Information
  - Interpretation
  - Expression and fluency
  - Understanding
  - Organization
  - Generalization
  - Application

The Dessert

A permanent interest in reading accompanied by
Taste for both literary and factual material

The Demitasse

A small portion of invigorating fluid that will go down easily and will leave one with the desire to keep coming back for more

and more

and more.

CONCLUSION

Reading is a highly individual process. When the child can learn to be an individual in his own right and still function in a group, then he has become a mature member of society ready to take his place and his responsibility in the family, in the classroom, in the community, and in the nation. Not until he has reached that stage has he really become mature either as a person or as a reader.

So you're TEACHING CHILDREN TO READ. I hope I have helped you to understand how to guide the individual as a member of the group. After all, individualized instruction is not only a matter of teaching the individual, but also a matter of meeting his needs within the group.

The teacher is the catalyst.

The child must do the learning.

The teacher can only set the conditions for learning.

The learning is not induced by the materials, the methods, the time, or the content.

The learning is induced only when the child wants to know or to know how.

All the teacher can do is to
Lead him to the brink;
Provide the materials;
Arrange the time;
Manage the setting;
Encourage him to try;
Keep the records;
Get out of his way;
And hope!

BIBLIOGRAPHY

Adams, Georgia Sacke, and Theodore Torgerson, *Measurement and Evaluation,* New York, Dryden, 1957.

Anderson, Freeman B., *et al., New Directions in English,* Teacher's Edition, New York, Harper & Row, 1969.

Bailey, Mildred Hart, "The Utility of Phonic Generalizations in Grades One through Six," *The Reading Teacher, 20,* no. 5 (February, 1967), 413–418.

Bond, Guy L., and Miles A. Tinker, *Reading Difficulties, Their Diagnosis and Correction,* New York, Appleton-Century-Crofts, 1957.

Bond, Guy L., and Eva Bond Wagner, *Teaching the Child to Read,* New York, Macmillan, 1966.

Cleland, Donald L., "Clinical Materials for Appraising Disabilities in Reading," *The Reading Teacher, 17,* no. 6 (March, 1964), 428–434.

Clymer, Theodore W., "The Utility of Phonic Generalizations in the Primary Grades," *The Reading Teacher, 16* (January, 1963), 252–258.

Cordts, Anna D., *Phonics for the Reading Teacher,* New York, Holt, Rinehart and Winston, 1965.

DeBoer, John J., and Martha Dallman, *The Teaching of Reading,* New York, Holt, Rinehart and Winston, 1964.

Dechant, Emerald V., *Improving the Teaching of Reading,* Englewood Cliffs, N.J., Prentice-Hall, 1964.

DeHirsch, Katrina, *Predicting Reading Failure,* New York, Harper & Row, 1966.

Della-Piana, Gabriel M., *Reading Diagnosis and Prescription,* New York, Holt, Rinehart and Winston, 1968.

Dolch, Edward M., *Methods in Teaching Reading,* Champaign, Ill., Garrard, 1955.

Durkin, Delores, "Phonics Materials: A Big Seller," *The Reading Teacher, 20,* no. 7 (April, 1967), 610–614.

Emans, Robert, "Phonics: A Look Ahead," *Elementary English, 46,* no. 5 (May, 1969), 575–582.

Evertts, Eldonna L., and Byron H. VanRoekel, *Seven Seas,* Basic Sixth Reader, Strand 1 (The Harper & Row Basic Reading Program), Evanston, Ill., Harper & Row, 1966.

Evertts, Eldonna L., and Byron H. VanRoekel, *Trade Winds,* Basic Fourth Reader, Strand 1 (The Harper & Row Basic Reading Program), Evanston, Ill., Harper & Row, 1966.

Fries, Charles C., *Linguistics and Reading,* New York, Holt, Rinehart and Winston, 1962.

Frost, Joe L., *Issues and Innovations in the Teaching of Reading,* Glenview, Ill., Scott, Foresman, 1967.

Harris, Albert J., *How to Increase Reading Ability,* New York, McKay, 1961.

Heilman, Arthur W., *Teaching Reading,* Columbus, Ohio, Merrill, 1961.

Ilg, Frances L., and Louise Bates Ames, *School Readiness,* New York, Harper & Row, 1964.

International Reading Association, *Corrective Reading in the Elementary Classroom* (Perspectives in Reading, No. 7), comp. and ed. Marjorie Seddon Johnson and Roy A. Kress, Newark, Del., International Reading Association, 1967.

International Reading Association, *The Evaluation of Children's Reading Achievement* (Perspectives in Reading, No. 8), comp. and ed. Thomas C. Barrett, Newark, Del., International Reading Association, 1967.

International Reading Association, *Organizing for Individual Differences* (Perspectives in Reading, No. 9), comp. and ed. Wallace Z. Ramsey, Newark, Del., International Reading Association, 1967..

Jones, Daisy M., "A Reading Fable," *The Clearing House, 43,* no. 1 (September, 1968), 39.

Jones, Daisy M., *Are You a Teacher or a Tester?* (Monograph No. 85), Evanston, Ill., Harper & Row, 1957.

Jones, Daisy M., "The Implications of Linguistics for the Teaching of Reading," *Elementary English, 46,* no. 2 (February, 1969), 176–183.

Jones, Daisy M., "Mechanics Versus Meaning—Teaching Versus Testing, A Plea for the Right Start in Comprehension," *The Reading Teacher* (January, 1953), 15–22.

Jones, Daisy M., and J. Louis Cooper, *From Actors to Astronauts,* Basic Fifth Reader, Strand 2 (The Harper & Row Basic Reading Program), Evanston, Ill., Harper & Row, 1964.

Jones, Daisy M., and J. Louis Cooper, *From Coins to Kings,* Basic Sixth Reader, Strand 2 (The Harper & Row Basic Reading Program), Evanston, Ill., Harper & Row, 1964.

Lamb, Pose, *Guiding Children's Language Learning,* Dubuque, Iowa, Brown, 1967.

Lamb, Pose, *Linguistics in Proper Perspective,* Columbus, Ohio, Merrill, 1967.
Lefevre, Carl A., "A Comprehensive Linguistic Approach to Reading," *Elementary English,* October, 1965, 651–659.
Monroe, Marion, and Bernice Rogers, *Foundations for Reading, Informal Pre-reading Procedures,* Glenview, Ill., Scott, Foresman, 1964.
Morrison, Ida E., *Teaching Reading in the Elementary School,* New York, Ronald, 1968.
National Society for the Study of Education, *Innovation and Change in Beginning Reading Instruction,* 67th Yearbook, Part II, Chicago, University of Chicago Press, 1968.
O'Donnell, Mabel, and J. Louis Cooper, *From Codes to Captains,* Basic Fourth Reader, Strand 2 (The Harper & Row Basic Reading Program), Evanston, Ill., Harper & Row, 1963.
O'Donnell, Mabel, and Byron H. VanRoekel, *All Through the Year,* Basic Second Reader, Strand 1 (The Harper & Row Basic Reading Program), Evanston, Ill., Harper & Row, 1966.
O'Donnell, Mabel, and Bryon H. VanRoekel, *Around the Corner,* Primer (The Harper & Row Basic Reading Program), Evanston, Ill., Harper & Row, 1966.
O'Donnell, Mabel, and Byron H. VanRoekel, *From Faraway Places,* Basic Third Reader, Strand 1 (The Harper & Row Basic Reading Program), Evanston, Ill., Harper & Row, 1966.
O'Donnell, Mabel, and Byron H. VanRoekel, *Janet and Mark,* Preprimer 1 (The Harper & Row Basic Reading Program), Evanston, Ill., Harper & Row, 1966.
O'Donnell, Mabel, and Byron H. VanRoekel, *Just for Fun,* Preprimer 4 (The Harper & Row Basic Reading Program), Evanston, Ill., Harper & Row, 1966.
O'Donnell, Mabel, and Byron H. VanRoekel, *Outdoors and In,* Preprimer 2 (The Harper & Row Basic Reading Program), Evanston, Ill., Harper & Row, 1966.
O'Donnell, Mabel, and Byron H. VanRoekel, *Real and Make-Believe,* Basic First Reader, Strand 1 (The Harper & Row Basic Reading Program), Evanston, Ill., Harper & Row, 1966.
Renshaw, Samuel, "The Visual Perception and Reproduction of Forms by Tachistoscopic Methods," *Journal of Psychology, 20* (October, 1945), 217–232.
Rosenthal, Robert W., and Lenore Jacobson, *Pygmalion in the Classroom,* New York, Holt, Rinehart and Winston, 1968, chap. 7.
Russell, David H., *Children Learn to Read,* New York, Ginn, 1961.
Shane, Harold G., *Linguistics and the Classroom Teacher: Some Implications for Instruction in the Mother Tongue,* Washington, D.C., Association for Supervision and Curriculum Development, NEA, 1967.
Shores, J. Harlan, "Are Fast Readers the Best Readers? A Second Report," *Elementary English, 38,* no. 4 (April, 1961), 236–245.
Shrewsbury, James B., Jr., "Linguistics and the Elementary Teacher: A Call for a Change in Certification Requirements," *Elementary English, 46,* no. 3 (March, 1969), 342–346.
Smith, Nila Banton, *American Reading Instruction,* Newark, Del., International Reading Association, 1965.
Smith, Nila Banton, *American Reading Instruction,* New York, Burdett, 1934.
Smith, Nila Banton, *Reading Instruction for Today's Children,* Englewood Cliffs, N.J., Prentice-Hall, 1963.
Spache, George D., and Mary E. Baggett, "What Do Teachers Know About Phonics and Syllabication?" *The Reading Teacher, 19,* no. 2 (November 1965), 96–99.
Spache, George D., and Evelyn B. Spache, *Reading in the Elementary School,* Boston, Allyn and Bacon, 1969.

Stauffer, Russell G., *Directing Reading Maturity as a Cognitive Process,* New York, Harper & Row, 1969.

Stauffer, Russell G., *Teaching Reading as a Thinking Process,* New York, Harper & Row, 1969.

Strang, Ruth, Constance M. McCullough, and Arthur E. Traxler, *The Improvement of Reading,* New York, McGraw-Hill, 1967.

Sullivan, Elizabeth T., Willis W. Clark, and Ernest W. Tiegs, *California Short-Form Test of Mental Maturity,* Elementary, Monterey, Calif., California Test Bureau, 1963.

Teacher's Guidebook, *Starting Out With Pictureforms* (The Harper & Row Basic Reading Program), Evanston, Ill., Harper & Row, 1966.

Tiegs, Ernest W., and Willis W. Clark, *California Reading Test,* Elementary, Monterey, Calif., California Test Bureau, 1963.

Tinker, Miles A., and Constance M. McCullough, *Teaching Elementary Reading,* New York, Appleton-Century-Crofts, 1968.

VanRoekel, Byron H., and Mary Jean Kluwe, *From Bicycles to Boomerangs,* Basic Third Reader, Strand 2 (The Harper & Row Basic Reading Program), Evanston, Ill., Harper & Row, 1966.

VanRoekel, Byron H., and Mary Jean Kluwe, *From Elephants to Eskimos,* Basic First Reader, Strand 2 (The Harper & Row Basic Reading Program), Evanston, Ill., Harper & Row, 1966.

VanRoekel, Byron H., and Mary Jean Kluwe, *From Fins to Feathers,* Basic Second Reader, Strand 2 (The Harper & Row Basic Reading Program), Evanston, Ill., Harper & Row, 1966.

Veatch, Jeannette, *Reading in the Elementary School,* New York, Ronald, 1966.

Wallen, Carl J., *Word Attack Skills in Reading,* Columbus, Ohio, Merrill, 1969.

Willson, Marcius, *The Second Reader of the School and Family Series,* New York, Harper & Row, 1864.

Wilson, Graham, *A Linguistics Reader,* New York, Harper & Row, 1967.

Wilson, Robert M., *Diagnostic and Remedial Reading for Classroom and Clinic,* Columbus, Ohio, Merrill, 1967.

INDEX

A

D

E

P

Q

R